History of
THE HOUSE OF
REPRESENTATIVES

Second Edition

GEORGE B. GALLOWAY

Revised by Sidney Wise

THOMAS Y. CROWELL COMPANY

New York | Established 1834

PHOTO CREDITS

Following page 112.
Pages: 1, Independence National Historical Collection (Photo by
Warren A. McCullough); 2-16, Library of Congress.

Following page 238.
Pages: 1-4, Library of Congress; 5 (top) Library of Congress,
(bottom) New York Public Library; 8, U.S. Navy Photo; 9,
Lloyd S. Jones; 14, The White House.

Manufactured in the United States of America

Library of Congress Cataloging in Publication Data

Galloway, George Barnes, 1898-1967.
    History of the House of Representatives.

    Previous editions published in 1962 and 1965 under title:
History of the United States House of Representatives.

    Bibliography: p.
    Includes index.
    1. United States. Congress. House—History.
I. Wise, Sidney. II. Title.
JK1316.G22 1976   328.73′07′2   75-35894
ISBN 0-690-01101-6

1   2   3   4   5   6   7   8   9   10

Dedicated to the Memory of

THE HONORABLE SAM RAYBURN

Speaker of the House of Representatives

Acknowledgments

THE AUTHOR DESIRES to express his sincere gratitude to several persons who assisted him in the preparation of this book: to Hon. Richard Bolling, member of Congress from Missouri, who first inspired the work; to Dr. Hugh L. Elsbree, Director of the Legislative Reference Service in the Library of Congress, who read the entire manuscript and made many valuable editorial suggestions; to Mr. D. B. Hardeman, research assistant to the Speaker, who did likewise; and to the following political scientists who read particular chapters and made helpful suggestions for their improvement: Prof. Stephen K. Bailey, Dean of the Maxwell Graduate School of Citizenship and Public Affairs, Syracuse University; Prof. Clarence A. Berdahl, University of Southern Illinois; Prof. Hugh A. Bone, University of Washington; Dr. Kurt Borchardt, professional staff member, Committee on Interstate and Foreign Commerce, U.S. House of Representatives; Prof. Paul T. David, University of Virginia; Dean Ernest S. Griffith, School of International Service, American University; Dr. Floyd M. Riddick, Assistant Parliamentarian, U.S. Senate; Dr. George Smith, Shelton, Connecticut; and Dr. Charles J. Zinn, Law Revision Counsel, Committee on the Judiciary, U.S. House of Representatives.

Grateful acknowledgment is also made to the *American Historical Review* for permission to reprint the article which appears herein as Chapter 6; and to the *Western Political Quarterly* for permission to reprint the articles which appear herein as Chapters 2 and 7.

The author also acknowledges with thanks permission received from the following publishers and authors to quote brief passages from their indicated published works:

American Political Science Review. Article by Richard E. Neustadt, December, 1955.

Annals of the American Academy of Political and Social Science. Article by Dorothy B. Goebel, September, 1953.

Current History. Article by Allan Nevins, July, 1932.

The Macmillan Company. Quotations from *The Federalists, The Jacksonians,* and *The Republican Era,* all by Leonard D. White; and from *The Memoirs of Herbert Hoover,* Vol. 3.

The New York Times and *Times Magazine.* Quotations from articles by Alben W. Barkley, June 20, 1948; and by Arthur Krock, November 13, 1956.

Charles Scribner's Sons. Quotation from *The Autobiography of Theodore Roosevelt,* Centennial Edition.

University of Chicago Press. Quotations from *The Philosophy and Policies of Woodrow Wilson,* edited by Earl Latham; Chapter 14, "Congressional Reorganization: Unfinished Business," by George B. Galloway.

University of Pittsburgh Press. Quotations from *The House of Representatives and Foreign Affairs* by Holbert N. Carroll.

Wilfred E. Binkley. Quotations from *President and Congress* (1947).

Floyd M. Riddick. Quotation from *Congressional Procedure* (1941).

Clinton Rossiter. Quotation from *The American Presidency* (1956).

Arthur M. Schlesinger, Jr. Quotation from *The Coming of the New Deal* (1959).

Finally the author acknowledges with deep gratitude the sustained interest and encouragement of his wife, Eilene-Marie Galloway, in the preparation of this work.

Introduction to the Second Edition

WHEN GEORGE B. GALLOWAY COMPLETED his work on the *History of the House of Representatives* in 1962, he could note with as much accuracy as melancholy that the study of Congress had received so little attention over the years. It was an assertion that would soon be undone by events. The next dozen years brought a significant increase in scholarly concern with Congress and an outpouring of books and articles on the nation's legislative process. One may take special note, for example, of the American Political Science Association Study of Congress project that was initiated in 1963 with a grant from the Carnegie Corporation and generated six distinguished monographs between 1967 and 1973 by some of the nation's leading scholars.

The period also saw an increasing interest in self-analysis by Congress. While the Legislative Reorganization Act of 1946 was regarded as a milestone by many and its passage as something of a "legislative miracle" by Dr. Galloway, the critics found the reforms incomplete. The act did succeed in reducing the number of legislative committees, strengthening the role of staff, and assigning greater responsibilities to the Legislative Reference Service (while increasing congressional salaries), but it was soon superseded by additional concerns. In 1965 a Joint Committee on the Organization of Congress held extensive hearings that finally culminated in the Legislative Reorganization Act of 1970. A major objective of that act was to alter the procedures in a manner that would allow a majority of a committee to cope with an overbearing and capricious chairman. In 1973 the House created a ten-member Select Committee on Committees which made an exhaustive study of its committee system and recommended extensive revisions of their jurisdictions. The modest plans that were eventually adopted were mainly the recommendations of a Democratic caucus committee on organization, study, and review. Some jurisdictional lines were altered; minority staffing was increased; proxies were banned (but not for long); the Ways and Means Committee, long under the leadership of a very powerful chairman, was forced to create subcommittees; and an additional emphasis was directed to legislative oversight. In 1975 the Senate established a Commission on the Operation of the Senate, although it specifically barred committee jurisdictional lines and Senate rules from its agenda.

Two distinct trends emerge from a study of recent years. From the election of John F. Kennedy in 1960 to about 1965, most critics of Congress were simultaneously enamored of the strong Presidency. An effective Congress was one that responded to White House initiative. The constituency of the President was the nation, and Congress was essentially a focus of parochial interests where the members were primarily concerned with the servicing of their states or districts. The power of the Committee on Rules to hold up bills, the excesses of committee chairmen who enjoyed their prerogatives solely because of seniority, and the deadening impact of the filibuster were all perceived as impediments which prevented the adoption of progressive measures that had originated in a State of the Union message. Thus such proposals as the four-year term for House members (their elections coinciding with the President's), the selection of chairman by "merit," the "twenty-one day" rule, the abolition of unlimited debate in the Senate. In 1961, Senator J. William Fulbright could state, "It is my contention that for the existing requirements of American foreign policy we have hobbled the President with too niggardly a grant of power."

The second wave of reform can be described as post-Great Society, post-Tet offensive, and most recently, post-Watergate. The frustrations that followed a war on poverty subtracted from the aura of presidentially inspired social programs. The stunning realization that Vietnam was a struggle that could never be won on our terms reflected on the assertion that the Commander in Chief knew more than the Committee on Foreign Relations. The catalog of abuses of presidential power, which is the story of Watergate, generated the new dialogue on how to stop "the imperial Presidency." The War Powers Act of 1973 and the Congressional Budget and Impoundment Control Act of 1974 were only the most apparent manifestations of a congressional quest for parity with the executive, and the support often came from those who had revered the F.D.R. Presidency as their model.

But there has been more to recent events than congressional machismo.

The efforts to strengthen party responsibility, to enlarge the roles of the caucus, and to expand the responsibilities of the policy committees stem from long-standing concerns among members of both parties and most assuredly among the scholars of Congress. These are themes that also concerned Dr. Galloway. His *History of the House of Representatives* was a careful, objective chronology, but it also sought to underscore the barriers that prevented the House from being more effective as a formulator of public policy. Thus his concern with the committee system, the role of staff assistance, and the special responsibilities of party leaders. He repeatedly stated the hope that the House could be organized in a manner that would allow its members to retain the virtues of specialization while at the same time allowing for greater co-ordination.

In many ways events have been kind to Dr. Galloway's aspirations. The House has changed considerably since those dramatic days of 1961 when it became necessary to enlarge the Rules Committee so that the proposals of a New Frontier President would at least get to the floor for a vote. If the House misses Sam Rayburn, it can look back a few months and recall how the Democratic caucus deposed three committee chairmen and thus announced that arbitrary chairmen did not enjoy infallibility or immortality. It can look back to the summer of '74 and recall how its Committee on the Judiciary comported itself with extraordinary dignity as it voted three articles of impeachment while millions of Americans watched the proceedings. And it most assuredly can recapitulate a decade when the tools of the party leaders have been sharpened and the concepts of party responsibility have become more meaningful even as the American people have shown a declining respect for the virtues of the party system.

The purpose of this revised edition is modest; it is merely to update each of its sections and in a few areas expand upon a work that has special relevance to those who recognize that the House of Representatives is a complex but vital institution. The reader will soon discover that change and innovation are no strangers to the House and indeed that yesterday's reforms are often considered today's agenda while the proposals of the moment are often a call to return to the customs of an earlier century. Because it is so large, because the nation's agenda is so overwhelming, and because public expectations are so great, the workings of the House will always be disparaged, particularly in an age when the Chief Executive can still dominate the media.

In 1971 a somewhat more mellow Senator Fulbright noted, "The greatest single virtue of a strong legislature is not what it can do but what it can prevent." Given the events since the first edition of this work, one need not minimize the quality of that insight by noting that in recent years the House has demonstrated considerably more than that. Dr. Galloway's monumental services to the Congress as a one-man task force that generated the 1946 Reorganization Act and his many years as the senior specialist in American Government and Public Administration in the Legislative Reference Service of the Library of Congress are all part of the background for many of those recent changes. Dr. Galloway was mindful of the rich history and the many achievements of the House, as well as its limitations as an architect of policy.

In a very effective but not flamboyant manner, Dr. Galloway's work was sensitive to the need for change, but it also insisted that an understanding of the history and organization of the House and an understanding of the intense and varied pressures on the members were a minimum prerequisite for the thoughtful reformer. His countless monographs, memoranda, and hours of testimony and conversation with House committees and members served to generate a concern with making the House a genuine "forge of democracy." That the reformist impulse in the House has momentarily paused is good reason to recapitulate and supplement Dr. Galloway's contribution to our understanding of one of the most complicated legislative bodies in the world.

In updating this volume, I particularly wish to express my appreciation to Mrs. Eilene-Marie Galloway for her enlightening conversations and encouragement. Her sharing of an unpublished autobiographical essay by her husband was especially helpful in appreciating the character and range of interests of a remarkable man. In any such venture, one also discovers the many helpful and friendly "staffers" on the Hill, those encyclopaedic and anonymous assistants who convert long days into memorable occasions. One is also forced to realize how all students of the legislative process owe an incalculable debt to the *Congressional Quarterly* and its many publications. There is also the helper who ends up doing so much so well that no thanks are adequate—for me that was Mrs. Jean G. Kerich. And finally, the wife who understandingly accepts preoccupation and even other misdemeanors. For me that was Eileen. The errors, alas, are mine alone.

—SIDNEY WISE
October, 1975

Preface

STRANGE AS IT MAY SEEM, the role of Congress in the American system of government has been largely neglected by American historians. In their *Basic History of the United States* the Beards devoted only 6 pages to the subject, and that only to the powers conferred on the national legislature by the Constitution of 1787, while discussion of Congress is largely omitted by Morison and Commager in their two-volume work, *The Growth of the American Republic*. In his *Democracy in America* (Bradley edition), de Tocqueville gave only 5 pages to Congress out of 434 pages of text.

The purpose of this book is to promote understanding of our national House of Representatives, where the public's business is performed. The American people have been legislation-minded for more than three centuries, and the legislature has long been the central institution of our democratic way of life. Despite its defects, the legislative process is vastly preferable to the way of dictators by whom we are now challenged. Upon this process depend the adjustment of our social disputes, the preservation of our individual liberties, and the peaceable solution of our public problems. Lawmaking involves the representation of all the various interests of the nation and the tolerance of many different points of view.

A former Congressman, who was also a philosopher, once said the legislature is a place where one learns that "all major interests in society are equally legitimate," that the "representatives of the great legitimate interests are equally honest," and that no man or group has a monopoly on justice or virtue. Although laws are seldom universally popular, "the legislature is, for all that, the only institution developed by man through the centuries which preserves individuals against gross invasion of their private rights and guarantees some minimum of benefits to all groups alike in their struggle for survival and supremacy. . . . It should be to us, therefore, a matter of great meaning and high hope that no modern nation long seasoned in our legislative way of handling common problems has yet voluntarily given it up."

Contents

History of the
House of Representatives

I

Planning the House in the Constitutional Convention

DURING THE DEBATES on the framing of the Constitution in the Federal Convention of 1787, a score of questions about the first branch of the national legislature were discussed and decided. These decisions were derived in large part from the constitutions of the individual states, from the experience of the colonial assemblies, and from the practice of the Continental Congresses and the Congress of the Confederation. According to Farrand: "Every provision of the federal constitution can be accounted for in American experience between 1776 and 1787."[1]* "Their experience with state legislatures," writes Binkley, "quite naturally led the framers of the Constitution to believe that the House of Representatives would possess a tremendous vitality as the immediate representative of the people. It would require no such special safeguards for its protection, as the other coordinate branches of the government."[2]

After deciding that a national government ought to be established consisting of a supreme legislative, executive, and judiciary, the Federal Convention took up the question: Should the national legislature be unicameral or bicameral? It was decided, apparently without debate, that it should consist of two branches. Benjamin Franklin, a member of the convention, preferred a single house, but he did not speak on this question. Although the Continental Congresses and the Congress of the Confederation had been unicameral, and likewise three state legislatures—Pennsylvania, Georgia, and Vermont—bicameralism was the prevailing form in most of the separate states and in the British Parliament from which the new republic inherited much of its parliamentary practice. So it was decided, first in committee of the whole, with Pennsylvania alone dissenting, and finally

* Notes begin on page 339.

in the convention itself by a vote of seven states to three (Maryland divided), that the new Congress should have two branches.

The next question was, Should the members of the first branch of the national legislature be elected by the people or by the state legislatures? This question was twice debated in committee of the whole and twice decided in favor of their election by the people of the several states. Some delegates, such as Sherman of Connecticut and Gerry of Massachusetts, distrusted the people and feared an excess of democracy, but the majority favored public election. Madison said that he "considered the popular election as essential to every plan of free government . . ." George Mason of Virginia asserted that the House "was to be the grand depository of the democratic principles of the Government. . . . The requisites in actual representation are that the Representatives should sympathize with their constituents, should think as they think and feel as they feel, and that for these purposes should even be residents among them." When this question came before the Convention for final action, nine states voted for election by the people, two dissented, and one divided.

The third question considered was that of the powers of the national legislature. Under the Articles of Confederation, Congress had been a weak and incompetent creature of sovereign states which retained control over the essential functions of government. To correct this condition, the Federal Convention (by a vote of six states to four) after debate, first conferred a broad grant of power upon Congress in the following terms:

> To enjoy the legislative rights vested in Congress by the Confederation, and moreover to legislate in all cases for the general interests of the Union, and also in those to which the States are separately incompetent, or in which the harmony of the United States may be interrupted by the exercise of individual legislation.

In the event, however, instead of this broad outline of authority, the convention enumerated eighteen specific powers of Congress, as reported by the Committee of Detail, which are set forth in Article I, Section 8, of the Constitution.

The next question, relating to the first branch of the legislature considered by the convention was upon the rule of suffrage in the House. Should the states be equally represented in the first branch or in proportion to their population? After long discussion in committee of the whole, it was agreed that members of the House should be elected in proportion to the population of the respective states, counting the whole number of free citizens and three-fifths of all others (slaves) except Indians not paying taxes. Later, after more than two weeks of discussion, this decision against equal representation of the states in the first branch of the legislature was confirmed by the convention by a vote of six states to four.

The term of office of members of the legislature next came up for discussion. Many delegates preferred annual elections for the first branch, following colonial practice which was designed as a check on the royal governors. But Madison argued for triennial elections, in order to enable representatives to acquire knowledge of the interests and needs of other states. After debate, the committee of the whole decided in favor of a three-year term for representatives, but the convention itself later fixed on biennial elections as a compromise between a one-year and a three-year term of office.

A long and hard fight took place in the convention over the power to originate money bills. Should this power be limited to the popular branch, as most of the state constitutions then provided; or should the second branch have the right to amend them, as it could in three states? On these questions the convention was deeply divided. Acting on a report from a compromise committee, it was first decided that money bills should originate in the first branch and should not be amended by the second branch. This was part of "the great compromise" of the convention between the large and small states. After reconsideration and vacillation, however, the convention finally decided (by a vote of nine states to two) that "all bills for raising revenue shall originate in the House of Representatives; but the Senate may propose or concur with amendments as on other bills"—the latter being the language of the Massachusetts state constitution.

A group of related questions now gave rise to a long and spirited debate: How many members should the lower house of the First Congress have? How should they be distributed among the original states? Should Congress have power to regulate the representation of all the states in the future? Should the representation of the states in the first branch of the legislature be based upon their wealth and number of inhabitants? After much disagreement, it was finally decided that the first house should have sixty-five members, divided among the thirteen original states in the numbers prescribed in Article I, Section 2, of the Constitution; and that Congress should itself determine future apportionments of representatives and direct taxes on the basis of the population of the states, counting three-fifths of the slaves and excluding Indians not taxed. Thus the principle that taxation and representation should be linked together was inserted in the Constitution. Lest Congress have the power of making future changes in the representation of the states, Randolph's motion for a decennial census of inhabitants was adopted so as to provide a basis for a reapportionment of representatives every ten years. Both wealth and population were at first accepted as bases of representation, but after strong opposition was voiced to the use of property as a basis, the word "wealth" was stricken. On the eve of final adoption of the Constitution, after George Washington had spoken in its favor, the convention unanimously agreed to change the ratio of representation in the lower house from one for every 40,000 inhabitants to one for every 30,000.

What qualifications should be required of those who were to elect the Congress? The population at that time comprised some seven classes: "first, the farmers, frontiersmen, and planters who formed the greatest single class, but almost all of whom owned land, even if they had no other property; second, the craftsmen and mechanics who largely worked on their own business; third, the mercantile interest composed of shopkeepers and their clerks; fourth, the commercial interest, most of whom were ship-owners or importers or exporters; fifth, the shipbuilding interest; sixth, apprentices, domestic servants, and farm laborers; seventh, the lawyers, doctors, and clergymen."[3] Property qualifications for voting varied so greatly among the states that it would have been difficult to devise any uniform rule for all the states. After debate, it was decided, therefore, to leave the qualifications of voters to regulation by the several states so as to avoid discriminating for or against any particular class of property owner. This the convention did by adopting without dissent the proposal of its Committee of Detail stating that the qualifications of electors for the House of Representatives "shall be the same . . . as those of the electors in the several states, of the most numerous branch of their own legislatures."

As regards the mode of congressional elections, the convention, after little debate, adopted the provision contained in Article I, Section 4, of the Constitution, that

> The times, places and manner of holding elections for Senators and Representatives, shall be prescribed in each state by the legislature thereof; but the Congress may at any time by law make or alter such regulations, except as to the places of choosing Senators.

What qualifications should members of Congress have? Each of the state constitutions at that time contained provisions establishing various qualifications for members of the state legislatures as to residence, age, property, religion, etc. Almost all the state constitutions contained property qualifications for members of their legislatures. The convention declined after debate, by a vote of seven states to three, to require members of Congress to possess property. As to residence, proposals for one, three, and seven years within the state were rejected, and the provision was finally approved that "no person shall be a Representative . . . who shall not, when elected, be an inhabitant of that state in which he shall be chosen." Residence in the congressional district was not required. After much disagreement, it was finally decided to require a member of the House of Representatives to be twenty-five years of age and seven years a citizen of the United States. Thus the qualifications of members of Congress were much more democratic and liberal than those in the state constitutions of the period for members of their own legislatures.

Meanwhile the convention without debate or dissent agreed to the provision that "each House shall be the judge of the elections, returns and qualifications of its own members"—a provision found in eight of the state constitutions at that time. A provision that "each House may determine the rules of its proceedings, punish its members for disorderly behavior, and, with the concurrence of two thirds, expel a Member" was also approved. And members of Congress, as well as all public officers of the United States, were exempted from any religious qualifications by the pronouncement that "no religious test shall ever be required as a qualification to any office or public trust under the authority of the United States."

On the adjournments of Congress and its place of sitting, the convention accepted the report of its Committee of Detail. Power to prorogue or dissolve the colonial assemblies had often been a bone of contention between them and the royal governors. Hence, the new state constitutions reserved control over their own sessions and adjournments to the legislatures themselves. And these provisions were copied in the Federal Constitution, the final version of the pertinent subsection reading as follows:

> Neither House, during the Session of Congress, shall, without the Consent of the other, adjourn for more than three days, nor to any other Place than that in which the two Houses shall be sitting.

The privileges of freedom from arrest and freedom of speech and debate, which are of great antiquity, dating far back in the practice of the English Parliament, and which were reaffirmed in the Articles of Confederation, were adopted by the convention without debate and appear in the Constitution as follows:

> The Senators and Representatives . . . shall in all Cases, except Treason, Felony and Breach of the Peace, be privileged from Arrest during their Attendance at the Session of their respective Houses, and in going to and returning from the same; and for any Speech or Debate in either House, they shall not be questioned in any other Place.

On the question whether legislative proceedings should be published or kept secret, there was considerable debate about the people's "right to know." Finally, the convention approved of the requirement that:

> Each House shall keep a Journal of its Proceedings, and from time to time publish the same, excepting such Parts as may in their Judgment require Secrecy; and the Yeas and Nays of the Members of either House on any question shall, at the Desire of one fifth of those Present, be entered on the Journal.

On the compensation of members of Congress, two questions gave rise to diverse views: Should members of Congress be paid by the states or out of the national treasury? And should the amount of their salaries be fixed in the Constitution or left to the discretion of Congress? Adherents of states' rights favored payment by the states, while the nationalists argued that Congressmen were to be national, not state, officers and should be paid out of the federal exchequer. Evidently the majority of delegates "were convinced of the necessity," as Dickinson expressed it, "of making the general government independent of the prejudices, passions and improper views of the state legislatures," for the convention finally decided by a vote of 9 to 2 to pay congressional salaries out of the national treasury in amounts "to be ascertained by law."

Two related questions provoked prolonged debate in the convention: Should members of Congress be ineligible to hold office under the state and national governments? And should they be ineligible to re-election? Great importance was attached to the first question by "the resentment of the delegates towards some of the appointments which had been made by the Congress under the Confederation" of its own members to diplomatic and executive posts; "but it was chiefly due to the fear lest the President should combine with the Congress in corrupt bargains as to his appointments."[4] Those opposed to a ban on such appointments argued that it would degrade the legislature and impair the calibre of its membership. The impasse was finally broken by a vote of five states to four when the Convention adopted the following provision:

> No Senator or Representative shall, during the Time for which he was elected, be appointed to any civil Office under the Authority of the United States, which shall have been created, or the Emoluments whereof shall have been increased during such time; and no Person holding any Office under the United States, shall be a Member of either House during his Continuance in Office.

The proposal to make members of Congress ineligible for re-election, at least for a period of time, which was incorporated in the Articles of Confederation, was favored by those who believed in the theory of rotation in office. But it had operated to deprive the Congress of the Confederation of the continued and valuable services of such delegates as James Madison, and it was rejected by the committee of the whole without debate or dissent.

During the debates in the convention, several proposals were made by individual delegates, and later in the report of the Committee of Detail, to restrict the powers of Congress in various respects. Eight of these restraints were ultimately approved and embodied in Article I, Section 9, of the Constitution.

Two other decisions of the convention affected the role of the House of Representatives. One concerned election of the President. Here it was finally agreed that if no person received a majority of votes for President in the electoral college, the eventual election should be by the House instead of the Senate, each state to have one vote. The convention assumed that this would happen in most cases, but it has actually occurred only twice in American history: in 1801, when the House chose Jefferson over Burr; and in 1825, when the House elected John Quincy Adams over Andrew Jackson.

The other decision affecting the House concerned the removal of the President. In all the state constitutions then in force the lower branch of the legislature was empowered to impeach. This precedent was followed by the Convention, and the House of Representatives was assigned "the sole power of impeachment."

Such were the momentous decisions relating to the House of Representatives that were made by the framers in Philadelphia in1787.

2

Precedents Established in First Congress

THE FIRST SESSION OF CONGRESS under the new Constitution was scheduled to meet in New York City on March 4, 1789. But only thirteen members of the House of Representatives, from five of the eleven states that had ratified the Constitution up to that time, appeared and took their seats on that day. So the House met and adjourned from day to day until a quorum finally appeared on April 1. They came by ship, wagon, and stagecoach; some were delayed by bad roads, others by storms and shipwreck.

In its composition the first House of Representatives resembled the membership of the state legislatures of that period. "The members were good eighteenth century Americans," Harlow remarks, "average representatives of the ruling class of the time."[1] Mostly men of moderate views, the first Congress "contained many men of talent, character, and wide legislative experience."[2]

We are indebted to Fisher Ames, a Federalist member of the first four Congresses from Massachusetts, for a contemporaneous description of his colleagues. An impulsive and prolific letter writer, Ames said of the first House: "The House is composed of sober, solid, old-charter folks. . . . There are few shining geniuses; there are many who have experience, the virtues of the heart, and the habits of business. It will be quite a republican assembly. . . ."[3]

The first House of Representatives contained fifty-five Federalists and ten Anti-Federalists. The South accounted for half the seats in the House; New England and the Middle Atlantic states for one-quarter each. In the first Congress, nine representatives had been members of the Constitutional Convention and thirty-six of the Continental Congress. Thirty-nine representatives had served in state legislatures, and fifty-two had been members of either a state legislature, the Continental Congress, or the Federal Convention. Nineteen members of the first House were college graduates, and nineteen others had some academic training. Twenty-four were lawyers. Their median age was forty-four.

Popular interest in the first congressional elections was slight, and only a small minority of interested property holders voted. Paullin estimates the total vote in the first congressional elections at from 75,000 to 125,000, or from 3 to 3½ per cent of the free population (3,200,000).[4]

Among the outstanding members of the first House were Frederick A. C. Muhlenberg, of Pennsylvania, the first Speaker; the studious James Madison of Virginia, who was regarded as the "first man" in the House; and the vigorous Fisher Ames of Massachusetts, who was often critical of the slow pace of the legislative process. The others spent their day on the legislative stage, played their parts, and then disappeared in the wings of oblivion.

Organization of the House

The Constitution was silent on the organization and structure of the House beyond saying that it should choose its Speaker and other officers, that it could determine the rules of its proceedings, and that it should keep and publish a journal of its business. But once a quorum appeared, the House lost little time in organizing itself for the tasks ahead of the new republic. This involved four steps: election of officers, adoption of rules, appointment of committees, and acceptance of credentials.

On April 1, 1789, the first day a quorum was present, the House chose Frederick A. C. Muhlenberg, a representative from Pennsylvania, as its Speaker by ballot by majority vote. A clerk of the House (John Beckley) was then elected in the same manner on the same day. On April 4 a doorkeeper and assistant doorkeeper were likewise appointed. A House chaplain, Rev. William Linn, was elected by ballot on May 1. And a sergeant at arms (Joseph Wheaton) was elected on May 12. Meanwhile the House approved the form of oath to be taken by members and the chief justice of New York state, on request, administered the oath of office to the Speaker and other representatives.

On April 2, a committee of eleven members was appointed, by order of the House, to prepare and report standing rules and orders of proceeding. Five days later, the report of this select committee was submitted by Mr. Boudinot, read at the clerk's table, and agreed to by the House. The simple code of initial rules then adopted dealt with four topics: the duties of the Speaker, decorum and debate, bill procedure, and committees of the whole house. On April 13, the House debated and adopted additional rules, as reported by the same committee, relating to committee service, leaves of absence, and appointment of a standing Committee of Elections. A resolution relating to joint rules with the Senate was laid on the table. And the next day the House agreed to an additional rule concerning its sergeant at arms: his appointment, symbol of office, and fees.

On April 18, the House received and agreed to a report from its Committee on Elections, accepting the credentials of forty-nine members from nine states. And on April 29, the House agreed to the procedure to be followed by its Elections Committee in handling contested election cases which arose in South Carolina and New Jersey. Thus the first House expeditiously completed its organization.

Early House Procedure

Compared with today's intricate, complex code, the parliamentary practice of the first House was simple indeed. Many of its members had previous legislative experience and were presumably familiar with the precedents available in contemporary state legislative practice. Yet they preferred at the outset to adopt a few simple rules and let experience guide them in making additions to the rule book.

Fisher Ames complained of the slow progress of business in the early days. "As we manage our time," he wrote, "I think we shall never get out of employment."[5] After two months, Madison wrote that "in every step the difficulties arising from novelty are severely experienced, and are an ample as well as just source of apology. Scarcely a day passes without some striking evidence of the delays and perplexities springing merely from the want of precedents. Time will be a full remedy for this evil; and will, I am persuaded, evince a greater facility in legislating uniformly for all the States than has been supposed by some of the best friends of the Union."[6]

The duties assigned to the Speaker of the House by the first standing rule were modeled on those of the Speaker of the English House of Commons. He was to preside at sessions of the House, preserve decorum and order, put questions, decide points of order, announce the result of divisions and teller votes, appoint committees of not more than three members, and vote in all cases of ballot by the House.

Decorum and debate, motions and balloting, were governed by the second standing rule. No member could speak more than twice to the same question without leave of the House. No member could vote on any question in the result of which he was immediately and particularly interested;[7] or in any other case where he was not present when the question was put. Every member present in the House when a question was put was required to vote for or against it, unless excused. The previous question was to be admitted upon demand of five members, and its form was defined. Committees of more than three members were to be chosen by ballot. And any fifteen members could compel the attendance of absentees.

According to the third rule, a committee was to be appointed to prepare every bill which should receive three readings; but no bill could be read twice on the same day without special order of the House. After second reading, a bill was to be engrossed or committed either to a select committee or to a committee of the whole house. After commitment and report, a bill could be recommitted at any time before its passage. But no bill amended by the Senate could be committed.

The fourth rule adopted on April 7, 1789, prescribed the procedure of committees of the whole house in which bills were to be twice read, debated by clauses, and subjected to amendment.

Several features of early parliamentary practice are interesting to recall. Conspicuous reliance was placed by the House, then as now, on the committee of the whole. The guiding principles of all the major measures of the first five Congresses, such as the first tariff bill and the acts organizing the executive departments, were formulated first in committee of the whole and were then referred to select committees to work out the details and draft the bills. A committee of the whole was the House itself under another name, and in those days the House was small enough (sixty-five members) to function as a genuine deliberative assembly and to stage great debates on national questions.

After a problem, such as the location of the permanent seat of the federal government, had been discussed from every angle in committee of the whole house on the state of the Union, it would be referred by House resolution to an *ad hoc* select committee with instructions to prepare and report a bill on the subject. Some days later, the select committee would present its bill to the House, according to order, and after second reading, the bill would be ordered committed to a committee of the whole house. The House would then resolve itself into a committee of the whole house; the Speaker would leave the chair; another member would take the chair; and the committee of the whole house would consider and probably adopt amendments to the bill. Then the Speaker would resume the chair, and the chairman of the committee of the whole would report its action to the House and deliver the proposed amendments at the clerk's table, where they would be read twice and usually agreed to by the House. The House would then order the bill, with the amendments, to be engrossed and read the third time the next day. After third reading, the House would adopt a resolution that the bill pass and be entitled. Finally the clerk of the House would be directed to carry the bill to the Senate and request their concurrence.

The quality of the debates in committee of the whole varied, of course, for not all the members were competent to elucidate general principles, and some of the more brilliant members were impatient at this time-consuming procedure. Fisher Ames, to quote him again, thought it was "certainly a bad method of doing business. Too little use is made of special committees."[8]

Writing to a friend in July, 1789, about a revenue collection bill, Ames described the procedure as follows: "The bill was at first very imperfect. We labored upon it for some time, settled some principles, and referred it to a large and very good committee. They met, agreed upon principles, and the clerk drew the bill which they reported. We consider it in committee of the whole, and we indulge a very minute criticism upon its style. We correct spelling, or erase *may* and insert *shall,* and quiddle in a manner which provokes me. A select committee would soon correct little improprieties. Our great committee is too unwieldy for this operation. A great, clumsy machine is applied to the slightest and most delicate operations—the hoof of an elephant to the strokes of mezzotinto. . . ."[9]

Another feature of early procedure was the election of House committees to confer with Senate committees on matters of mutual interest—such as the use of titles for the President and Vice President, the enrollment of bills, and the presentation of bills to the President for his approval—and to consider the remaining business of the session and the prospects of adjournment. In a bicameral legislature, conference committees were from the start an essential feature.

Four instances of the use of the previous question are found in the *House Journal* of the first session of the First Congress. On the demand of five members that "the main question be now put," it was twice resolved in the negative and twice in the affirmative.[10]

The standing rules of the House were twice amended during the First Congress: first, on June 9, 1789, by changing the procedure when a division was called for; and, second, on January 12, 1791, by rescinding the rule that no bill amended by the Senate should be committed.

Only one instance is recorded during the first session of an appeal from a decision of the chair. On September 11, 1789, an appeal was taken from a decision of the chair that a motion to reconsider the proceedings of the previous day on the congressional salary bill was in order. After debate, the Speaker's ruling was upheld.[11]

The annals disclose that the first election contest arose during the first session of Congress. The question was whether William Smith of South Carolina had been seven years a citizen of the United States at the time of his election. After due consideration, the House resolved the question in his favor.[12]

Committees in the First Congress

In the light of frequent criticisms that the modern Congress has lost control of its autonomous standing committees, it is interesting to recall that the early practice of the House of Representatives was to set up a select committee on every bill. Whether it was to provide for the first census or to regulate the importation of slaves prior to 1808, or whatever the subject matter, Congress retained control of its committees by giving them specific instructions as to their authority and duties.

The First Congress relied, as we have seen, on Committees of the Whole House for developing the general principles of legislation, and upon numerous select committees to perfect the details of bills. Thus on April 11, 1789, the House elected by ballot a select committee of nine to draft a bill to regulate import duties.

Only one standing committee dates from the First Congress—the Committee of Elections—whose seven members were elected by ballot on April 13, 1789, to examine and report upon the certificates of election and to investigate election contests. On February 1, 1790, after the opening of the second session, this committee was reappointed with three of its original members and four new ones.

In approving joint rules between the two houses on July 27, 1789, the House authorized the creation of a joint standing Committee on Enrolled Bills to be composed of one Senator and two members of the House of Representatives, who were named a few days later.

During debate on the bill to establish a Treasury Department, the question of creating a Committee of Ways and Means arose. Several of the state legislatures had finance committees, and many members felt that Congress should have a committee to advise it on fiscal matters. The House agreed and ordered the appointment of a Committee of Ways and Means, consisting of a member from each state; they were named on July 24, 1789. But on September 17 this committee was "discharged from further proceeding on the business referred to them," and it was "referred to the Secretary of the Treasury, to report thereon."[13] Evidently the House, or at least the Federalists, had more confidence at that time in Alexander Hamilton, who had just become Secretary of the Treasury, than in its own committee. Not until 1795 was a permanent standing Committee on Ways and Means created.

Relations with the Senate

By the great compromise of 1787, the Constitution created a bicameral legislature in which the House was to represent the people of the several states, and the Senate, whose members were to be elected by the state legislatures, was to represent the "sovereign states" themselves. Since all legislative powers "herein granted" had been vested in a Congress composed of two houses, it was obviously necessary for them to devise methods of communication and co-operation with each other in order to carry out their concurrent functions.

Important precedents were established during the First Congress regarding the forms of joint action between the two bodies. Within the first six weeks of their organization, the two houses had met in joint sessions, had set up several joint committees, and had adopted joint rules.

The first communication between them took place on April 6, 1789, the day on which the Senate organized, when the House received a message from the Senate, delivered by Mr. Ellsworth of Connecticut, that a quorum of that body had formed and was now ready in the Senate chamber to proceed, in the presence of the House, to count the votes of the electors for President and Vice President. Whereupon the House resolved to proceed to the Senate chamber for this purpose and appointed two of its members to make a list of the votes in cooperation with a member of the Senate. Accordingly, the two houses held their first joint session in the Senate chamber and canvassed the votes of the electors. After the House had withdrawn, Mr. Madison conveyed a message to the Senate saying that it was the desire of the House that the notifications of the election of the President and Vice President of the United States should be made by such persons and in such manner as the Senate should be pleased to direct.

Congress met again in joint session on April 30 in the Senate chamber to hear the inaugural address of President Washington and then the members of both houses accompanied the President and Vice President for divine services at St. Paul's Chapel, performed by the chaplain of Congress.

The House resolved on June 16, 1789, that seats be provided, "within the bar," for the accommodation of the President and members of the Senate, presumably in order to facilitate joint sessions. The first joint committee was set up, at the initiative of the Senate, to prepare a system of rules to govern the two houses in cases of conference and to regulate the appointment of chaplains. Upon receipt of a letter from Senator Ellsworth stating that the Senate had appointed its members of this committee, the House on April 9 elected a committee of five for these purposes. The joint committee's report was agreed to by the House on April 17. In seven lines, it stated the rule for a free conference between committees of the two houses in cases of disagreement on amendments to bills, the law and practice of which now occupy sixteen pages in the *Senate Manual*. Each house was also to appoint a chaplain, and they were to "interchange weekley."

Later, after a year's experience, supplementary rules were adopted on the recommendation of a joint committee appointed to consider what additional regulations were necessary for conducting the business between the houses. These rules prescribed that when a bill, passed by one house, was rejected by the other, notice of such rejection should be given to the house which had approved. Moreover, a bill thus rejected should not be brought in during the same session, without ten days' notice and leave of two-thirds of that house in which it should be renewed. It was also provided that each house should transmit to the other the papers pertinent to any pending bill or resolution; and that after each house should have adhered to its disagreement, a bill or resolution should be lost.[14]

Legislative Output

The First Congress enacted many important and useful laws. It met for three sessions, lasting a total of 519 days. It had not only to organize itself and to establish the basic institutions of the new government, but also to lay the foundations of the American economy. More than threescore major statutes were the legislative fruit of its efforts. It created the War, Treasury, and Foreign Affairs (State) Departments. It established the judicial courts of the United States, a Land Office, and a government for the Northwest Territory. It passed a tariff bill, an invalid-pensions measure, and a bill for the regulation of the coastal trade. It established the permanent seat of the national government and fixed the compensation of executive and judicial officers and employees. It enacted the first annual appropriations acts, passed several relief bills, and submitted the first Ten Amendments to the Constitution. It considered scores of memorials and petitions, as well as laws regulating patents and copyrights, bankruptcies, harbors, the punishment of crimes, naturalization, the importation of slaves, and intercourse with the Indian tribes.

The House and the Senate divided the honors in originating this vast legislative output. The bills creating the new departments, the financial measures, the tariff bill, and the bill for the assumption of the state debts started in the House of Representatives. On the other hand, the Senate took the initiative in the act establishing the temporary and permanent seat of the government; it started the bill for incorporating the first bank of the United States; and it originated the procedure for the organization of new states and territories. The Senate also took the lead in the measures establishing the judicial courts of the United States, regulating their procedure, and providing for the punishment of crimes against the United States. From the earliest days, the Senate functioned not only as a chamber of revision but also exercised its right to originate legislation. However, its sessions were held in secret while those of the House were open to the public, which thronged its galleries.

Relations with the President

During the first decade of the new republic, when the sessions of Congress were held in New York City and Philadelphia, the office of the President was located in the same building where Congress met. This physical propinquity combined with the need of collaboration in organizing the new government to make for closer relations between Congress and the Chief Executive than obtained after the seat of the government was transferred to the District of Columbia.

The first contact occurred on April 23, 1789, when a joint committee composed of five members of the House and three members of the Senate, appointed for the purpose, met President Washington at Elizabethtown, New Jersey, and escorted him by vessel to New York and to the house selected for his residence. Meanwhile a joint committee of three members of the House and two members of the Senate waited upon Vice President Adams and congratulated him upon his arrival in the city.

The day after Washington's inauguration, the Speaker laid a copy of the President's address before the House, which considered it in committee of the whole and then appointed a committee of five members, chaired by James Madison, to prepare a reply. The Madison committee prepared an eloquent reply, congratulating the First Magistrate upon his election to the highest honor in the land and expressing sentiments of affection and esteem, which was read to the House on May 5 and unanimously approved. On May 8, the Speaker attended by the members of the House presented their reply to the President in a room adjoining the House chamber.

On January 8, 1790, President Washington delivered his State of the Union message in person to a joint session of Congress in the Senate chamber. After considering his address in committee of the whole on the following day, the House appointed a committee of three to prepare a reply "with assurances that this House will, without delay, proceed to take into their serious consideration the various and important matters recommended to their attention."[15] And when on January 14 the entire House presented their reply to the President at his residence, he said to them: "I have full confidence that your deliberations will continue to be directed by an enlightened and virtuous zeal for the happiness of our country."[16] When the same ritual was repeated the following December, Fisher Ames confided to a friend: "We have had the speech from the throne, have answered it, and tomorrow we are to present our answer. Both contain some divine molasses."[17]

Relations with the Departments

The First Congress, as we have seen, established three executive departments—Foreign Affairs (State), War, and Treasury—each headed by a Secretary removable by the President. It also passed an act for the temporary establishment of the Post Office.

While these new department heads were executive officials and were designed to be instruments of the President, and while the statutes creating them did not authorize the Congress to give them orders, nevertheless we find the First Congress soon issuing them a series of directives. Thus the Secretary of State, Thomas Jefferson, was "ordered" by the House on January 15, 1790, to prepare and report "a proper plan or plans for establishing uniformity in the currency, weights, and measures of the United States."[18] And on February 23, 1791, the House "ordered" the Secretary of State to report to Congress the nature and extent of the privileges and restrictions of the commercial intercourse of the United States with foreign nations and measures for the improvement of our commerce and navigation.[19] Again, on April 23, 1790, the House directed the Secretary of War, Mr. Knox, to submit an account of the troops and ordnance stores furnished by the several states toward the support of the late war.[20]

These early precedents were overshadowed, however, by the relations between the First Congress and the Secretary of the Treasury—Alexander Hamilton. As noted above, the House of Representatives set up a Committee of Ways and Means on July 24, 1789, to advise it on fiscal matters, but eight weeks later the House discharged this committee and referred its business to the Secretary of the Treasury "to consider and report thereupon."[21] Simultaneously it ordered him to report an estimate of the sums required to defray the expenses of the civil list and the War Department for the current year. This precedent was followed by a long series of House directives to Mr. Hamilton which made it evident that Congress regarded him as its agent and adviser in matters of public finance and the national economy.

Such heavy congressional reliance upon the Secretary of the Treasury, in lieu of its own Ways and Means Committee, reflects the intimate relationship that existed between the first Congresses and Alexander Hamilton. The statute creating his department evidently permitted a closer relationship between Congress and the Treasury than with the State and War Departments, for it required the Secretary of the Treasury "to digest and prepare plans for the improvement and management of the revenue, and for the support of the public credit . . . to make report, and give information to either branch of the legislature, in person or in writing . . . respecting all matters referred to him by the Senate or House of Representatives, or which shall appertain to his office; and generally to perform all such services relative to the finances, as he shall be directed to perform."[22] The absence of similar language in the laws creating the State and War Departments, and the failure of this statute to authorize the President to assign duties to the Secretary of the Treasury, seem to signify a congressional intent to give this official a unique status.

Hamilton's successful influence with the first Congresses and their early use of the department heads to prepare plans, draft bills, handle petitions, etc., explain perhaps why the system of standing committees did not develop until later. It appears that the early Federalists may have conceived of the heads of departments as constituting a ministry in the British sense of the term. Under this concept it was the proper function of a finance minister to take the initiative in fiscal policy formation, to supervise the legislative process, and to promote the adoption of his policies.

Be this as it may, Hamilton's power in Congress caused deep distress among some Republican members. Thus Senator Maclay confided to his diary: "Where Eloquence personified and reason flowed from her tongue, her talents would be in vain in our assembly; . . . Congress may go home. Mr. Hamilton is all-powerful, and fails in nothing he attempts."[23] Maclay goes on to cite four measures: the assumption, bank, and excise bills, and a resolution regarding the mint, all of which, despite opposition, were passed largely as a result of Hamilton's personal efforts and influence.[24] Harlow concludes his description of these events by saying that "the Secretary of the Treasury was the most important factor in Congress during its first session."[25]

Relations with the States

Official relations with the governments of the states were rare during the first session. In May, 1789, applications were received by the Congress from the legislatures of Virginia and New York for the calling of a convention to consider the "defects" of the federal Constitution and to report amendments thereof designed to secure "the great and unalienable rights of mankind." In the same month the House received an offer from the legislature of Virginia of ten square miles of territory anywhere in the state for use as the seat of the federal government. A similar offer was received from the Maryland legislature. On June 5, 1789, the House concurred with a Senate resolution requesting the President to transmit two copies of every act of Congress to the governors of each of the states.

Evolution of Party Organization

The early months of the First Congress were marked by a notable absence of party spirit. Peace and brotherly love prevailed at the outset, induced perhaps by a sense of historic responsibility for launching the new regime. It was not long, however, before controversies arose, inspired by underlying sectional and philosophical differences among the members. These were reflected in the arguments over legislative proposals to regulate the slave trade and in the debates over the location of the permanent seat of the federal government.

These disputes gave rise, in turn, to the first meetings of like-minded members of the legislature which gradually evolved into party organizations of Federalists and Republicans. At these meetings party policies on current issues were discussed, crystallized, and embodied in drafts of bills which were subsequently introduced in Congress. Thus the actual initiative in legislation came to be transferred from the committee of the whole to the party caucus.

The Federalists were the first to develop a parliamentary party in Congress because they were in the majority in the early years and because they also had the advantage of the superlative leadership of Alexander Hamilton, who was a master of the arts of political organization. As Secretary of the Treasury he was in close touch with Congress, and according to contemporary observers he dominated it behind the scenes through what were, in effect, party caucuses. Thus Maclay refers to "the rendezvousing of the crew of the Hamilton galley," and to a "call of the gladiators this morning," and to the statement of Speaker Muhlenberg that "there had been a call of the Secretary's party last night."[26]

The gap between the legislature and the Executive, created by the constitutional system of separated powers, was thus bridged by the Hamiltonian or Federalist party organization before the First Congress ended. "Instead of being a forum, where every member was a peer and no man led, where great principles of government were evolved through the give and take of unrestricted discussion, Congress as such had become in effect a mere ratifying body. The real work of legislation was put in shape, not in the legislature, but in secret session of the majority party. In this organization, unknown to the Constitution and beyond the reach of the rules of either chamber, the executive could work with the party-following in Congress, and secure the adoption of a prearranged program."[27] Thus party tactics, already familiar in state legislatures, made an early appearance in Congress. They attained their peak of perfection a century later under the astute leadership of Speakers Reed and Cannon.

3

The Composition
of Congress

As THE YOUNG NATION GREW in population and expanded westward toward the Pacific, the size of the House of Representatives increased, although not at a corresponding pace. During the first half century the population quadrupled in number, growing from some 3.9 million in 1790 to 17 million in 1840, while representatives in Congress were increasing from 65 to 232 members. By 1890 the population had almost quadrupled again, rising to 63 million persons who were represented in Washington by 357 Congressmen. After another half century of amazing expansion, the nation had 132 million inhabitants in 1940, while the House of Representatives had limited its size since 1913 to 435 members. By 1960 the population had reached 180 million; and by 1975 it had climbed to 210 million.

Since the population grew more rapidly than the membership of the House of Representatives, the effect of these changes was gradually to increase the average number of inhabitants represented by each member. Thus during the First Congress the constituencies averaged about 33,000 persons compared with an average of 71,000 in 1840, 176,000 in 1890, 303,000 in 1940, 410,000 in 1960, and 495,000 in 1970. In other words, a member of the House today has fifteen times as many constituents on the average as he had in 1790.

It is also interesting to note the effect of these changes upon the distribution of seats in the House of Representatives among the principal geographical regions of the country. The South controlled half the seats in the House in the First Congress and today accounts for 134 seats, 31 per cent of the total. New England, which had about one quarter of the seats in 1790, now has about 6 per cent of the total. The Middle Atlantic states, which were on a par with New England in the beginning, now have 18 per cent or about three times as many representatives as New England. The North Central region, whose twelve stars did not appear upon the flag until the nineteenth century, now controls 121 seats (27 per cent) in the House— the second largest single regional bloc. And the eleven Western states, last to be admitted to the Union, prior to Alaska and Hawaii, account for 16 per cent of the present membership with seventy-three members.

History of Apportionment

Recalling the old system of "rotten" or "pocket" boroughs represented in the British House of Commons, the Founding Fathers provided in the Constitution of the new republic that representation in Congress should be apportioned among the several states according to their respective numbers and that the actual enumeration should be made within three years after the first meeting of the Congress, and within every ten years thereafter "in such manner as they shall by law direct." Article I, Section 2, further provided that "the number of Representatives shall not exceed one for every thirty thousand, but each state shall have at least one Representative." In the event of vacancies in the representation from any state, the governor thereof was to issue writs of election to fill them. The growth in the size of the House since 1789 is shown in the table below.

GROWTH IN SIZE OF HOUSE, 1789-1970

Year	Number of Representatives *	Year	Number of Representatives *
1789	65	1880	332
1790	106	1890	357
1800	142	1900	391
1810	186	1910	435
1820	213	1930	435
1830	242	1940	435
1840	232	1950	435
1850	237	1960	437
1860	243	1970	435
1870	293		

* No apportionment was made in 1920.

As the nineteenth century advanced and the country grew, the question of the formula to be employed in distributing representation among the states provoked bitter arguments on the House floor between spokesmen for the slow-growing and fast-growing commonwealths. Whether or not one representative should be added for each major fraction over the ratio was a particular bone of contention. The disuse of fractions in some of the early apportionment acts deprived some states of full representation in the House, notably the New England states. In 1832, for example, John Quincy Adams confided to his diary: "I passed an entirely sleepless night. The iniquity of the bill and the disreputable means by which so partial and unjust a distribution of the representation had been effected, agitated me so that I could not close my eyes. I was all night meditating in search of some device, if it were possible, to avert the heavy blow from Massachusetts and from New England."[1] Advocates of a small body argued, meanwhile, that it would result in economy and less confusion on the floor, more efficient transaction of business and greater opportunity for the individual member, reduced power of committees and less rigid rules. James Bryce suggested that it would also spare the House the hazards of a crowd psychology.[2]

There has been a readjustment of House representation every decade except during the period 1911 to 1929. The present total membership of 435 was first attained in 1913 and has not been changed since then. Congress has by law provided for the automatic apportionment of the 435 representatives among the states according to each census including and after that of 1950. After the admission of Alaska and Hawaii as states during the Eighty-sixth Congress, the size of the House temporarily increased to 437 members. The apportionment acts formerly provided that the districts in a state should equal the number of its representatives, with no district electing more than one member, and that the districts were to be composed of contiguous and compact territory containing as nearly as practicable an equal number of inhabitants; but the acts of 1929 and 1941 omitted such provisions. After any apportionment, until a state is redistricted in a manner provided by its own law, the question whether its representatives shall be elected by districts, at large, or by a combination of both methods, is determined by the Apportionment Act of 1941. The House has always seated members elected at large in the states, although the law required election by districts. Questions have arisen from time to time, when a vacancy has occurred soon after a change in districts, whether the vacancy should be filled by election in the old or new district. The House has declined to interfere with the act of a state in changing the boundaries of a district after the apportionment has been made.

Legislative Apportionment Procedure

The Apportionment Act of November 15, 1941, makes the procedure for apportioning representatives entirely automatic, requiring no action by Congress other than review. The right of Congress to change the procedure whenever it deems such action advisable has in no way been relinquished. As the first step in the procedure of apportionment, the Bureau of the Census enumerates the population and tabulates state totals within eight months after the start of the enumeration. As part of the report to accompany these population figures, a table shows the distribution of the existing number of representatives among the states, using the method of equal proportions. The report containing this information is transmitted to the Congress by the President within the first week of the next session of that body. In fifteen days the clerk of the House of Representatives informs the executive of each state of the number of members of the House of Representatives to which the state will be entitled in the following Congress, to meet about two years hence. Thus Congress has eliminated the possibility of a decade passing without a redistribution of seats, such as occurred during the decade 1920-1930. The use of a method based upon sound mathematical principles has been combined with an automatic procedure for putting the results of this method into effect.

The need for an automatic procedure that would assure a reapportionment after each decennial census was apparently felt at an early date, as the legislation for the seventh (1850) decennial census contained such a provision. The method specified by this act was the "Vinton Method." When, however, a new census act was passed in 1870, no mention was made of any reapportionment procedure, automatic or otherwise. Apparently the apportionments of both 1850 and 1860 as calculated under the procedures set up by the act of 1850 were not satisfactory, for in both years changes in assignments to certain states were made by supplementary legislation.

An automatic procedure was not discussed again to any extent until late in the decade 1920-1930. At that time a great many persons were disturbed by the failure of Congress to redistribute seats on the basis of the 1920 census, for it was felt that many states were not properly represented. Until the Seventy-third Congress, which convened in 1933, the number of representatives from each state remained as assigned on the basis of the census of 1910. Because of different rates of growth of the various states and because of the large migrations of people from one state to another during and after World War I, major injustices occurred. For example, one such injustice was corrected when the apportionment based on the census of 1930 went into effect and the state of California gained nine members, increasing its representation from eleven to twenty, although the size of the House did not change.

Major Fractions Versus Equal Proportions

As a result of feeling aroused by inequalities in apportionment, Congress took steps to prevent a repetition of such injustices and inserted an apportionment section in the act for the taking of the fifteenth (1930) and subsequent decennial censuses. The procedure adopted called for a report that included calculations by two methods—major fractions and equal proportions. If Congress did not act on this report within a year, an apportionment by the method last used went into effect automatically. When the Fifteenth Decennial Census Act was passed on June 18, 1929, the proponents of the methods of major fractions and of equal proportions were unable to come to an agreement. It was decided to require computations by both methods and then permit a period for debate after which a decision could be made between the two. When the computations based on the census of 1930 were made, however, they showed no difference between the results of the two methods. Thus the need for a decision did not arise, and an apportionment was effected without further action by Congress.

In the computations based upon the census of 1940, however, a difference between the methods in the allocation of one representative did occur. If the method of major fractions had been used, the number of representatives from the state of Arkansas would have decreased from seven to six, while an additional representative would have been added to the seventeen for the state of Michigan. By the method of equal proportions, the representations from Arkansas and Michigan remained at seven and seventeen respectively. The volume of other legislation in Congress caused a delay in the consideration of this topic until after the period of debate had expired, but Congress wished to consider further the issues raised by the apportionment report. The primary issue in this instance appears to have been the question of which method of apportionment was to be used. After extensive debate, Congress decided that the method of equal proportions was the more desirable, and the present procedure was established. Thus, after 150 years of discussion and debate, the procedure for reapportioning representatives in Congress has developed until now a reapportionment based on a sound statistical approach is assured after each decennial census.

Through the co-operation of legislator and technician, the fundamental adjustment of representation to population has been made the subject of a scientific procedure, thereby eliminating an important source of possible discontent with the workings of our government.

Reapportionments After 1960 and 1970

As a result of the reapportionment of 1960, nine states gained nineteen seats in the House of Representatives, and sixteen states lost twenty-one seats. Two of these twenty-one seats were those that had been temporarily allocated to Alaska and Hawaii upon their admission into the Union (thus raising the statutory limit temporarily from 435 to 437 seats) and that were dropped in the reapportionment after 1960. From a regional viewpoint, gains were registered by the East North Central (one), South Atlantic (three), Pacific (nine), and Mountain (one) states; losses were sustained by the New England (three), Middle Atlantic (four), East South Central (three), West South Central (one), and West North Central (five) states. After the 1970 census, the regional gains were in the Pacific (five), Mountain (two), South Atlantic (two), and West South Central (one) states; losses were sustained by the Middle Atlantic (four), West North Central (two), East North Central (two), and West South Central (two) states.

REGIONAL APPORTIONMENT OF SEATS IN THE HOUSE OF
REPRESENTATIVES BASED ON SELECTED CENSUSES

	1789 (Constitutional Apportionment)	1840 (6th Census)	1890 (11th Census)	1940 (16th Census)	1960 (18th Census)	1970 (19th Census)
New England	17	31	27	28	25	25
Middle Atlantic	18	63	72	92	83	79
North Central	0	50	128	131	125	121
South Atlantic	30	47	50	56	63	65
South Central	0	39	62	79	70	69
Mountain	0	0	7	16	17	19
Pacific	0	2	11	33	52	57
Total	65	232	357	435	435	435

Thus the past thirty years have seen considerable shifts in voting power in the House. The New England and Middle Atlantic states have gone from 120 seats, or 28 per cent of the total, to 105 seats, or 24 per cent of the total, while the Pacific states have gone from thirty-three seats to fifty-seven seats, or from 8 per cent to 13 per cent of the total. In the reapportionments after the 1960 census and the 1970 census, the largest gains were achieved by California (total of thirteen) and Florida (total of seven).

Disparities Within States

Although Congress determines the number of representatives, the state legislatures determine the boundaries of congressional districts. The long domination of these bodies by their rural members, party considerations, deadlocks following reapportionments, etc., have often resulted in some disparities in the population of congressional districts within states, as well as some rural-urban discrepancies, some gerrymandering, and on occasion selection of members-at-large. These conditions have been reflected in some rural overrepresentation, or urban underrepresentation, in Congress. During the decade 1940-1950, for example, rural districts were overrepresented in Congress by a margin of twelve members, and urban districts were underrepresented by fourteen, or seventeen if the District of Columbia is included. A prime example of rural-urban discrepancies was in Illinois where no redistricting occurred between 1901 and 1948. The Chicago area, with more than half the state's population, elected ten representatives, the remainder of the state fifteen. Congressmen added through federal reapportionment were elected at large.[3]

From time to time Congress has set up federal standards for the drawing of district lines by state legislatures. In 1842, when the practice of electing representatives by districts had become well established, the apportionment act of that year provided that representatives "should be elected by districts composed of contiguous territory equal in number to the representatives to which said state may be entitled, no one district electing more than one representative." The apportionment act passed after the census of 1850 contained no provision regarding districts. The requirement of 1842 was revived in 1862 and repeated in the act of 1872 with the added requirement that the districts should contain "as nearly as practicable an equal number of inhabitants." The 1872 act provided that if there were an increase in the quota of any state the additional members might be elected at large. These provisions were repeated after the census of 1880 and in 1891. In 1901 an act added the words "compact territory," and the clause read "contiguous and compact territory and containing as nearly as practicable an equal number of inhabitants." The act of 1911 repeated the 1901 requirement. Congress passed no apportionment act after the census of 1920, and the permanent act of June 18, 1929, contained no provision for compactness, contiguity, or equality in population. In 1932 the Supreme Court held, in the case of *Wood* v. *Broom,* that these requirements "did not outlast the apportionment to which they related," namely, the one made after the census of 1910. The act of 1940, which amended the act of 1929, likewise contained no such requirements.

In a special message to Congress on January 9, 1951, President Truman transmitted the results of the 1950 census of population by states and the number of representatives to which each state was entitled. He said that widespread discrepancies had grown up between the populations of the various congressional districts that should be corrected, and that several states had added Congressmen-at-large instead of redistricting as they should. From 1842 through 1911, said the President, the apportionment statutes had usually required the states to divide themselves into single-member districts composed of contiguous and compact territory and containing as nearly as practicable an equal number of inhabitants. He recommended that Congress promptly enact legislation reaffirming these basic standards and that it consider establishing limits of permissible deviation in population between districts of about 50,000 above and below the average size of about 350,000. Congress should also take steps, he said, to see that these standards were complied with.

President Truman's suggestions closely resembled recommendations made on December 22, 1950, by the Committee on Reapportionment of Congress of the American Political Science Association, under the chairmanship of Professor Arthur N. Holcombe of Harvard University. The A.P.S.A. committee recommended that the size of the House should not be changed; that the method of equal proportions be retained; that all members of Congress be elected by single-member districts rather than at large; that new legislation should contain express standards of equality and fairness in redistricting; that the deviation in size of congressional districts from the state average should preferably be kept within a limit of 10 per cent and should never exceed 15 per cent; and that the standards of approximate equality should be enforceable through an express sanction administered by Congress. The committee rejected suggestions that states maintaining unequal districts should be sued in the federal courts, deprived of their representation in the House, or compelled to elect their Congressmen at large. Instead, it urged that if the states do not create satisfactory districts for themselves, Congress should do it for them.

Following these political-science and presidential recommendations, Representative Celler, chairman of the House Judiciary Committee, introduced a bill (H.R. 2648) to amend the apportionment act of 1929 so as to require the states to establish congressional districts composed of contiguous and compact territories that should not vary by more than 15 per cent from the average size of districts in each state. The Celler bill also provided that "any Representative elected from a district which did not conform to these requirements should be denied his seat in the House of Representatives, and the clerk of the House should refuse his credentials." The Judiciary Committee held hearings on the Celler bill during 1951, but it was not reported. It also held hearings in 1959 on four similar bills establishing standards for congressional districts, but none of them went beyond the committee stage.

Although congressional efforts continued into the sixties, they became much less significant because of a series of important decisions by the Supreme Court. In 1962 the Court finally stated in *Baker* v. *Carr* that legislative apportionment was indeed a justiciable issue, abandoning the position it had taken in *Colegrove* v. *Green* in 1946 that the issue was a "political thicket." In 1964 the Court ruled in *Wesberry* v. *Sanders* that congressional districts must be "substantially equal." Relying on Article I, Section 2, of the Constitution, which states that the House of Representatives "shall be composed of members chosen every second year by the people of all the several states," the 6-to-3 opinion held that "one man's vote in a congressional election is to be worth as much as another's" and that "while it may not be possible to draw congressional districts with mathematical precision, there is no excuse for ignoring our Constitution's plain objective of making equal representation of equal numbers of people the fundamental goal of the House of Representatives."

The Supreme Court, while eschewing "mathematical precision," has nevertheless insisted on precise standards. In 1973 the Court in *White* v. *Weiser* invalidated a Texas reapportionment plan where the population differences between the largest and smallest districts was 19,275 persons and the total percentage deviation was 4.13 per cent. The plan was defended on the grounds that it met the intent of *Wesberry* v. *Sanders* and simultaneously protected a maximum number of incumbent members of the House and their seniority. The Court nevertheless selected an alternate plan where the absolute deviation between the largest and smallest districts was 696 persons, or .159 per cent. The Court, however, has yet to get involved in cases of gerrymandering, so that state legislatures are still free to employ highly partisan criteria in establishing district lines as long as they do so with considerable mathematical precision.

Qualifications for Election

The Constitution requires that a member of the House of Representatives must have attained the age of twenty-five, have been a citizen of the United States for seven years, and be an inhabitant of the state in which he is elected. In practice he is usually a resident of the district that he represents, but that is not a constitutional requirement. The American "locality rule," as it is called, reflects and supports the prevalent belief that a Congressman's primary obligation is to his own district rather than to the country as a whole. He is responsible to a local, not a national, electorate. His chief objective is re-election, so as to gain influence and political advancement. To this end he must spend much of his time promoting the interests of his district and running errands for the folks back home. No one has compiled a catalog of the very rare exceptions to this "locality rule." There have been a few such cases, particularly in New York City, where residents of uptown districts have occasionally sat for downtown districts.

Among the more prominent "carpetbaggers" of recent times are Ken Hechler, who was elected to the House in 1958 from a district in West Virginia in which he had resided for less than two years, and John V. Tunney, a New Yorker who won election to the House only four years after moving to California. In 1970, he was elected to the Senate. The late Robert F. Kennedy was elected to the Senate in 1965, shortly after moving from Massachusetts to New York. Yet a recent survey showed that 58 per cent of the members of the House were born in the districts they represent, while in the Senate, 75 per cent of the members were born in the states they represent.[4]

Qualifications for Voters

Members of Congress are elected by popular vote. The qualifications of voters in congressional elections, which are the same as for the electors of the most numerous branch of the state legislature, have changed over the years. After the Revolutionary War, property qualifications for voting existed in each of the thirteen states. Five states required the ownership of real estate; five states required either real estate or other property; while three states required no real estate but the possession of fifty pounds in money (New Jersey), or property of ten pounds' value (Georgia), or the payment of public taxes (Pennsylvania). The Revolution coincided with a gradual transition that was taking place from the ownership of real estate to taxpaying as a qualification for voting in the states.[5] It is estimated that between one-fifth and one-third of the adult white males were disfranchised by state law at the time of the adoption of the Constitution and that not more than 25 per cent of them voted on the ratification of that document.

The last decade of the eighteenth century witnessed further progress in the democratization of the franchise as four states—Georgia, South Carolina, Delaware, and New Jersey—adopted the taxpaying qualification; and four other states—New Hampshire, Kentucky, Maryland, and Vermont—provided for manhood suffrage.[6] Property qualifications for voting were dropped by South Carolina in 1778, New Hampshire in 1784, Georgia in 1789, and Delaware in 1792. Taxpaying qualifications expired in New Hampshire in 1792, in Georgia in 1798, and in South Carolina in 1810.

After 1800, party rivalry and the need of immigrants to settle the new states west of the Alleghenies led to the gradual extension of the franchise and the eclipse of the Federalist party which favored a limited suffrage. Ohio came into the Union in 1803, Louisiana in 1812, and Mississippi in 1817 without property qualifications. Thereafter no state entered the Union with either a property or taxpaying qualification. Maryland dropped its property requirement in 1810 and Connecticut in 1818; Massachusetts and New York followed suit in 1821.

By the 1830's practically all the original thirteen states had acquired a wide, if not universal, suffrage; and by the end of the Civil War almost universal manhood suffrage had been established for all whites. In the thirty-four states of the Union in 1860, the essential voting requirement was residence which ranged from six months to two years, and was typically one year in the state and from one to six months in the county. Free Negroes were allowed to vote in six states in 1860 and aliens in five states.[7] Meanwhile the taxpaying test had almost disappeared from all but four states. North Carolina abolished hers in 1868, and Delaware gave it up in 1897. Pennsylvania and Rhode Island abandoned theirs, which was only a registry fee, in 1933 and 1950 respectively. By the time of the Civil War all the new states either had been admitted with white male suffrage, or had achieved it under the influence of the Jacksonian philosophy.

Under the Fifteenth Amendment to the Constitution, adopted in 1870, "the right of citizens of the United States to vote shall not be denied or abridged by any State on account of race, color, or previous condition of servitude." Despite this provision, Blacks have long been systematically disfranchised in various states, and it was not until the Civil Rights Acts of 1957 and 1960 that Congress began to implement this article by legislation. Meanwhile, after long agitation, suffrage for women was achieved by adoption of the Nineteenth Amendment in 1920.

In the past decade the trend toward expanding the electorate has accelerated dramatically. In 1964 the Twenty-fourth Amendment outlawed the poll tax as a requirement for voting in federal elections. The Twenty-sixth Amendment in 1971 lowered the voting age to eighteen in all elections. The variety in state residence requirements was struck down by the Supreme Court in 1972 when it held in *Dunn* v. *Blumstein* that a residency requirement of more than thirty days was a violation of equal protection, although the rule was modified slightly in 1973 to allow states to impose residency requirements of up to fifty days for voters in state and local elections.[8]

In 1970 amendments to the Voting Rights Act of 1965 banned literacy tests and character tests in all states. The 1965 act even provided for the appointment of federal examiners to register persons to vote in those states or counties where less than 50 per cent of the voting-age registrants were registered to vote on November 1, 1964, and required the covered jurisdictions to obtain the approval of the Department of Justice before they could make any changes in their voting laws. That act was renewed for an additional seven years in 1975, and its coverage was extended to include significant population concentrations of Spanish-speaking Americans, American Indians, Alaskan natives, and Asian Americans.

Since 1965, about 1.5 million Blacks in the South have become registered voters, about 1.1 million in the states covered by the Voting Rights Act. Lowering the voting age added some 10.5 million voters to the rolls for the 1972 election.

Election Contests

Under Article I, Section 5, of the Constitution, "Each House shall be the judge of the elections, returns, and qualifications of its own members." Both houses may exclude members-elect by majority vote and may expel sitting members by a two-thirds vote. In practice, they have done so not only for failure to satisfy the constitutional requirements for membership, but also for other reasons. The Supreme Court has ruled that the power to expel a member after he has been seated extends to all cases where the offense is such, in the judgment of the House or Senate, as to be inconsistent with the trust and duty of a member.

The procedure with regard to contested elections for seats in the House of Representatives is prescribed by law and practice.[9] From 1789 down through 1951, some 541 election contests were decided by the House, an average of almost seven cases per Congress. The Sixth and Twentieth Congresses alone were barren of such contests. Their number reached a peak during the Civil War sessions (1861-1865), when 36 House contests were instituted, and a record high during the Fifty-fourth Congress (1895-1897), when there were 38 election contests. The House decided 126 contested-election cases from the Sixtieth Congress (1908) through the first session of the Eighty-second Congress (1951); but only thirteen contestants were seated. In two of these instances the election out of which the contest arose was declared null and void or the seat vacant.

Since 1957 there have been fourteen challenges, each of which has been dismissed. Five of those challenges were instituted in 1965 by the Mississippi Freedom Democratic Party, which insisted that the entire delegation of the state should be unseated because of racial discrimination in the electoral process. In rejecting the challenges, the House appears to have been persuaded by the arguments that precedents precluded noncandidates from contesting elections and that the alleged voter discrimination "even if true, is now a moot question" because of the enactment of the Voting Rights Act of 1965.

The Committee on Elections, which was the first standing committee appointed by the House in 1789 and which had a continuous history down to 1947 when it became a standing subcommittee of the Committee on House Administration, has jurisdiction over election contests and expulsions. Its reports and the action of the House upon them for more than a century and a half have developed a fairly coherent body of the law and practice of congressional contested-election cases, which have been compiled and digested by Rowell and Moores for the first sixty-four Congresses.[10]

Exclusion, Expulsion, and Censure

On various occasions the House has exercised its power to exclude members-elect, to expel members, or to censure them.

In 1870, for example, one B. F. Whittemore resigned from the House to escape expulsion for the sale of appointments at the Military Academy, but when he was promptly re-elected to the same House, it declined to let him take his seat. In 1882 the House excluded a delegate-elect from the territory of Utah for the disqualification of polygamy.[11]

The power of expulsion has frequently been discussed but seldom exercised by the House, especially in relation to offenses committed before election. In 1861, John B. Clark, a member-elect from Missouri who had not appeared or taken the oath, was expelled for treason. Later in the same year, Representatives John W. Reid of Missouri and Henry C. Burnett of Kentucky were expelled for treason. In general, the House has been dubious of its power to punish members for offenses committed before their election. In the South Carolina election case of Richard S. Whaley in 1913, it was held that the power of the House to expel one of its members is unlimited, a matter purely of discretion to be exercised by a two-thirds vote, from which there is no appeal. But the charges against Whaley were dismissed. The resignation of an accused member has always caused a suspension of expulsion proceedings. No cases of expulsion from the House since Civil War days are reported in *Hinds'* and *Cannon's Precedents*.[12]

While the composition of the House is not affected by the censure of members, this subject is worthy of our attention. Under Rule XIV, "If any Member, in speaking or otherwise, transgress the rules of the House, and, if the case require it, he shall be liable to censure or such punishment as the House may deem proper." The annals of Congress disclose only sixteen cases in which members have been censured by the House. The last recorded censure case occurred in October, 1921, and involved Representative Thomas L. Blanton of Texas.[13]

Certainly the most celebrated attempt at expulsion in modern times involved Representative Adam Clayton Powell, Jr., of New York. In 1967 the House voted to exclude Powell from the Ninetieth Congress primarily because of his misuse of congressional funds. A select committee had investigated those charges and had recommended only that Powell be fined $40,000, stripped of his seniority, and censured. In upholding his contention that he had been illegally excluded, the Supreme Court ruled that the House could not exclude an elected representative who met the constitutional requirements of age, residence, and citizenship. However, the opinion did not affect the right of the House to expel a member, an action which, as already noted, requires a two-thirds vote.[14]

Term of Office

Representatives are elected for two-year terms in general elections held in the fall of the even-numbered years and take office the following January 3. Before the ratification of the Twentieth Amendment, the terms of Representatives began on March 4 and terminated on March 3. This resulted from the action of the Continental Congress on September 13, 1788, in declaring, on authority conferred by the Federal Convention, "the first Wednesday in March next" to be "the time for commencing proceedings under the said Constitution." Every Congress formerly had a long and a short session. The long session began early in December after the November elections and continued, with a Christmas recess, until the following summer. The short session began in December after the summer recess and lasted until the fourth of the following March. This schedule meant that the business of the short session was often greatly congested and that it contained numerous "lame duck" representatives who had lost their seats but continued to legislate for three months. It was not until 1932 that the House reluctantly joined the Senate in proposing a constitutional amendment abolishing the short session of Congress. As ratified in 1933, the Twentieth Amendment changed the congressional calendar by providing that the annual sessions shall begin on January 3.

The House as a Career

Despite a new pension law in 1969, which appears to have increased the number of House members who retired in 1972 and 1974, and despite the Democratic landslide in the post-Watergate election, the Ninety-fourth Congress convened in 1975 with 41 per cent of its members having been elected to six or more terms, 14 per cent having been elected to ten or more terms.[15] When the Fifty-eighth Congress (1903-04) convened, only 13.2 per cent of its members had six or more terms.[16] Of the 391 members of the House in 1900, 36 had served five or more consecutive terms; 3 had served ten or more consecutive terms; and 2 had been in the House for thirty years or longer. Of the 435 members in the House in 1975, 206 had served five or more consecutive terms; 61 had served ten or more consecutive terms; and 18 had been in the House for thirty years or longer.

Thus the major characteristic of the twentieth-century House is that it has become "institutionalized." As Nelson W. Polsby has put it, "As an organization institutionalizes, it stabilizes its membership, entry is more difficult, and turnover is less frequent. Its leadership professionalizes and persists."[17] For example, in 1875 nearly three out of five members of the House were in their first term; a century later only about one-fifth were freshmen. Before 1899 there were thirty-three Speakers, none of whom had served in the House for more than fourteen years. Since 1899 there have been thirteen Speakers, all of whom have had more than fifteen or more years of service.[18] The present Speaker, Carl Albert, has served since 1947; his predecessor, Sam Rayburn, was elected to twenty-five terms.

Thanks to its habit of re-electing the same legislators term after term, the South has long occupied a leading place in congressional councils. During the Eighty-fifth Congress, continuity of service reaped its reward in the twelve chairmanships out of the nineteen standing committees of the House that were held by Southerners, including such significant committees as Rules, Ways and Means, Interstate and Foreign Commerce, Agriculture, and Banking and Currency. Despite the increased competitiveness of many Southern districts, in the Ninety-fourth Congress Southerners still chaired eleven of the twenty-two standing committees, including Appropriations, Education and Labor, Interior and Insular Affairs, Public Works and Transportation, and Interstate and Foreign Commerce.

The rule of seniority is a factor not only in the choice of committee chairmen, but also in the distribution of office suites in the House Office Buildings, in committee assignments, in the appointment of members of the influential conference committees, and even in the protocol of social life in the nation's capital. Seniority in the House of Representatives is a major factor in giving a member position and influence in the Congress and in Washington.

Speaking to the "baby Congressmen" on "The Making of a Representative," Speaker Clark once said: "A man has to learn to be a Representative just as he must learn to be a blacksmith, a carpenter, a farmer, an engineer, a lawyer, or a doctor." And "as a rule," he continued, "the big places go to old and experienced members" of the House. Recent modifications of seniority have not been so significant as to diminish the accuracy of that observation.

Membership Characteristics

Some impression of the character of Congress in the early part of the nineteenth century is gained from the letters of contemporaries. In a letter to his son dated December 30, 1805, Senator William Plumer of New Hampshire described his messmates as follows:[19]

> . . . A better collection or more agreeable society cannot be found in this wilderness city than at Coyle's. There you will find in Pick the stern severity of a Roman Cato; in Tracy genius, wit, poetry, and eloquence; in Dana extensive information, deep erudition and the correct scholar united with an inexhaustible fund of wit and pleasantry; in Hillhouse a sample of court cunning mingled with the manners of low life; in Mosely a chesterfield in dress and address with a tincture of true attic salt; in Pitkin application and shew united; in Davenport the manners of a blunt unpolished countryman— zeal and bigotry of blind superstition; in Smith manners more polished, some knowledge of the world, and much of that which floats on the surface; in Talmadge much of that plain sound sense which is so necessary to render any man what he is, a man of business and honesty; in Stedman wit, shrewdness, good sense, and prudence; in Chittenden good sense and frankness who directly pursues the object; in Ellis information, caution, and reserve with the timidity and taciturnity of an old bachelor; in Sturgis plain unaspiring common sense; and of Betton you know what.

In the same year Augustus Foster, Secretary of the British Legation, sent his mother, the Duchess of Devonshire, the following impressions of Washington and Congress:[20]

> This undoubtedly is a miserable place, but the elect of all the states are assembled in it, and really such a gang to have the affairs of an empire wanting little of the size of Russia entrusted to them, makes one shudder. Imagination is dead in this country. Wit is neither to be found nor is it understood

among them. All the arts seem to shrink from it, and you hear of nothing but calculation and speculation in money or in politics. . . . People's depth of reading goes no farther than Tom Paine's muddy pamphlets or their muddier political newspapers. In Congress there are about five persons who look like gentlemen. All the rest come in the filthiest dresses and are well indeed if they look like farmers—but most seem apothecaries and attorneys. . . . Randolph alone speaks well; strangest looking demagog you ever set eyes on, but gentlemanlike and for this country a prodigy. . . .

Occupationally the House of Representatives, like the House of Commons, has never been a mirror to the nation. Some occupations are greatly overrepresented in Congress, notably the legal profession which accounted for 37 per cent of the membership of the House in 1790, 70 per cent in 1840, 67 per cent in 1890, 54 per cent in 1957, and 47 per cent in 1975. Other occupational groups such as workers in manufacturing and farming, persons employed in the service trades, and domestic servants have been greatly underrepresented in Congress or not directly represented at all. The table on the next page shows the occupations and professions of the members of the Seventy-second, Eighty-fifth, and Ninety-fourth Houses.

The first woman ever to become a member of Congress was Jeannette Rankin (Republican, Montana) who was elected to the Sixty-fifth House in 1916. She served one term and was elected again in 1940 to the Seventy-seventh Congress. Beginning with the Sixty-seventh Congress, there have always been one or more women in the national legislature. Several of them succeeded their deceased husbands in the House. There were ten women in the Seventy-ninth House and fifteen in the Eighty-fifth, including such veterans as Frances P. Bolton of Ohio, Edith Nourse Rogers of Massachusetts, and Katharine St. George of New York. In the Ninety-fourth Congress there were eighteen women. Leonor K. Sullivan of Missouri began her congressional career in 1951, Patsy T. Mink of Hawaii in 1965, and Margaret M. Heckler of Massachusetts in 1967. Seven of the women were first elected in 1972, and six in 1974.

Political Complexion

Five major political parties vied for control of the House of Representatives after 1789: the Federalists versus the Jeffersonian Republicans, 1789-1828; the Whigs versus the Democrats, 1829-1855; the Republicans versus the Democrats, 1856-1975. The Federalists were in power in the First Chamber for six years (1789-1793, 1799-1801) and later the Whigs for an equal span (1839-1843, 1847-1849).

Occupation	72d	85th	94th
Accounting		2	1
Advertising and Public Relations		5	8
Agriculture	12	20	12
Banking		5	3
Business and/or Manufacturing	82	49	43
Civil Service		2	1
Dentistry	2	1	
Education	12	23	31
Engineering	5	1	1
Investments		3	5
Journalism, including Radio	14	23	18
Labor		4	5
Law	274	234	204
Medicine and Surgery	5	5	3
Pharmacist		1	
Public Official		23	48
Real Estate and/or Insurance		16	16
Secretary (Congressional)		7	11
Social Welfare		4	2
Miscellaneous	4	8	22
Not indicated	20		
Vacancies	5		1
	435	435	435

Over the 186-year period since 1789, the Jeffersonian Republicans and the Democrats have controlled the House for 116 years and the Republicans for 58. After the decline of the Federalists, the Jeffersonian Republicans and the Jacksonian Democrats held sway for thirty-eight years (1801-1839), but almost a century passed before they enjoyed another long period of supremacy during the New Deal era when they controlled the House for fourteen years (1933-1947). From 1801 down to the eve of the Civil War, the Democrats kept control of the House of Representatives in all but four Congresses. Then, during the Civil War and Reconstruction period, the Republicans were in power for sixteen years (1859-1875). Thereafter the political pendulum swung back and forth between the two major parties, with the Republicans controlling the House for two long periods: from 1895 to 1911 and from 1919 to 1933. During the past century the dominant political complexion of the House was Republican for forty years and Democratic for sixty years. Since 1933, the Republicans have controlled the House only during 1947-1948 and 1953-1954.

More than 500 seats in the House have been held over the years by the representatives of minor parties and by a few Independents. During the

Thirty-fourth to Thirty-seventh Congresses, inclusive, 108 seats were occupied by members of the American Party one of whom, Nathaniel P. Banks of Massachusetts, was chosen Speaker in the Thirty-fourth Congress. Upwards of 40 "Independents" have sat in the House of Representatives in the course of time, among them such memorable figures as George W. Norris of Nebraska and Fiorello La Guardia of New York.

Various Evaluations

Political cartoonists have lampooned Congress down through the years as a body composed of middle-aged windbags with open mouths, ten-gallon Texas hats, and flowing coattails. But the conventional picture underestimates the real character of our national legislature. "In plain fact," remarks a close observer, "Congress is neither as doltish as the cartoonists portray it nor as noble as it portrays itself. While it has its quota of knaves and fools, it has its fair share of knights. And sandwiched between these upper and nether crusts is a broad and representative slice of upper-middle-class America."[21]

Of the thousands of members who have sat in the Hall of the House since 1789, the overwhelming majority have been patriotic, conscientious, hard-working men and women. Many historic personages have marched across the congressional stage during its 186 crowded years and passed into the annals of history. Most of them have disappeared into the oblivion of the past, leaving only their biographies in the records of Congress. But a few mighty men of old writ large their names on the scroll of time and linger on in political memory.[22] Every decade in the history of the House has seen a little group of great debaters in that chamber, arguing the changing issues of national concern and adorning the pages of the *Congressional Record* with their brilliant speeches. "As one studies the great debates of the past century," remarked Alexander, "the fact appears that speakers who have commanded the country's attention come in groups. Indeed, it may be said that the congressional firmament reveals constellations of genius as clearly as the heavens disclose brilliant star clusters."[23] Behind the bright stars in every session, however, have been the unsung heroes—the old professionals and committee specialists, the John McCormacks and Thor Tollefsons—who have carried on the unspectacular but essential work of lawmaking.

In fact, it seems difficult to generalize regarding the quality of the membership of Congress down through the years. Any body as numerous as a national legislature has had its share of both mediocre and outstanding men. It seems safe to say that, in the long view, the calibre of Congress compares favorably with that of most other legislatures in the modern world.

When Alexis de Tocqueville first visited the American House of Representatives during the Jacksonian era, he was "struck by the vulgar demeanor of that great assembly. "Often," he wrote, "there is not a distinguished man in the whole number. Its members are almost all obscure individuals . . . village lawyers, men in trade, or even persons belonging to the lower classes of society."[24]

Fifty years later James Bryce offered this evaluation.[25]

> Watching the House at work, and talking to the members in the lobbies, an Englishman naturally asks himself how the intellectual quality of the body compares with that of the House of Commons. His American friends have prepared him to expect a marked inferiority. . . . A stranger who has taken literally all he hears is therefore surprised to find so much character, shrewdness, and keen though limited intelligence among the representatives. Their average business capacity did not seem to me below that of members of the House of Commons of 1880-85. True it is that great lights, such as usually adorn the British chamber, are absent; true also that there are fewer men who have received a high education which has developed their tastes and enlarged their horizons. The want of such men depresses the average. . . . In respect of width of view, of capacity for penetrating thought on political problems, representatives are scarcely above the class from which they came, that of second-rate lawyers or farmers, less often merchants or petty manufacturers. They do not pretend to be statesmen in the European sense of the word, for their careers, which have made them smart and active, have given them little opportunity for acquiring such capacities. As regards manners they are not polished, because they have not lived among polished people; yet neither are they rude, for to get on in American politics one must be civil and pleasant. The standard of parliamentary language, and of courtesy generally, has been steadily rising during the last few decades. . . . Scenes of violence and confusion such as occasionally convulse the French chamber, and were common in Washington before the War of Secession, are now unknown.

Certain historical changes in the composition of the House are also worth noting, as well as a more recent development. Since the Civil War, the tendency has been for the age of first-term members to increase, for the length of service to increase, and for the average age of all the members of the House of Representatives to rise. For example, in the Forty-first Congress (1869-1971), the median age of all members was forty-five; of first-term members it was forty-two; and the average number of terms served was 1.04. In the Sixty-eighth Congress (1923-1925), the median age of all Representatives was fifty-one; of first-term members, forty-seven; and the average period of legislative service was 2.5 terms.[26] The long-run trends continued up to the 1970's. In the Seventy-ninth Congress (1945-1947), the median age of all Representatives was fifty-two. In the Ninety-third (1973-1975), it was fifty-three, but in the Ninety-fourth (1975-1977), it was fifty. The median age of the House freshmen in those three Congresses was forty-six, forty-two, and forty-one and a half respectively. And the average number of terms served was 4.5, 5.7, and 5.3.

However, several additional data are worth noting in assessing the situation in 1975. In 1972 the first year of eligibility for the new retirement benefits, twenty-nine incumbents retired. In 1974 twenty-five House incumbents retired. These figures should be contrasted with 1970 and 1968, when only eight and thirteen retired.[27] While this trend may continue for several more sessions, it is obvious that it is a movement that will flatten out. In addition, speculations on turnover in the House which may result from increased Republican activity in the South or the more recent speculation that the restrictions on campaign financing enacted in 1974 will work to the advantage of incumbents, do not impinge on the insistence that for most members the House is, hopefully, a home.

4

Organization of the House

UNDER THE CONSTITUTION as amended, Congress assembles at least once each year at noon on January 3, unless it shall by law appoint a different day.[1] At the opening of the first regular session of each new Congress in the odd-numbered years, the House and Senate organize themselves anew. The manner in which the House organizes itself for business may be illustrated by the proceedings in that chamber on January 3, 1957. Promptly at noon on that day, Ralph Roberts, clerk of the House during the Eighty-fourth Congress, called it to order and, after the chaplain's prayer, directed a clerk to call the roll by states of members-elect whose credentials had been received. When the roll call had been completed, the clerk of the House announced that 428 members-elect had answered to their names and that a quorum was present. He also announced that credentials in regular form had been received showing the election of the delegates from Alaska and Hawaii and of the resident commissioner from Puerto Rico.

The chairmen of the Republican and Democratic party conferences then nominated Mr. Joseph W. Martin, Jr., and Mr. Sam Rayburn, respectively, for the office of Speaker. The clerk appointed tellers to canvass the vote on the election of the Speaker, and Mr. Rayburn was elected, having received a majority of the whole number of votes cast. Thereupon the clerk declared that Mr. Rayburn had been elected Speaker of the House of Representatives for the Eighty-fifth Congress and appointed a committee to escort the Speaker to the chair. The Speaker was escorted to the chair by the committee and was introduced to the House by Mr. Martin. Mr. Rayburn then addressed the House, voicing his appreciation of his election and paying tribute to the principles and responsibilities of representative government. Mr.

Vinson of Georgia, next ranking member of the House in point of continuous service, then administered the oath of office to Mr. Rayburn. The members-elect and delegates-elect then rose in their places and took the oath of office prescribed by law.

The respective conference chairmen then announced that the Hon. John W. McCormack of Massachusetts had been selected as majority leader of the House and that the Hon. Joseph W. Martin, Jr., of Massachusetts had been chosen as minority leader.

Resolutions were then offered by the chairmen of the party conferences nominating their respective candidates for the offices of clerk of the House, sergeant at arms, doorkeeper, postmaster, and chaplain; and the candidates of the Democratic party, which was in the majority, were elected. The officers then presented themselves at the bar of the House and took the oath of office.

Then, in quick succession, the House adopted resolutions notifying the Senate that it had assembled and chosen its Speaker and clerk, and authorizing the Speaker to appoint a committee of three members to join with a similar Senate committee to notify the President of the United States that Congress had assembled and was ready to receive any communication that he might be pleased to make.

Mr. Smith of Virginia, who was to be the chairman of the Committee on Rules, then offered a resolution for the adoption of the rules of the Eighty-fifth Congress, which was agreed to. Before the adoption of rules, the House proceeds under general parliamentary law. The rules and orders of a previous Congress are not in effect until adopted by the sitting House.

Resolutions authorizing a joint session of Congress on January 7 to count the electoral vote and providing for the creation of a joint committee to make necessary arrangements for the inauguration of President-elect Eisenhower were then agreed to. Thus, in little less than two hours, the House of Representatives had organized itself, elected its officers, and adopted its rules for the next two years.

The solemnity and pomp of the opening-day ceremonies often fail to reflect the considerable controversy that frequently accompanies the beginning of the new session. These struggles are usually a feature of the respective party caucuses that precede the first day of the session. For example, shortly before the Eighty-ninth Congress convened on January 4, 1965, the Democratic caucus censured and stripped of their seniority rights Representative John Bell Williams of Mississippi and Representative Albert W. Watson of South Carolina. Both had campaigned for the Republican presidential candidate, Senator Barry Goldwater. It was the first time a House Democrat had been punished for party disloyalty since 1911.[2] On the morning of January fourth, the Republican Conference (caucus) had spent several abrasive hours as Representative Gerald R. Ford, Jr., of Michigan defeated Representative Charles A. Halleck of Indiana for the post of minority floor leader by a vote of 74 to 70 and elected Representative Melvin R. Laird of Wisconsin over Representative Peter Frelinghuysen of New Jersey as chairman of the conference by a vote of 75 to 62.[3]

A similar contrast between the sobriety of the opening ceremonies and the caucuses that preceded them took place in 1971 when Representative Hale Boggs needed two ballots to defeat Representative Morris K. Udall of Arizona as the Democratic majority leader while Representative John B. Anderson of Illinois was winning over Representative Samuel L. Devine of Ohio in a close vote for the chairmanship of the Republican Conference.[4] As we have already noted, the most intense opening-day atmosphere took place in 1975. By the time the Ninety-fourth Congress had convened, the Democratic caucus had created a new Committee on Committees, launched an assault on the seniority system, and abolished the Internal Security Committee. An opening-day debate saw the Democrats defeating a Republican attempt to amend the rules with a near party-line vote.[5]

Election Contests

In normal times the organization of the House has proceeded in a congenial manner. But during the first half of the nineteenth century the election of the Speaker gave rise to several minor contests, and on at least four occasions to sharp contests that ran on for days or weeks. From 1820 on, the slavery question underlay these disputes, which grew more and more violent during the 1840's and 1850's. Before he left the House in 1861 to join the Confederacy, Representative John H. Reagan of Texas attributed the dissolution of the Union in large part to these passionate arguments.

Ordinarily a Speaker is chosen on the first ballot, if one political party in the House has a clear majority and if party lines are tightly held. But at least ten contests for the Speakership took place during the decades before the Civil War. The first occurred in 1809 when the vote was divided among five candidates on the first ballot, with none receiving a majority. On the second ballot Nathaniel Macon of North Carolina, who had served as Speaker from 1801 to 1807, withdrew for reasons of health, and Joseph B. Varnum of Massachusetts was elected.

The next contest took place in November, 1820, after Henry Clay resigned the Speakership. On that occasion there were three candidates: John W. Taylor of New York, William Lowndes of South Carolina, and Samuel Smith of Maryland. The contest lasted two days and twenty-two ballots before Taylor, the antislavery candidate, was elected over Lowndes, the compromiser.

In 1821, Philip C. Barbour of Virginia was chosen on the second day and the twelfth ballot over Taylor of New York by a majority of one. Taylor won in 1825 on the second ballot over two other candidates. In 1834, after Stevenson's resignation, John Bell of Tennessee was finally elected on the tenth ballot. In 1847, Robert C. Winthrop of Massachusetts was elected on the third ballot, and in 1861 Galusha Grow of Pennsylvania on the second vote.

The great prebellum fights for the Speakership came in 1839, 1849, 1855, and 1859 and imposed a severe test upon our representative institutions. Those were exciting days in which the passions of sectional conflict and party strife inflamed the House and the qualifications and politics of candidates were closely inspected.

Contest of 1839

The first session of the Twenty-sixth Congress met on December 2, 1839, but did not succeed in electing a Speaker until December 16. The delay was caused by the fact that five of the six New Jersey seats were contested and by the refusal of the clerk, who was presiding according to established usage, either to decide between the conflicting claimants or to put any question until a quorum of the House was formed. The effect of these two decisions was to prevent the transaction of any business as well as the organization of the House. Excluding the New Jersey delegation, there were 119 Democrats and 118 Whigs in the House. Control of the House depended upon which delegation from New Jersey was admitted.

After four days of debate and disorder, during which the clerk persisted in his refusal to put any question until the House should be organized, John Quincy Adams arose and earnestly appealed to the House to organize itself by proceeding with the roll call and ordering the clerk to call the members from New Jersey who held credentials from the governor of the state. When someone asked who would put the question, Adams replied: "I will put the question myself." And when a resolution was offered that Adams be appointed chairman of the meeting, it was carried "by an almost universal shout in the affirmative."[6] Such was the confidence of that body in its leading statesman.

Under Adams' firm guidance the House finally agreed to vote on December 14. On the first day of voting an attempt was made to postpone election of a Speaker and to hear and decide the New Jersey contest first, but the House declined to let either delegation from that state take part in its organization. There were six candidates for Speaker on the first vote and thirteen on the final eleventh vote on December 16. Robert M. T. Hunter of Virginia was finally elected Speaker over John W. Jones of the same state who fell only five votes short of election on the first vote and who led the balloting on the first five rounds. As Adams concluded his eye-witness account of this furious struggle, Hunter "finally united all the Whig votes, and all the malcontents of the Administration."[7]

Contest of 1849

In 1849 a great battle for the Speakership took place that lasted for three weeks and 63 ballots. No party had a majority in the chamber when the Thirty-first Congress met because several Free-Soil Whigs and Democrats acted independently. The basic issue was whether or not the District and Territorial committees were to have proslavery majorities, which would be determined by the identity of the Speaker who had the power to appoint the committees. The two leading candidates were Robert C. Winthrop of Massachusetts, the Whig candidate, who had been Speaker of the previous House; and Howell Cobb of Georgia, the Democratic candidate. At one stage in the proceedings it was proposed, in an effort to facilitate organization, that whoever was elected Speaker should be divested of power to construct the committees, but no action was taken on this motion.[8] According to one member, the committees had long been composed so as to pigeon-hole all petitions for the abolition of the slave trade.

On the first vote, on December 3, 1849, there were eleven candidates led by Howell Cobb who received 103 votes, 8 short of a majority. Viva-voce voting for a Speaker continued daily until December 22. After the thirteenth vote a motion to elect a Speaker by a plurality of votes (made by Andrew Johnson) and a motion to select a Speaker from the top four or two candidates (made by Frederick P. Stanton) were made and tabled. After the thirtieth vote Lewis C. Levin proposed that the Speaker's chair be filled by lottery. Five names would be placed in a box, one by each of the five political parties or factions, and the first name drawn from the box by the Clerk would be Speaker. The five factions were the Whigs, Democrats, Native Americans, Free Soilers, and Taylor Democrats. This motion was also tabled. A similar proposal that the Speaker be chosen by lot, with only the names of Cobb and Winthrop in the box, was likewise tabled.

Other efforts to resolve the prolonged deadlock met a similar fate, including motions to elect a Speaker by ballot, or by plurality, or by less than a majority vote, or from the top three or two on the list, or to elect a Speaker pro tempore and other officers. After the forty-fourth vote, proposals were made but not adopted that Congressmen should receive no salary or mileage until a Speaker had been elected. On December 17 a proposal to appoint a committee to recommend some practicable and acceptable method of expediting the organization of the House was tabled by the margin of a single vote; and a motion to appoint certain named persons as officers of the House was also lost. Two days later, Andrew Johnson suggested that ministers of the gospel be invited to attend and pray for a speedy and satisfactory organization, but even this appeal to the Deity was tabled, as was another motion to appoint a committee of one from each state delegation "to concert and report suitable measures for the speedy organization of this House."[9] Meanwhile the Whig and Democratic parties had appointed committees to confer and report some solution to the dilemma.

After a struggle of unprecedented duration and gravity, it was clear that a Speaker could not be elected by majority vote. Finally, on December 22, 1849, the House agreed by a vote of 113 to 106 to Stanton's motion to elect a Speaker by a plurality, provided it be a majority of a quorum. For the first time in its history the House surrendered the principle of majority rule. For sixty votes Cobb and Winthrop had been alternately in the lead. At long last, on the sixty-third vote, amid intense excitement, Howell Cobb received 102 votes out of 222, and Winthrop received 100, with 20 votes scattered among eight others. Cobb was chosen by a plurality of votes, being a majority of a quorum of the House, which then confirmed his election by majority vote.

Commenting on this contest in 1895, Mary P. Follett wrote:[10]

> Southern suspense was now relieved. If the Whigs had elected their candidate in 1849 the Civil War might have been delayed, for the committees of this Congress affected the Compromise of 1850. It is probable that Mr. Winthrop's prestige would have carried him into the Senate and eventually have affected the makeup of the Republican Party. The choice of a very pronounced proslavery and Southern man at this crisis undoubtedly aggravated the struggles of the following decade.

Contest of 1855

Another prolonged struggle over the election of a Speaker took place at the opening of the Thirty-fourth Congress in December, 1855. It continued for two months and took 133 ballots to decide. Here again the basic issue was whether the committees of the House would be organized in a manner hostile or friendly to slavery. The candidates were examined with respect to their political opinions, reflecting the political character of the contest and the power of the Speakership position. Since 1849 the irrepressible conflict over slavery had gained momentum, and the overriding question was whether Kansas should be on the side of freedom or slavery. The two leading political parties in the House were now the Republican party, which had emerged in the congressional elections of 1854 and replaced the Whigs, and the Democratic party. The "Anti-Nebraska men" had a majority in the Thirty-fourth Congress, but were unable to unite behind a single candidate.

On December 3, 1855, on the first vote for Speaker, votes were cast viva voce for twenty-one candidates, but none received a majority. William A. Richardson of Illinois led with 74 out of 225 votes. After the twenty-third vote, Mr. Lewis D. Campbell of Ohio, one of the top two candidates in the voting, withdrew from the race. After the fifty-ninth vote, a motion to drop the lowest candidates on the list progressively until two only should remain and that the higher of these two should then be the duly elected Speaker, was tabled. After two weeks of deadlock, a motion was offered that, after organizing, the House should do no business except pass the necessary appropriation bills and that then all the members should resign their seats; but this, too, was tabled. As in 1839, it was suggested that the House solve the problem by appointing certain committees itself, but this proposal was not accepted. Weeks of maneuvering and negotiating passed, but neither the Democrats nor the Free-Soilers would yield in their determination to control the committees for or against slavery.

Meanwhile, on a long series of votes, Mr. Nathaniel P. Banks of Massachusetts fell only half a dozen votes short of the number necessary to a choice. After two months of tedious roll calls, the House finally decided to settle the contest, as it had in 1849, by a resort to plurality rule. And on February 2, 1856, on the one hundred and thirty-third vote, Banks was declared Speaker of the House, having received 103 out of 214 votes cast. William Aiken of South Carolina was second with 100 votes.[11] Banks' election was subsequently confirmed by a resolution adopted by a majority vote. The House then proceeded to complete its organization by the election of a Clerk and other officers. According to Miss Follett, "Mr. Banks was elected above all because it was expected that he would constitute the committees in favor of the Free-Soilers. He justified this expectation by putting a majority of antislavery men on the Kansas Investigation committee, which act practically delayed the settlement of the Kansas episode until after 1857, and thus gave time for the antislavery forces to organize."[12]

Contest of 1859

The last great contest for the Speakership in the nineteenth century occurred at the opening of the Thirty-sixth Congress on the eve of the Civil War. The first session of this Congress met on December 5, 1859, but the House did not succeed in electing a Speaker until February 1, 1860, when

William Pennington of New Jersey, a new member, was chosen on the forty-fourth ballot. No political party had a majority of the House, which was then composed of 109 Republicans, 88 administration Democrats, 13 anti-Lecompton Democrats, and 27 Americans. The agitated state of public opinion on the slavery question was reflected in the desperate fight for the Speakership that ensued.

After the first vote, on which sixteen candidates received a total of 230 votes, the highest having 86 votes, which was not a majority, Mr. John B. Clark of Missouri offered a resolution that no member of the House who had endorsed and recommended a book hostile to slavery called *The Impending Crisis of the South: How to Meet It,* written by one Hinton R. Helper, was fit to be Speaker.[13] The next day Mr. John A. Gilmer of North Carolina offered a second resolution, calling on all good citizens to resist all attempts at renewing the slavery agitation in or out of Congress and resolving that no member should be elected Speaker whose political opinions were not known to conform to such sentiments.[14] These resolutions were aimed at John Sherman, the Republican candidate, who had endorsed Helper's book. They set the stage for the bitter struggle that followed.

Voting for Speaker proceeded very slowly, amid scenes of uproar and confusion, as the clerk who was presiding declined to decide any questions of order. All such questions were submitted to the House and debated, so that it was impossible to expedite the proceedings. Sometimes only one vote would be taken during a day, the remainder of the time being consumed in passionate arguments. The galleries were packed with partisans of both sides, whose applause and hisses goaded the gladiators on the floor. Members came armed with revolvers and bowie knives, and it looked as if the Civil War might begin in the House itself. Filibustering by the Southern Democrats was chiefly responsible for the long delay in the organization of the House.

On the second vote for Speaker, John Sherman of Ohio received 107 out of 231 votes, and on the third vote he had 110, only six short of the necessary majority. But by the end of January, the Republicans realized that Sherman could not be elected because of the bitterness over the slavery issue, and so they swung their support to Mr. Pennington of New Jersey, a new member and a political unknown. Finally, on February 1, 1860, almost two months after the beginning of the session, he was chosen Speaker of the House on the forty-fourth vote, receiving 117 votes out of 233, the exact number necessary to a choice. Pennington's name first appeared on the thirty-eighth ballot on which he received one vote. On the fortieth vote he jumped from 1 to 115, from the bottom to the top of the list, and remained in the lead until he was elected. In his speech of acceptance he said in part:[15] "After witnessing the almost insurmountable obstacles in the way

of the organization of this House, I came to the conclusion that any gentleman, of any party, who could command a majority of the votes for Speaker,
was bound, in deference to the public exigencies, to accept the responsibility as an act of patriotic duty. . . ."

Contest of 1923

No serious contest for the Speakership took place on the floor of the House
after the Thirty-sixth Congress until the opening of the Sixty-eighth Congress on December 3, 1923. At that time the political complexion of the
House consisted of 225 Republicans, 205 Democrats, 1 Independent, 1
Farmer-Laborite, and 1 Socialist; but the balance of power in the chamber
was held by about 20 Progressives who wore the Republican party label,
but who presented a candidate of their own—Mr. Cooper of Wisconsin—as
a "protest to the rules that have grown up in this body."[16] The regular Republicans nominated Mr. Frederick H. Gillett of Massachusetts for Speaker,
the Democratic nominee was Mr. Finis J. Garrett of Tennessee, while Mr.
Martin B. Madden of Illinois was also nominated by Mr. Reid of that state
as a Republican candidate from the Middle West.

Four roll calls were held on the first day, and four more on the second
day, all without result. On the first roll call Gillett received 197 votes, Garrett 195, Cooper 17, and Madden 5. On the evening of the second day Mr.
Longworth, the Republican floor leader, arrived at a gentlemen's agreement
with the Progressives regarding a revision of the House rules, as a result of
which Mr. Gillett was elected Speaker on the ninth roll call on December 5,
receiving 215 votes to 197 for Garrett and 2 for Madden.[17]

Since the Sixty-eighth Congress there have been no unusual contests for
the Speakership, one party having always been in the majority and its candidate having always received a majority of the votes cast on the first ballot.

Seating Arrangements

During the nineteenth century it was customary, following the organization
of the House and the adoption of the usual resolutions, for the members to
draw lots for their seats in the hall. Up to the Twenty-ninth Congress, when
the drawing began, seats were taken on a first-come, first-choice basis.
Members living near Washington who arrived early for a session secured
the best seats and kept them for the duration of the session. Before the
drawing began, ex-Speakers and one or two members of long service in the
House were allowed to select their seats.

On February 13, 1847, while the House was in committee of the whole house on the state of the Union, John Quincy Adams entered the Hall for the first time since his attack of paralysis. At once the committee rose in a body to receive him, and Mr. Andrew Johnson said: "In compliance with the understanding with which I selected a seat at the commencement of the present session, I now tender to the venerable member from Massachusetts the seat which I then selected for him, and will furthermore congratulate him on being spared to return to this House."[18]

In 1857, when the House moved into its present chamber, Congressmen had individual carved oak desks and chairs. These were replaced in 1859 by circular benches with the parties arranged opposite each other, but the desks were restored in 1860. As the membership grew, smaller desks were installed in 1873 and again in 1902. The places at the extreme right and left of the rostrum were the least desirable. Members usually tried to secure seats near their friends or colleagues from the same state. The Republicans sat, as now, on the left of the Speaker, and the Democrats on his right. But when one of these parties was in a small minority, the surplus of the majority party sat to the extreme left or right of the Hall.

Commenting on these arrangements in 1888, James Bryce said: "It is admitted that the desks are a mistake, as encouraging inattention by enabling men to write their letters; but though nearly everybody agrees that they would be better away, nobody supposes that a proposition to remove them would succeed."[19] But by 1914, when the membership had grown to 435, the House was forced to remove the desks and replace them with chairs arranged in long benches. Today there are 448 medium-tan, leather-covered chairs with walnut frames, bronze feet, and leather-padded arm rests. This change put an end to the drawing of seats by lot, and members now occupy any vacant chair on their side of the aisle.

5

Evolution of the House Rules

UNDER THE CONSTITUTION, each house of Congress may determine the rules of its proceedings. And in practice each House of Representatives has done so from the beginning of congressional history, either by explicitly adopting rules or by acquiescing in those of a preceding House. As we saw earlier, the House of Representatives adopted a short code of four rules on April 7, 1789, and agreed to six additional rules a few days later. From then until 1860, the House rule book gradually expanded by a process of accretion, as the rules were enlarged by amendments offered mainly by individual members. Each new House customarily adopted the rules of its predecessor, sometimes with changes or additions, thus erecting a code that became continuous in character and substantially constant in content.

After seventy years of gradual expansion, the rules of the House had grown to more than 150 in number, consuming some twenty pages of the journals, when a select committee of five was appointed, at the close of the first session of the Thirty-fifth Congress on June 14, 1858, "to digest and revise the rules . . . and to suggest alterations and amendments" therein.[1] From time to time over the years, they had been criticized as cumbersome and useless. Warren Winslow, ex-Speaker of the North Carolina Senate, was the author of this resolution, which provided that the Speaker, James L. Orr of South Carolina, should be a member of the select committee. This was the first time in the history of the House that its presiding officer had served on one of its committees. On December 20, 1858, the select committee reported some thirty-one amendments of the rules, a dozen of which were to strike out existing rules.[2] Its report was recommitted without further action in that Congress.

Continued criticism of the rules and parliamentary practice of the House led to the reappointment of the select committee on February 1, 1860, under the chairmanship of Israel Washburn, Jr., of Maine, a distinguished parliamentarian. Six weeks later the Washburn committee submitted its famous report which embraced some thirty-eight amendments of the rules, consisting mainly of the changes that had been recommended in December, 1858. "They need to be amended," Washburn declared. "But their observance is most needed. The good nature of members in granting unanimous consent breeds ignorance, and when applied they provoke criticism because a different practice obtains."[3] After extensive debate, the House agreed to numerous amendments on March 16 and 19, 1860.[4] Just as the Union was breaking up on the eve of the Civil War, the House of Representatives adopted the first sweeping revision of its rules since 1789.

Many of the changes in the revision of 1860 were technical in character, correcting inconsistencies, combining related rules, and adjusting others to the existing practice. But several drastic modifications were made. "One destroyed the trick of striking out the enacting clause in Committee of the Whole and then disagreeing to the report in the House. [Bills are considered in committee of the whole before they are reported to the House. When the enacting words of a bill are stricken out, the bill is rejected.] Another provided that the previous question, when negatived, should leave the pending business undisturbed, and when ordered on a motion to postpone, should act only on such motion; or, if on an amendment or an amendment thereto, that it should not preclude debate on the bill. This gave the House the facility for amendment enjoyed in Committee of the Whole. To avoid a repetition of the riotous scenes preceding the election of Speaker Pennington, the rules of one House were made binding upon its successors, unless otherwise ordered. Although parliamentarians generally held this rule invalid whenever seriously questioned, it survived for thirty years."[5]

With the postwar increase in the size and business of the House, dissatisfaction with the strictness of its rules recurred—the burden of complaint being that the liberty of the individual member suffered under them. On May 24, 1872, the House agreed to the Banks resolution, providing for the appointment of a commission to revise the rules and report "such changes as will facilitate the presentation of reports of committees, enlarge the means of an intelligent transaction of general business, and secure to every member a proper opportunity to examine all legislative measures before they are submitted for consideration and action by the House."[6] This commission does not appear to have reported, but meanwhile more than forty rules were added to the House *Manual* and many new precedents were established.

In response to continued criticism, the House in 1879 instructed a committee of able parliamentarians to sit during the recess in order to revise, codify, and simplify the clumsy accretion of 169 rules that had accumulated since the revision of 1860. Samuel J. Randall, Joseph C. S. Blackburn, Alexander H. Stephens, James A. Garfield, and William P. Frye composed the committee. Their unanimous report rearranged and grouped the orders by subject into forty-four main rules with the avowed object to "secure accuracy in business, economy of time, order, uniformity, and impartiality." Thirty-two rules were dropped as obsolete or unnecessary; twelve were retained intact; and one hundred and twenty-five were condensed into thirty-two, making a total of forty-four, each subdivided into clauses. The House debated the new code at intervals for two months and finally adopted it as the general revision of 1880.[7]

Hailed as a brilliant achievement, the new code had far-reaching effects on committee access to the floor, the distribution of the appropriation bills, the privilege of reporting at any time, on suspension of the rules, special orders, and the Committee on Rules which became a standing committee at this time. De Alva S. Alexander has summarized the historic revision of 1880 as follows: "It stopped voting after the second call of the roll; it dropped the penalty system of absenteeism without leave; and it authorized the clerk to announce 'pairs' instead of members. It abolished the practice of changing a few words in a pending bill to make it germane as an amendment; it caused a motion to reconsider, made during the last six days of a session, to be disposed of at the time; it sent a bill, to which objection was made to its present consideration, to the Committee of the Whole or to the House calendar; it gave preference to revenue and appropriation bills in Committee of the Whole; it required bills on the private calendar to be taken up and disposed of in order; and it provided that the previous question should bring the House to a direct vote upon a single motion, a series of allowable motions, or upon an amendment or amendments, the effect being to carry the bill to its engrossment and third reading, and then, on a renewal of the motion, to its passage or rejection."[8] But the revisers of 1880 left untouched such "disreputable practices" as "riders" on appropriation bills and the "disappearing quorum" (members present but refusing to vote).

Except for the exciting contests that marked the general revisions of 1860 and 1880, the customary practice in postbellum days, when a new House met, was to proceed under general parliamentary law, often for several days, with unlimited debate, until a satisfactory revision of former rules had been effected. Proposed changes in the old rules were discussed on these occasions in a leisurely, good-natured way, and the meaning of the complex code of the House was explained to the new members.

Reed Rules of 1890

The next major development in the evolution of the House rules came in 1890 with the adoption of the famous "Reed Rules." Thomas Brackett Reed had entered Congress from Maine in March, 1877; during the intervening years he had often seen how the business of the House could be paralyzed and the will of the majority frustrated by minority groups. The tactics of obstruction then employed included such devices as the "disappearing quorum," repeated roll calls, and various dilatory motions.

Reed was a bold and courageous man with a powerful personality and an acid tongue. He had been a leading figure in the Maine legislature, and he was destined to become a masterful Speaker of the House of Representatives. In his view the business of an organism was to function and the duty of a legislature was to legislate. During the 1880's, Mr. Reed became an expert in parliamentary strategy and tactics, biding his time until he should be in a position to overcome the techniques of minority rule. The need of reform in House procedure impressed him deeply, and he was convinced that the traditional practice must be changed. Minority rights, he felt, should not be allowed to override the rights of the majority.

Reed's opportunity to carry out his ideas came with his elevation to the Speakership in the Fifty-first Congress. When the House met in December, 1889, it declined to adopt rules at its organization, thus bringing general parliamentary law into operation. On January 29, 1890, the contested election case of *Smith* versus *Jackson* was called up for consideration. When Mr. Crisp of Georgia raised the question of consideration, the vote stood: yeas 161, nays 2, not voting 165—less than a quorum. But when the objection of "no quorum" was raised, the Speaker directed the clerk to record the names of those present and refusing to vote (members using a long-standing minority maneuver), and then he declared a quorum present and consideration of the election case in order.

Immediately the House was in an uproar. Members poured into the aisles and denounced the Speaker as a "tyrant" and a "czar." The commotion continued for several hours amid scenes of unprecedented disorder. In support of his ruling Mr. Reed cited the practice of the English House of Commons, the rules and precedents of the House of Representatives, and the Constitution. A Democratic member appealed from the decision of the chair, but the appeal was tabled by a majority of a quorum.

The next day the Speaker again counted those present but not voting in order to make a quorum for the approval of the *Journal* and refused to entertain any appeal from his decision, stating that the House had already decided the question of a quorum. Despite violent abuse, Mr. Reed maintained his position with calmness and dignity until at last the crisis passed. And he declared his intention thenceforth to disregard all motions and appeals, however parliamentary in themselves, which were made merely for the sake of delay.

These two historic decisions of the chair—that a vote is valid if a quorum be actually present, though not voting; and that obviously dilatory motions designed to obstruct business need not be entertained—were both incorporated among the forty-five rules that the House adopted after long debate on February 14, 1890. Thus, after a century of warfare over minority obstruction, the adoption of the Reed rules in 1890 finally doomed the dilatory tactics of a minority in the House to defeat.[9]

In addition to these major reforms, the Reed rules as adopted in 1890 also provided for: a readjustment in the order of business, reduction of the quorum in committee of the whole to one hundred, the relief of the morning hour by filling bills and reports with the clerk, and the adoption of special orders by a majority vote (a major change). Under the new system, the Speaker referred all public bills to their respective committees and was authorized to dispose of business "on the Speaker's table" without action by the House—except on House bills with Senate amendments, which usually go to conference without debate. Likewise he minimized "unfinished business" by limiting its jurisdiction to business transacted by the House in its general legislative time as distinguished from business transacted in special periods. Under the revised "order of business," adopted in 1890, the House has since been able to move freely from one calendar to another and from the House to the committee of the whole.

By empowering the Speaker to prevent obstruction, the reforms of 1890 went far to regularize House procedure, to expedite the conduct of its business, to enhance its dignity, and to fix legislative responsibility upon the majority. The Reed rules won lasting fame for their author in the annals of Congress and have proved generally satisfactory in practice.[10]

Revolution of 1910

Under the operation of the Reed system, the Speaker of the House developed far-reaching powers. They included his power to appoint the standing committees of the House, to designate their chairmen, and thus determine the legislative opportunities of the individual members. As chairman of the Committee on Rules he was able to determine what business the House should consider. And through his unlimited power of recognition he could decide what matters would come before the House and discipline members who failed to comply with his wishes. After a long process of evolution the Speaker of the House had become an officer second only to the President of the United States in influence and power.

It was not long, however, before a reaction set in. Under Speaker Cannon, first elected to that office in 1903, there developed growing discontent both in Congress and throughout the country with the manner in which and the purposes for which the powers of the Speaker were being exercised. This discontent finally broke out in open rebellion on the floor of the House on March 16, 1910, when a coalition of insurgent Republicans and Democrats, led by George Norris of Nebraska, succeeded in effecting a radical revision of the House rules. They removed the Speaker from the Rules Committee, of which he had formerly been chairman. They stripped him of the power to appoint the standing committees of the House and their chairmen, which he had previously possessed and exercised as a powerful weapon of party discipline. And they restricted his former right to recognize or refuse to recognize members seeking to address the House. It also provided that the Committee on Rules, which had been composed of five members appointed by the Speaker, should henceforth be elected by the House and be composed of ten members, six from the majority party and four from the minority. The Speaker was excluded from membership on this committee which was to elect its chairman from its own members.

The Norris resolution was adopted by a vote of 191 to 156, on March 19, after a great debate and continuous session lasting twenty-nine hours. In a vivid description of this successful coup d'état, which he had witnessed from the press gallery, George Rothwell Brown wrote that "as Mr. Cannon's gavel fell, an epoch in the long and brilliant history of the American House of Representatives came to an end. A new era had begun."[11]

The revolution of 1910 was not only political in character; it was also social in the sense that it reflected an aroused public opinion which felt that legislative power, under "Czar" Cannon's leadership, had grown so great as to upset the balance of power in the American constitutional system. The insurgents who thus succeeded in destroying the strong system of party government, party discipline, and majority rule in the House of Representatives, which their party had erected under the masterful leadership of Mr. Reed and Mr. Cannon, sought to liberalize the rules of the House as a prelude to the introduction and passage of measures liberalizing the laws. Their grievances were voiced by Mr. Nelson of Wisconsin who said: "Have we not been punished by every means at the disposal of the powerful House organization? Members long chairmen of important committees, others holding high rank—all with records of faithful and efficient party

service to their credit—have been ruthlessly removed, deposed, and humili-
ated before their constituents and the country because, forsooth, they would
not cringe or crawl before the arbitrary power of the Speaker and his House
machine. . . . We are fighting for the right of free, fair, and full representation in this body for our respective constituencies. . . . We are fighting
with our Democratic brethren for the common right of equal representation
in this House, and for the right of way of progressive legislation in
Congress. . . ."[12]

When the House adopted the Norris resolution amending its rules on
March 19, 1910, Speaker Cannon signified his recognition of its importance by announcing that he would entertain a motion that the chair be
vacated so that the House could elect a new Speaker. Such a motion was
made, but defeated. The Republican insurgents were willing to form a
coalition with the Democrats to revise the rules, but not to elect a Democratic Speaker. The Democrats captured control of the House, however,
in the following November, and when the Sixty-second Congress convened
in special session on April 4, 1911, Champ Clark was chosen Speaker.

Back in power after sixteen years, the Democrats proceeded to adopt
a radically revised code of rules based upon the Crisp rules of the Fifty-
third Congress and incorporating substantially all the changes effected by
the Norris resolution. The rules of the Sixty-second House dealt the final
coup de grâce to the traditional powers of the Speaker by depriving him of
the right to appoint the standing committees of the House, providing instead that they should be "elected by the House, at the commencement of
each Congress." They provided further that committee chairmen should be
elected by the House and not be appointed by the Speaker. They retained
and strengthened the Calendar Wednesday rule, first adopted in 1909,
under which every standing committee had a chance to call up its reported
bills without getting a "green light" from the Rules Committee. And they
also preserved the unanimous consent calendar, another 1909 procedural
innovation of Progressive origin, whereby two days a month were expressly
reserved for the consideration of minor bills, important to individual members, without requiring the recognition of the chair.

On the surface, the 1911 rules had apparently succeeded in transferring
control of the legislative process in the House of Representatives from the
Speaker to the House itself. To many students of these tremendous events
it appeared, not that the House had rejected the principle of leadership,
but rather that the House had rebelled against the dictatorial manner in
which Speaker Cannon exercised his powers and had determined to shift
the leadership of the House from the chair to the floor, leaving the Speaker
on the rostrum as merely a moderator of the legislative machine.[13] This
interpretation of these events seemed to be confirmed by the role assumed

in the Sixty-second Congress by Oscar W. Underwood, who was, at once, both the majority floor leader and the chairman of the Ways and Means Committee, to which the Democratic caucus assigned the function of naming the committees of the House, including the Committee on Rules.

In looking back, however, the changes made in 1911 have proved to be less drastic than they appeared at the time. In 1973 the Democratic caucus placed the Speaker and other leaders on their Committee on Committees and on a newly created Steering and Policy Committee to formulate party policies. Two years later, that committee supplanted the Ways and Means Committee as the Democratic Committee on Committees, with the Speaker being empowered to nominate all the Democratic members of the Rules Committee, subject to the subsequent approval of the caucus. The Speaker exerts considerable influence in the selection of conference committees, appoints select committees, and the chairman of the committee of the whole. The Speakership continues to be an immensely influential office, particularly in an era when an increasing number of House members see merit in the co-ordination of legislative policy. How the power and prestige of that office will be utilized will, to some extent at least, be a function of the Speaker's personality and perception of his role.

Developments Since 1912

Since the revision of 1911, many noteworthy developments have taken place in the rules of the House. The first of these concerned jurisdiction over appropriations for the support of the government. The Committee on Appropriations was first established in 1865, and for twenty years it reported all the general appropriation bills. But in 1885 authority to report the supply bills was divided among nine committees of the House, and this allocation continued until July 1, 1920, when by an amendment of the rules the House again concentrated in the Committee on Appropriations the power to report all the general appropriation bills and readopted the rule in the form provided by the revision of 1880. Meanwhile, Congress enacted the Budget and Accounting Act of 1921, and the change in the general supply bills to conform to the new budget law was made in the second session of the Sixty-seventh Congress.[14] Thus, since 1920, the Committee on Appropriations has had exclusive jurisdiction over all the general appropriation bills.

Another significant development took place on December 5, 1927, when some eleven separate committees on expenditures in the executive departments were consolidated into a single such committee. The first of these expenditure committees had been created in 1816, and others were added as new departments were established. In reporting a resolution from the Committee on Rules to abolish these "deadwood committees," Chairman Snell of the Rules Committee remarked:

> I think there is no one on either side but that will agree that it is foolish and ridiculous for us to carry from year to year sixteen committees [of which eleven were expenditures committees] that have practically no work to do in connection with the work of the House and are only deadwood, used simply to furnish assignments to Members. The majority of the committees that we are abolishing have not met in several years and there is no probability that there will be any work for them in the immediate future.

The resolution was passed on the same day it was reported, and the eleven expenditures committees, which Mr. Alvin Fuller of Massachusetts described as "ornamental barnacles on the ship of state," were abolished.[15] On July 3, 1952, the name of this committee was changed from "Expenditures in the Executive Departments" to "Government Operations."

Reforms of 1946

An outstanding development in the organization and operation of Congress during the past fifty years was the Legislative Reorganization Act of 1946. Hailed at its passage as a legislative miracle, this act was the culmination of a long and sustained campaign in Congress and the country to "modernize" the national legislature. The alleged decline of Congress in relation to the Executive was a widely observed phenomenon. For several years members of both houses and both political parties had been offering various proposals for specific reforms or wider action, which had been the subject of lively discussion on the floor of the House and Senate. These members recognized that the problem of making Congress a more efficient democratic machine was becoming increasingly acute, that it was not a party problem, and that it required solution regardless of the party situation in Congress. Meanwhile articles urging legislative rehabilitation were appearing in the lay and learned magazines, while the press, ever alert to significant public questions, was arousing and informing public opinion on the need for "congressional reform." The radio networks broadcast debates on the machinery and methods of Congress as part of their educational programs, and various civic and professional groups put their weight behind the movement.

Congress responded to this campaign by setting up a joint select committee of its own members which held extensive hearings and produced an act "to provide for increased efficiency in the legislative branch of the Government" which was approved by President Truman on August 2, 1946. The Legislative Reorganization Act had ten objectives:

1. To streamline and simplify the committee structure
2. To eliminate the use of special or select committees
3. To clarify committee duties and reduce jurisdictional disputes
4. To regularize and publicize committee procedures
5. To reduce the work load on Congress
6. To strengthen legislative oversight of administration
7. To reinforce the power of the purse
8. To improve congressional staff aids
9. To regulate lobbying, and
10. To increase the compensation of Members of Congress and provide them retirement pay

Of these objectives, the first seven found expression in extensive changes in the rules of the House and Senate and were set forth in the first title of the 1946 act. This title was divided into three parts of which the first amended the standing rules of the Senate by streamlining its committee system; Part 2 amended the rules of the House of Representatives in the same way; and Part 3 contained twelve sections applicable to both houses of Congress.

Modernization of the standing committee system was the first aim of the act and the keystone in the arch of congressional "reform." By dropping minor, inactive committees and by merging those with related functions, the act reduced the total number of standing committees from forty-eight to nineteen in the House of Representatives and from thirty-three to fifteen in the Senate. Since 1947, the House has added standing committees on Science and Astronautics (1958), Standards of Official Conduct (1968), and Budget (1975). In 1975, the House made the Select Committee on Small Business a standing committee and dropped its Internal Security Committee. The Senate has since added committees on Aeronautical and Space Sciences (1958), Veterans' Affairs (1970), and Budget (1975).

In the form in which it passed the Senate, the act prohibited special committees. Although this provision was stricken in the House, the spirit of the act clearly frowned on the creation of special committees. Its authors had recommended that the practice of creating special investigating committees be abandoned on the ground that they lack legislative authority and that the jurisdiction of the new standing committees would be so comprehensively defined, in the reformed rules, as to cover every conceivable subject of legislation. In practice, special committees have not been abandoned, but their number has diminished, and their influence is not great.

The act also amended Rule XI of the House rules by clarifying the duties of the reorganized standing committees, which were defined in terms of their jurisdiction over specific subject-matter fields and administrative agencies. Although House bills are occasionally re-referred by unanimous consent, open conflicts between committees in the first chamber have almost disappeared. But it must be admitted that jurisdiction over the various aspects of several subject-matter fields is still split among many standing committees in both houses of Congress. National defense policies, transportation, energy, education, and expenditures are reviewed in piecemeal fashion by several committees in both houses; jurisdiction over various phases of our foreign relations is widely scattered; and the fiscal machinery of Congress is also splintered and fragmented.[16]

Under Section 133 of the 1946 act, committee procedure has been regularized in regard to periodic meeting days, the keeping of committee records, the reporting of approved measures, the presence of a majority of committeemen as a condition of committee action, and the conduct of hearings. Under the rule, proxy voting would be permissible in committee only after a majority was actually present. Each committee could fix the number of its members to constitute a quorum for taking testimony and receiving evidence, which would be not less than two. The requirement that witnesses file written statements of their testimony in advance of hearings has been observed by some committees and ignored by others; hearings are sometimes called on too short notice for this action to be possible. Most committees held open hearings, except the House Committee on Appropriations which availed itself of the allowed option of holding its hearings *in camera*.[17] Committee offices, staff personnel, and records are now kept separate and distinct from those of committee chairmen (another requirement of the 1946 act). In practice, to be sure, these committee regulations have not always been followed.

Section 131 of the act sought to reduce the work load on Congress by banning the introduction of four categories of private bills, e.g., pension bills, tort claims bills, bridge bills, and bills for the correction of military or naval records. But this gain was offset by a postwar flood of private immigration bills that engulfed the Judiciary Committees: 2,181 were introduced in the House in 1955.

Another main objective of the 1946 act was to strengthen legislative "oversight" of administration. To this end, Section 136 provided that "each standing committee of the Senate and the House of Representatives shall exercise continuous watchfulness of the execution by the administrative agencies concerned of any laws, the subject matter of which is within the jurisdiction of such committee. . . ." This provision, coupled with the professional staffing of congressional committees, contributed mightily to the extraordinary increase in the exercise of the investigative function of Congress after World War II. In practice, the armory of legislative surveillance of the executive has included such weapons as committee investigations, question periods at the committee stage, the statutory requirement of prior committee clearance of contemplated administrative action, the requirement of periodic reports to Congress, the control of administrative action by congressional resolutions, and demands for the production of executive documents and testimony—all of which have been increasingly used in recent years to strengthen the "watchdog" function of Congress.[18]

A final major aim of the 1946 act was to strengthen the congressional power of the purse. There was a growing feeling in Congress and the country that Congress was losing control of the purse strings. This aim found expression in several sections of the act of which the most ambitious was that (Section 138) for the creation of a Joint Committee on the Budget, which was to formulate a "legislative budget" and fix a ceiling on expenditures. Attempts to carry out the legislative budget provision during 1947-1949 proved abortive, and the joint budget committee failed to function.

The enactment of budget-reform legislation in 1974 and the creation of standing committees on the budget in the House and the Senate in 1975 are only the most recent attempts to achieve the goals set in 1946. Under the new legislation the Congress would examine the proposed budget in its entirety and would then set a target through a budget resolution before dealing with appropriations and authorizations.

For the most part, the reforms of 1946 were enacted by Congress as an exercise of the rule-making power of the respective houses and were incorporated in their standing rules. Since 1946, the number of standing committees has expanded somewhat, but the increase in joint committees and subcommitteees has been dramatic. The increasing complexities of the issues confronted by Congress, the continuous expansion of executive initiatives since the beginnings of the Vietnam War, the reactions to President Nixon's use of impoundments, and the general disenchantment called Watergate have all contributed to the subsequent attempts to increase congressional effectiveness in formulating policy and legislative oversight. Yet these more recent changes should not diminish our regard for the 1946 act, and the significant contributions of such House members as Mike Monroney of Oklahoma, Everett M. Dirksen of Illinois, E. E. Cox of Georgia, Thomas J. Lane of Massachusetts, Earl E. Michener of Michigan, and Charles A. Plumley of Vermont.

Reforms of 1970

Within a few years, it became obvious that the Legislative Reorganization Act of 1946 had set goals that could not be reached. On the level of housekeeping, the provision that except in times of war or national emergency

Congress should adjourn by the end of July was quickly forgotten. The requirement that all committees set a regular day for meetings was set but often ignored. The number of subcommittees continued to proliferate, and the congressional machinery seemed to be creaking. Within the Congress, Representative Richard Bolling of Missouri was the author of *House Out of Order* (1964), and Senator Joseph S. Clark of Pennsylvania wrote *Congress: The Sapless Branch* (1964), insisting that the distribution of power in Congress rendered it ineffective. In 1964 the American Assembly pondered *The Congress and America's Future* and was pessimistic, while in 1965 NBC News aired a TV special "Congress Needs Help," the result of a management study by Arthur D. Little, Inc.[19] The result was the creation in 1965 of the Joint Committee on the Organization of Congress, co-chaired by Senator Mike Monroney of Oklahoma and Representative Ray J. Madden of Indiana. The committee heard 199 witnesses, published fifteen volumes of testimony, and in 1966 made some 120 recommendations. The major focus of these recommendations was on committee procedures, and the intent was to reduce the power of committee chairmen by reducing their discretion. The proposals were subjected to extensive debate, delay, and amendment, finally emerging after "five years, seven months, and fifteen days."

Our concern here is in noting the major provisions of the act that modified the House rules. These would include such provisions as

1. Each standing committee was required to fix regular meeting days and outline a procedure by which members of a committee could force the calling of a special meeting.

2. Each standing committee was required to make its meetings and hearings open to the public, unless the committee, by majority vote, determined otherwise, and to give one week's notice of hearings.

3. All committees were required to make public all roll-call votes and note whether the vote was made in person or by proxy.

4. Allowed a majority of a committee to require the filing of a committee report within seven calendar days after the committee had approved the measure.

5. Banned the use of general proxies in all committees of the House and allowed the use of special proxies only if the committee adopted a written rule to do so.

6. Permitted any committee member three calendar days to file his views on a measure given final approval by the committee.

7. Gave the minority members of committees the right to call witnesses at any hearing.

8. Under carefully defined circumstances, allowed points of order to be raised against a measure on the floor of the House on the grounds that hearing procedures were violated.

9. Permitted any committee to allow, by majority vote, the broadcast or

televising of any of its public hearings, subject to certain basic regulations.

10. With certain exceptions, allowed committees to meet during House sessions except when amendments were considered under the five-minute rule.

11. Provided that committee rules were also the rules of its sub-committees.

12. Formulated a procedure which would require the recording by name of the members in teller votes.

13. Authorized the use of electronic equipment for the recording of roll calls and quorum calls.

The overall objective of the act was to democratize procedures and give the legislative process in the House much greater visibility. By choosing to modify the rules in a manner that allowed more precise codification of committee and floor practices, the House added to the rights of all members without directly threatening the prerogatives of its chairmen. The cumulative effect of these changes in the rules, however, was to contribute to a momentum that did indeed diminish their status.

Reforms of 1974

In 1973 the House established a ten-member bipartisan Select Committee on Committees for the purpose of studying House Rules X and XI, the rules that establish the standing committees and define their jurisdiction. The committee was chaired by Representative Richard Bolling of Missouri, a longtime advocate of congressional reform; the vice chairman was Representative Dave Martin of Nebraska. In its report, the committee argued that the Legislative Reform Act of 1946, by reducing the number of standing committees and "hardening their jurisdictional lines" had strengthened the autonomy of the committees and made them less able to deal with contemporary problems. The committee also insisted that since 1946 the legislative branch had been confronted by increased activism in the executive and judicial branches and that accordingly

> Congress must put its house in order if the imbalance of powers is to be combatted. Imbalances frequently occur not because one branch usurps another's powers, but because one branch moves into a vacuum created by another's ineffectiveness. To the extent that congressional powers have ebbed as a result of failure to develop timely and coherent responses to public problems, Congress has itself to blame for the predicament. And to the extent that better organization will strengthen the ability of Congress to fulfill its constitutional duties, periodic changes are justified to help preserve congressional powers from further decline.[20]

After extensive hearings over a period of six months, which even included a panel of legislative scholars and a month of public markup sessions, the committee unanimously proposed a very ambitious set of reforms. Adoption of these proposals would have resulted in a wholesale reorganization of the jurisdiction of House committees. For example, Education and Labor would have been divided into two committees; Post Office and Civil Service would have been abolished; and major areas of jurisdiction of Ways and Means and Merchant Marine and Fisheries would have been redistributed to other committees. Indeed the proposed changes in the rules which would have been required by the committees' reallocation of committee responsibilities required fifty-four pages of its report. The committee also proposed limiting each member to one major committee; it would have required each standing committee (other than Appropriations) to establish a subcommittee on oversight and banned all forms of proxy voting in committees and subcommittees. It recommended a change in Rule X, so that at least a majority of House conferees would be in support of the position of the House as determined by the Speaker. Another recommendation would have allowed the Speaker to refer bills to more than one committee or to split the legislation for purposes of referral or even to appoint *ad hoc* committees. The committee also recommended an increase in the staffing of the committees, with one-third of the staffing going to the minorities.

Predictably these proposals were regarded as highly controversial, if only because they would reduce the historical prerogatives of senior members as well as intrude on the long-standing relationships that had developed between the standing committees and various interest groups.

When the Democratic caucus considered these recommendations, it voted to send the report to a committee chaired by Representative Julia Butler Hansen of Washington. A much more modest set of proposals emanated from that committee, and they became the basis of floor action. Most of the jurisdictional shifts had been dropped as well as the one-committee-per-member proposal and the requirement for oversight subcommittees. After eight days of debate, the House finally agreed to a vast number of changes that seemed minor when contrasted with the original Bolling proposals. The changes included the ban on proxies, the increase in minority staffing, a requirement that all committees with more than fifteen members establish a minimum of four subcommittees (directed at the Ways and Means Committee which had no subcommittees), allowing the Speaker greater discretion in assigning bills to committees and the requirement that a majority of House conferees support the House position on the proposal. While the House also approved a considerable number of jurisdictional shifts in committees, it is safe to suggest that the present committee structure has not been significantly modified since 1946. Other changes since

1970, which affect the role of committee chairmen and which were initiated by actions of the Democratic caucus, will be considered in our next chapter.

Struggle Over the Twenty-one-day Rule

One recurring rule struggle that merits special note is the intermittent concern over the twenty-one-day rule, if only because of the insights it offers about the relations between the leadership and the committee system. In 1937 the New Deal lost control of the House Rules Committee when three of its Democratic members joined with the four Republican members to block floor consideration of controversial administration bills. The coalition succeeded in preventing a score or more of New Deal–Fair Deal measures from reaching the House floor, except by the laborious discharge route, which requires 218 signatures on a discharge petition to take a bill away from a committee. After World War II a rising demand developed for reform of the powers of the Committee on Rules. Rebellion against the committee found expression in a letter that Representative Eberharter wrote his House colleagues in December, 1948. "In theory," he said, "the Rules Committee is a traffic director on the legislative highway, determining the order of business on the floor of the House. In practice this committee has become an obstruction to orderly traffic. The committee often allows bills to come before the House only on its own terms. It frequently usurps the functions of the regular legislative committees of the House by holding hearings and reviewing the merits of bills that have already been carefully studied by the proper legislative committees. A reform of this undemocratic system is long overdue. Congress is constantly engaged in a struggle for the respect of the people. The people never have and never will be able to understand how the will of a majority of the House of Representatives can be set aside by the judgment of a few men on a powerful committee."

The fight against the "obstructive tactics" of the Rules Committee finally came to a head on January 3, 1949, when the House adopted the so-called twenty-one-day rule by a vote of 275 to 142. Under this rule, the chairman of a legislative committee that had favorably reported upon a bill could call it up for House consideration if the Rules Committee reported adversely on it or failed to give it a "green light" to the House floor within twenty-one days. The twenty-one-day rule remained in effect throughout the Eighty-first Congress (1949-1950), despite a determined effort to repeal it early in the second session. A coalition led by Congressman Cox of Georgia was defeated on January 20, 1950, by a vote of 236 to 183. Eighty-five Southern Democrats voted for the Cox repeal resolution, while sixty-four Republicans sided with the administration against their own leadership.

During the first session of the Eighty-first Congress, the twenty-one-day rule brought the anti-poll-tax bill to the House floor for a successful vote, and forced action on the housing and minimum-wage bills. During the second session it enabled the House to vote for the National Science Foundation, Alaskan and Hawaiian statehood legislation, and other important measures. Altogether during this Congress, eight measures were brought to the floor of the House and passed by resort to the twenty-one-day rule, and its existence caused the Rules Committee to act in other cases.

On January 3, 1951, a hostile coalition regained control of the situation and obtained repeal of the twenty-one-day rule by a vote of 247 to 179 after a bitter fight. As a result, the power of the Rules Committee to blockade bills was restored. After continued frustration with the Rules Committee during the Kennedy administration, the House adopted a new version of the twenty-one-day rule at the opening of the Congress in 1965. The new rule gave the Speaker, not the committee chairman, the discretion to recognize the chairman or any other member of a committee for consideration of a bill which had been favorably reported by the committee but which had been before the Rules Committee for twenty-one days without receiving a vote. The new rule was used six times in 1965 and twice in 1966, and undoubtedly contributed to favorable action by the Rules Committee on several other occasions. However, an increase in the number of Republicans and Southern Democrats in the elections of 1966 led to the repeal of the rule, and it has not returned.[21]

Two opposing principles were involved in the struggle over the powers of the House Committee on Rules: whether legislative action should be controlled by a majority of the entire House, or whether the majority party should control through its nominal agent. Those who believed in the principle of majority rule by the whole House favored reducing the Rules Committee to a traffic director on the legislative highway and a more liberal discharge rule. Their fundamental objection to the existing setup was that it vests power in a small group of Rules committeemen to prevent the House from considering and taking action upon measures not favored by the committee. Under the present system, they say, many cases arise where a bill or resolution that would receive favorable action by the House, if it had a chance to consider it, is killed in committee. Such a system, it is argued, denies the House its constitutional right to legislate and violates the principle of representative government.

On the other hand, those who believed that the party in power should control legislative action, as a means of fulfilling its responsibility to the electorate, favored strengthening party government in the House through a strong Rules Committee and a strict discharge rule. To curtail the authority of the committee, they asserted, would (1) go far to destroy the effective working of party government and responsibility, and (2) tend to facilitate the attempt of self-seeking special interests and minority groups to secure the passage of legislation detrimental to the general welfare.

While conceding the force of these objections, advocates of a change maintained that, under existing political conditions in the Rules Committee, it is possible for the will of the majority party, as expressed at the polls, to be frustrated by a hostile coalition within the committee. Under these circumstances, ran their argument, only a reform of the powers of the committee would, in crucial cases, enable the true majority will to prevail. The action of the Democratic caucus in 1974, which now allows the Speaker to nominate, subject to approval of the caucus, all the Democratic members of the Rules Committee, suggests that the Democrats have chosen to strengthen the role of the leadership and party government in its relationship with that important committee.

6

Development of the Committee System

FROM THE BEGINNING, our national legislature has conducted its work in large part through committees of its members. The use of select and standing committees, as well as the committee of the whole, was derived by Congress from the practice of the English House of Commons via the colonial assemblies, especially those in Pennsylvania and Virginia.[1] In the early days the House of Representatives referred its business to a host of select committees. For every bill and petty claim a special committee was "raised." Select committees are special or temporary groups created for a particular purpose, whereas standing committees are permanent groups that continue from Congress to Congress.

Although select committees and the committee of the whole were largely relied upon by the House during its first quarter century, the standing committee system had its inception in the earliest days. The Committee on Elections created in 1789 (since 1946 a standing subcommittee of the Committee on House Administration) has the honor of being the oldest standing committee of the House. Claims, established in 1794, was the second to join this category. It was followed in 1795 by Interstate and Foreign Commerce and Revisal and Unfinished Business. As the nineteenth century advanced, the select committees were converted into standing committees which gradually grew in number. Six of them were set up in the first decade of that century and eleven in the second decade. By mid-century the House had thirty-four standing committees, and by 1900 it had fifty-eight. Nine more were added during the twentieth century up to 1930 when the process of fission stopped, save for the creation of the Committee on Un-American Activities in 1945 and in 1958 of the Committee on Science and

Astronautics. With the consolidation in 1920 of jurisdiction over appropriations in a single Committee on Appropriations (previously divided among nine committees), and with the merger in 1927 of eleven expenditures committees into a single Committee on Expenditures in the Executive Departments, a net reduction of eighteen in the number of standing committees in the House was effected. In 1946 the committee structure in the first chamber was streamlined when forty-eight standing groups were reduced to nineteen.

Chronological Development

The following tables reflect the chronological development of the standing committee system of the House of Representatives.

GROWTH OF STANDING COMMITTEES BY DECADES

1789-1800	4
1801-1810	6
1811-1820	11
1821-1830	6
1831-1840	6
1841-1850	1
1851-1860	1
1861-1870	7
1871-1880	4
1881-1890	3
1891-1900	9
1901-1910	3
1911-1920	3
1921-1930	2
1931-1940	0
1941-1950	1
1951-1960	1
1961-1970	1
1971-1975	1

Congress	Number
14th	20
28th	36
42d	42
56th	58
70th	45
86th	20
94th	22

CHRONOLOGY OF HOUSE STANDING COMMITTEES

Committee	*Created*
Elections No. 1	1789
Claims	1794
Interstate and Foreign Commerce	1795
Revisal and Unfinished Business	1795
Ways and Means	1802
Accounts	1805
Public Lands	1805
District of Columbia	1808
Post Office and Post Roads	1808
Library	1809
Judiciary	1813
Revolutionary Claims	1813
Public Expenditures	1814
Private Land Claims	1816
Expenditures in Executive Depts. (5)	1816
Manufactures	1819
Agriculture	1820
Indian Affairs	1821
Military Affairs	1822
Naval Affairs	1822
Foreign Affairs	1822
Military Pensions	1825
Territories	1825
Invalid Pensions	1831
Railways and Canals	1831
Militia	1835
Patents	1837
Public Buildings and Grounds	1837
Mileage	1837
Engraving	1844
Expenditures in Interior Department	1860
Coinage, Weights, and Measures	1864
Appropriations	1865
Banking and Currency	1865
Mines and Mining	1865
Pacific Railroads	1865
Education and Labor (separated in 1883)	1867
Revision of the Laws	1868
War Claims	1873
Expenditures in Department of Justice	1874
Levees and Improvements of Mississippi River	1875
Rules	1880
Rivers and Harbors	1883

Committee	Created
Merchant Marine and Fisheries	1887
Expenditures in Department of Agriculture	1889
Election of President, Vice President, and Representatives	1893
Immigration and Naturalization	1893
Irrigation and Reclamation	1893
Civil Service	1893
Alcoholic Liquor Traffic	1893
Ventilation and Acoustics	1895
Elections No. 2	1895
Elections No. 3	1895
Insular Affairs	1899
Census	1901
Industrial Arts and Expositions	1901
Expenditures in Department of Commerce and Labor	1905
Roads	1913
Flood Control	1916
Woman Suffrage	1917
World War Veterans' Legislation	1924
Memorials	1929
Un-American Activities	1945
Science and Astronautics	1958
Standards of Official Conduct	1967
Small Business	1975
Budget	1975

A mere listing of the names of the standing committees set up by the House of Representatives over a period of nearly two centuries reflects the growing diversity of interests in the expanding nation and, concomitantly, the rising business of the House. With a little imagination the committee list may be viewed as an outline of American history, for the creation of each major committee was associated with some important historical event or emerging public problem. Thus, the increasing domestic and foreign trade of the new republic was soon followed by the creation of the Committee on Interstate and Foreign Commerce in 1795. The Louisiana Purchase in 1803 gave rise to the Committee on Public Lands in 1805. And so on, down the long list to the creation of the Un-American Activities Committee in 1945, reflecting postwar fears of internal subversion, and the Committee on Science and Astronautics in 1958, marking the advent of the space age, the Committee on Standards of Official Conduct in 1967, showing increased concern with the publicity attending the misuse of funds by some members, and the Budget Committee in 1975, which demonstrated congressional frustrations with executive discretion in spending policies.

Appointment of Committees

From 1790 until 1911, the Speaker generally appointed the members and the chairmen of the standing and select committees of the House of Representatives, although the annals reveal several instances in which committees chose their own chairmen.[2] From 1857 he made these appointments, with few exceptions, at the commencement of each Congress. But this power was taken away from the Speaker in 1911, as we have seen, and since that time the committees and their chairmen have been elected by the House as soon as the two political parties in the chamber have had time to perfect their lists and present resolutions for their ratification.[3] In the earlier usage the member moving a select committee was named as its chairman. Prior to 1880, when the rule relating to the appointment of select committees was adopted, the House occasionally deprived the Speaker of the appointment of a select committee; but the practice of leaving the appointment of House members of conference committees and the chairman of the committee of the whole to the Speaker dates from the earlier days.

During early Congresses an attempt was made to give each state representation on important committees. As the number of states in the Union gradually grew, this practice was discontinued but geographical representation remains a significant factor in committee assignments. Formerly members sometimes complained about undue delay on the part of the Speaker in assigning committee posts. In the Forty-second Congress (1871) the Speaker waited 275 days (March 4 to December 4) before submitting committee lists.

In the modern practice the lists of committee assignments are prepared by the "committees on committees" of the major parties. The Republican Committee on Committees consists of one Representative from each state having at least one Republican member; however, voting on that committee is based on the number of Republicans in the state's delegation. The nominees for ranking member are then submitted separately to the Republican Conference for approval by secret ballot. As the result of a Democratic caucus in December, 1974, the Democratic Committee on Committees is its twenty-four-member Steering and Policy Committee, which consists of the Speaker, the majority leader, the caucus chairman, nine members appointed by the Speaker, and twelve members elected by regions. The recommendations must then be approved by the caucus. The lists are subsequently approved by the House. Party representation on the standing committees of the House is determined by the selection committee of the majority party and reflects the party ratio in the chamber. For example, in 1975 all committees except Standards of Official Conduct had a 2-to-1 Democratic majority, plus one additional Democrat.

In filling vacancies in committee chairmanships the unwritten rule of seniority has usually, but not invariably, been followed. Seniority is the custom by which the chairmanships of the standing committees automatically go to the majority party members who have the longest continuous service on the committees. On rare occasions this custom has not been followed. For example, in 1903, Representative Jesse Overstreet of Indiana was appointed chairman of the Committee on Post Offices and Post Roads, giving him precedence over two members who had served sixteen and thirty-two years respectively. In 1905, Representative James A. Tawney of Minnesota was made chairman of Appropriations although two other members outranked him. Both of these departures were made by Speaker Cannon in order to promote his policies. In 1909, Representative James R. Mann of Illinois was advanced to the chairmanship of Interstate and Foreign Commerce out of his turn. In 1915, Representative Claude Kitchin of North Carolina was promoted to the chairmanship of Ways and Means over Representative Shackleford of Missouri, who stood next in line, because the incumbent of this post at that time was also the Democratic floor leader, a position for which Mr. Kitchin was preferred. And in 1921, Representative Martin B. Madden of Illinois was elevated to the chairmanship of Appropriations, of which he had only recently become a member, because the committeeman next in line was considered too old to assume the heavy duties of launching the new budget system.[4]

Between 1971 and 1975 a series of actions by the Democratic caucus have brought about the most serious incursions in the past sixty years on the automatic relationship between committee chairmanships and the principle of seniority. At the opening of the Congress in 1971, the Democratic caucus adopted a rule that allowed a separate vote on chairmen or any committee member recommended by the Committee on Committees if any ten members demanded it. The only use of the new rule that year was on Representative John L. McMillan as chairman of the District of Columbia Committee, on the grounds that he had frequently abused his privileges as chairman. The caucus, however, voted in favor of McMillan, 126 to 96. When a number of House Democrats sought to overrule the caucus and tried to invoke a literal construction of Rule X which calls for the House to elect chairmen, they were rebuffed by a 258 to 32 vote with Minority Leader Gerald R. Ford of Michigan insisting that the majority party should select chairmen in their caucus.[5]

The Democratic caucus modified its rule further in 1973, adopting a requirement that voting be by secret ballot if 20 per cent of the caucus members requested it. Even though all the senior members were re-elected as chairmen, the fact that a considerable number of negative ballots were cast against Representatives W. R. Poage of Texas, Wayne L. Hays of Ohio, Chet Holifield of California, and Wright Patman of Texas, and that the voting results became public, put each chairman on notice that his style was not beyond criticism.[6] It should also be noted that the increased interest of the Democratic caucus in challenging the automatic seniority system was influenced considerably by the Democratic Study Group. Founded in 1959 as a research and action arm for Democratic liberals in the House, the Study Group has devoted much of its energies in recent years to revitalizing the role of the caucus and trying to make committee chairmen more responsive to the caucus. By 1973 its membership had grown to more than 160; by 1975, it numbered more than 220.[7]

When the Congress convened in 1975, it began with a sequence of events which one member called "an earthquake." Most significant was the arrival of seventy-five freshmen Democrats, most of whom were anxious to challenge seniority. The first opportunity came unexpectedly in December, 1974, when they and many other Democrats made it known that they would not accept Representative Wilbur D. Mills as chairman of the Ways and Means Committee because of his bizarre conduct involving a strip-tease dancer. Mills resigned the chairmanship, although the Democratic caucus had already reduced the powers of that post. During December, Common Cause had circulated a lengthy report on the conduct of committee chairmen which received considerable attention.[8] Even though the report touched on the voting records of many of the chairmen, its primary emphasis was on their compliance with the rules of the House and the caucus, their regard for the rights of their committee members, and their fairness in managing the staff and calendar. The report concluded that fourteen chairmen were deficient. Many of these chairmen had already appeared at unprecedented meetings with freshmen Democrats where they were questioned on a wide range of legislative matters.

On January 15, the new Committee on Committees—the Steering and Policy Committee—decided to vote on each chairman separately and by secret ballot. At their initial meeting, they voted to unseat Representative Patman, chairman of the Banking, Currency and Housing Committee in favor of Representative Henry S. Reuss of Wisconsin, and Representative Hays, chairman of the House Administration Committee, in favor of Representative Frank Thompson of New Jersey.

A full week of back-and-forth activity followed, with caucus votes which often strayed from the recommendations of the Committee on Committees. When the final results were compiled, three incumbent chairman had been deposed. Representative Patman was succeeded by Representative Reuss;

Representative W. R. Poage of Texas was unseated as chairman of the Committee on Agriculture, and Representative Thomas S. Foley of Washington was chosen to replace him; and Representative Melvin Price of Illinois was elected to succeed F. Edward Hebert of Louisiana as chairman of the Armed Services Committee. Representative Hays retained his chairmanship by a vote of the caucus. The possibility that the unseated chairmen might appeal the decision to the full House was snuffed out when Majority Leader Thomas P. O'Neill said that any member who opposed the recommendations of the caucus "should be expelled from the party" and Speaker Carl Albert stated that such appeals would be ruled out of order as a violation of House rules.[9]

While it would be a mistake to exaggerate the significance of these events, they certainly stand as an extremely important passage in the history of the House. Without formally erecting a routinized alternative to seniority, these votes demonstrated that chairmen would always recognize that untoward conduct could have consequences. The probability is that the House will continue to venerate seniority, but that it will never be quite the same.

Role of Committee Chairman

The powers and duties of the chairmen of the standing committees of Congress gradually evolved over the years and have not been codified, but are scattered through the rules and statutes. Statements on the subject are found in House Rule XI, in the standing orders adopted by some committees, in certain sections of Title 2 of the United States Code, in the Legislative Reorganization Act of 1946, and in *Hinds'* and *Cannon's Precedents of the House of Representatives*. In addition, the role of chairmen has been affected by the Legislative Reorganization Act of 1970, reforms recommended by the Democrats' Committee on Organization, Study and Review which were adopted in 1971, the Committee Reform Amendments of 1974, and most assuredly by the events of 1975.

The earliest light on the role of committee chairmen is shed by Jefferson's famous manual of parliamentary procedure. Although this manual was prepared by Thomas Jefferson for his own guidance as president of the Senate from 1797 to 1801, it reflects both the theory and practice of the House of Representatives in the last decade of the eighteenth century, in relation to the functioning of committees and their chairmen. In the early Congresses most important matters were first considered in a committee of the whole for the purpose of rational discussion and the definition of guiding principles, before bills were allowed to be introduced and before reference to smaller committees which were appointed to establish facts and arrange details. When standing committees were appointed, *Jefferson's Manual* states in Section XI: "The person first named is generally permitted to act as chairman. But this is a matter of courtesy; every committee having a right to elect their own chairman, who presides over them, puts questions, and reports their proceedings to the House." If a bill or resolution were committed to a select committee, the member who moved its appointment was usually named as chairman. The Jeffersonians believed that these committees and their chairmen should be sympathetic to the purpose of the matters committed to them.

The *Annals* of the early Congresses indicate that special knowledge or experience of a particular subject was sometimes considered a qualification for committee appointment, but that the principle of seniority had not yet become customary in selecting committee chairmen. Joseph Cooper reports that the standing Committee on Elections in the Third Congress and the standing Committees on Claims and on Commerce and Manufacturing in the Fourth Congress had different chairmen in one session than in another. The successive chairmen were not the ranking members, members were not listed by party on the committee lists, and the composition of the standing committees underwent substantial changes from session to session.[10]

As regards committee reports, Jefferson notes in Section XXVI of his manual that

> A committee meet when and where they please, if the House has not ordered time and place for them; but they can only act when together, and not by separate consultation and consent—nothing being the report of the committee but what has been agreed to in committee actually assembled. A majority of the committee constitutes a quorum for business.

During the first twenty years (1789-1809), when the House largely relied on select committees to perfect the details of bills after their general principles had been formulated in committee of the whole, committee reports were made by the chairman standing in his place on the House floor. He would read the committee amendments and explain the reasons for them and then deliver the bill at the clerk's table. The clerk would read the reported amendments and the papers would lie on the table until the House, at its convenience, took up the report. The report being made, the committee was dissolved (*Jefferson's Manual,* Section XXVII). This procedure has long been obsolete. In the modern practice, most of the reports of committees are made by filing them with the clerk without reading, and only the reports of committees having leave to report at any time are made by the chairman or other member of the committee from the floor. While privileged reports are frequently acted upon when presented, the general rule is that reports shall be placed on the calendars of the House, there to await action under the rules for the order of business. Since 1946, it has been the duty of the chairman of each committee to report or cause to be reported promptly to the House any measure approved by his committee and to take or cause to be taken necessary steps to bring the matter to a vote (Rule XI, para. 2l[1] [A]).

As time went on, disparities developed between theory and practice regarding the role and prerogatives of committee chairmen. Originally conceived as merely the moderator or agent of the committee, the chairman began to play a more active part both in advancing and retarding committee reports. Evidence of this is reflected in two resolutions introduced in the House at the end of the first session of the Ninth Congress (1805-1806) by Representative James Sloan of New Jersey. One resolution required all committees to make weekly reports unless excused from so doing by unanimous consent. The other required that all standing committees be elected by ballot and choose their own chairmen. These resolutions were aimed at John Randolph, chairman of Ways and Means, in order, said Sloan, "to prevent in future the most important business of the nation from being retarded by a Chairman of the Committee of Ways and Means, or any other committee, by going to Baltimore or elsewhere, without leave of absence . . . to prevent in future the Chairman of the Committee of Ways and Means from keeping for months the estimates for the appropriations necessary for the ensuing year in his pocket, or locked up in his desk . . . and, finally, to prevent hereafter bills of importance being brought forward, and forced through the House, near the close of a session, when many members are gone home. . . ."[11] In the first session of the Tenth Congress (1807-1808), John Randolph was removed from Ways and Means when the committee was completely reformed. Meanwhile the House adopted a rule in the second session of the Eighth Congress (1804-1805), and renewed it in the Ninth and Tenth Congresses, allowing committees to choose their own chairmen if they wished. Through the nineteenth century, however, previous service on a committee increased in importance, and the tendency grew to appoint the senior members of the House to the committee chairmanships.

The *Precedents* of the House of Representatives, as compiled by Asher Hinds and Clarence Cannon, shed further light on the evolution of the role of committee chairmen during the nineteenth century. The rule providing for the appointment of clerks of committees dates from December 14, 1838, when Representative Samuel Cushman of New Hampshire proposed that no committee should be permitted to employ a clerk at public expense without first obtaining leave of the House for that purpose. This suggestion was adopted and became old rule Number 73. In the rules revision of 1880

it became Section 4 of Rule X (*Hinds' Precedents,* Vol 4, Section 4533).
In 1911 an amendment was added to this rule including other committee
employees, making the rule read as follows:

> The chairman shall appoint the clerk or clerks or other employees of his
> committee, subject to its approval, who shall be paid at the public expense,
> the House having first provided therefor (*Cannon's Precedents,* Vol. 8, Sec-
> tion 2206).

Under the Legislative Reorganization Act of 1946, as amended, each
standing committee of the House was authorized to appoint professional
and clerical staffs, by majority vote of the committee, who could be assigned to the chairman and ranking minority member, as the committee
deemed advisable, and whose compensation could be fixed by the chairman. As a result of rule changes adopted in 1975, the number of statutory
staff positions for the standing committees was set at forty-two, with the
majority receiving twenty-six and the minority sixteen.

As regards their meetings, committees of the House originally met when
and where they pleased, as noted above, the time and place being largely
determined by the chairman. The failure of chairmen to take action responsive to the wishes of committees occasioned discussion in later Congresses, and on December 8, 1931, the first rule on this subject was
adopted by the House (*Cannon's Precedents,* Vol. 8, Section 2208). The
present rule, which combines the 1931 rule, Section 133 (a) of the Legislative Reorganization Act of 1946, and Section 102 (b) of the Legislative
Reorganization Act of 1970, provides that

> Each standing committee of the House shall adopt regular meeting days,
> which shall be not less frequent than monthly, for the conduct of its busi-
> ness. Each such committee shall meet, for the consideration of any bill or
> resolution pending before the committee or for the transaction of other
> committee business, on all regular meeting days fixed by the committee,
> unless otherwise provided by written rule adopted by the committee.
>
> The chairman of each standing committee may call and convene, as he or
> she considers necessary, additional meetings of the committee for the con-
> sideration of any bill or resolution pending before the committee or for the
> conduct of other committee business. The committee shall meet for such
> purpose pursuant to that call of the chairman [Rule XI, paragraphs 2 (b)
> (c)].

As regards committee procedure, the House amended its rules on March
23, 1955, by adopting a set of standards for the conduct of investigative
hearings which imposed certain duties on the chairman at such hearings,
including the making of an opening statement, the punishment of breaches

of order and decorum, and the disposition of requests to subpoena witnesses (Rule XI, para. 2[k]).

It often happens in human affairs that law or theory and actual practice do not precisely correspond. An account of the powers of committee chairmen would be incomplete, therefore, which did not include some description of the actual operation of the rules as seen by close students of congressional government down through the years.

Writing in 1885, Woodrow Wilson said:[12]

> It is now, though a wide departure from the form of things, no great departure from the fact to describe ours as a government by the Standing Committees of Congress . . . The leaders of the House are the chairmen of the principal Standing Committees. Indeed, to be exactly accurate, the House has as many leaders as there are subjects of legislation; for there are as many Standing Committees as there are leading classes of legislation, and in the consideration of every topic of business the House is guided by a special leader in the person of the chairman of the Standing Committee, charged with the superintendence of measures of the particular class to which that topic belongs. . . . I know not how better to describe our form of government in a single phrase than by calling it a government by the chairmen of the Standing Committees of Congress. . . .

Writing in 1953, George B. Galloway summed up the practice at that time by saying:[13]

> Just as the standing committees control legislative action, so the chairmen are masters of their committees. Selected on the basis of seniority, locally elected and locally responsible, these "lord-proprietors" hold key positions in the power structure of Congress. They arrange the agenda of the committees, appoint the subcommittees, and refer bills to them. They decide what pending measures shall be considered and when, call committee meetings, and decide whether or not to hold hearings and when. They approve lists of scheduled witnesses, select their staffs and authorize staff studies and preside at committee hearings. They handle reported bills on the floor and participate as principal managers in conference committees. They are in a position to expedite measures they favor and to retard or pigeonhole those they dislike. Strong chairmen can often induce in executive sessions the kind of committee actions that they desire. In the House of Representatives, where debate is limited, the chairman in charge of a bill allots time to whomever he pleases during debate on the floor; he also has the right to open and close the debate on bills reported by his committee; and he may move the previous question whenever he thinks best. In short, committee chairmen exercise crucial powers over the legislative process.

This is obviously a summary that has been tempered by subsequent events. Both parties in the House now have procedures that allow the members to reject the nominations of party leaders for the positions of chair-man or ranking member. In the case of the Democrats, the procedures have been tested with considerable vigor. In addition, in 1971, the Democratic caucus adopted new rules which prevent the chairman of a committee from heading more than one subcommittee of that committee, which prevent any member from chairing more than one legislative subcommittee and forbid a member from being a member of more than two committees with legisla-tive jurisdiction. As Representative Morris K. Udall of Arizona has put it, these changes, which resulted in about forty new subcommittee chair-men, "gave a piece of the action to all kinds of bright young men and women who otherwise would have been frozen out for years."[14] Among the other changes which have subtracted from the historical prerogatives of the chairmen is the 1973 rule that ended the practice of closed rules for bills coming from the Ways and Means Committee by allowing floor con-sideration of amendments if fifty or more members obtain a majority vote in the caucus. The 1975 change which calls for the approval by the caucus of chairmen of subcommittees of the Appropriations Committee is also a substantive change, as is the adoption by most committees of rules that al-low members to take the initiative when confronted by a recalcitrant chair-man. While it is still true that committee chairmen have immense influ-ence, it is a fact of legislative life now that there are extensive formal methods which will minimize their conducting themselves in a capricious or arbitrary manner.

Regional Distribution of Chairmanships

In view of the potent place of committee chairmen in the power structure of Congress, it is interesting to note the regional distribution of these influ-ential posts. When the Republicans controlled the House in the Eighty-third Congress, the Central states had fourteen of the nineteen standing-committee chairmanships; the Middle Atlantic states had four; and New England had one. Illinois alone had five chairmanships, including Foreign Affairs, Judiciary, and Rules. Michigan had three: Banking and Currency, Government Operations, and Public Works. In the second session of the Eighty-fifth Congress, when the Democrats were in power, the South had twelve of the nineteen chairmanships in the House; the Middle Atlantic states had four; the Central states had two; and the Pacific Coast one. This pattern of committee power has existed for many years, with the Middle West in the seats of the mighty when the Republicans dominate the House, and the South controlling the committee strongholds when the Democrats are in the ascendancy. There are, however, indications that this pattern may be altered considerably in the future as more Northern districts become Democratic safe seats and more Southern districts become competitive. For example, between the presidential elections of 1968 and 1972, the number of Northern representatives who were elected by 65 per cent or more of a two-party vote went from sixty-six to eighty while the number of Southern representatives from similarly safe seats declined from sixty-eight to fifty-five.[15] The long-run trends in the geographical distribution of committee chairmanships in the House since 1820 are reflected in the accompanying table.

REGIONAL DISTRIBUTION OF COMMITTEE CHAIRMANSHIPS
IN THE HOUSE OF REPRESENTATIVES, 1820-1975

Region	Dem. 1820	Rep.* 1860	Rep. 1900	Dem. 1940	Dem. 1960	Dem. 1975
New England	4	7	8	0	0	0
Middle Atlantic	11	13	12	8	4	2
North Central	2	9	33	10	2	6
South Atlantic	8	2	1	10	6	4
South Central	5	3	0	13	7	7
Mountain	0	0	0	2	1	0
Pacific	0	0	3	4	0	3
	30†	34	57	47	20	22

* In 1860 the Republicans had a plurality, not an absolute majority, of House seats.
† Includes several committees that were standing in fact though not in name.
SOURCE: *Congressional Directories,* 16th Congress, 2d Session; 36th Congress, 1st Session; 56th Congress, 2d Session; 76th Congress, 3d Session; 86th Congress, 2d Session; 94th Congress, 1st Session.

Jurisdiction and Duties

From the earliest days the rules of the House have given its standing committees jurisdiction over the various subjects of legislation. The entire legislative domain has been divided into distinct categories defined by the rules, and jurisdiction over each category has been allocated to a separate standing committee. The Legislative Reorganization Act of 1946 not only streamlined the committee structure of the House, but also redefined and clarified the jurisdiction of the nineteen streamlined committees. Every subject of legislation then conceivable was listed under the appropriate standing committee, no one then foreseeing that the amazing advance of science and the exploration of outer space by manmade moons and satellites would create new fields of legislative interest and inquiry. The same act sought to reduce the scope of lawmaking by prohibiting the reception or consideration of certain private bills relating to claims, pensions, construction of bridges, and the correction of military or naval records. Upon their introduction all bills are referred to the appropriate standing committees which must consider and report them before they can be taken up on the floor.

As we have noted, in 1974 the Select Committee on Committees made a vigorous but unsuccessful attempt to modify substantially the jurisdictions of the standing committees. The committee concluded that in the twenty-eight years since the Reorganization Act, "the shape of national problems has changed so dramatically that jurisdictional lines are tangled, workloads unbalanced, and overlap and confusion all too frequent."[16] It noted that twelve House committees had significant jurisdiction in energy matters and that five committees were dealing with environmental problems. The committee recommended an extensive revision of jurisdictional lines, proposing a new structure consisting of fifteen ("A") committees on which membership would be limited to one per member and seven ("B") other committees on which members could serve in addition to the fifteen. Obviously a massive reorganization of jurisdictional lines, whatever its merits in terms of organizational theory, alters relationships between interest groups and committees which have evolved over a very long period of time. It also means a reduction of power for those committees and subcommittees which presently enjoy that jurisdiction. The benefits are abstractions, but the number of aggrieved members is a reality. Having undertaken a review of the entire committee structure, it was inevitable that the committee would seek to achieve a comprehensive revision. The dimension of the proposals then worked against its success.[17]

As for the procedures of the standing committees, it is important to note that the rules of the House are the rules of the committees and their subcommittees insofar as applicable. House Rule XI now requires each standing committee to adopt, at a meeting that is open to the public, written rules governing its procedure. It also requires that the rules be published in the *Congressional Record*.

Evolution of Committee Powers

During the Federalist and Jeffersonian periods, it was the general practice of the House of Representatives to refer legislative subjects to a committee of the whole in order to develop the main principles of legislation, and then to commit such matters to select committees to draft specific bills. In those early years, before the rise of the standing committee system, the committees were regarded as agents of the House which kept control over them by giving them specific instructions as to their authority and duties. *Jefferson's Manual,* in Section XXVI, provided:

> The committee have full power over the bill or other paper committed to them, except that they can not change the title or subject.
>
> The committee may not erase, interline, or blot the bill itself; but must, in a paper by itself, set down the amendments, stating the words which are to be inserted or omitted, and where, by reference to page, line, and word of the bill.

And in Section XXVIII:

> If a report be recommitted before agreed to in the House, what has passed in committee is of no validity; the whole question is again before the committee, and a new resolution must again be moved, as if nothing had passed.

The guiding principles of legislation were settled in the House before a matter was referred to a committee, and a committee in reporting a bill back to the House was obliged to conform to the terms of the resolution of reference. The decisions reached in the House were binding to its committees.

The House retained control of its committees in early days, first, by assigning specific tasks to *ad hoc* groups; second, by requiring them to report back favorably or unfavorably; third, by dissolving a select committee when it had completed its work; and fourth, by passing judgment upon the committee reports. Scores of special committees were raised by the Federalists and the Jeffersonian Republicans to consider specific matters or draft bills and were dismissed upon the submission of their reports. There was no discharge problem in those days because committees were expected to report back, one way or another; should a committee fail to report, a discharge motion could easily be made and carried by a simple majority vote.

Moreover, at the outset, the introduction and reference of bills was strictly controlled by the House. The power of a committee to report by bill was not allowed until principles had first been settled by the House, usually in committee of the whole. And the right of an individual member to introduce a bill depended upon a grant of leave so to do by the House, in striking contrast to the modern practice under which Congressmen enjoy complete freedom in this respect. This rule was adopted by the House in the First Congress:

> Every bill shall be introduced by motion for leave or by an order of the House on the report of the committee; and in either case a committee to

> prepare the same shall be appointed. In cases of a general nature, one day's
> notice at least shall be given of the motion to bring in a bill; and every such
> motion may be committed.

In the early decades, bills were customarily introduced on the report of a
committee by order of the House, but as time went on the practice developed of permitting committees to report by bill at their own discretion; and
finally in 1822 a rule was adopted which recognized this practice and provided that "the several standing committees of the House shall have leave
to report by bill or otherwise."[18] Meanwhile the introduction of bills on
leave by individual members revived after 1835 and has been unchecked
since 1880.

As regards the reference of bills, the original practice, as we have seen,
was to refer important matters to a committee of the whole for a decision
on principles and this continued to be prevailing practice down to the end
of Jefferson's first administration. But with the growth of the standing committee system in 1816 and thereafter, the Committee of the Whole declined
and their roles were reversed. With increasing frequency, legislative subjects came to be referred initially to the smaller standing committees which
grew in power and prestige. "Thus, by 1825, if not earlier," writes Joseph
Cooper, "we may conclude that both in theory and in fact the standing
committee had become predominant with regard to the first reference of
legislative subjects."[19]

As regards committee meetings, the original rule provided that

> A committee meet when and where they please, if the House has not or-
> dered time and place for them; but they can only act when together, and not
> by separate consultation and consent—nothing being the report of the com-
> mittee but what has been agreed to in committee actually assembled (*Jeffer-
> son's Manual*, Section XXVI).

A long-standing rule dating back to 1794 provided that no committee of
the House could sit, without special leave, while the House was in session.
Exceptions were inserted for the Committee on Rules in 1893 and for the
Committee on Government Operations and on Un-American Activities in
1953. The rule was considerably changed by the Legislative Reorganization
Act of 1970, and committees may now sit at any time except when amendments under the five-minute rule are being considered. However, the Committees on Appropriations, Government Operations, Rules, and Standards
of Official Conduct may meet at any time. In 1952, Speaker Sam Rayburn
ruled that committees could not televise or otherwise broadcast their proceedings either in Washington or elsewhere.[20] Subsequently the Reorganization Act of 1970 permitted any committee, by majority vote, to allow its

public hearings to be televised or broadcast, subject to certain rules. For example, commercial sponsorship was forbidden and no subpoenaed witness could be televised or broadcast without his permission. Nor could members subsequently make use of the tapes as partisan political campaign material.

Four years later, a joint committee proposed "a carefully designed but limited test to determine the ultimate feasibility and desirability of a permanent system for broadcasting activities in the House and Senate Chambers. . . ."[21] Many members have reservations about full coverage and wonder if it may adversely affect the nature of the legislative process. Television executives envision many technical and schedule problems. Nevertheless it seems safe to forecast that the immense public interest generated by the televised impeachment hearings by the Committee on the Judiciary in 1974 and the perception by members of Congress that presidential domination of the media needs to be redressed will eventually lead to greater television coverage of the Congress.

From earliest days the House has delegated the conduct of investigations to its select and standing committees and has authorized them to send for persons and papers. This power, whose origin has been traced back to the ancient practice of the English House of Commons in the sixteenth century, was first conferred by the House on a select committee that investigated the defeat of General St. Clair by the Indians in 1792 and compelled witnesses to attend and testify under oath.[22] Since then the House has frequently granted the power to compel testimony, even to subcommittees, and it has been used in scores of cases down through the years in investigations of the conduct of public officials, members of Congress, election contests, and economic and social problems. The power to send for persons and papers has been upheld by the courts, within certain limits, and many contumacious and recalcitrant witnesses have been cited for contempt of the House for their refusal to answer questions or produce papers. During the nineteenth century the House of Representatives was the chief inquisitor, and much American history can be gleaned from the reports of its investigating committees. In recent years the pace of the investigative process has increased, partly as a result of the authority granted each standing committee of the House and Senate in 1946 to "exercise continuous watchfulness" of the execution of the laws within its jurisdiction. Reacting to the abuses of the McCarthy period, some committees adopted rules of procedure for the conduct of their inquiries, and on March 23, 1955, the House adopted a set of rules for the guidance of all its investigating committees (Rule XI, paragraphs h-k). These rules are still in effect.

The role of the House as the "inquest of the nation" and the proper scope of committee inquiries into the conduct of administration was a subject of frequent debate during the early Congresses. Federalists and Jeffersonians argued at length over the appropriate limits of legislative oversight of the executive. Joseph Cooper identifies three areas in which this debate raged:[23]

1. Investigations of offenses committed by executive officers to ascertain whether they were serious enough to sustain an impeachment proceeding;
2. Investigations aimed at informing the nation as to possible abuses in the administration of the law or aimed at supplying the House with sufficient information to enable it to control administration legislatively; and
3. Investigations into the use of public money to secure the information necessary to enable the House to appropriate wisely.

The Jeffersonians believed that these were proper fields for congressional inquiry of administration, but that Congress should not interfere with the administration of the law. Discrepancies developed, however, between their theory and practice, and after 1809 the practice of the House was marked by a noteworthy expansion of special investigations into administrative conduct of the government and of the exercise of the oversight function by House committees. In a searching and original analysis of the "postnatal role" of the House and its committees during the period, 1789-1829, Joseph Cooper concludes that after 1809 there was[24]

a turning away from oversight or superintendence toward supervision, a turning away from the notion that the President is primarily responsible for administration toward the notion that all rests with Congress . . . it is clear that a different sense of responsibility for administration activated the generations of Republicans who served in Congress after 1809 and that the thrust of that new sense of responsibility was toward Congressional supremacy in administration as well as in legislation.

Beginning with the Committee on Enrolled Bills in 1812, several House committees at intervals over the years were granted leave to report at any time on stated matters, as a method of expediting the most important matters of business. The privilege carried with it the right of immediate consideration by the House. Privileged reports are made from the floor. In the revision of the rules in 1880 these various privileges were consolidated in one rule. The rule was amended in 1946 to provide that no general appropriation bill shall be considered in the House until printed committee hearings and a committee reoprt thereon have been available for the members of the House for at least three calendar days. The privilege of reporting at any time is now enjoyed by the following committees: Appropriations, House Administration, Budget, Standards of Official Conduct, and Rules on the matters specified in paragraph 21 of Rule XI.[25]

From this review of the development of committee powers, it will be seen that the committees were regarded in early years as creatures of the House and were subject to its direction, that they received most of their major rights and powers during the first quarter century of congressional history, and that by 1825 at the latest, the pattern of committee powers had assumed its modern form. No basic change in this pattern took place thereafter. However, as the nineteenth century advanced and the standing committee system expanded, the prestige and influence of committees were steadily enhanced, and they became increasingly autonomous in their operations. By 1885, Woodrow Wilson correctly described congressional government as "government by the standing committees of Congress." And at the end of the century Miss Follett truthfully remarked that "Congress no longer exercises its lawful function of lawmaking; that has gone to the committees as completely as in England it has passed to the cabinet."[26]

Summarizing this section, the standing committees of the House have acquired power over the years to receive legislative proposals, messages, petitions, and memorials on matters within their defined jurisdiction; to sit and act when and where they deem it advisable during sessions (by special leave), recesses, and adjourned periods; to send for persons and papers; to take testimony and make expenditures; to conduct authorized investigations and to report by bill or otherwise upon any matter within their jurisdiction; to oversee the execution of the laws; to certify contumacious witnesses for contempt; to adopt rules and appoint subcommittees; to report in certain cases at any time or not to report. Measures that the whole House might approve are sometimes "killed in committee" by a few members. Congressional committees usually report only those bills that a majority of their members favor, unlike some state legislatures and the English House of Commons where all referred bills are reported back one way or another.

Subject to some limitations, the committees of Congress have thus come to play a leading role in lawmaking. Each composed of comparatively few members, each normally acting independently of the others, they have long determined the agenda of the House which has largely delegated to its standing committees the power to decide what matters shall be considered on the floor and to control the proceedings there, subject to the terms of the Rules Committee. They can amend or rewrite bills to suit themselves. They can report bills or pigeonhole them. They can initiate measures they desire and bury or emasculate those they dislike. They can proceed with dispatch or deliberate at length. Thus the real locus of the legislative power is not in the House or Senate; it is in their standing committees. The tendency is for the standing committees to frame policy that the whole legislature usually follows.

Types of Committees

There are four types of congressional committees: (1) standing or permanent committees that continue from Congress to Congress; (2) special or temporary committees created for a particular purpose; (3) joint committees (including conference committees) composed of members from both houses; and (4) subcommittees (both standing and special) created to divide the labor of the standing committees.

In the House of Representatives there are also two committees of the whole, in effect standing committees: the Committee of the Whole House, which considers business on the private calendar; and the Committee of the Whole House on the State of the Union, which considers business on the Union Calendar.

The committees of Congress may also be classified by function as (1) legislative committees having jurisdiction defined in the rules over the several fields of legislation; (2) supervisory committees concerned with supervising the administration of the laws; (3) fiscal committees, which handle the revenue and appropriation bills; (4) investigating committees, which make inquiries of various kinds; (5) housekeeping committees, which oversee the internal housekeeping functions of Congress; and (6) political committees, which perform various functions for the political parties.

The size of the standing committees is fixed by the rules of the House; of special committees by the resolutions creating them; and of joint committees by the statutes or resolutions establishing them. In 1975 the standing committees ranged in size from twelve to fifty-five members, but typically they had twenty-five, thirty-seven, or forty-three members. Appropriations, with its heavy work load had fifty-five members; Ways and Means had thirty-seven; Rules had sixteen.

Composition of Committees

Various criteria have been used in making the committee assignments. The most influential considerations are seniority of service in the chamber, geography, personal preference, and previous committee service. Seniority is governed by continuous, uninterrupted service; a member's seniority dates from the beginning of his last uninterrupted service, regardless of previous service in the House, and determines his rank on committees and his place at the committee table.[27] If a veteran member of the House loses his seat for a single term and returns to his former committee, he begins again at the foot of the committee table despite his previous service. This happened, for example, to Representative Earl C. Michener of Michigan, who served from March 4, 1919, to March 3, 1933, and enjoyed a long tenure on the Rules Committee, but was defeated for re-election to the Seventy-third Congress. Mr. Michener returned to the House on January 3, 1935, and served until his voluntary retirement on January 3, 1951, but his absence of two years during 1933-1934 cost him his high place on Rules and the chairmanship of this committee during the Eightieth Congress. In 1975, however, when Representative John Jarman of Oklahoma switched from the Democratic to the Republican party, he went from second ranking member of the Committee on Interstate and Foreign Commerce to third ranking Republican on the Committee on Science and Technology. When Jarman made the switch, he automatically became the senior House Republican.

Party ratios on the standing committees have been customarily determined by agreement between the majority and minority leadership. For many years, that of Ways and Means was at 15-10, that of Rules at 10-5, with the remaining committees divided roughly according to the party division in the chamber. In the Democratic caucus of 1974, the rule that was adopted for the Ninety-fourth Congress gave the Democrats twice as many seats plus one on every committee except Standards of Official Conduct. Ways and Means was expanded to thirty-seven (25-12), and Rules is now sixteen (11-5).

From the Sixty-fourth to the Eightieth Congress, when the Legislative Reorganization Act became effective, the House had eleven major or "exclusive" committees whose chairmen served on no other standing committee of the House while the Democrats were in power. The eleven "exclusive" committees were Agriculture, Appropriations, Banking and Currency, Foreign Affairs, Interstate and Foreign Commerce, Judiciary, Military Affairs, Naval Affairs, Post Offices and Post Roads, Rules, and Ways and Means.

Under the one-committee-assignment rule adopted in 1946, all the standing committees of the House were "exclusive" committees, except that members who were elected to serve on the District of Columbia Committee or on the Un-American Activities Committee might be elected to serve on two committees and no more, and members of the majority party who were elected to serve on the Committee on Government Operations or on the Committee on House Administration might be elected to serve on two standing committees and no more. These exceptions were made so that the majority party could maintain control of all the committees. In the Eighty-third Congress, however, when the Republicans had a "paper-thin" majority of only seven seats in the House, eighteen Republicans were given second committee assignments so as to enable them to control all the standing committees of the House.[28] This necessary departure from the one-committee-assignment rule apparently marked the beginning of the breakdown of that rule, for an examination of committee assignments in the second session of the Eighty-fifth Congress showed that 118 members of the House had two or more committee assignments in 1958. In addition to the four excepted committees mentioned above, five more had been added to the list of those groups upon which some Representatives had second seats: Education and Labor, Interior and Insular Affairs, Merchant Marine and Fisheries, Public Works, and Veterans' Affairs.

The trend to increased committee responsibilities has continued to accelerate, if only because of the increased size of the standing committees. The number of standing committee assignments in 1949 was 480; in 1965, 507; and in 1975, 771. In 1949, 89 per cent of the members had only one committee assignment; in 1965, the figure had declined to 60 per cent, and in 1973, it had gone down to 33 per cent. By 1973 the average number of standing committee assignments per member was 1.82; in addition the proliferation of subcommittee assignments over the years put each member on 3.74 subcommittees. Indeed, by 1973 the only committee assignments that exempted a member from significant additional committee assignments were Appropriations, Ways and Means, and Rules.[29]

The committees of Congress have varied in their representative character, some being fairly representative of the House and the country, others being dominated by members from particular regions or economic interests. It has often happened, for example, that most of the members of the Agriculture Committee were farmers or members from rural districts; that the Interior Committee was largely composed of members from the "public lands" states and districts; and that spokesmen for the coastal districts have sat on Merchant Marine and Fisheries. Congressmen naturally seek assignment to committees that have jurisdiction over matters of major concern to their districts and states. The effect of this practice tends to give a special-interest character to the composition of these panels.

Committee Procedures

During the time he served as Vice President of the United States and president of the Senate, 1797 to 1801, Thomas Jefferson compiled a *Manual of*

Parliamentary Practice in which he acknowledged his debt for information to Hatsell, clerk of the House of Commons from 1760 to 1797. *Jefferson's Manual* is said to have been his penance to England for the Declaration of Independence. From it we learn, among other things, something of the procedure of congressional committees in those early days. It shows that committee proceedings were not published; that committees were forbidden to receive petitions except through the House, or to sit when notified that the House was in session. When select committees conducted inquiries, only the chairman was to question witnesses; testimony was to be taken in writing for submission to the House.

Committees were to be appointed by the Speaker, but the House was to control their names and number. A bill should be committed only to those friendly to its chief features, for "the child is not to be put to a nurse that cares not for it." Unless the House named the place and the hour, the committee might sit anywhere and at any time. A majority was the committee quorum. Any member of the House could attend the meetings of a select committee, but only its members could vote. It had full power to alter a bill or other paper committed, except the title. Committees themselves could originate bills, resolutions, and addresses. Reports were to be made by the chairman; and when concluded, unless the bill were recommitted to it, the committee was dissolved.

Since Jefferson penned his famous *Manual* in the days of the stagecoach, House procedure has evolved as its business and membership increased until today the parliamentary precedents of that body occupy eleven large volumes. As regards committee procedure, we may examine a few significant features of the modern practice: committee meetings, secrecy versus publicity of their sessions, their rules of procedures and proxy voting, the hearings process, quorums and reports, and discharge.

Under the rules each standing committee of the House (other than the Committee on Appropriations) fixes regular weekly, biweekly, or monthly meeting days for the transaction of its business. Additional meetings may be called by the chairman as he may deem necessary. The committees customarily meet to consider their pending business on their regular meeting days as well as upon the call of their chairmen. Special meetings may be called upon the written request of a majority of a committee if the chairman, after three days' consideration, refuses or fails to call a special meeting; but committeemen seldom overrule their chairmen in this way. A committee scheduled to meet on stated days, when convened on such a day with a quorum present, may proceed to the transaction of business regardless of the absence of the chairman. If the chairman of any standing committee is not present at any meeting of the committee, the ranking member of the majority party on the committee who is present presides at that meeting. Typically, a quorum for doing business is a majority of the committee, except that two members must be present at meetings where testimony is taken, one of them, whenever possible, a member of the minority party. On a typical day of a modern Congress, the Daily Digest of the *Congressional Record* will show a score of House committees and subcommittees in session.

Secrecy versus Publicity

Whether committee meetings should be open or closed to the public has long been a controversial question. Although the House galleries have been open from the beginning, secrecy customarily veiled committee sessions during the nineteenth century and sometimes aroused public suspicions of evil. During the Credit Mobilier scandal after the Civil War, it was charged that certain members of Congress[30] had sought to bribe their congressional colleagues with gifts of railway stock. Two House committees set up to investigate these charges in 1872-1873 proceeded at first in closed sessions, but the pressure of an excited public opinion forced the House to open these hearings to reporters. Occasional exposures of wrongdoing gave rise to public distrust of star-chamber proceedings and to the demand that the searchlight of publicity be trained upon them.

During the twentieth century the long-run trend has been in the direction of greater publicity for committee activities. Under Rule XI, as amended by the House in 1973, all committee meetings for the transaction of business, including the markup of legislation, are open to the public unless the committee votes in open session and by a roll-call vote decides that the meeting should be closed. Internal budget or personnel matters were exempted. The rule also states the sole grounds for closed hearings would be that the disclosure of testimony or evidence "would endanger the national security or would violate any rule or law of the House of Representatives."

The results of this new rule have been dramatic. A survey by the *Congressional Quarterly* notes that in 1972—the year before the new rule—25 per cent of the committee meetings in the House were closed, while in 1973 the figure dropped to 10 per cent, and in 1974 to 8 per cent.[31] The trend to even more open meetings will undoubtedly continue. The House Republican Task Force on Reform, chaired by Representative Bill Frenzel of Minnesota, has recommended that even conference committees and party caucuses and conferences should be open whenever votes are taken that decide public questions or bind members.[32] The Democratic caucus had already approved the idea of open conference committees at a meeting in 1975, but the change could only become effective if the Senate approved.

Recent Developments

Several provisions of the Legislative Reorganization Act of 1946 were designed to regularize committee procedure and have since been made a part of the standing rules of the House. Each committee was required to keep a complete record of all committee action, including a record of the votes on any question on which a record vote is demanded. All committee hearings, records, data, charts, and files are to be kept separate and distinct from the congressional office records of the chairman of the committee; such records are the property of the House and all members of the House shall have access to them. Each committee is authorized to have printed and bound testimony and other data presented at its hearings. It is the duty of the committee chairman to report or cause to be reported promptly to the House any measure approved by his committee and to take or cause to be taken necessary steps to bring the matter to a vote. But no measure or recommendation shall be reported from any committee unless a majority of its members were actually present. So far as practicable, all witnesses appearing before a committee are required to file in advance written statements of their proposed testimony, and to limit their oral presentations to brief summaries of their argument. Digests of such statements are to be prepared for the use of committee members. As noted above, the rule was also adopted in 1973 that all hearings conducted by standing committees or their subcommittees should be open to the public, except under carefully stipulated circumstances.

The demand for congressional control of committee conduct finally led the House on March 23, 1955, to adopt ten rules of procedure for its investigating committees that were designed to assure majority control of these groups and to safeguard the rights of witnesses. Under these rules, not less than two members of a committee shall constitute a quorum for taking testimony and receiving evidence. They direct the chairman to announce the subject of an investigation in his opening statement, to make a copy of the committee rules available to witnesses, and to punish breaches of order and decorum. Witnesses at investigative hearings may be accompanied by their own counsel to advise them concerning their constitutional rights. If a committee determines that evidence or testimony at an investigative hearing may tend to defame, degrade, or incriminate any person, it shall receive such evidence or testimony in executive session; afford such person an opportunity voluntarily to appear as a witness; and receive and dispose of requests from such a person to subpoena additional witnesses. Evidence or testimony taken in executive session may not be released or used in public sessions without the consent of the committee. In the discretion of the committee, witnesses may submit brief and pertinent sworn statements in writing for inclusion in the record. And a witness may obtain a transcript copy of his testimony at cost. While this "code of fair play" fell somewhat short of the recommendations of a House Rules subcommittee, its adoption marked a notable milestone in regularizing the rules of House committee procedure.

From the viewpoint of the witnesses modern congressional procedures seem considerably safer than those occasionally employed in the more turbulent past. John Quincy Adams told of an incident that occurred in 1837, while he was serving in the House of Representatives after being President. Adams wrote:[33]

> When Reuben Whitney was before a committee of investigation in 1837, Bailie Peyton of Tennessee, taking offense at one of his answers, threatened him fiercely, and when he rose to claim the committee's protection, Mr. Peyton, with due and appropriate profanity, shouted:
> "You shan't say one word while you are in this room; if you do, I shall put you to death."
> The chairman, Henry A. Wise, added: "This insolence is insufferable."

Adams commented wryly:

> As both of these gentlemen were armed with deadly weapons, the witness could hardly be blamed for not wanting to testify again.

Proxy Voting in Committees

Until the Legislative Reorganization Act of 1970, the rules of the House of Representatives did not deal with proxy voting. But the *House Manual* did state that the rules of the House were the rules of its committees. From this, it was sometimes argued that use of proxies in committees was illegal.

On the two occasions when the question was raised, however, the Speaker stated an "opinion" that the use of proxies was at the discretion of each committee. On February 16, 1929, Speaker Nicholas Longworth said a proxy may be voted "only by unanimous consent of the committee itself. . . . A proxy on one particular vote must have the unanimous consent of the committee." On January 26, 1946, Speaker Sam Rayburn was asked to rule on proxy voting. He said, "That is a matter for the committee to determine. The Chair may make this statement: He served on one committee for twenty-four years [Interstate and Foreign Commerce], and never was a proxy voted on that committee, because the present occupant of the chair always voted against it."

Defenders of proxy voting argued that overlapping official duties made it impossible for members to attend all meetings of the committees to which they are assigned. Proxies permitted them to vote their convictions when circumstances prevented them from attending committee meetings.

Opponents of proxy voting argued that proxy voting actually encouraged absenteeism by permitting a member to disguise his absence from important sessions of committees. Proxy voting encouraged irresponsibility; absent members could not be acquainted with the arguments or even the substance of proposals on which their proxies are cast.

Another problem concerned the pros and cons of general versus special proxies. Some members objected to general proxies on the ground that they had a tendency to promote absenteeism. This objection was reflected in the pertinent rule of the Committee on Interior and Insular Affairs which provided, in part, that "no general proxies shall be given or recognized . . ." On the other hand, the Committee on the Judiciary allowed the use of both general and special proxies.

A survey of the rules and practice of all the standing committees of the House of Representatives during the first session of the Eighty-fifth Congress indicated that proxy voting was not permitted in six committees, and that the use of special proxies was allowed in thirteen committees. The 1957 practice is summarized in the table below.

PROXY VOTING PRACTICE IN COMMITTEES
OF THE HOUSE OF REPRESENTATIVES

Committee	Special Proxies Permitted	Not Permitted
Agriculture	x	
Appropriations		x
Armed Services	x	
Banking & Currency		x
District of Columbia	x	
Education & Labor	x	
Foreign Affairs	x	
Government Operations	x	
House Administration		x
Interior & Insular Affairs	x	
Interstate & Foreign Commerce		x
Judiciary*	x	
Merchant Marine & Fisheries	x	
Post Office & Civil Service	x	
Public Works	x	
Rules		x
Un-American Activities	x	
Veterans' Affairs		x
Ways & Means	x	
	13	6

* Permitted both general and special proxies.

The 1970 Act sought to regularize committee procedure by stipulating that the use of proxies was forbidden unless the committee adopted a specific rule that allowed it. The Act outlawed general proxies and permitted special proxies only under certain conditions. The general proxy was defined as a proxy that did not "identify the specific measures or matters with respect to which the proxy is to be voted" and a specific or special proxy as one that is "stated in terms specifically identifying one or more measures or matters with respect to which the proxy is to be voted." The new rule stated that if a committee adopted a proxy rule, the proxy had to be in writing, must designate the person executing it, and was limited "to a specific measure or matter and any amendments or motions pertaining thereto."[34]

In 1974, the Select Committee on Committees recommended a total ban on proxy voting, and the proposal became a part of the reforms adopted by the House that year. There was considerable concern about the action, for as Representative Bolling pointed out, the proposal was an integral part of a package, i.e., the ban on proxies was linked to the reduction in the number of standing committees and subcommittees.[35] To retain the ban on proxies while maintaining a situation where members had to be at several meetings at the same time seemed to make little sense. When Congress convened in 1975, the Democratic caucus therefore voted to delete the ban from the House rules, and instead adopted a procedure for committees to follow in adopting a proxy rule. In the Ninety-fourth Congress, all committees permitted some form of proxy voting with the exception of Appropriations, House Administration, and Rules.

Typical of the proxy rules adopted in the Ninety-fourth Congress is the one reprinted below from the Committee on Science and Technology:[36]

> No general proxies may be used for any purpose; however, a Member may vote by special proxy. The special proxy authorization shall be in writing, shall assert that the Member is absent on official business or is otherwise unable to be present at the meeting of the committee, shall designate the person who is to execute the proxy authorization and shall be limited to a specific measure or matter and any amendments or motions pertaining thereto; except that a Member may authorize a general proxy only for motions to recess, adjourn or other procedural matters. Each proxy to be effective shall be signed by the Member assigning his or her vote and shall contain the date and time of day that the proxy is signed.

Committee Hearings

"It is not far from the truth to say," remarked Woodrow Wilson in 1885, "that Congress in session is Congress on public exhibition, whilst Congress in its committee-rooms is Congress at work."[37] Long located in the Capitol and later also in the House office buildings, the committee rooms have been the chief "workshops" of the House. Here in these spacious chambers with their frescoed domes and swinging chandeliers, their walls adorned with the portraits of former chairmen, their cushioned chairs and long committee table on a raised dais, the visitor sees the fountainhead of the legislative process. Here come the spokesmen for all the competing interests of American society: the lobbyist and the expert, the captain of industry and the labor official, the military men from the Pentagon and the financiers from Wall Street, the Cabinet member and the bureau chief, the merchant and the farmer, the lawyer and the judge—all seeking to influence these "little legislatures" whose reports may prescribe the action of the House itself. Here in the committee room is the meeting ground between the public and the Congress, the citizen and the legislator, where hearings have been held since earliest days on a host of legislative proposals designed to meet the needs of a changing society.

Thousands of bills are introduced in every session of Congress and are referred to the appropriate committees. The committees usually hold hearings on legislative proposals which are administration measures or in which the majority party or the chairmen are sufficiently interested or which are strongly favored by some organized interest group. The hearing on a bill is important because it is practically the only stage in the legislative process in which there is an opportunity to make a critical evaluation of a proposed piece of legislation. Theoretically the floor stage also offers an occasion to debate the merits of a measure, but debate on the House floor is often sparsely attended and is usually "after the fact," so to speak; it is designed to explain to the country decisions already arrived at in committee rather than to analyze the facts or elucidate the rationale underlying a legislative proposal.

Due notice of the hearings is customarily given; government officials from the agencies concerned and representatives of interested private organizations are invited to appear, and other witnesses are heard at their own request in favor of or opposed to the pending measure. Notices and brief summaries of committee hearings, with the names of witnesses, are published in the Daily Digest section of the *Congressional Record*. During a week in July, 1975, for example, various House committees and subcommittees held hearings on topics as diverse as the financing of public broadcasting, international commodity agreements, revenue sharing, a contested election in Maine, public-works jobs on railroads, a nationwide surface-transportation policy, nuclear safety, and the trade embargo on Cuba. The hearings may run from one day to several weeks depending upon the number of witnesses, the controversial character of the subject, and the wishes of the committee. When the hearings have been completed and printed, the committee goes into executive session, reviews the testimony heard, considers amendments, examines the bill and report on it that has been drafted by the staff, and finally decides whether or not to report the revised measure to the House.

Congressional committee hearings as they have developed down through the decades have served a variety of practical uses. Their most important function has been to collect facts so as to enable committee members to make informed judgments regarding legislative proposals. Their printed hearings are a gold mine of factual information about all the public problems of the nation. A second use of the hearing process is the safety-valve function: an opportunity for individuals and groups who feel strongly about a matter to "blow off steam." In this way social tensions are often relaxed even though legislation may not be the end result. A third use of committee hearings is as a political sounding board for the legislature, furnishing a barometer to gauge public opinion and to identify and assess the strength of conviction and relative power of the political forces that are lined up for and against the pending bill. This function helps legislators estimate the political consequences of their votes on a measure when and if the bill reaches the House floor.[38]

In modern practice the committee hearing has been the scene of some useful innovations. One of these has been to make use of panels of experts to assist committees in clarifying the facts relating to complex legislative problems. During the Eighty-fourth Congress, for example, when questions arose regarding the safety and efficacy of the Salk vaccine, the National Academy of Sciences co-operated with the House Committee on Interstate and Foreign Commerce in selecting a panel of experts who discussed the scientific problems involved in open hearing before the committee under the guidance of an impartial moderator. This technique was so successful that it was repeated in 1957 at hearings before the Subcommittee on Health and Science where another panel of experts discussed the scientific problems involved in testing and evaluating the safety of chemical additives. Similarly, panels of leading economists have frequently debated questions of monetary and fiscal policy before subcommittees of the Joint Economic Committee. In 1973, when the Select Committee on Committees was holding hearings on the committee structure of the House, it conducted twelve days of panel discussions with forty-six scholars and other experts either participating in the discussions or presenting "working papers."

Another innovation in committee procedure has been the scheduling of "docket days" at which a committee has invited the authors of bills referred to it to appear at a preliminary hearing early in a session and speak in behalf of their proposals. This procedure serves to give the committee a better understanding of the proposals before it and gives rank-and-file members of the House a closer working relationship with the committee and its problems. This sensible procedure was launched by the Committee on Foreign Affairs in 1952.

The coming of radio and television and the popularity of legislative broadcasts of the Kefauver Crime Committee hearings, as well as of the proceedings of the United Nations and several parliaments, led to many proposals for putting House committee hearings on the air. But Speaker Rayburn ruled on February 25, 1952, as noted above, that radio broadcasting and televising of hearings before House committees were not authorized by existing rules. However, as we have noted, the Legislative Reorganization Act of 1970 allowed committees to determine if they wished to allow broadcast coverage, and the likelihood was that by 1976 the House and the Senate would even allow televised coverage of floor debates. The movement was undoubtedly accelerated by the successful televising of the impeachment hearing in 1974.

Quorums at Committee Hearings

A summary of the modern practice of the standing committees of Congress as regards the presence of a quorum at committee hearings leads to the following general conclusions:

1. While committees and subcommittees frequently meet with fewer than a quorum, the House rules now require that for taking testimony or receiving evidence, at least two members must be present.

2. So far as the presence or absence of a quorum is concerned, it makes no difference whether or not the testimony is sworn.

3. It is the accepted modern custom that a committee of Congress, once having convened with a quorum, may without maintaining a quorum, continue to conduct a hearing and take testimony.

4. Some committee clerks recall fairly recent instances when the point of no quorum was raised during committee hearings, but they are not able to give definite citations to such cases. Hinds cites a case in 1862 when the validity of testimony taken when a quorum of a committee was not present was questioned (3 *Hinds' Precedents* 1774). On December 17, 1862, the select committee appointed to investigate government contracts adopted the following:

> Resolved, that inasmuch as certain testimony has been taken by one member of the committee, in the absence of a quorum, touching the official conduct of certain Federal officers in New York, under objection from them, therefore the committee will examine such testimony, and whenever it appears that the testimony of any such witness so taken is found to affect the official character of any such persons, such witness shall be reexamined,

and so far as his testimony on reexamination affects the official conduct of any Federal officer in New York, it shall be submitted to him for his inspection (37th Congress, 3d Session, House Report No. 49, pp. 25, 26).

5. The only imaginable motives for objecting to the lack of a quorum during a hearing would be in order to delay the proceedings until some absent committeeman could attend or to cancel the hearing.

6. While a House rule states that no committee can report any "measure or recommendation" unless a majority of the committee was actually present, the House simply assumes that those actions were taken in accordance with the rule unless a point of order is raised.

Three other more or less pertinent precedents are cited by Hinds and Cannon, as follows:

1. On January 25, 1864, the Joint Committee on the Conduct of the War ordered that less than a quorum should be sufficient for taking testimony (4 *Hinds' Precedents* 4424).

2. In the case of Robert W. Stewart, who declined to answer certain questions propounded by the Senate Committee on Public Lands and Surveys during the first session of the Seventieth Congress, the witness was indicted for perjury and tried in the Supreme Court of the District of Columbia and acquitted on the ground that a quorum of the committee was not present on the occasion of the inquiry which resulted in the indictment. But in charging the jury in this case, Justice Jennings Bailey said in part that, if a quorum be present and subsequently members leave temporarily or otherwise, a quorum is presumed to be present until and unless the question of no quorum is raised (6 *Cannon's Precedents* 345).

3. On June 17, 1922 (Sixty-seventh Congress, Second Session), the chair ruled that no report is valid unless authorized with a quorum of the committee present. The discussion prior to the chair's decision distinguished between the requirement of a quorum in the House and in a committee. In the course of this discussion, Representative James R. Mann of Illinois said in part:

> The House does business on the theory of a quorum being present, but it has always been my understanding since I have been a Member of this House that a committee must develop a quorum before it can transact any business. And it is the practice, at least in most of the committees, to call the roll of the committee . . . to ascertain whether a quorum is present (8 *Cannon's Precedents* 2222).[39]

Section 133(d) of the Legislative Reorganization Act of 1946 reads: "No measure or recommendation shall be reported from any such committee unless a majority of the committee were actually present." This provision relates, of course, to reports and not to hearings, and is still a House rule.

In the case of *Christoffel* v. *U.S.* (338 U.S. 84), decided in 1949, the United States Supreme Court decided, in effect, that a quorum of a committee must be actually physically present when a perjurious offense is committed. In the Christoffel case the House Labor Committee was investigating the political affirmations of an individual rather than holding a hearing on a piece of proposed legislation. It does not necessarily follow, therefore, from the decision in this case that a standing committee of the Congress is not a competent tribunal unless it maintains a quorum of its members present throughout a hearing held preparatory to reporting legislation as distinguished from a hearing held to investigate individual conduct.

Inquiry among the clerks of the standing committees of the House and Senate indicated (1) that, as a rule, they do not require the presence of a quorum for the taking of testimony; and (2) that they do not consider the holding of a hearing as the transaction of business. Some committee clerks stated that, in practice, a quorum is usually or often present at hearings on important bills, but not at hearings on minor bills, e.g., those which, when reported, are referred to the Consent Calendar.

In the Ninety-fourth Congress each of the standing committees had adopted the rule that a majority constituted a quorum, although inquiry among staffers disclosed that points of order had not been raised at those meetings which had no quorum. Rule XI allows each committee to set a quorum figure; however, on February 19, 1975, the Democratic caucus adopted a resolution offered by Representative James G. O'Hara of Michigan which would have allowed each committee to set one-third as a quorum for taking any action other than "the reporting of a measure or matter." The resolution, obviously one further attempt to deal with the problem of multiple committee assignments, was sent to the House Rules Committee, but no action has resulted. The constitutionality of the proposal was questioned by Representative John B. Anderson of Illinois, but a memorandum from the Congressional Research Service concluded that the proposal "was not subject to serious constitutional question." Obviously the decision to set a quorum of only one-third raises questions that are more political than legal.[40]

Committee Reports

Since 1880, a rule of the House has required that all bills, petitions, memorials, or resolutions from the committees shall be accompanied by reports in writing, which shall be printed. A report is not necessarily signed by any or all of those concurring in it, but minority views are signed by those submitting them. In 1946 another House rule provided that no general appropriation bill shall be considered in the House until printed committee hearings and a committee report thereon have been available to the members of the

House for at least three calendar days. By a rule change in 1970, all committees "shall make every reasonable effort" to have printed hearings available before floor consideration of the matter involved. The purpose of this provision is to allow members time to study the committee hearings and reports before their floor consideration.

The House has adhered to the principle that a report must be authorized by a committee acting together, and a paper signed by a majority of a committee acting separately has been ruled out. Since 1946, it has been the duty of the chairman of each committee to report or cause to be reported promptly any measure approved by his committee and to take or cause to be taken necessary steps to bring the matter to a vote. In 1970 the rules were modified so that once a committee has approved a measure, a majority of the members of that committee may file a written request to have it reported to the House. Committee reports must also now include the roll-call vote totals on motions to report as well as a statement of the bill's impact on "prices and costs in the national economy." But no measure or recommendation may be reported from any committee unless a majority of the committee are actually present. In the modern practice, most committee reports are made by filing them with the clerk of the House without reading them on the floor, and only the reports of committees having leave to report at any time are made by the chairman or other member of the committee from the floor. While privileged reports are frequently acted on when presented, the general rule is that reports shall be placed on the calendars of the House and there await action under the rules for the order of business.

Discharge Procedure

The annals of Congress reveal frequent use of the motion to discharge a committee from consideration of a bill in the early practice of the House.[41] But use of the discharge motion was discontinued in the House at an early date and by the time of the Fortieth Congress (1867-1869) had ceased to be privileged in the order of business. The subject was discussed from time to time, and resolutions to re-establish the privilege of the discharge motion were introduced in Congress at intervals. But it was not until June 17, 1910, that the House adopted its first discharge rule.[42]

The 1910 rule provided for filing with the clerk motions to discharge committees from consideration of bills at any time after reference. Such motions were placed on a special calendar, to be called up on suspension days after the call of the consent calendar, and on being seconded by tellers, when called up, were placed on their appropriate calendar as if reported by the committee having jurisdiction.

In this form the rule proved ineffective, and it was amended in the revision of 1911 by restricting the presentation of the discharge motion to not less than fifteen days after reference and by requiring the reading of the bill by title only when the motion was called up to be seconded. In this form the rule was employed to such advantage in obstructive tactics that it was further amended in the second session of the Sixty-second Congress (1911-1912) by making it the third order of business on suspension days to follow the call of the consent calendar and the disposition of motions to suspend the rules.

According to Clarence Cannon:[43]

> This change rendered the rule inoperative, and it remained practically nugatory until the Sixty-eighth Congress, when the Committee on Rules reported a substitute which was agreed to after five days debate and under which motion to discharge a committee when signed by 150 Members was entered on a special calendar and after seven days could be called up under privileged status. This rule was invoked but once and while on that occasion the bill to which it was applied failed to reach final consideration, so much time was consumed, sixteen roll calls being had in one day during its consideration, that a further revision of the rule was effected in the succeeding Congress, making it still more difficult of operation. Under this revision the requirement of 150 Members was increased to 218 Members, a majority of the House, and further safeguards were included which rendered the rule wholly unworkable. Only one attempt was made to utilize it during the Sitxy-ninth Congress and at the opening of the Seventy-second Congress it was completely redrafted and adopted in its present form with the exception that 145 signatures were sufficient to secure reference to the Calendar. The amendment requiring a majority of the membership of the House was incorporated in the resolution providing for the adoption of the rules of the Seventy-fourth Congress (1935).

Many petitions to discharge committees have been filed under the discharge rule, but of the 388 petitions filed between 1923 and 1974 only twenty-five bills have been freed from committees by this procedure. Twenty of these were passed. In the entire history of the discharge rule, however, only two bills have ever become law by the discharge route: the Fair Labor Standards Act of 1938, and the Federal Pay Raise Act of 1960.

But it should also be noted that there have been times when the use of the discharge procedure as a threat has also been important. In 1960 a discharge petition came within ten of the required number of signatures for discharging the Rules Committee of a civil rights bill. The committee then granted a rule for debate on the bill, and it subsequently was enacted. In 1970 the rule was used to force the Judiciary Committee to release the constitutional amendment guaranteeing equal rights for women; it passed the House and the Senate. In 1971 the rule was again successful in discharging a school-prayer amendment from the Judiciary Committee, but it did not receive the required two-thirds vote.[44]

Sentiment in the House varies widely on the discharge rule. Some legislators favor its use as an appropriate means to enable the House to work its will on bills that have been pigeonholed in committees. They believe that, in the last analysis, the legislative power should belong to the whole House and not to any one of its committees. Other legislators believe that taking legislation from the consideration of the properly designated committee disrupts the orderly functioning of the legislative process. Many members make it a rule not to sign discharge petitions on the ground that floor consideration of bills that have not been fully heard and considered in committee lacks proper safeguards and is a dangerous practice.

Evaluation of Committee System

Congress, a microcosm of the nation, is in turn epitomized in its committees. From a few select panels at the outset, the system even now continues to expand dramatically. In 1947 there were nineteen standing committees in the House; in 1975 there were twenty-two. In 1947 the standing committees had eighty-nine subcommittees; in 1975 they had 142. Congressional government is, in large part, government by committee. Is the House well organized internally for the performance of its lawmaking, supervisory, and informing functions? An objective appraisal suggests that the congressional committee system has both advantages and disadvantages.

At a time when public problems of bewildering variety and baffling complexity crowd the calendars of the national legislature, the committee system serves the indispensable function of dividing the labor of screening and digesting the legislative proposals to which these problems give rise. A system of standing committees, subdivided into many subcommittees, allows deliberation on many different matters to proceed simultaneously. Thus, the first advantage of the system is that it enables the House to cover a much wider range of subjects than it could in committee of the whole, and makes a fuller use of the talents of its members.

In the second place, the committee system provides invaluable training in the public business by enabling the members to specialize in a few related subject-matter fields. In Congress the individual member has a chance to learn the legislative trade more easily than his British counterpart by reason of his continuing service on one or two specialized standing committees. Long service on the same committees develops in the American legislator an expertise that makes him more of a match for the transient department head.

Committee government also facilitates close inspection and review of administrative performance which has become a major activity of the Congress. In practice, legislative surveillance of the executive branch is chiefly exercised by particular committees which operate as overseers and watchdogs of downtown departments. A variety of oversight devices: committee investigations, question periods, departmental reports, the requirement of prior committee approval, concurrent resolutions, and demands for documents and testimony have been increasingly used in recent years to implement the "oversight" function of Congress.

Committee hearings have the further advantage, as we have seen, of serving as political sounding boards for legislative policy makers, enabling them to ascertain the intensity of support for and opposition to legislative proposals on the part of interested groups in the country. In a democracy where preponderant public opinion is supposed to be the source of law, this function of discovering the attitudes of the interested and informed public is obviously an essential one. In cases where a general consensus of opinion has not yet emerged on a legislative proposal or where some regional or sectional group is strongly opposed to a measure, the hearing process will reveal this condition and serve at least as a safety valve for the release of social tensions.

The operation of the committee system is recognized as the heart of congressional activity. Here, in practice, Congressmen organized in "little legislatures" consider legislative and spending proposals, review the operations of administration, and at times themselves initiate new law. Committee work includes hearings as well as discussion in closed meetings. It involves contact with experts and written material. It is the center of legislative activity where criticism of administration and decision upon proposed legislation is largely made.

On the other hand, the congressional committee system is not without some drawbacks that could be corrected. As noted above, these miniature legislatures have acquired such power and prestige over the years that they are largely autonomous in the House itself which created them and whose agents they are supposed to be. Functions which are the constitutional birthright of Congress as a whole—the making of policy and the conduct of investigations—have in practice been delegated by the House and Senate to their standing committees. It is often charged that role of the House is now largely limited to ratifying decisions made by its committees.

The autonomy of the committees gives rise in turn to the problem of coordination. Since the committees usually have a decisive voice in lawmaking, the committee system makes for the decentralization of legislative policy formation. Jealous of their jurisdictions and acting independently of each other, these little legislatures go their own way at their own pace. Although there is no central or advance planning of the legislative program on a scale comparable with the British practice, the leadership of the House does plan a general outline of the major bills which it hopes to get through at a given session, thus deciding which measures to leave until the second session of the Congress or to a subsequent Congress. This is done informally by the Speaker, the majority leader, the majority whip, the policy committees, and the chairmen of the committees handling major measures. Precise, long-range planning as to the exact day or week when a bill is to be voted upon in the House is hardly possible, of course, because of unforeseeable delays in committee action. Closer intercommittee coordination is deemed desirable in order to avoid jurisdictional disputes, promote consistency and coherence between related areas of legislative policy making, and accelerate the legislative process. The proliferation of subcommittees seems to have carried the process of fission too far. Problems of environmental policy, energy, and transportation, for example, often reside in many subcommittees, further complicating the problem of co-ordination.

Yet there has been considerable progress in dealing with the defects of the committee system. Chairmen can be arbitrary only at their peril. The committees are better staffed, and their procedures are not subject to the charges of capriciousness that so frequently characterized the 1950's. Vietnam, Watergate, and the Nixon Presidency have left as a major heritage a greater congressional concern with the problem of oversight. Insofar as the attempts at major restructuring of the ·committee system in 1970 and 1974 sought to challenge the predilection for incremental change, they were in the main unsuccessful. But, as we have seen, the tools of party leadership for co-ordination have been sharpened considerably in recent years. On balance, the manifold advantages of the committee system clearly outweigh its drawbacks.

7

Leadership in the House

POLITICAL LEADERSHIP is a fascinating subject for study, and nowhere more so than in nations with democratic forms of government. Such countries are governed in large part by their national legislatures, the role of whose leaders excites perennial interest. Writing in 1885, Woodrow Wilson remarked that "in a country which governs itself by means of a public meeting, a Congress or a Parliament, a country whose political life is representative, the only real leadership in governmental affairs must be legislative leadership—ascendancy in the public meeting which decides everything. The leaders, if there be any, must be those who suggest the opinions and rule the actions of the representative body."

The position of Congress in the American system of government may not be so supreme today as it was when Wilson wrote his little classic on *Congressional Government*. But the leadership of Congress continues to intrigue the interest of scholars and laymen alike. Especially is this true in the case of the House of Representatives, where the character and conditions of leadership have had a most interesting history.

In any large assembly leaders must arise or be chosen to manage its business, and the American House of Representatives has long had its posts of leadership. Outstanding among them have been the Speaker, the floor leader, majority whip, and the chairman of the Committee on Rules. The chairmen of Ways and Means and of Appropriations have also long been top-leadership positions in the hierarchy of the House, followed by the chairmen of the other great standing committees of that body.

During the first twenty years of congressional history, the Speakers were mere figureheads. They presided over the House, to be sure, but actual legislative leadership and control were exercised by the Chief Executive with the aid of trusted floor lieutenants, especially during the Jeffersonian regime. Harlow gives a lucid description of the system of executive control of the legislative process as it operated in that early period:[1]

> It is evident that both in methods and in effectiveness, the Republican legislative machine differed little from that evolved by the severely criticized Federalists. The president and his Secretary of the Treasury were responsible for the main outlines, and in some cases for the details as well, of party measures. Policies were evolved, programs laid before Congress, and bills passed, all under the watchful eye of the chief executive. Jefferson was so successful that he was called a tyrant, but his methods were more like those of the Tudor kings than of the Italian despots. Everything that he did had to be done through Congress. Congress, to be sure, was usually ready to follow Jefferson's lead, but the compliance of that body was due to nothing else than the constant and never ending vigilance of Jefferson and Gallatin.
>
> In one important particular, Jefferson improved upon Federalist legislative methods. Hamilton had his followers in Congress, and there was usually some one leader of prominence in charge of the party forces, but this floor leader was not looked upon as the personal representative of the president himself. He was rather an assistant to the Speaker. From 1801 to 1808, the floor leader was distinctly the lieutenant of the executive. William B. Giles, who was actually referred to as "the premier, or prime minister," Caesar A. Rodney, John Randolph of Roanoke, and Wilson Cary Nicholas all held that honorable position at one time or another. It was their duty to look after party interests in the House, and in particular to carry out the commands of the president. The status of these men was different from that of the floor leader of today, who is given his position because of long service in the House. They were presidential agents, appointed by the executive, and dismissed at his pleasure. . . .

Thus, in the beginning, "leadership was neither the prerogative of seniority nor a privilege conferred by the House; it was distinctly the gift of the president." During the Jeffersonian period the President kept a recognized leader in the House in order to see that members "voted right." Party caucus and House floor leaders took their orders from the White House. "The infallibility of Jefferson in the political field was like unto that of the pope in the spiritual, and denial of his inspiration was heresy, punishable by political death. Good Republicans, such as John Randolph, for instance, who insisted upon the right of independent judgment, were promptly read out of the party. It seemed a far cry to democracy when the President insisted upon doing the thinking for Congress and regulating the actions of its members."[2]

After Jefferson's retirement, the balance of power shifted from the President to Congress. Several factors contributed to this transfer: the weakness of President Madison, a rebellion in the House against executive control, factional fights within the Cabinet, and the appearance on the legislative scene of the "war hawks" of 1812—that famous group of young and energetic men, including Calhoun and Clay, who became the new Speaker. It took some time for Henry Clay and his followers to restore party unity and recover control of the administration, but by the end of the second war with England they had succeeded in erecting a new system, based on the party caucus, in which legislative leadership was now the prerogative of a group of prominent men in the House of Representatives. No longer subject and submissive to the dictates of a strong President, Congress developed its own internal leadership structure. Under Henry Clay, the Speakership emerged as an office of greatly enhanced power and prestige. Merely chairman of the House and subordinate in actual influence to the floor leader during the Jeffersonian regime, the Speaker now became both presiding officer and leader of the majority party in the chamber. Meanwhile the development of the standing committee system in 1816 and afterward, with the appointment of their chairmen by the Speaker, completed the transformation. "Thus, by 1825," as Harlow observes, "so far as its organization was concerned, the House of Representatives had assumed its present form."[3]

With the evolution of the committee system during the nineteenth century, as sketched in the preceding chapter, and with the gradual delegation of functions by the House to these "little legislatures," their chieftains acquired enlarged powers and enhanced importance as leaders in the legislative process. The chairmanships of the great committees called for steering qualities of a high order. Those who demonstrated the most skillful generalship in the arts of floor management were promoted by the Speaker from one committee headship to another, gradually rising in the committee hierarchy to preside over Appropriations and Ways and Means, the most prized posts next to the Speakership in the leadership structure of the House.

Thus, as the nineteenth century advanced, the leadership of the House came to be divided among the chairmen of its standing committees. The more numerous the committees, the more was leadership diffused. By 1885, Woodrow Wilson reported that "the House has as many leaders as there are subjects of legislation; for there are as many standing committees as there are classes of legislation . . . The chairmen of the standing committees do not constitute a cooperative body like a ministry. They do not consult and concur in the adoption of homogeneous and mutually helpful measures; there is no thought of acting in concert. Each committee goes its own way at its own pace."[4]

Diffusion is still the characteristic feature of leadership in Congress. In practice, Congress functions not as a unified institution, but as a collection of autonomous committees that seldom act in unison. The system of autonomous committees and the selection of committee chairmen on the basis of seniority render difficult the development of centralized legislative leadership and the adoption of a coherent legislative program. The function of leadership was dispersed in 1975 among the chairmen of approximately 350 committees of all types in both houses: standing, special, joint, and subcommittees. The chairmen and ranking minority members of the House are described as "seniority leaders" as distinguished from the "elective leaders" who are chosen by their respective party caucuses: the Speaker, floor leaders, party whips, and conference chairmen.[5] Party caucuses or conferences are infrequently held to determine the party stand on legislative issues, and they are rarely binding. And party responsibility for policy making is weakened by the operation of the seniority system.

Formally, the existence in the House of Representatives of twenty-two standing committee chairmen, plus the various political committees and elective leaders, gives an appearance of widespread diffusion of leadership functions in the first chamber. But, paradoxically, in practice, leadership in the House is more effectively centralized in the Speaker, the Rules Committee, and the floor leaders than is the case with their senatorial counterparts. Several factors contribute to this result. These include the powers, prestige, and personal influence of the Speaker; the stricter rules of the House; the tighter organization of its business and debates; and the greater discipline of its members. The larger size of the House and the shorter term of office also combine to reduce the members' comparative independence.

The leadership of the modern House of Representatives is composed of a group of men on both sides of the party aisle. On the majority side of the aisle the "leadership" includes the Speaker of the House, who presides over its sessions; the majority (or floor) leader, who manages its business on the floor; the majority whip, who rounds up party members for floor votes and keeps in touch with party sentiment; and the chairman of the party conference, who presides at general meetings or party caucuses. On the minority side of the aisle the "leadership" includes the minority (floor) leader, who is the chief spokesman for his party on the House floor; the minority whip, who is the opposite number of the majority whip; the chairman of the party conference; the chairman of the party policy committee; and the ranking minority member of the Rules Committee. The last two officials mentioned are included by the House Republicans in their top leadership group.

The Office of the Speaker

In the American system of government, the Speakership of the national legislature is rated as the second most powerful office in the land. Only the Presidency stands higher in the political hierarchy.

FREDERICK AUGUSTUS CONRAD MUHLENBERG
January 1, 1750–June 4, 1801

A native of Montgomery County, Pennsylvania, Frederick A. C. Muhlenberg was educated in Germany and ordained as a Lutheran clergyman in 1770. At the age of twenty-nine, he turned to a political career, serving in the Continental Congress and in the General Assembly of Pennsylvania, of which he was speaker, 1780–1783. His correspondence reflected a lively interest in contemporary politics. In 1787 he presided over the state convention that ratified the Federal Constitution, and was elected as a Federalist to the First Congress from Philadelphia. The House of Representatives chose him as its first Speaker in part because of his previous experience and reputation as speaker of the Assembly, in part to balance a Southern President and a New England Vice President with a Speaker from the strongest of the middle states. He served four terms in the House, and two terms as its presiding officer. As time went on, his Federalist zeal waned, and not long before his death, he switched to the Republican party. He was a very corpulent man, and his death in 1801 was attributed to a stroke of apoplexy.

JAMES MADISON *March 16, 1751–June 28, 1836*

James Madison, after serving as a member of the Virginia Assembly and the Governor's Council, was a delegate to the Continental Congress (1780–1783). Returning to Virginia, he served for three years as a leading member of the House of Delegates, playing an active part in legislative projects for the development of the resources and commerce of the state, and in the interstate conferences that led to the Federal Constitutional Convention at Philadelphia in 1787. Long a student of the history of confederacies, ancient and modern, Madison drew upon his studies and his experience of the weaknesses of the existing confederation to formulate a set of proposals for constitutional reform which were embodied in the Virginia Plan and submitted to the Constitutional Convention to which Madison was a delegate. He kept a journal of the convention, and played such an influential part in its proceedings that he has been

Fisher Ames served as a Federalist in the first four Congresses where he promoted the commercial and tariff interests of New England and supported the policies of Alexander Hamilton. Attractive in appearance, conciliatory in manner, possessed of high character and great talents, and well fortified with facts, Ames was an effective debater and the intellectual superior of most of his fellow members. Accused by the Republican press as a speculator, Ames replied that the interest on the investments of the Massachusetts delegation would not pay for the oats of the Southern members' coach horses. He was burned in effigy in Charleston, South Carolina, together with Benedict Arnold and the devil because of his speech in the House on January 27, 1794, opposing Madison's resolutions for a commercial war with England. The historian Channing described Ames's speech on Jay's treaty (April 28, 1796) as "one of the greatest speeches ever made in Congress," and Dr. Priestley, who heard it, called it "the most bewitching piece of parliamentary oratory he had ever listened to." Ames retired from public life at the close of Washington's administration, preferring the life of a squire even to the presidency of Harvard to which he was elected but which he declined.

FISHER AMES
April 9, 1758–July 14, 1808

described as the chief architect of the Constitution. In the struggle for ratification of that document, Madison was co-author (with Hamilton and Jay) of the famous *Federalist* essays that have been accepted as the authoritative exposition of the Constitution and this country's major contribution to political science. He was elected as a Democrat to the First and to the three succeeding Congresses (1789-1797) and soon became a recognized leader of the Jeffersonian party in the House, where he opposed many of Hamilton's financial measures. In 1798 Madison collaborated with Jefferson in framing the famous Virginia Resolutions declaring the Alien and Sedition Laws unconstitutional and affirming the right of the states to "interpose" their enforcement within their respective limits. Later he served as Jefferson's Secretary of State (1801-1809), and finally as President of the United States (1809-1817).

ALBERT GALLATIN *January 29, 1761–August 12, 1849*

Born of aristocratic lineage and educated in Geneva, Switzerland, Albert Gallatin came to America in 1780 in quest of personal freedom. Influenced by Rousseau to seek freedom in a romantic return to nature, Gallatin invested his patrimony in the wilderness of western Pennsylvania on the banks of the Monongahela. In 1793 Gallatin was elected to the United States Senate, which denied him his seat on the ground that he had not been a United States citizen for nine years. Elected to Congress in 1794, Gallatin served three terms (1795–1801) in the House during one of the stormiest periods in American political history. In 1797, after Madison's retirement from that body, Gallatin became the recognized leader of the Republican minority and the outstanding authority in the House in the field of finance. Appointed by President Jefferson as Secretary of the Treasury in May, 1801, Gallatin held that office until February, 1814. His statesmanlike administration of the Treasury was seriously handicapped by the costs of the Barbary wars, the purchase of Louisiana, commercial losses from embargoes and nonintercourse, the War of 1812, and factional opposition in the Senate. Named a peace commissioner by President Madison in 1813, Gallatin spent the next decade in diplomatic services abroad. He played a crucial role in negotiating the Treaty of Ghent, served seven years (1816–1823) as the U.S. minister to France, and ended his public career with his mission of 1826–1827 to England.

JOHN QUINCY ADAMS *July 11, 1767–February 23, 1848*

After long, varied, and distinguished public service in many posts, including the Presidency, John Quincy Adams was elected to the Twenty-second Congress (1831–1833), where he represented Quincy, Massachusetts, for seventeen years. His varied experience at home and abroad over a period of forty years as U.S. Senator, diplomat, Cabinet minister, and President; his knowledge, industry, and integrity; and his talents as a debater combined to make his service in Congress the most important part of his career. In the House, Adams opposed the annexation of Texas, the war with Mexico, and the extension of slavery. He presented to the House hundreds of petitions relating to slavery that had been sent him. These

petitions were tabled under a "gag" rule for eight years (1836–1844). Southern members sought to discipline and even expel Adams for his persistent and courageous defense of the right of petition, but his view finally prevailed and the "gag" rule was repealed. His opposition to slavery involved him in a series of dramatic conflicts with Southern members, but he always managed to weather these parliamentary storms. Adams was a lifelong student of political institutions, and he was deeply devoted to human freedom for all men. An aggressive and belligerent debater, he enjoyed controversy and relished combat. Known to his contemporaries as "Old Man Eloquent," he was stricken on the floor of the House and died in the Speaker's room on February 23, 1848.

JOHN RANDOLPH
June 2, 1773–May 24, 1833

A man of brilliant talents and fiery temper, John Randolph "of Roanoke" entered the House as a Jeffersonian in 1799 and served continuously until 1813. He was appointed chairman of the Ways and Means Committee at the early age of twenty-eight, and functioned as majority leader of the House during Jefferson's first term. "Booted and spurred, he swaggered about the House, whip in hand," writes Dumas Malone, "but in labors he was indefatigable and in parliamentary matters a master." By 1806, however, Randolph's violent and uncompromising nature caused him to break with the administration and cost him his leadership position. Because of his hostility to the War of 1812, he lost his seat in the House in 1813, but was re-elected in 1815; he strongly opposed a charter for the Second Bank of the United States and other nationalistic measures. Not a candidate for the Fourteenth Congress, Randolph was re-elected in 1819 and served continuously until 1825. In 1826 he fought a duel with Henry Clay, whose alliance with John Quincy Adams he had described as the combination "of the puritan with the blackleg." After serving two years (1825-27) in the Senate, Randolph was replaced by John Tyler, but was returned to the House for his last term in that body (1827-1829), leading the opposition to President Adams. Mentally deranged at intervals during his later years, he died in Philadelphia on May 24, 1833. Randolph has been described as an irritable and eccentric genius, an incomparable orator, and a vitriolic adversary.

HENRY CLAY
April 12, 1777–June 29, 1852

Henry Clay was first elected to the House of Representatives in 1810. He entered the Twelfth Congress as the leader of the young "War Hawks," was elected Speaker, and soon pushed President Madison into the second war with England. After serving as one of the commissioners who negotiated the Treaty of Ghent, he returned to the House and the Speakership. After 1817, Clay became a critic of the national administration, a role that he maintained until the end of his life. He long aspired to the Presidency and suffered a long series of disappointments in a futile quest for that office. He was a strong and eloquent advocate of national defense, and an "American system" of protective tariffs and internal improvements. The emerging struggle over the slavery question and his belief in a union of equal states led Clay to propose the Missouri Compromise in 1820. In the presidential election of 1824, Clay ran last of the four candidates at the polls, and then voted for Adams in the House, thus effecting his election, although the Kentucky legislature had instructed Clay to vote for Jackson who had received a plurality in the nation. When Adams appointed Clay as Secretary of State and Clay accepted, the suspicion of duplicity hung over him throughout his life. Disillusioned by the election of Jackson to the White House in 1828, Clay retired to private life in Kentucky.

Returning to the Senate in 1831, he opposed Jackson on many fronts, but was overwhelmingly defeated by him in the presidential election of 1832. In an effort to save the Union from disruption when South Carolina nullified the Tariff Act of 1832, Clay formulated the Compromise Tariff of 1833 and secured its passage. Regarding Andrew Jackson as a menace to the liberties of the people, Clay battled him on many issues and induced the Senate to censure Jackson for the removal of the deposits from the Bank of the United States, only to see the censure resolutions expunged from the record in 1837. After a series of defeats by the Tyler administration, Clay resigned his seat in the Senate on March 31, 1842. In 1844, he was nominated by the Whigs for the Presidency, but was defeated by Polk, much to the dismay of many admirers. A candidate for the Whig presidential nomination in 1848, Clay lost out to General Zachary Taylor, a military hero who, Clay felt, was not qualified for civil leadership. In 1849, Clay returned to the Senate and made there a last great effort to settle the sectional struggle over slavery and save the Union. A man of great personal magnetism, he excelled in the arts of political debate and enjoyed undisputed popularity among all sections of the American people.

DANIEL WEBSTER *January 18, 1782–October 24, 1852*

A conservative by temperament and a Federalist by inheritance and conviction, Daniel Webster began his career in national politics when he was elected to Congress from Portsmouth, New Hampshire, in 1812. Assigned to the Committee on Foreign Affairs, he opposed the second war with England and the administration's tax and manpower measures for the support of that conflict. He became a champion of the mercantile interests of New England and an authority on public finance. While serving his second term in the House, Webster participated as counsel in a series of Supreme Court cases, including the celebrated Dartmouth College case involving basic constitutional issues, winning victories that brought him a national reputation. After moving to Boston in 1816, he retired for a season from national office, but kept himself in the public eye by delivering a series of brilliant orations on historic anniversaries. In 1823, Webster returned to Congress as a representative of Boston and was appointed chairman of the Judiciary Committee. During the administration of John Quincy Adams, Webster supported the programs of his fellow statesman. Elected to the Senate in 1827, he became a strong advocate of the protective tariff, especially on woolens, and the leading opponent of Calhoun's doctrine of nullification. In the famous debate of January, 1830, with Robert Y. Hayne, Webster won nationwide fame as the defender of the Constitution with his eloquent appeal for "Liberty *and* Union, now and forever, one and inseparable!" Re-elected to the Senate in 1833, Webster joined the newly formed Whig party, but broke with President Jackson over the latter's war on the Bank of the United States. Re-elected again in 1839, he served as Secretary of State in the Harrison-Tyler administration, completing a series of successful diplomatic negotiations, including the settlement of the Maine boundary dispute with England in the Webster-Ashburton Treaty of 1842. He resigned from the Cabinet under Whig pressure in May 1843, and returned to the Senate in 1844 where he worked to protect the industrial interests of New England and opposed the acquisition of Texas and the war with Mexico. In 1848, Webster had hope of the Presidency, but his party preferred a military hero, General Zachary Taylor. He regarded the rising sectional controversy over the slavery question as a serious threat to the Union and he sought to avert it by supporting Clay's compromise measures. After Taylor's death Webster served with distinction as Secretary of State in the Fillmore Cabinet. In 1852 he again aspired to the Presidency, but the Whigs again turned to a military man, General Winfield Scott. Webster was a man whose talents and ambitions exceeded his achievements, so that life for him was a series of great frustrations. But his eloquent and articulate dedication to the preservation of the Union won him a lasting place in the congressional hall of fame.

JAMES KNOX POLK
November 2, 1795–
June 15, 1849

Entering Congress from Tennessee in 1825, James K. Polk became a leader of the Administration forces in the House of Representatives during the Jackson presidency. Named chairman of the Ways and Means Committee in December, 1833, he was the main defender of the President in his struggle with the Bank of the United States. In 1836 Polk was elected Speaker of the House, in which office he bore with dignity the brunt of much abuse and vituperation from his own and Jackson's enemies. After serving a term as governor of Tennessee, Polk's stand in favor of the annexation of Texas, plus the support of "Old Hickory," won him the Democratic presidential nomination in 1844; in the election he defeated Clay who had unwisely voiced his opposition to annexation. Entering the White House at the age of forty-nine, younger than any previous President, Polk announced a fourfold program of tariff reduction, an independent treasury, settlement of the Oregon boundary question, and the acquisition of California—all of which were consummated before he left the White House in 1849: a great achievement in the short span of four years.

First elected to Congress as a Democrat in 1862, Samuel Jackson Randall represented the old first Philadelphia waterfront district. He gained fame in the House by his brilliant filibusters against the Civil Rights and Force Bills in 1875, and by his part in launching the investigations of the Credit Mobilier, the Sanborn contracts, and the Pacific mail subsidy. "Retrenchment and Reform" was the slogan with which he led the Democratic party out of the postwar wilderness. As Speaker of the Forty-fifth and Forty-sixth Congresses, Randall's rulings strengthened the power of the Rules Committee. He played a key role in the rules revision of 1880, which cleared a path for the subsequent adoption of the Reed rules a decade later. In 1883, Randall lost the Speakership to John G. Carlisle because of his protectionist position on the tariff issue, but as chairman of the Committee on Appropriations he attained the peak of his powers and was able to dictate both appropriations and general legislation. Randall lost control of federal patronage and hence of the Democratic organization in Pennsylvania in 1888 when he broke with President Cleveland over the "tariff for revenue only" stand of his party. But he remained to the end an indefatigable worker and the best-informed member of the House on the business of government.

SAMUEL JACKSON RANDALL
October 10, 1828–April 13, 1890

JAMES GILLESPIE BLAINE
January 31, 1830–January 27, 1893

James G. Blaine combined a commanding figure with a dignified manner, powerful oratorical ability, and a magnetic personality. His assets included a talent for political management and a sense of humor which he used effectively in debate. Blaine was one of the founders of the Republican party, a delegate in 1856 to its first national convention, and long the acknowledged leader of the party in Maine, his adopted state. He was a member of the national House of Representatives from 1863 to 1876, serving as Speaker from 1869 to 1875, and then as minority leader until his election to the Senate where he sat from 1876 to 1881. Candidate for the Presidency in 1876, Blaine was nominated as the "Plumed Knight" in a brilliant speech by Robert G. Ingersoll, but his implication in charges of railroad graft in the Credit Mobilier scandals was probably responsible for his loss of the Republican nomination to Rutherford B. Hayes, governor of Ohio. Again a candidate in 1880, Blaine lost out to James A. Garfield on the thirty-sixth ballot. He served as Secretary of State in the Garfield Cabinet, but resigned after Garfield's assassination. In 1884, Blaine received the Republican presidential nomination on the first ballot, but was defeated by Grover Cleveland in a very close election. His defeat has been attributed to the unfortunate remark made by the Reverend S. D. Burchard, a Blaine supporter, in a New York speech at the close of the campaign, that the Democratic party was "the party whose antecedents are rum, Romanism, and rebellion." In 1888, Blaine declined to be a presidential candidate, but became Secretary of State in the Cabinet of Benjamin Harrison, where he exerted a powerful influence on American foreign policy. Meanwhile he produced his *Twenty Years of Congress, from Lincoln to Garfield* (2 vols., 1884–1886), an outstanding work in its field.

JAMES ABRAM GARFIELD *November 19, 1831–September 19, 1881*

The last President to be born in a log cabin, James A. Garfield served with distinction as a Union general in the Civil War. Aided by his victories on the battlefield, he was elected to the Thirty-eighth Congress in 1863 as representative of the Nineteenth Ohio District, and served nine consecutive terms. By 1876 he had become the unrivaled leader of the Republican party in the House and an accomplished parliamentarian. During his years in Congress he served on the Military Affairs, Appropriations, and Ways and Means Committees. In 1877 he was a member of the electoral commission that settled the Hayes-Tilden controversy. Elected to the Senate in 1880, Garfield never took his seat there, having meanwhile received the Republican presidential nomination, after seeking it for his fellow statesman, John Sherman. During the first two months of his administration, President Garfield was involved in a struggle with the Senate over the confirmation of various minor nominees, including those for the New York Customhouse posts. Garfield was shot on July 2, 1881, in the Washington railroad station by a disappointed office seeker, Charles J. Guiteau, and died on September 19, 1881.

JOSEPH GURNEY CANNON *May 7, 1836–November 12, 1926*

Joseph Gurney Cannon served as a Republican Congressman from Illinois from 1873 to 1923, save for the Fifty-second and Sixty-third Congresses. He was known as "the Hayseed Member from Illinois" during his early years in the House because of his bucolic speech and uncouth manner, and later as "Uncle Joe." He first served as a member of the Committee on Post Offices and Post Roads, later on the Committee on Rules (1883–1889), and as chairman of the Committee on Appropriations (1889–1891) and (1897–1903). Cannon was elected Speaker at the opening of the Fifty-eighth Congress (1903) and retained that office until March 3, 1911. He developed a system of arbitrary and partisan control of procedure which became known as "Cannonism" and which finally led to his overthrow in March, 1910, by a combination of Democrats and insurgent Republicans. He received fifty-eight votes for President on the first ballot at the Republican National Convention of 1908. A reactionary in politics, he opposed President Wilson and the League of Nations. Although his name was not associated with any major legislative act, and although his conduct as Speaker evoked bitter attacks, he maintained his personal popularity in the House for half a century.

THOMAS BRACKETT REED *October 18, 1839–December 7, 1902*

A native of Portland, Maine, and a lawyer by profession, Thomas B. Reed served in the state legislature, as attorney general of Maine, and also as city solicitor, before his election to Congress in 1876 from the First Congressional District which he continued to carry by large majorities for twenty-two years. In the House, Reed soon became known as a formidable debater, famous for his invective and sarcasm.

He once described James G. Blaine as a burden to the Republican party, like unto "the gentleman Sinbad carried." To Theodore Roosevelt, he once remarked: "Theodore, if there is one thing for which I admire you, it is your original discovery of the Ten Commandments." "A statesman," he said, "is a successful politician who is dead."

Reed became a member of the Rules Committee in January, 1882, and represented the Republicans on the Ways and Means Committee from 1884 to 1889. He was the undoubted leader of his party in the House after 1882. For several years he fought to reform the rules of the House which, he said, was trying "to run Niagara through a quill." Elected Speaker on December 2, 1889, Reed finally succeeded, by a series of rulings described elsewhere, in establishing majority rule and the efficient transaction of public business. Under the Reed rules, adopted on February 14, 1890, the Republican majority in the Fifty-first Congress enacted the greatest legislative program since the Civil War. After Democratic victories in 1890 and 1892, the Republicans captured control of the House in 1894, restored Reed to the Speakership, and re-enacted the Reed rules. He remained as leader of the Republican party in the House until September 4, 1899, when he resigned his seat, disgusted by American intervention in Cuba and the annexation of Hawaii.

WILLIAM MCKINLEY *January 29, 1843–September 14, 1901*

After practicing law in Canton, Ohio, William McKinley was elected to Congress as Republican representative of the Seventeenth Ohio District in 1876. He remained in the House until 1890 (except for the Forty-eighth Congress when a Democratic House unseated him in an election contest) when he lost his seat in a Democratic landslide. While in the House, McKinley specialized in the tariff, becoming a leading protagonist of protection, and played an active part in state and national party politics. In 1880 he became a member and in 1889 the chairman of the Ways and Means Committee where he steered to passage the McKinley Tariff Bill of 1890. The following year he was elected governor of Ohio, with the help of Mark Hanna, and he served two terms. McKinley received the Republican presidential nomination in 1896 and, after conducting a dignified front-porch campaign, while his eloquent opponent William Jennings Bryan toured the country, was elected with a majority of the popular votes. Re-elected in 1900 after the victory over Spain, McKinley had served only six months of his second administration when he was shot by an anarchist, Leon F. Czolgosz, and died at Buffalo on September 14, 1901.

CHAMP CLARK *March 7, 1850–March 2, 1921*

Elected as a Democrat from Missouri to the Fifty-third Congress (1893–1895), Champ Clark remained a member of the House until his death, except for the Fifty-fourth Congress (1895–1897). He was long a member of the Foreign Affairs and Ways and Means Committees. He became party leader in the Sixtieth Congress (1907-1909), succeeding John Sharp Williams, and served as Speaker of the House from April, 1911, to March, 1919. His successful leadership of the fight against "Czar" Cannon and "Cannonism" was Clark's outstanding achievement in Congress. In the Baltimore convention of the Democratic party in 1912, Champ Clark was the leading candidate for the presidential nomination on the first fourteen ballots, but was finally defeated by Woodrow Wilson when Bryan threw his support to Wilson. He served as minority floor leader in the Sixty-sixth Congress (1919–1921), but was defeated for re-election in the "great and solemn referendum" of 1920.

The Constitution says that "the House of Representatives shall choose their Speaker and other officers," but remains silent upon his status and functions. Historians regard him as a direct descendant of the Speaker in the colonial assemblies. Asher C. Hinds, former parliamentarian of the House, held that the Constitution did not *create* the Speaker, but merely adopted an existing officer. His office is thus a colonial heritage whose importance and influence have varied down through the passing years, depending upon the personal force of the incumbents.

Selection and Qualifications

We do not know what the intent of the Founding Fathers was with respect to the Speakership. They did not say whether he must be a member of the House, although he always has been. Nor did the framers say how he should be selected. At first he was elected by ballot, but since 1839 he has been chosen by voice vote, on a roll call. In 1809 it was held that he should be elected by a majority of all present, and in 1879 that he might be elected by a majority of those present rather than a majority of all members—if those present and voting constituted a quorum.

In fact there is a discrepancy between the law and the practice in the choice of the Speaker. For, in actual practice, the Speaker is chosen by the caucus of the majority party in the House, whose choice is then ratified by the House itself. Prior to the meeting of each new Congress, the congressional parties hold caucuses or conferences at which they nominate their respective candidates for the elective offices in the House. On rare occasions there is a lively contest for the nomination for the Speakership. On the eve of the Sixty-sixth Congress, for example, a spirited campaign was waged between Mr. Gillett of Massachusetts and Mr. Mann of Illinois. Gillett won. In the Ninety-first Congress, Speaker John McCormack easily beat off a challenge for re-election by Representative Morris K. Udall of Arizona. The contest is keenest in the caucus of the majority party, because its nomination is equivalent to election in the House.

Contests for the posts of party leadership in the House have usually occurred over vacancies, but on rare occasions an incumbent party leader has been forcibly displaced. This happened at the opening of the Eighty-sixth Congress when Representative Charles Halleck of Indiana was selected as Republican floor leader in place of Representative Joseph W. Martin, Jr., of Massachusetts. Martin had served continuously as Republican floor leader since January 3, 1939, except for the years 1947-1948 and 1953-1954, when Republicans controlled the House, and Martin was Speaker, and Halleck was floor leader. In the 1959 Republican caucus, Halleck ousted Martin by a 74-70 secret-ballot vote. The Martin-Halleck struggle was not a "liberal-conservative" fight. It reflected, in part, a belief that Halleck, at fifty-eight, could provide more vigorous leadership than the seventy-four-year-old Martin, who had been handicapped by a blood clot on his leg. Some Republicans also complained that Martin had co-operated too closely with Speaker Rayburn in the past and had not been sufficiently partisan in his leadership efforts. Martin attributed his defeat in part to GOP election reverses, saying a "fall guy" was needed. In another close vote (73-67) in 1965, Representative Gerald R. Ford defeated Representative Halleck for the post of floor leader. Again the issue appears to have been "forceful leadership" rather than ideology.

In nominating their candidates for the Speakership, the congressional parties usually lay stress on length of congressional service, among other factors. Long legislative experience is a criterion that seems to carry more weight in the twentieth century than it did in the nineteenth, with the increasing rigidity of the seniority system. Before 1896, the average length of congressional service before election to the chair was seven years. Henry Clay of Kentucky and William Pennington of New Jersey were elected to the Speakership on their first appearance in the House, something that would never happen in our time. Since 1896, however, the average length of service of Speakers has been about three times as long as before. "Uncle Joe" Cannon was elevated to the chair in his thirty-first year in the House of Representatives. Champ Clark was chosen in his sixteenth year of service, Gillett in his twenty-seventh, Longworth in his twenty-first; Sam Rayburn, at the time of his first election was in his twenty-eighth year in the House; John W. McCormack became Speaker after thirty-three years in the House; and Carl Albert was elected twenty-four years after becoming a member.

Aside from having seen long service, the modern Speakers are men who have won the confidence and esteem not only of their own party, but also of the general membership of the House. They have usually served as chairmen of important committees of the House or as floor leaders. Thus Rayburn was long chairman of the Committee on Interstate and Foreign Commerce and later was the Democratic floor leader; McCormack had been floor leader or whip for twenty-two years; and Albert had been floor leader for nine years.

It has been a long-standing custom of the House to re-elect a Speaker to that office as long as his party remains in control of the House and he retains his seat. Both Speaker Cannon and Speaker Clark were re-elected consecutively for four terms, until a change of party control took place. Mr. Rayburn was elected Speaker on September 16, 1940, and was serving his tenth term in that post at his death, having held the office longer than any predecessor in the chair. He was his party's top leader in the House for more than ten terms.

When a change in party control of the House occurs, the elective party officers rotate under a system by which the Speaker shifts down to minority leader, the former majority leader becomes the minority whip, and the majority whip returns to the role of a rank-and-file member. At the same time, when the minority party becomes the majority party, the former minority leader ascends to the Speakership, and the minority whip becomes the new majority leader. Thus when the Democrats captured control of the House in the Fifty-second Congress (1891-1893) and retained control in the Fifty-third Congress (1893-1895), former Speaker Reed became minority leader during Charles F. Crisp's two terms in the chair. Then, with another switch in party control in the Fifty-fourth Congress (1895-1897), Mr. Reed returned to the speakership. Likewise, Champ Clark served as minority leader of the House in the Sixty-first Congress (1909-1911) and, after eight years in the Speaker's chair (1911-1919), became minority leader again in the Sixty-sixth Congress (1919-1921). Similar shifts in party-leadership posts occurred with the changes in party control of the House that took place between the Seventy-ninth and the Eighty-fourth Congresses.

Powers and Duties

The Speaker of the House derives his powers and duties from the Constitution, the rules of the House, previous decisions of the chair, and general parliamentary law. He presides at the sessions of the House, announces the order of business, puts questions, and reports the vote. He also decides points of order and can prevent dilatory tactics, thanks to the earlier rulings of Speaker Reed. He appoints the chairman of the committee of the whole and the members of select and conference committees. He chooses Speakers pro tem and refers bills and reports to the appropriate committees and calendars. He also enjoys the privileges of an ordinary member of the House, and may vote and participate in debate on the floor. When the Speaker is a Democrat, he may also nominate the Democratic members of the Rules Committee, subject to approval of the caucus, and he is chairman of the Steering and Policy Committee.

When Henry Clay took the Chair as Speaker on December 1, 1823, he described the duties of the office in terms that are still apropos today:

> They enjoin promptitude and impartiality in deciding the various questions of order as they arise; firmness and dignity in his deportment toward the House; patience, good temper, and courtesy towards the individual Members, and the best arrangement and distribution of the talent of the House, in its numerous sub-divisions, for the dispatch of the public business, and the fair exhibition of every subject presented for consideration. They especially require of him, in those moments of agitation from which no

deliberative assembly is always entirely exempt, to remain cool and un-
shaken amidst all the storms of debate, carefully guarding the preservation
of the permanent laws and rules of the House from being sacrificed to temporary passions, prejudices, or interests.

A Triple Personality

In contrast to his English counterpart, the Speaker of our House is a triple
personality, being a member of the House, its presiding officer, and leader
of the majority party in the chamber. As a member of the House he has the
right to cast his vote on all questions, unlike the Vice President, who has
no vote except in case of a tie. Usually the Speaker does not exercise his
right to vote except to break a tie or when he desires to make known how
he stands on a measure. As a member, he also has the right to leave the
chair and participate in debate on the House floor as the elected representative of his district, unlike the Vice President, who may not do likewise in
the Senate. The Speaker seldom exercises this right, but when he does, as
on close party issues, the House fills up, and everyone pays close attention.

As presiding officer of the House, the Speaker interprets the rules that
the House has adopted for its guidance. Customarily he performs this duty
as a judge, bound by the precedents created by prior decisions of the chair.
But in 1890 Speaker Reed broke with all past practice by refusing to entertain a motion on the grounds that it was dilatory and by including members
physically present but not voting in counting a quorum. With significant exceptions, appeals are in order from decisions of the chair, but are seldom
taken; when taken, the chair is usually sustained.

The Speaker's power of recognition is now narrowly limited by House
rules and conventions that fix the time for the consideration of various
classes of bills; require recognition of the chairmen of the Appropriations,
Budget, House Administration, Rules and Standards of Official Conduct
Committees for the consideration of certain measures specified in the House
rules; and allow committeemen in charge of other legislation to control all
the time allotted for general debate. The chair still has discretion, however,
in determining who shall be recognized while a bill is being debated under
the five-minute rule in committee of the whole; but then the Speaker is not
in the chair. He still has complete discretion also as to whom he will recognize to make motions to suspend the rules, on days when such motions are
in order. The rules of the House may be suspended by a two-thirds vote on
the first and third Mondays of the month and on the last six days of the
session.

As party leader, the Speaker prior to 1910 had certain additional powers: to appoint all standing committees and to name their chairmen; to se-

lect the members of the Rules Committee; and, from 1858, to serve as its chairman. By the exercise of these powers he was in a position to influence greatly the action taken by the standing committees, the order of business in the House, and the character of the action taken by the House itself. His political powers evolved gradually during the nineteenth century, reaching a peak under the masterful leadership of Speakers Reed and Cannon. Taken together, the powers of the Speaker prior to 1910, as a member of the House, as its presiding officer, and as majority leader were so far-reaching that the Speakership was regarded as second only in power and influence to the Presidency, and as supreme in relation to the legislative process. After a long process of evolution, the problem of leadership in the House of Representatives seemed to have been finally solved.*

In the revolution of 1910, however, a coalition of Democrats and insurgent Republicans, led by George W. Norris, rebelled against the despotism of "Czar" Cannon, dethroned the Speaker from his post of power, and deprived him of most of the great powers he formerly possessed.

Although, in 1910, the Speaker lost his power of appointing the standing committees of the House, he still appoints the select committees, the House members of conference committees, and the chairman of the committee of the whole. Prior to 1910, the Speaker controlled the House in collaboration with a coterie of trusted party lieutenants; since 1910 the leadership of the House has been in consortium. Thus, despite the overthrow of Cannonism, the Speakership continues to be the most powerful office in Congress and in recent years has acquired even more formal powers.

Contrast with English Speaker

The Speaker of our own House of Representatives offers an interesting contrast with the Speaker of the English House of Commons. Formerly the "King's man," and later the majority leader, the Speaker of the House of Commons has been its impartial umpire since 1839. He is elected by the Commons from among its members, subject to the approval of the Crown. Upon election, he gives up his former political affiliations and becomes the impartial servant of the whole House, its presiding officer, and the protector of its rights and liberties. It seems probable that his role evolved as it did because the government was present on the Front Bench as a group of members, plus the strength of the leadership and the role of the opposition party in the House.

The English Speaker holds a position of great dignity and authority, enhanced by the wig and gown he wears. Without a bell or gavel to keep or-

---

* See Chapter 9 for a fuller description of the powers of the Speaker during this period.

der, he rules the House with a firm hand. The English Speaker does not intervene in committee or make political speeches outside Parliament; he keeps aloof from party contacts and does not even enter a political club. After resigning from the chair, he also retires from the House, being rewarded by the Crown with a peerage. He is not opposed on re-election in the House as long as he wishes to serve.

In his capacity as chairman of the House of Commons, the English Speaker presides over its deliberations, maintains order in its debate, decides questions arising on point of order, puts the question for decision, and declares the decision. However, like the Speaker of our House of Representatives, he does not act as chairman when the House is sitting as committee of the whole.

Rayburn and Martin, McCormack and Albert

Sam Rayburn and Joseph W. Martin, Jr., as Speakers of the House of Representatives, enjoyed responsibilities beyond those of the typical Speaker of earlier days. Mr. Rayburn was a close friend and trusted adviser of both President Franklin D. Roosevelt and President Harry S. Truman. He also believed so strongly that President John F. Kennedy should have the opportunity to have his program considered by the House that in 1961 he committed his full prestige to an expansion of the Rules Committee and then influenced the appointment of the new members. He was also instrumental in starting the regular White House meetings with congressional leaders. Mr. Martin met with President Dwight D. Eisenhower in his weekly conferences at the White House with the Republican leaders of Congress, inheriting a tradition that was continued by his successor, Charles A. Halleck. During the past decade, the most frequent judgments made about the styles of Speaker McCormack and Speaker Albert are that they are reluctant to exert influence on the members of the House. One scholar has described them as leaders whose personal appeals were "flavored with a large degree of understanding for members who cannot go along on any given bill."[6] The question of how persuasive the Speaker can be is still a matter of considerable conjecture.

William S. White, who covered Congress for the *New York Times,* described the Speaker as "the second most influential elected official" in Washington. "Officially, his job is in many respects comparable to the job of heading any great corporation or enterprise. He is the ultimate chief of everything in the House, from the nature of its legislative program to the conduct of its dining room, and the direction of its personnel—hired and elected—is his endless concern.

"He performs this job with economy of motion, with scant and infrequent but heady praise for those about him, with a ready and easy delegation of authority and with a somewhat amused deference to perhaps the most temperamental of all men—a politician at work."[7]

Compensation and Allowances

For the fiscal year 1974, Congress appropriated $316,000 for compensation for the office of the Speaker, of which $62,500 was salary. The Speaker has a suite of rooms in the Capitol building. Attached to his office is the office of the parliamentarian and his assistants, for which $182,000 was appropriated for the fiscal year ending June 30, 1975.

Floor Leader

In the history of the evolution of the office of floor leader, the year 1910 marks a major dividing point. For the reform of the House rules adopted in that year brought about a redistribution of the powers of the Speakership and a significant change in the position of the floor leader.

During the nineteenth century the majority floor leader was customarily selected by the Speaker who often designated either his leading opponent within the party or the chairman of Ways and Means or of the Appropriations Committee or one of his faithful lieutenants. Thus Winthrop appointed his opponent Samuel F. Vinton in 1847; Banks designated Lewis D. Campbell in 1856; Pennington named John Sherman in 1859, and Reed selected McKinley in 1889. Ranking membership of Ways and Means accounted for Clay's appointment of Ezekiel Bacon in 1811; Stevenson's choice of Gulian C. Verplanck in 1822; Polk's selection of Churchill C. Cambreleng in 1835; Orr's promotion of James S. Phelps in 1858; Randall's advancement of Fernando Wood in 1879; Keifer's appointment of William D. Kelley in 1881; Carlisle's designation of Roger Q. Mills in 1887; and Henderson's selection of Sereno E. Payne in 1899. Faithful lieutenants were rewarded by the appointment of James J. McKay by Jones in 1843; Thomas S. Bayly by Cobb in 1849; George S. Houston by Boyd in 1851; William H. Morrison by Kerr and Carlisle in 1875 and 1883; and William M. Springer by Crisp in 1891.[8]

According to Floyd M. Riddick, "in the House, the early titular floor leaders were at the same time the chairmen of the Ways and Means Committee. Before the division of the work of that committee, the duties of its chairmen were so numerous that they automatically became the actual leaders, since as chairmen of that committee they had to direct the consideration of most of the legislation presented to the House. [Ways and Means handled both the revenue and the appropriations bills down to 1865.] From 1865 until 1896 the burden of handling most of the legislation was shifted to the chairman of the Appropriations Committee, who then was designated most frequently as the leader. From 1896 until 1910 once again the chairmen of the Ways and Means Committee were usually sought as the floor leaders."[9]

Since 1910 the floor leader has been elected by secret ballot of the party caucus. During the Wilson administrations, the Democrats resumed their former practice of naming the chairman of Ways and Means as floor leader, but since the Seventy-second Congress (1931-1933), when the Democrats recovered control of the House, their floor leaders have not retained their former committee assignments. John W. McCormack, who was elected Democratic floor leader on September 16, 1940, and who held that office longer than any predecessor, resigned his seat on Ways and Means when he became floor leader. In 1919, when the Republicans captured control of the House, they elected as their floor leader the former chairman of Ways and Means and made him ex-officio chairman of their Committee on Committees and of their Steering Committee. He gave up his former legislative committee assignments in order to devote himself, with the Speaker, to the management of the business of the House.

Changes after 1910

After the congressional elections of November, 1910, in which the Democrats won full control of the House, they held a party caucus on January 19, 1911, and chose Champ Clark as Speaker and Oscar Underwood as their floor leader and as chairman of the Ways and Means Committee. Under the new system that became effective in the 1911-1912 session of the Sixty-second Congress, the Speaker was largely shorn of power, and the majority party caucus became the dominant factor. The Rules Committee was controlled by the floor leader and the caucus; it made the rules and retained all its former powers. The Democratic members of Ways and Means organized the House by naming its standing committees.

As floor leader, Underwood was supreme, the Speaker a figurehead. The main cogs in the machine were the caucus, the floor leadership, the Rules Committee, the standing committees, and special rules. Oscar Underwood became the real leader of the House. He dominated the party caucus, influenced the rules, and as chairman of Ways and Means chose the committees. Champ Clark was given the shadow, Underwood the substance of power. As floor leader, he could ask and obtain recognition at any time to make motions to restrict debate or preclude amendments or both. "Clothed with this perpetual privilege of recognition, and backed by his caucus," remarked a contemporary observer, "the floor leader had it in his power to make a Punch and Judy show of the House at any time."[10]

After World War I the party caucus gradually fell into disuse: the Democratic floor leader ceased to be chairman of Ways and Means; the standing committees continued to function as autonomous bodies; and the Rules Committee became a more influential factor in the power structure of the House. After 1937 this powerful committee ceased to function as an agent of the majority leadership and came under the control of a bipartisan coalition that was often able to exercise an effective veto power over measures favored by the majority party and its leadership.

The net effect of those changes in the power structure of the House of Representatives was to diffuse the leadership, and to disperse its risks, among a numerous body of leaders. The superstructure which came to control "overhead" strategy now included the Speaker, the floor leader, the chairman of Rules, and the party whip. At a somewhat lower echelon behind this inner "board of strategy" were the chairman and the secretary of the party caucus or conference; the majority members of Rules; and the members of the Republican Policy Committee and of the two Committees on Committees. Thus, the top leaders of the House were no longer "the chairmen of the principal standing committees," as Woodrow Wilson described them in 1885, although the chairmen still have large powers over bills within their jurisdiction.

In recent years, the Democrats have revitalized their caucus (see Chapter 9) and in 1975 adopted caucus rules that require monthly meetings. A Democratic Speaker can now nominate the Democratic members of the Rules Committee. The Democrats have also converted the Steering and Policy Committee into a much more vigorous body. The Republican Conference has also become more active as has its Policy Committee. Thus leadership may be said to be more diffused in the House than it was, even though the formal powers of the top leaders are also greater.

So far as the position of the floor leader is concerned, he no longer occupies the post of supremacy that Oscar Underwood held. There is still no provision for his office in the standing rules of the House. Nevertheless he stands today in a place of great influence and prestige, the acknowledged leader of his party in the chamber, its field general on the floor, first or second man in the party hierarchy, and one of the potential successors to the Speakership. All the Speakers of the past century have been advanced to the Speakership from either the minority or majority floor leadership position, except in 1919 when James R. Mann of Illinois, Republican floor leader, was defeated for the speakership by Frederick H. Gillett of Massachusetts.

Qualifications and Previous Experience

After retiring from the House of Representatives, where he represented
Buffalo from 1897 to 1911, DeAlva Alexander wrote an informative history of that body which contains a series of character sketches of the floor
leaders of the House from Griswold in 1800 to Underwood in 1911. Most
of these mighty men of old are now forgotten, but to their contemporaries
they were men of exceptional capacity. "In interesting personality and real
ability the floor leader is not infrequently the strongest and at the time the
best-known man in the House."

Alexander went on to give his own evaluation of the characteristics of a
good leader as follows:[11]

> It certainly does not follow that a floor leader is the most effective de-
> bater, or the profoundest thinker, or the accepted leader of his party, al-
> though he may be and sometimes is all of these. It should imply, however,
> that in the art of clear, forceful statement, of readily spotting weak points in
> an opponent's argument, and in dominating power to safeguard the interests
> of the party temporarily responsible for the legislative record of the House,
> he is the best equipped for his trade. It is neither necessary nor advisable for
> him to lead or even to take part in every debate. The wisdom of silence is a
> great asset. Besides, chairmen and members of other committees are usually
> quite capable and sufficiently enthusiastic to protect their own measures.
> But the floor leader must aid the Speaker in straightening out parliamentary
> tangles, in progressing business, and in exhibiting an irresistible desire to
> club any captious interference with the plans and purposes of the majority.

Eighteen men have held the office of majority or minority floor leader
of the House of Representatives since 1919. Eight of them were Republicans: Mondell, Longworth, Tilson, Snell, Martin, Halleck, Ford, and
Rhodes. Ten were Democrats: Garrett, Garner, Rainey, Byrns, Bankhead,
Rayburn, McCormack, Albert, Boggs, and O'Neill.

All the floor leaders since World War I have also enjoyed long service
on some of the most eminent committees of the House. Of the eight Republicans, three had served on the Rules Committee; two ranked high on
Ways and Means; and three on the Appropriations Committee. Of the ten
Democrats, four were high-ranking on Ways and Means; three on Rules;
one on Appropriations; one on Agriculture; and one (Rayburn) had been
chairman of Interstate and Foreign Commerce.

Functions and Duties of Floor Leader

The standing rules of the House are silent on the duties of the floor leaders who, as we have seen, are selected by the caucus or conference of their

respective parties. As his title indicates, the principal function of the majority leader is that of field marshal on the floor of the House. He is responsible for guiding the legislative program of the majority party through the House. In co-operation with the Speaker, he formulates and announces the legislative program, keeps in touch with the activities of the legislative committees through their chairmen, and stimulates the reporting of bills deemed important to the nation and the party. After conferring with the Speaker and majority leader, the majority whip customarily sends out a "whip notice" on Fridays to the party members in the House, indicating the order of business on the floor for the following week, and the majority leader makes an announcement to the same effect on the floor in response to an inquiry from the minority leader. The legislative program is planned ahead on a weekly basis according to the readiness of committees to report, the condition of the calendars, the exigencies of the season, and the judgment of the party leaders. Advance announcement of the weekly program protects the membership against surprise action.

The role of the majority leader was lucidly summarized in a statement inserted in the *Congressional Record* on May 11, 1928, when the Republicans were in power, by Representative Guy U. Hardy of Colorado:[12]

> The floor leader, especially the leader of the majority side, has much to do with the legislative program. The majority leader, of course, represents the majority on the floor. Motions he makes are usually passed. He endeavors to represent the majority view and the majority follow his leadership. He leads in debate on administration matters and gives the House and the country the viewpoint of his party on the legislative program.
>
> The leader keeps in touch with proposed legislation, the status of bills of importance, with the steering committee of which he is chairman, and with the attitude of the Rules Committee. He confers with committee chairmen and Members in general. The majority leader often confers with the President and advises with him regarding administrative measures. He takes to the President the sentiment of the party in the House and he brings to the party in the House the sentiment of the President. The majority leader acts also as chairman of the committee on committees and of the steering committee. . . .

The duties of the minority floor leader were described by Representative Bertram H. Snell in a statement on March 5, 1934, as follows:[13]

> The Minority Floor Leader is selected at a conference of the minority members. Usually he is his party's candidate for Speaker. . . . He is also chairman of a steering committee whose members are his chief advisers. He is spokesman for his party and enunciates its policies. He is required to be alert and vigilant in defense of the minority's rights. It is his function and duty to criticize constructively the policies and program of the majority,

and to this end employ parliamentary tactics and give close attention to all proposed legislation. The minority leader must keep in constant touch with the ranking minority members of committees, he himself not being a member of any committee although indirectly acquainted with the work of all committees.

Through another party functionary called the "whip" the minority leader informs the minority members of the order of business from time to time and secures their attendance when important votes are to be taken. By this method also the attitude of members toward a given proposition is ascertained, looking to unanimity of action.

Various parliamentary procedures are employed by the floor leader in directing and expediting the legislative program. The floor leader uses the device of unanimous consent to fix the program of business. Members know that it would be futile to object to his unanimous consent requests to consider legislation because the same end could be achieved via a simple majority vote on the floor. Similarly, if a member sought to bring up a matter out of its turn, without prior agreement with the leadership, the floor leader could defeat him by objecting.

The floor leader can also limit debate on a bill, if it tends to get out of control, by making the point of order that debate is not germane to the pending subject or by moving that all debate on the pending bill and all amendments thereto close in a certain time. By his temper and spirit he can also influence the tone of debate.

As the end of a session approaches, with many measures pressing for passage, the Speaker and the floor leader co-operate closely to avoid a last-minute jam. The procedural devices employed at this time are largely unanimous consent, special orders, and motions to suspend the rules which are in order on the last six days of a session and require a two-thirds vote. "There is a usual speeding up of the program during the last days. But there is also a tightening of control. In strong contrast to the Senate, the House remains a poised, businesslike body as it approaches adjournment. The men in the cab hold the legislative train steady to the very end of its run."[14] At the end of each session the floor leader customarily extends his remarks by inserting a record of its accomplishments, showing the major legislative actions taken and the number of public and private laws enacted, viewing with pride the role of his party in the legislative process.

In 1909 the House adopted a rule whereby Wednesdays were set apart for the consideration of unprivileged bills on the House and Union Calendars. Under this "Calendar Wednesday" rule, when invoked, the clerk calls the roll of the committees in turn and authorized members call up bills that their committees have reported. At the time of its adoption this rule was regarded as perhaps the most vital of the reforms that the progressives won under Cannonism. For it reserved Wednesday as the one day of each week which had to be given to the consideration of bills upon the House Calendar. Before its adoption, the "call of committees" was rarely reached as the result of the accidental or intentional manipulation of privileged matters. To remedy that condition, the new rule provided that on one day each week no business, regardless of its privileged character, should be allowed to interfere with the regular routine. In obtaining its adoption the progressives demanded, and thought that they had secured, one day so guarded that nothing could interfere with the consideration and final passage of general legislation.

For many years, however, the Calendar Wednesday rule has been more honored in the breach than in the observance. Session after session passes without a call of the committees. In practice, Calendar Wednesday is usually dispensed with by unanimous consent at the request of the majority leader. If there is objection, it requires a two-thirds vote to dispense with it, but no one ever objects. The leadership has evidently felt that there is little, if any, need for Calendar Wednesday because of the alternative methods by which bills can be brought up and over which they have more control. In the modern practice there are five routes by which bills and resolutions reach the floor of the House: (1) by the leave of certain committees to report at any time; (2) under unanimous consent, on call of the Unanimous Consent Calendar or the Private Calendar; (3) on special days, as on District Day, when particular types of business are privileged; (4) under suspension of the rules on the first and third Mondays and the last six days of the session; and (5) under special orders reported by the Committee on Rules.

Since the floor leader is responsible for the orderly conduct of the business of legislation on the floor, it is necessary for him to keep in close touch with the sentiment of the House and with the chairmen of committees that have under consideration bills of interest to the House, the country, and the party. To this end he holds frequent conferences with those concerned with prospective measures in order to compose any differences that may arise, as well as to plan the strategy and tactics of his campaign. Information as to party sentiment on a particular bill is also obtained, with the aid of the party whips, by polls of the state delegations.

In summarizing the resources that are available to the leadership for affecting legislative results, Randell B. Ripley notes how the leaders can make use of the rules to assist the members in passing their favored bills, influence appointments to desirable committees, single out members in a manner that enhances their prestige, and effectively control a communications system that allows them to possess the most reliable information about key bills, the presidential position, etc.[15]

Whip Organization

In the practice of the United States Congress, party whips are used in both houses and both political parties. The first person officially known as a whip in Congress was Republican Representative James E. Watson of Indiana, so designated by his party in 1899. In the Senate, the first official Democratic whip was James H. Lewis of Illinois, named in 1913. Two years later the Republicans designated Senator James W. Wadsworth of New York as their whip.

In the Ninety-fourth Congress, the Democratic "whip organization" consisted of a chief whip, a chief deputy whip, and three deputy whips appointed by the majority leader in consultation with the Speaker, and twenty-one assistant whips selected by the Democrats from their zones. In addition, in 1975, Majority Leader O'Neill appointed three at-large whips, representing freshmen, black, and women members.[16] The Republican "whip organization" consisted of a whip chosen by the Committee on Committees, four regional assistant whips chosen by the whip, and twelve additional assistant whips selected to cover specific states.

The whips send out weekend "whip notices" to party members about next week's legislative program, conduct polls of party members through a "whip check" to estimate the prospective vote on bills, round up members for the actual votes, arrange "pairs" between opposing members, and serve as assistant floor leaders in the absence of their leaders.

Obviously the information that the whips bring to the leadership can be of great value. Their reports that attendance may be low can lead to a rescheduling of floor action. Adverse member reaction to a bill may result in returning the proposal to the appropriate committee for further consideration. The whips can also advise the leaders on which members are in need of additional persuasion or about those members who will be immune to persuasion.

Beginning in the Ninety-third Congress, the majority whip began a series of "Whip Advisories," summarizing the provisions of a bill and the possible amendments. The chief deputy whip can also supply information for speeches, testimony for hearings, and reviews of legislation which has already passed the House.

The tasks of the whips are obviously extensive in a legislative body where every member's primary concern is with the impact of a proposal on his district.

Party Caucuses

Under the old system the congressional parties held frequent caucuses at which party policies were vigorously discussed and differences settled. Every major measure of a session was considered in party caucus and members were bound to abide by its decisions. The leadership then knew exactly where it stood, whether bills could be passed on the floor without amendment or whether compromises would have to be made. After Champ Clark became floor leader in 1909, the House Democrats held many binding caucuses, and much of the success of the legislative program of the Wilson administration was attributed to the effective use of the caucus by the Democratic Party in both houses of Congress. For many decades, House Republicans also held frequent party conferences which, although they were not binding, made for a consensus among the party membership and helped a succession of strong GOP Speakers and floor leaders to hold the party reins tightly. Thus, at the opening of the Sixty-ninth Congress in 1925, the members of the Wisconsin delegation, who had supported Senator La Follette in the presidential campaign of 1924, were barred from the Republican caucus and reduced in rank on the standing committees of the House.

From about 1918 to 1968, party caucuses were seldom held except at the opening of a new Congress to nominate House officers and approve recommendations of the leadership for committee appointments. Perhaps the party leaders considered those meetings too hazardous. The leadership could not compel members to vote against their will or conscience nor could it discipline them any longer by removal or demotion from committees. The floor leader had to rely for the co-operation of his followers not upon the compulsion of party rules but upon his own powers of logic and persuasion and considerations of party welfare. "Under the new system the Floor Leader is dependent not upon his power under the rules, but upon his own personality and character, upon the esteem in which he is held in the House for his political sagacity and his wisdom as a statesman, and upon the natural instincts which prompt men belonging to a party, and held together by natural selfish instincts for mutual protection, for his success in harmonizing differences and thus being able to go into the House with a measure assured of sufficient support to secure its enactment . . . the Floor Leader has become the general manager of his party in the House, the counselor of his colleagues, the harmonizer of their conflicting opinions, their servant, but not their master."[17]

During the late 1960's, the Republicans and the Democrats began to infuse new life into the caucus system. The full implications of this movement will be treated in our discussion of "Party Government in the House," yet we have already noted that the Democratic caucus in 1975 deposed three senior committee chairmen. Both caucuses now have rules that require monthly meetings. Since 1966, the Republican conference has had a paid staff, and in 1975 the House passed a resolution funding staff for the Democratic caucus. Despite the reappearance of the caucus as a viable part of the House scene, the failure of the House to override several vetoes by President Ford in 1975 did not exempt the Democratic leadership from considerable criticism.

Thus as long as the caucus cannot bind members on policy matters, it will still be the responsibility of the leadership to utilize all the nuances of their power and prestige. In short, the function of a leader is still to lead. In the case of a majority leader of a legislative assembly, leadership involves planning the legislative program, scheduling the order of business on the floor, supporting legislation calculated to implement the party's platform pledges, co-ordinating committee action to this end, and using his individual influence to keep the members of the party in the House in line with party policies. The majority leader's task is to steer his party in the House toward the formulation and adoption of policies and strategy designed to carry out the administration's legislative program, where the House and the Presidency are controlled by the same political party. As floor leader his function is to employ all the arts of parliamentary procedure to expedite the enactment of that program.

Relations with Committees

During the nineteenth century, as already noted, the actual floor leader was often the chairman of Ways and Means prior to 1865 when this committee handled both the revenue and appropriation bills. In that year the supply bills were given to the Committee on Appropriations and thereafter the floor leader was often the chairman of Appropriations. When the Sixty-second Congress (1911-1913) transferred the power to appoint committees from the Speaker to the Democratic members of Ways and Means, its chairman (Underwood) who was also floor leader thus acquired an indirect influence over legislation not enjoyed by his predecessors. Today Democratic nominations to fill vacancies on all committees must be made by the Steering and Policy Committee, twelve of whose twenty-four members are either the party's leaders or are appointed by the Speaker, a procedure which increases the influence that the leadership can have on a vast range of legislative issues.

As already noted, the Republican floor leader always ex officio, serves as chairman of the Republican Committee on Committees of the House, which has the task of filling its party vacancies on the legislative committees. This involves hearing the claims of interested candidates and deciding who should be chosen.

The floor leader on both sides of the House aisle is a member of his party's Steering or Policy Committee. The Republican floor leader is also a member of the party's Policy Committee. That committee has twenty-five members, including the nine major leaders of the party and seven at-large members chosen by the chairman and the minority leader. The Republicans also have a Committee on Research of seventeen members; while the chairman is elected by the conference, all the leaders are included, and the remaining members are nominated by the leaders and approved by the conference.

Republican leadership in the House is less centralized than is the Democratic leadership. Thus by a resolution of the conference in the Ninety-fourth Congress, the Republican leadership was defined as the floor leader, the whip, the chairman, vice chairman, and secretary of the conference, the chairmen of the Policy, Research, and Congressional (campaign) Committees, and the ranking member of the Rules Committee.

Relations between the leadership of the House and the Rules Committee have varied over the years. From 1890 to 1910 they were merged, for Rules was then a triumvirate composed of the Speaker and his two chief lieutenants, often the chairmen of Ways and Means and of Appropriations. After 1910, the speakership was "syndicated," and the leadership was separated from the members of the Committee on Rules who ceased to be the dominant figures in the House, although their chairman continued to be an important personality because of his position.[18] Writing in 1927 Paul H. Hasbrouck said of the Rules Committee:[19]

> It is the trump card of the Floor Leader, but he himself is not officially identified with it. True, he must appeal to the reason of twelve men, and win a majority of them to the support of his proposals. But the mainspring of action is not in the Rules Committee. The impulse comes from the Floor Leader after consultation with his "board of strategy" or, for purposes of more formal and routine action, with the Steering Committee.

In 1939 the leadership lost control of the House Rules Committee, thanks to the seniority custom, when two of its Democratic members joined with the four Republican members to block floor consideration of controversial administration bills. The coalition succeeded in preventing many

New Deal–Fair Deal measures from reaching the House floor except by the laborious discharge route. After World War II a rising demand developed for reform of the Rules Committee whose powers were temporarily curbed during the Eighty-first Congress (1949-1950) by adoption of the so-called twenty-one-day rule. This rule strengthened the position of the chairmen of the legislative committees of the House vis-à-vis both the Rules Committee and the leadership. While it was in effect, the twenty-one-day rule brought the anti-poll-tax bill to the House floor for a successful vote and forced action on the housing and minimum wage bills. It also enabled the House to vote for the National Science Foundation, Alaskan and Hawaiian statehood legislation, and other important measures. Altogether, during the Eighty-first Congress eight measures were brought to the House floor and passed by resort to the twenty-one-day rule, while its existence caused the Rules Committee to act in other cases. Repeal of this rule in January, 1951, restored the check-rein power of the Rules Committee which it has since exercised on various occasions.

The role of the leadership in influencing the Rules Committee has increased considerably since its expansion from twelve to fifteen members in 1961. One scholar notes that in 1973, when the Democratic caucus added the Speaker, the majority leader, and the caucus chairman to the Committee on Committees, "Speaker Albert used his newly acquired power on the Committee on Committees to insure that the Committee on Rules, the principal scheduling body of the House, would remain loyal to his direction."[20] The ability of the leaders to exert influence on the Rules Committee was also strengthened by the Democratic caucus adopting a rule in 1973 that allows fifty or more members to bring to the caucus any amendments to bills granted only a closed rule by the Rules Committee. If those amendments are approved by a majority of the caucus, the amendments must receive consideration by the full House. The 1975 rule change, which allows the Speaker to nominate all the Democrats on the Rules Committee, suggests even further co-ordination between the leadership and that important committee. There may well be occasions in the future when the Rules Committee will be accused of holding up proposals that some members wish to vote on, but the likelihood is that those decisions will be made only with considerable leadership guidance.

Relations with the President

Since 1937, when Franklin D. Roosevelt began the practice, regular conferences have been held at the White House between the President and his party leaders in Congress—the "Big Four": the Speaker and majority leader of the House and the Vice President and majority leader of the Senate, when they belong to the President's party. Inclusion of the majority whips in recent years has made it a "Big Six." When opposing political parties control Congress and the Presidency, the minority leaders attend these meetings at the White House, which are usually weekly while Congress is in session, if the President is in town. These "Big Six" meetings have helped to bridge the gap between the legislative and executive branches of the national government created by our inherited system of separated powers. Subsequent Presidents have continued the practice of holding weekly leadership meetings at the White House.

When President Roosevelt took office in 1933, he launched such a varied legislative program that it was necessary for him to keep in close touch with Congress through the leaders of both houses. He consulted with his party leaders and committee chairmen with respect to the New Deal measures before they were introduced as administration bills, usually by the majority leaders. Sometimes he called the majority leader of the House or Senate individually to the White House to confer about some problem peculiar to one chamber or the other. After his return from trips abroad he sometimes asked the floor leaders of each house to brief him on legislative developments during his absence.

When opposing parties control the two branches, the President is more likely to discuss domestic legislative matters with the congressional leaders of his own party, although in the early days of the Eightieth Congress, President Truman occasionally conferred with Messrs. Vandenberg, White, Martin, and Halleck, especially on legislation of a nonpartisan nature. In view of the vital role of Congress in the field of foreign relations, the President must sometimes take the leaders of both political parties in both houses into his confidence. In the days before World War II, when President Roosevelt was seeking to strengthen our defenses, he frequently conferred with both Democratic and Republican leaders in both houses of Congress. Such a conference was the famous night meeting at the White House late in July, 1939, when the President and Secretary of State Cordell Hull urged that Congress repeal the Embargo Act. Among those in attendance were the chairmen of the Foreign and Military Affairs Committees, members of the Cabinet, and the majority and minority leaders of the House and Senate.[21] However, in 1970, when President Nixon announced that United States combat troops had been sent into Cambodia, there was no prior consultation with legislative leaders. Five years later, when President Ford ordered the use of troops to free an American ship that had been captured by Cambodian Communists in the Gulf of Siam, the President's staff informed legislative leaders of a decision that had already been made. By then the President could take the position that he had acted in accord with the War Powers Act of 1973 which required that within forty-eight hours he report to the House Speaker and president pro tem of the Senate any commitment of combat forces abroad.

The full range of topics that are appropriate to a study of the relationship between the President and Congress are, of course, beyond our concern here. Obviously the modern Presidents have gone beyond consulting with just the legislative leaders. In a system characterized by the decentralization of power, Presidents have often found it necessary to court committee chairmen. Since 1953, when President Eisenhower gave official status to the post of White House liaison man with Congress, every President has had at his command an enormous staff system capable of effectively lobbying the full membership of Congress. Yet the ability of the White House to influence the legislative process did not prevent the tragic erosion of executive-legislative relations during the Nixon Presidency.

Compensation and Allowances

The Legislative Branch Appropriation Act for the fiscal year 1974 appropriated $149,805 for the office of the majority floor leader; $133,190 for the office of the minority floor leader; $9,500 for each leader's automobile; and $107,810 each for the offices of the majority and minority whip. Only since 1965 have the majority and minority floor leaders received a salary greater than the other members. Their salary in 1974 was $49,500, with an additional $3,000 for official purposes.

8

The Business of Congress

THE BUSINESS OF CONGRESS in modern times is as varied and multifarious as the affairs of the American people. Once relatively limited in scope, small in volume, and simple in nature, it has now become almost unlimited in subject matter, enormous in volume, and complex in character.

The Founding Fathers had expected that Congress would confine itself, for the most part, to the external affairs of the new nation, leaving the conduct of internal affairs to the states and communities. The national legislature would have little to do, Alexander Hamilton thought, after the central government was firmly established and a federal code formulated. But with the steady expansion of the national domain, the rapid growth of population, and the development of commerce and industry, this expectation proved to be chimerical. As the new republic grew greater, the demand for congressional action increased apace. From the opening day of the First Congress on March 4, 1789, to the adjournment of the Ninety-third Congress on December 20, 1974, no less than 1,051,085 bills and resolutions—public and private—were introduced in both chambers: an average of 11,302 for each of the first ninety-three Congresses.

Some conception of the enormous expansion of the business of Congress is afforded by a comparison of the work of the First (1789-1791) and the Ninety-third (1973-1974) Congresses.

The table on the next page measures the great growth in legislative business since 1789 and reflects the attendant burdens. The sheer bulk of bills introduced increased more than eightyfold, while the number of standing committees available to receive and handle the rising flood grew from two to forty-five. Total committee reports jumped from 155 to 3,095 and the number of laws produced by the legislative mills multiplied six times. Meanwhile, as the population of the country expanded from 4 to 210 million, and thirty-seven new states were admitted to the federal Union, the membership of Congress available to handle the added work load multiplied almost six times.

FIRST AND NINETY-THIRD CONGRESSES COMPARED

Points of Comparison	1st Congress	93d Congress
Number of bills introduced:	268	21,950
House of Representatives	142	17,690
Senate	126	4,260
Number of laws enacted:	118	´772
Public	108	649
Private	10	123
Number of Members	91	535
Representatives	65	435
Senators	26	100
Days in session	519	334
Number of Committees (standing, joint):	2	47
House of Representatives	1	22
Senate	0	18
Joint	1	7
Committee reports:	155	3,095
House of Representatives	85	1,668
Senate	70	1,427
Nominations confirmed	211	131,264
Petitions filed	650	598
Presidential messages received	12	213
Executive Dept. communications received	72	3,122

Comparative data reflecting the work load and output of single Congresses are available as far back as the Forty-ninth Congress (1885-87). The following table gives a comparative statement of the work of five selected Congresses (House only) over the past eighty-nine years.

Congress	No. of Bills	No. of Reports	Public Laws	Private Laws	Total Laws	Length in Days
49th (1885-87)	11,260	4,181	424	1,031	1,455	330
56th (1899-1901)	14,339	3,006	443	1,498	1,941	277
62nd (1911-13)	28,870	1,628	530	186	716	500
69th (1925-27)	17,415	2,319	808	537	1,423	297
85th (1957-58)	15,660	2,719	936	784	1,720	469
93d (1973-74)	21,095	1,666	649	123	772	688

SOURCE: Final edition, House Calendars, 56th, 70th, 85th, and 93d Congresses.

Business of First Congress (1789-1791)

Such legislative statistics afford no measure, however, of the changes in the range and complexity of public problems facing Congress then and now. The First Congress established the State, War, and Treasury Departments; fixed import and tonnage duties and regulated their collection; appropriated revenue and provided for a public debt; admitted Kentucky and Vermont to the Union and settled certain state accounts; established courts of justice and fixed the compensation of public officers; provided for the census of 1790 and regulated trade with the Indians; and otherwise dealt with the comparatively simple problems of the federal government in that remote age. Many problems in the early days of the Republic were state and local in scope, as they still are, and were left to the states and localities or to the private forces of the frontier to settle. Accordingly, the legislative process in Washington was much more leisurely and the life of a Congressman far more tranquil than it is today.

Of the 108 public laws approved by the First Congress, 18 dealt with foreign affairs (including tariff duties), 16 with relations between the central government and the states, 10 with the defense of the infant nation; 18 were concerned with administrative matters (including salaries); 15 with questions of public finance, and 9 with the judiciary. Only 3 were pension acts, and only 2 for the relief of private claimants.

Work Load of the Eighty-fourth Congress (1955-1956)

Contrast this with the work load of the Eighty-fourth Congress. Almost half the laws it passed—893 out of 1,921—dealt with private and local matters which diverted its attention from national policymaking and with which it need not have been burdened. These included measures relating to the District of Columbia, the settlement of private claims and immigration cases, and other private and local legislation. Much of the work of this Congress was devoted to considering and enacting thirty-three appropriation bills involving a total of $137 billion, almost two-thirds of it for national defense.

Of the 1,028 public laws enacted by the Eighty-fourth Congress, the most important dealt with military defense and foreign economic aid, federal aid to education and social security, the farm program, highways and housing, immigration and labor legislation, public power, industrial health and safety, unemployment compensation and natural gas regulation.

The Ninety-third Congress (1973-1974)

Whatever its other achievements, the Ninety-third Congress would undoubtedly be recorded as the Congress that sought to retrieve its status as a co-equal branch of the government. For many months, its energies were also in the shadow of scandals in the executive branch. In 1973, the Congress found itself deliberating and then ratifying President Nixon's choice of Minority Leader Gerald R. Ford as Vice President, following the resignation of Spiro T. Agnew after he had pleaded no contest to a charge of income tax evasion. And in 1974 came the first presidential resignation, after the House Judiciary Committee had voted three articles of impeachment, and the subsequent congressional acceptance of President Ford's choice of Nelson A. Rockefeller as Vice President.[1]

The Vietnam War had led to the Congress overriding a Nixon veto of a measure that limited the power of a President to wage undeclared war. Congressional insistence that President Nixon had abused his fiscal powers also brought a budget reform act that was designed to give Congress more control over federal spending while restricting the power of the President to impound funds. Watergate also contributed to the passage of a campaign finance law that limited campaign contributions and expenditures, allowed for public financing of presidential elections, and set up a commission to monitor enforcement.

Expansion Since 1911

In volume, scope, and complexity the legislative agenda of the past decade was obviously a far cry from that of 1790. It was a far cry, too, from the days when Congress struggled with Andrew Jackson over the Bank of the United States and the sale of public lands. It was a far cry even from 1911, when Robert Ramspeck, Democratic whip in the Seventy-ninth House, came from Georgia to Washington to work in the Capitol Post Office and serve as a congressional secretary. Congress was then in session only nine months out of twenty-four, and the members spent the remainder of their terms at home practicing law or attending to their private business. The mail they received then dealt largely with free seed, rural routes, Spanish-American War pensions, and occasionally a legislative matter. Members had ample time to attend to their congressional duties. "It was a pretty nice job that a Member of Congress had in those days," Representative Ramspeck reminisced when he appeared thirty-four years later before a joint committee studying the burdens of legislators. "At that time the Government affected the people directly in only a minor way. . . . It was an entirely different job from the job we have to do today. It was primarily a legislative job, as the Constitution intended it to be."

The enormous expansion in the work load of Congress dates back, in fact, only to World War I. A succession of crises in our national life, marked by our participation in two world wars within a single generation, plus the intervening depression of 1929-1933 and the following recovery efforts, imposed vast new responsibilities upon Congress and the administration for the conduct of national and international affairs. Making up as if for lost time, Congress delegated large powers over American economy and society to a score of regulatory commissions, credit corporations, and developmental authorities. Responding to the exigencies of events and the requirements of the times, Congress and the federal government took almost all human affairs as their province. So great, indeed, was the gradual expansion of federal authority and activity from Woodrow Wilson's administration on that no important field of human interest and endeavor failed to feel its impact.

This past half century has witnessed a striking expansion of public policy into many new fields of activity under the successive impact of Wilsonian and New Deal reforms, two World Wars, and the intervening depression. During the New Freedom era an extraordinary series of reforms were enacted into law, including the Underwood Tariff, the Clayton Act designed to strengthen antitrust policy, and the federal child labor laws. Although these measures proved to be short-lived or were later diluted or invalidated by the courts, Congress added several important and permanent weapons to the arsenal of federal control of the economy during the first Wilson administration, including the Federal Reserve Board, the Federal Trade, Power, and Tariff Commissions, and the Federal Farm Loan Board.

World War I saw the creation of numerous emergency wartime agencies in Washington with legislative sanction, such as the War Labor Board which gave government recognition for the first time to the right of labor organization and collective bargaining, federal operation of the railroads followed by the Transportation Act of 1920, the activities of the Shipping Board which continued into the postwar period, an industrial mobilization plan of unprecedented scope directed by the War Industries Board, the Food and Fuel Administration, a War Trade Board established to control

154 The Business of Congress

foreign trade, and the creation of the U.S. Employment Service and the War Finance Corporation to mobilize labor and capital for the war effort.

With the return of peace, most of the emergency wartime machinery was quickly demobilized, and a reaction ensued against government control of economic life. During the decade of the 1920's the political climate of the country was hostile to further experiments in the social control of business, yet this period witnessed the establishment of the Inland Waterways Corporation in 1924 on a permanent basis, creation of the Federal Radio Commission in 1926, and a series of legislative measures designed to help farmers cope with the postwar agricultural depression, including the Packers' and Stockyards Act of 1923, the Cooperative Marketing Act of 1926, and the Agricultural Marketing Act of 1929.

With the coming of the Great Depression and the New Deal, Congress collaborated with the Roosevelt administration in a series of novel economic and social experiments designed to promote recovery and conserve natural and human resources. In the agricultural field, steps were taken to increase farm income and expand farm credit facilities. In the labor field, the Walsh-Healey Act and the Fair Labor Standards Act were passed to improve wages and working conditions, and the National Labor Relations Board was created to stimulate labor organization. Meanwhile the range of regulatory authority was widened by the creation of the Securities and Exchange Commission and the Federal Communications Commission, and by expanding the jurisdiction of the Interstate Commerce Commission and the Federal Power Commission. Public enterprise was greatly enlarged in the electrical utility field, in banking and credit, and in the provision of low-cost housing and slum clearance. And Congress approved a broad new program of social security by providing such measures as old-age insurance, unemployment compensation, public assistance, work relief, and long-range public works programs. During the New Deal era, in short, the role of government in the American economy was vastly enlarged.

During World War II, Congress made many important legislative decisions in major areas of wartime policy. It made decisions respecting the conversion and control over manpower, money, and supplies; labor policy, price control, and monetary policy; military policy and the conduct of the war; foreign policy and postwar commitments; and reconversion to peace after the war. Congress performed three major functions during the war: it made both broad and specific grants of power to the President; it adjusted conflicts of interest; and it supervised the execution of policy. Many difficult decisions were made by the national legislature on organizing the resources of the nation and allocating men, money, and materials among competing claimants.[2]

During the postwar period Congress was called upon to play its essential part in handling many important domestic and international public problems. Passage of the Employment Act of 1946 involved legislative recognition of a new public responsibility for maintaining high production and full employment in the domestic economy. Enactment of the Taft-Hartley Act in 1947 marked a significant reversal of public policy in the labor field and struck a new balance in labor-management relations. Adoption of many of the recommendations of the Hoover Commissions and admission to statehood of Alaska and Hawaii reflected the expanding scope of public activity in the field of government organization. Passage of the Civil Rights Act of 1957, 1960, and 1964 witnessed the first legislative steps in this field since Reconstruction days.

The landslide election of President Lyndon B. Johnson and a heavily Democratic Congress in 1964 led to even greater congressional activity. The next few years saw the enactment of legislation that vastly increased federal aid to education, brought medical care to the aged, expanded manpower training programs, and added greatly to consumer protection. A war on poverty was declared; the most comprehensive Voting Rights Act in the nation's history became law and a vast program of space exploration was encouraged.

While much of the foregoing was the response of sympathetic Congresses to a President deeply interested in domestic programming, most of the legislation continued even after the election of a more conservative President in 1968. Although President Nixon sought to reduce the level of expenditures for many of these programs, he nevertheless supplied the initiative for the enactment of a plan for revenue sharing and unsuccessfully attempted to achieve a family assistance plan, a form of guaranteed annual income. During President Nixon's first term, the Congress continued its support of education, established a government-owned postal corporation, gave extensive support to water- and air-pollution legislation, enacted the first national occupational safety legislation, and lowered the voting age in federal elections to eighteen. The split between a Republican President and a Democratic Congress continued into 1974; nevertheless the Congress did enact an emergency job program, established federal standards for private pension plans, and increased the minimum wage.[3]

By 1975 it was possible to conclude that the Congress had demonstrated its ability to enact a considerable amount of legislation despite presidential wishes, but that it also had great difficulty in overriding presidential vetoes, even though the Democrats had apparent 2-to-1 majorities.

Meanwhile, in the foreign field, Congress and the administration assumed new tasks after World War II in organizing and supporting the United Nations, in underwriting the reconstruction of western Europe by the Marshall Plan, in extending aid to Greece and Turkey, in waging the war in Korea, in promoting the fuller development of international trade, in the provisions of the mutual security programs, in the development and control of atomic energy, in the exploration of outer space, and in many other vital areas of international responsibility.

Most of these actions were initiated by Presidents, with successive Congresses responding to White House urgings. The pattern continued through most of the nation's tragic involvement in Vietnam. In 1964 the Congress passed the Gulf of Tonkin Resolution, which allowed the President to "take all necessary measures" to halt aggression in Southeast Asia. The Senate vote was 88-2; the House vote was 414-0. The doctrine that Congress should allow presidential initiative in foreign policy was eroded by the seemingly endless involvement in Vietnam. In 1970, Congress repealed the Gulf of Tonkin resolution and also passed an amendment to a supplementary foreign aid authorization bill that prohibited the use of any funds to pay for the introduction of American troops into Cambodia. Three years later came the War Powers Act, a statute that sought to prevent any lengthy American involvement in a war that did not have congressional approval. In all these and many other areas the developments of the past sixty years at home and abroad have combined with the increasing complexity and technical nature of modern public problems, and with the multiplying interests of constituents in public affairs, to magnify greatly the work load on Congress.

In the post-Vietnam and post-Watergate age, it was obvious that the role and responsibilities of the national government continued to overwhelm the nation. The country's international responsibilities were still massive; the state of an economy that confronted inflation and recession simultaneously, and the sudden emergence of an energy crisis meant a continued reliance on governmental power to meet new challenges. Yet the historical reliance on presidential initiatives had lost its attractiveness, especially when an activist Congress confronted a conservative President. At the same time there was an increasing unease among liberals that many of the ambitious programs of the 1960's had failed to achieve their goals.

Work Load

Since the end of World War II, Congress has grappled with the problem of its work load. The increased specialization of its legislative concerns, the proliferation of subcommittees, the growth of pressure groups, and the greater involvement of constituents with the federal government have intensified the day-to-day pressures on the members. One consequence of having members who were so thoroughly preoccupied with the day-to-day operations of their offices was an increasing reliance on the executive branch for expertise on major policy questions.

One of the objectives of the Legislative Reorganization Act of 1946 was to provide more staff for the members and the committees. That act authorized four professional staff positions for each standing committee. In 1965 the Joint Committee on the Organization of Congress noted that twenty-seven of the thirty-six standing committees exceeded the statutory provision by the use of annual resolutions requesting funds for inquiries and investigations and that, in fact, all of those committees had more than twelve staffers. The Reorganization Act of 1970 increased the number to six, and in 1974 the number went to eighteen professionals.

In 1953 the members of the House received an allowance that permitted the average member to employ a secretary and two clerks.[4] Twelve years later, half the members employed between seven and nine persons.[5] In 1971 the staff allowance for each member was increased from fifteen to sixteen, and in 1975 was increased again to eighteen. Senate staff size is not a fixed number because the states vary in population; one commentator has noted that the size of the staffs of the two Senators from California went from 40 to 118 between 1955 and 1974, and that Senator Sam Ervin of North Carolina had an office staff of 7 in 1954 and a staff of 70 when he left in 1974.[6] In 1975 the Senate voted to allow each Senator to hire three additional legislative assistants.

According to a U.S. Civil Service Commission report, the total staffs of Congress had gone from about 5,500 in 1955 to about 8,800 in 1965 to over 15,000 in 1975, with both the House and Senate authorizing increases since that report.[7] Before 1908, all members of the House and Senate and their staffs were located in the Capitol. In 1975 there was a strong likelihood that soon there would be a fourth office building for the House and a third one for the Senate.

Some of the work load of the members has been assisted by the Congressional Research Service. In 1914 it was established as the Legislative Reference Service. In 1946 it was expanded and made a separate department in the Library of Congress. It was again expanded by the Reorganization Act of 1970, when it received its new title. The service now has greatly increased responsibilities. Upon request it can assist and advise all committees in evaluating proposals and can even provide the committees with a list of topics it believes a committee might profitably study. In recent years the service has also developed a very sophisticated computerized system of information retrieval on legislative topics, issues, and bibliography. In 1953 the Legislative Reference Service budget was approximately $890,000; for 1976 its budget was about $17,000,000. In 1953 it received about 51,000 congressional inquiries; in 1973 it received over 180,000; in 1974, over 200,000.[8]

Despite the assistance given to the members, their agenda seems to have expanded. A press release from Representative Wayne L. Hays of Ohio on April 21, 1975, described the Congress as "battling to keep up with an ever increasing work load brought on by heavier constituent mail, more complex federal problems and public cries for legislative investigations on a wide variety of issues." The release noted that on an average day of the previous week no fewer than seventy committees or subcommittees had scheduled meetings and that during the previous four years the amount of mail received by congressional offices had tripled. According to Hays, the mail count in 1971 was about fourteen million pieces annually, but had since gone up to nearly a million letters per week. He also noted that most members travel back to their districts at least three weekends each month and that "the job of a Congressman often means fourteen-hour days, six or seven days per week."

A month after this press release, the Committee on House Administration, of which Representative Hays is chairman, increased the number of free round trips a member could make to his district from thirty-six per congress to thirty-two per year. It also increased the size of the staff, raised the telephone allowance, and allowed the House to pay for the production and printing of two newsletters each year for each member.

If the public seems to believe that the Congress is lethargic in its attack on the issues of the day, the members are equally depressed by their constituents' impressions of their daily schedule. Thus the following letter was sent by Representative David R. Obey of Wisconsin to a constituent who wondered how his Congressman spent his time:

Dear Art:

I received your note in which you state that Congress was in session 180 days last year and wondering what I did the other 185.

Anyone who assumes that a member of Congress is only working when he is on the House floor is either a charter member of the flat-earth society or he is just about as uninformed about the legislative process as I would be about business if I suggested that the only time a hardware dealer is working is when he is standing behind the cash register.

Time spent on the House floor represents a small portion of the working day of any member of Congress and I am sure you know that.

Most of my time is spent in Appropriations Committee hearings. The remainder is spent in dozens of meetings weekly with constituents, government agency people, and a great variety of people representing virtually every interest group in my district: doctors, lawyers, businessmen, workers, state and local officials, students, bankers, savings and loan representatives, farmers, scientists, clergymen, consumers, senior citizens, and virtually anyone else you can name. Occasionally, I even find time enough to meet with my own staff preparing legislation and preparing for hearings. We also must handle the nearly 1,000 pieces of mail I receive every week. And that is just a summary of the time I spend in Washington.

In addition, I spend a great deal of time, as you know, back home in Wisconsin attending countless meetings with people who have elected me to deal not only with national problems, but also with their own problems.

When Congress is in session, I am in Washington five days a week with rare exceptions. That fact is borne out by my 97.6% attendance record on House votes last year. I am on Capitol Hill by 8:00 in the morning and get home, if I am lucky, after 7:30 in the evening.

In addition to the time my job requires in Washington, I also spend over half of my weekends away from home meeting with constituents throughout the 18,000 square mile 7th District—my wife and kids really love that.

I really never have kept very good track in my own mind of how I have spent my time on a day-to-day basis over a given period of time. But, after receiving your note, I asked my secretary to go back over the record of appointments and schedules she kept for me during 1974. This is what she found:

1—The House was in session on 160 days (not your 180). There were 537 recorded votes during those sessions and, as previously noted, I was present for 524 of them, or 97.6%.

2—I spent 41 days in my Washington office when the House was not in session. There were usually Appropriations Committee or other meetings on these days, and even when there weren't, the more than one hundred pieces of mail per day kept coming.

3—I spent 127 days in Wisconsin. In fairness, those 127 days included 5 days which I spent fishing up North and the two days after the election when I escaped to the woods. Specifically, I was away from my family 28 of the 52 weekends last year. That doesn't leave much time for golfing, fishing, playing with my two sons, or just plain loafing.

Art, if you still think that a member of Congress has such a soft life and if you wonder what we do on those so-called "vacations"—as they are euphemistically called by some—I would invite you to travel with me through the 7th District on my next so-called "vacation" which is scheduled for May 23rd through June 2, 1975. For your information, I am enclosing a sample schedule for one of my recent weekend "vacations."

It has been my experience that the vast majority of members of Congress work pretty damn hard and that is not confined to my colleagues on the Democratic side of the aisle. Some of the people with whom I disagree the most around here work long hours just about every day of the year. If you don't, you simply get buried.

I don't think anyone in Wisconsin has heard me complain that I have too much work to do. I have asked for this job and despite the long hours, and despite what it takes from my family, I enjoy it immensely. But there are two things which make it difficult occasionally.

The worst problem is that by the time we attend hearings, meet with every group in sight who wants to talk with us about legislation and meet with every group at home ranging from mayors and county boards, to private citizens, we have precious little time to do what is most important—to think and read about problems that we have been sent here to deal with in the first place.

The second thing which is incredibly time-consuming is the necessity to respond to the over 50,000 letters a year which come into this office. Most of them are legitimate letters asking questions or expressing opinions on issues facing the country but more and more these days, we're also finding some that represent downright foolishness from people like yourself who should know better.*

In recent years, the House has attempted to modify its legislative schedule, introduced electronic voting in the House, enlarged its staff, reduced the number of private bills, and tampered with jurisdictional lines. Yet the members appear to be inundated with greater responsibilities than ever before. The beginning of a new anti-executive age when coupled with a greater public stake in the workings of Congress suggests that life on Capitol Hill will become less demanding only when the nation's business is simpler.

* May 19, 1975, reprinted by permision of Representative Obey.

9

Party Government in the House

POLITICAL PARTIES and party leadership found no explicit basis in the American Constitution, but they soon developed as a means both of expressing conflicting sectional and economic interests in the new republic and of bridging the gap between Congress and the Executive created by the constitutional system of separated branches and shared powers. James Madison with shrewd insight set forth in Number 58 of *The Federalist* the general principle that "in all legislative assemblies, the greater the number composing them may be, the fewer will be the men who will in fact direct their proceedings." And the history of the House of Representatives affords convincing proof of this principle.

Practice in Early Congresses: 1790-1816

Partisanship was noticeably absent from the early deliberations of the First Congress, as we saw in Chapter 2. But factional disputes soon dispelled this calm, and partisan controversies gave rise behind the legislative scenes to the formation of party groups in the House. The accounts of the time clearly reveal the appearance of an embryonic party organization in the House as early as 1790. Under Alexander Hamilton's masterful leadership, the Federalists in Congress were soon holding party caucuses and translating his financial policies into legislation. Later, the Jeffersonians when they came to power in 1801 made similar use of the party caucus and entrusted the conduct of the legislative process to an inner circle of majority leaders. According to Lord Bryce, political parties made their first appearance in Congress in the presidential election of 1796.[1] But Harlow's evidence dates the beginning of party organization in the House back to the First Congress.[2]

During Washington's first administration, James Madison, then a member of the House, became involved in a struggle with Alexander Hamilton over Treasury domination of Congress. Madison inspired and managed a series of moves against the Treasury forces, which led Fisher Ames to write in January 1793:[3]

> Virginia moves in a solid column, and the discipline of the party is as severe as the Prussian. Deserters are not spared. Madison is become a desperate party leader, and I am not sure of his stopping at any ordinary point of extremity. We are fighting for the asssumption of the balances, which shall be declared due the creditor states. He opposes, *vi et armis*.

During the Jeffersonian regime (1801-1809), the Republicans in Congress followed Federalist precedent and made regular use of the party caucus to determine their attitude on important legislation. "Through the caucus the jarring, discordant elements of the party were reconciled and made to work together, so that concerted policies and harmonious action were no longer the exclusive possessions of the Federalists."[4] From 1800 to 1824 the most noteworthy caucuses were those that nominated the party candidates for the Presidency.[5] During the Jeffersonian period, frequent reference to Republican *caucuses* appeared in the Federalist press. "The Democrats in Congress," according to an item in the *Washington Federalist,* "are adopting of late quite an economical plan of making laws. All business is to be settled in *caucuses* before it comes before the House; and the arguments or motives be given in *newspapers* afterwards. The federal members are to be treated as nullities."[6] It was charged that either Jefferson or Duane (publisher of the Philadelphia *Aurora*) always presided at these meetings. Apparently the first mention of the device on the House floor occurred in 1802 when Representative Bayard referred to the caucus during the debate on the repeal of the act establishing the district courts.[7]

What the Federalists thought of the caucus when it was used by their Republican opponents was reflected in a letter written by Representative Roger Griswold of Connecticut on January 25, 1802: "The Jacobins, finding themselves unable to manage their business on the questions in the House, have adopted the plan of meeting in divan and agreeing on measures to be pursued and passed in the House and then they vote in mass without admitting any alteration in the plan proposed. The wickedness of such a course has never been equalled but by the Jacobin club in Paris; the spirit is intolerant and must lead to ruin."

The way in which the caucus functioned as the "real legislature" was perhaps best described in a speech by Representative Josiah Quincy of Massachusetts in 1809. In speaking of a bill for an extra session, he said:

> "But, sir, with respect to this House, I confess I know not how to express my opinion. To my mind, it is a political non-descript. It acts, and reasons, and votes, and performs all the operations of an animated being, and yet, judging from my own perceptions, I cannot refrain from concluding that all great political questions are settled somewhere else than on this floor."[8]

Some conception of Jefferson's role in developing and controlling his party organization in Congress is afforded by the later observations of Henry Adams in his history of that period. "In ability and in energy," wrote Adams, "the Executive [Jefferson] overshadowed Congress, where the Republican party, though strong in numbers and discipline, was so weak in leadership, especially among the Northern democrats, that the weakness almost amounted to helplessness . . . the Northern democrats were and always remained, in their organization as a party, better disciplined than their opponents . . . while senators had not yet learned their power, representatives were restrained by party discipline. . . ."[9]

Madison's first administration was apparently marked by a breakdown of the Jeffersonian system of party organization and strict discipline. But by 1813, Henry Clay and the leaders of the House were in control of the situation; the balance of power had been transferred from the President to Congress; and the party caucus had been revived. Thus Daniel Webster wrote on June 4, 1813, that all really important business was being carried on outside the House. "In our political capacity we, that is, the House of Representatives, have done little or nothing. The time for us to be put on the stage and moved by the wires, has not yet come. I suppose the 'show' is now in preparation, and at the proper time the farce of legislating will be exhibited . . . before any thing is attempted to be done here, it must be arranged elsewhere."[10]

Ten months later, Webster's correspondence was reporting the success of Republican party discipline. Writing about the restrictions on commerce in force during the War of 1812, he said that the system had been supported "because it was attended with a severe and efficacious discipline, by which those who went astray were to be brought to repentance. No Saint in the Calendar ever had a set of followers less at liberty, or less disposed to indulge troublesome inquiry, than some, at least, of those on whom the system depended for support."[11] Evidence of the effectiveness of Republican party organization in Congress was seen in the enactment during Madison's second term of the bills for the Second Bank and for internal improvements and the tariff of 1816. Party measures were carefully canvassed in caucus before being admitted to the floor of the House where the party edicts were faithfully enforced. Meanwhile, with the establishment of the standing committee system in 1816, the majority party extended its control over these important panels through Speaker Clay who was chosen by the party caucus and who in turn selected the committees.[12]

Developments During the Nineteenth Century

With the development of the committee system in 1816 and thereafter, and with the nomination of presidential candidates by national conventions in 1832 and afterwards, the congressional caucus yielded its early pre-eminence to these new devices. During the period, 1816-1860, the standing committee system became the established device for the consideration of congressional business. In 1841 the Rules Committee, which hitherto had lacked special privileges, received authority to report "at all times"; in 1853 its reports were given priority; and in 1858 the Speaker became its chairman. The fragmentary party records of the period show, however, that the party caucus continued to be employed to nominate party candidates for Speaker and other House officers and, occasionally, to shape legislative policy.[13] But party discipline and the power of the caucus were weakened by sectional disputes over the slavery question as the irrepressible conflict approached.

The period from 1860 to 1890 was marked by a growing complexity in the economic and social organization of the nation which was reflected in turn in a more intricate organization of the House. It was a period characterized by intense resistances within Congress both to organizational change and to legislation of any sort. The minority became adept in the utilization of the rules to block the will of the majority, and the end of the period found an extremely decentralized power system prevailing within the House.

The condition of party organization in Congress during the decades after the Civil War was well described by Woodrow Wilson. Writing in 1885, he said: "Outside of Congress the organization of the national parties is exceedingly well-defined and tangible . . . but within Congress it is obscure and intangible. Our parties marshal their adherents with the strictest possible discipline for the purpose of carrying elections, but their discipline is very slack and indefinite in dealing with legislation. At least there is within Congress no *visible,* and therefore no *controllable* party organization. The only bond for cohesion is the caucus, which occasionally whips a party together for cooperative action against the time for casting its vote upon some critical question." Wilson attributed this condition to the bipartisan composition of the committees. "It is plainly the representation of both parties on the committees," said he, "that makes party responsibility indistinct and organized party action almost impossible. If the committees were composed entirely of members of the majority . . . committee reports would be taken to represent the views of the party in power" and the leaders of the opposition "could drill their partisans for effective warfare and give shape and meaning to the purposes of the minority. But of course there can be no such definite division of forces so long as the efficient machinery of legislation is in the hands of both parties at once; so long as the parties are mingled and harnessed together in a common organization."[14] Wilson believed that party government in the United States was complicated by the possibility of party diversity between Congress and the President and that real party government could exist only when Congress possessed complete control of the administration.[15]

During the Forty-eighth, Forty-ninth, and Fiftieth Congresses (1884–1889) the House of Representatives had been reduced to a condition of legislative impotence by abuses of its then existing rules of procedure. Not only was its legislative output small and insignificant, but the use of dilatory motions combined with the disappearing quorum and a series of filibusters to make the House an object of public ridicule and condemnation. For example, during a filibuster against a bill refunding to the states taxes collected under the war revenue legislation of 1861, eighty-six roll calls were taken, each consuming about half an hour. In January, 1889, James B. Weaver of Iowa led a famous filibuster in an effort to compel consideration of a bill organizing the Territory of Oklahoma. The defects of the existing system of congressional procedure were repeatedly demonstrated during these years and evoked widespread public criticism.

For example, on January 19, 1888, the *Washington Post,* in an editorial captioned "Slowly Doing Nothing," observed that the House had passed only four bills, none of them important, in more than six weeks, and explained that "the system of rules is the prime cause of the wonderful inertia of this unwieldy and self-shackled body. . . . In stalling legislation and keeping everybody else from doing anything a few members are all powerful, but when it comes to passing laws little can be done except by what is practically unanimous consent." In a series of editorials the *New York Tribune* attacked the rules of the House as a system of "Legislative Lunacy" and demanded their amendment as "an absolute and paramount necessity" in order "to permit the majority to control the business for which it is responsible."[16] At the close of the Fiftieth Congress the *Washington Post* denounced the "un-Democratic, un-Republican, and un-American rules of the House of Representatives which have submitted that body to a petty committee of debaters." It was time for a change and "the proper time to establish republican government is at the opening of the next session."[17] The *Post* conducted a nationwide survey of public opinion on the situation, the results of which were extremely critical of the futility, complexity, and wastefulness of House procedure.[18]

Representative Reed of Maine, the minority leader of the House who was destined to be Speaker in the Fifty-first Congress, had observed the parliamentary situation in that body with disgust and indignation. He had repeatedly expressed the view that "the rules of this House are not for the purpose of protecting the rights of the minority, but to promote the orderly conduct of the business of the House," in contrast to the Democratic doctrine, voiced by Representatives Randall and Crisp, that the object of the House rules was to protect the minority's rights from an arbitrary and despotic majority.

To the public discussion of the issue, Reed now made two important contributions. In an article on "The Rules of the House of Representatives" in the *Century Magazine* for March, 1889, he demanded a check on dilatory motions, a restoration of the "morning hour," and the establishment of majority rule in the House. And in another article on "Obstruction in the National House" in the October issue of the *North American Review,* Reed compared the situation here with that in the House of Commons in 1881 where the Irish obstructionists had forced Speaker Brand to close debate and the Commons to adopt a closure rule in 1882. Reed predicted that an effort would be made at the opening of the Fifty-first Congress "to establish rules which will facilitate the public business—rules unlike those of the present House, which only delay and frustrate action."

In the September, 1889, issue of the same *Review,* Henry Cabot Lodge dealt with the same problem. The rules had been so perverted, he said, that "the American House of Representatives today is a complete travesty upon representative government, upon popular government, and upon government by the majority." In the coming session drastic changes in the rules would be necessary in order to "change the condition of the House from dead rot to vitality. . . . The people of this country," continued Mr. Lodge, "are, as it seems to me, thoroughly tired of the stagnation of business and the general inaction of Congress. They are disgusted to see year after year go by and great measures affecting the business and political interests of the country accumulate at the doors of Congress and never reach the stage of action. They have also waked up to the fact that this impotence and stagnation are due to the preposterous fabric known as the rules of the House, and they are prepared to support heartily that party and those leaders who will break down these rules and allow the current of legislation to flow in its natural channel and at its proper rate."[19]

Dominance of the Speaker

The period 1890-1910 witnessed an inevitable reaction against the earlier decentralization of power in the House, a reaction that took the form of a tremendous growth in the power of the Speaker of the House. The period began with the elevation of Thomas B. Reed to the Speakership in 1889 and ended with a revolt against the concentration of power in that office under Speaker Cannon in 1910.

When the Fifty-first Congress convened on December 2, 1889, Reed was elected Speaker by a margin of twelve votes over Carlisle. The membership of the House then consisted of 170 Republicans and 160 Democrats. On December 3, the rules of the Fiftieth House were referred to the Committee on Rules for consideration and report. Its members were the Speaker, and Representatives McKinley, Cannon, Carlisle, and Randall. For ten weeks the House operated under general parliamentary law while the Rules Committee drafted a new code which was largely the personal work of Reed himself. On December 9, the Speaker appointed McKinley as chairman of Ways and Means and floor leader, an appointment which proved to be a major steppingstone in McKinley's progress toward the Presidency. Reed had defeated McKinley for the Republican nomination for the Speakership, but the Ohio member later triumphed over Reed in winning the Republican nomination for the Presidency. On December 21, Reed announced the other committee appointments, assigning twenty-five out of forty-nine standing committee chairmanships to the North Central states, fifteen to the Middle Atlantic states, seven to New England, one to the South, and one to the Mountain states.

The opening weeks of the session went quietly, being interrupted by the Christmas recess from December 21 to January 6. But this was only the lull before the expected storm. Several election contests were pending, and in view of the narrow Republican majority it was anticipated that the election cases would be taken up before the adoption of the rules. Everything depended upon the ability of the leadership to maintain a quorum in a chamber in which the Republicans calculated that they had only three more than the quorum of 165. The Democrats caucused on January 24, and the Republicans on January 27.

Finally the storm broke on January 29, 1890, when the West Virginia election case of *Smith* versus *Jackson* was called up and promptly challenged by Mr. Crisp, the Democratic leader. On the ensuing roll calls the Democrats, though present, declined to vote, thus causing the lack of a voting quorum. Whereupon Speaker Reed ruled that members present but not voting should be counted as part of the quorum necessary to do business and that a quorum was present within the meaning of the Constitution. This innovation precipitated a great parliamentary battle which continued for three days amid scenes of unprecedented turbulence and disorder. The Democrats, led by Carlisle and Crisp, defended the traditional practice of the House, while the Republicans, led by Cannon and McKinley, upheld the Speaker. Reed's ruling was eventually sustained by a straight party vote. During the battle, Reed also made his famous ruling that he would deny recognition to members rising to make dilatory motions. Said he: "There is no possible way by which the orderly methods of parliamentary procedure can be used to stop legislation. The object of a parliamentary body is action, and not stoppage of action. Hence, if any member or set of members undertakes to oppose the orderly progress of business, even by the use of the ordinarily recognized parliamentary motions, it is the right of the majority to refuse to have those motions entertained, and to cause the public business to proceed. . . ."[20]

Speaker Reed interpreted his victory in the great quorum battle as a verdict in favor of majority rule and party government in the House of Representatives. On February 5, the House Republicans held an extended caucus on the new code of rules that was largely Reed's own handiwork, and the next day the "Reed rules" were reported to the House. The new code revolutionized House procedure by outlawing dilatory motions, which the Speaker was forbidden to entertain, thus setting up safeguards against obstruction; by authorizing a count of members present in the hall of the House in determining the presence of a quorum; by reducing the quorum in committee of the whole to one hundred members; by authorizing that committee to close debate on any section or paragraph of a bill under consideration; and by completely revising the order of business. The House debated the new code for four days and then adopted it by a vote of 161 to 144, with twenty-three not voting. Some of the changes were lost in the Fifty-second Congress, but were restored in the Fifty-third Congress when the Democrats themselves adopted the new quorum rule.

The net effect of the Reed rules was a great increase in the powers of the Speaker. Reed ruled the House with an iron hand for six years. "He established beyond dispute the principle of party responsibility in the lower chamber. . . . As a parliamentary leader he was the greatest ever produced by the Republican party, perhaps by any party in American history."[21] He created precedents and practices that were continued by Speaker Crisp and later by Speaker Cannon when he assumed the speakership in 1903. Reed's own view of the effect of the reforms of 1890 was summed up in this statement to his own constituents:[22]

Party responsibility has begun, and with it also the responsibility of the people, for they can no longer elect a Democratic House and hope the minority will neutralize their action or a Republican House without being sure that it will keep its pledges.

If we have broken the precedents of a hundred years, we have set the precedents of another hundred years nobler than the last, wherein the people, with full knowledge that their servants can act, will choose those who will worthily carry out their will.

When Speaker Cannon succeeded to the scepter in 1903, he continued and expanded the Reed techniques until by 1909 the power of the Speaker had been extended to a quasi dictatorship. He had the power to appoint the committees of the House and to designate their chairmen. He had the unlimited power to grant or withhold recognition of members who might rise to move the consideration of bills. And as chairman of the Rules Committee he could largely determine what business the House should consider. These powers in combination were so far-reaching that "the speaker came to be considered as an officer second only in power and influence to the President of the United States himself, and so far as the enactment of legislation was concerned to exercise powers superior to his."[23]

Such was the situation in the House on the eve of the insurrection of 1909 and the revolution of 1910. Signs of insurgency had appeared, but Speaker Cannon used his great powers to penalize the rebels. For the most part these penalties consisted in unattractive committee assignments and failure to recognize the offending members. As his private secretary and biographer later wrote: "Mr. Cannon . . . believed that parties were necessary in the American form of government; that power must be entrusted to the party having the support of the majority of the voters of the country, and that without parties a democratic form of government can not exist. He had an utter contempt for the so-called Independent . . . who refused to submit to party discipline and considered his conscience a safer guide than the judgment of his associates."[24]

King Caucus Supersedes Czar Cannon

The revolution of March, 1910, that dethroned Speaker Cannon has been described elsewhere.[25] It terminated the Speaker's twenty-year reign and achieved a certain dispersion of leadership, although by and large sufficient concentration of power remained to ensure a measure of party responsibility. The underlying causes of Cannon's overthrow must be sought partly in the background of progressivism under Theodore Roosevelt and partly in the inevitable swing of the pendulum away from too much centralization of power. Cannon's leadership had grown more and more arbitrary, and the contrast between the democratic mood of the nation and his conduct as Speaker had become too pronounced to be ignored.

The major change effected was in the power of the Speaker himself. No longer was he to be a member of the Rules Committee. A new Rules Committee, composed of ten members instead of five, was elected by the House, the chairman to be chosen from this number by the committee members themselves. In actual practice this meant selection by party caucus; and within the party caucuses by a Committee on Committees of the Republicans and by the Democratic members of the Ways and Means Committee serving for that party.

During the decade 1910-1920, the party caucus functioned as the keystone in the arch of party government in the House of Representatives. Already used to choose caucus officers and to nominate party candidates for the Speakership and other House offices, the caucus during this period was also employed to consider matters of legislative policy and to define the legislative program for the session. Thus, on April 1, 1911, the Democratic *Caucus Journal* noted this resolution offered by Mr. Underwood, the floor leader: "Resolved, That the Democratic members of the various committees of the house are directed not to report to the house during the first session of the Sixty-second Congress, unless hereafter directed by this caucus, any legislation except with reference to the following matters."[26] Two years earlier, in the Sixty-first Congress, the House Democratic caucus had agreed to support the Republican insurgents in their drive to reform the House rules, to discipline those Democrats who had accepted committee assignments from Speaker Cannon without the approval of Champ Clark, the minority leader, and had adopted a set of caucus rules "or scheme of government for the Democratic party in the House, intended to define more clearly the rights and obligations of Democratic party membership, prevent such breaches of discipline as had just occurred, and thus promote unified and harmonious party action." This marked the beginning, says Berdahl, of the more formal party organization in Congress.[27]

Although the Democrats were in control of the House for eight years during this period (Sixty-second to Sixty-fifth Congresses, inclusive), the Republicans also utilized the party caucus to consider questions of organization, party loyalty, and legislative program. Thus on January 14, 1910, a White House statement was issued in which an agreement was foreshadowed "that caucuses should be held from time to time, to which all elected as Republicans should be invited, to take up the various measures recommended by the Administration as performances of party pledges, the subject of each caucus to be announced in advance." This statement was confirmed by the leaders of both the regular and progressive factions, Representative Dwight, the Republican whip, giving positive assurance that the regular Republicans were prepared to go into caucus upon any proposition and abide by the result.[28] Both factions attended a party caucus on March 23, at which the GOP's six representatives on the new Rules Committee were selected.

After capturing control of the House in the congressional elections of 1910, the Democrats promptly erected on the ruins of Cannonism a new political structure based on the secret caucus. In a caucus held on January 19, 1911, they decided that Champ Clark should be Speaker, that Oscar Underwood should be floor leader and chairman of Ways and Means, that the Democratic members of that committee should organize the House by naming its committees, that the selection of Republican committee members should be left to the determination of a majority of the minority party, that the Democratic caucus should not be open, and that their caucus should determine the attitude and legislative action of the majority.[29]

Democratic Caucus Rules

During the reign of King Caucus, the scope of caucus action was reflected in the preamble to the Democratic caucus rules, as follows:[30]

    a. In essentials of Democratic principles and doctrine, unity.
    b. In non-essentials, and in all things not involving fidelity to party principles, entire individual independence.
    c. Party alignment only upon matters of party faith or party policy.
    d. Friendly conference, and whenever reasonably possible, party cooperation.

As adopted in 1909, there were eleven House Democratic caucus rules:[31]

DEMOCRATIC CAUCUS RULES

1. All Democratic Members of the House of Representatives shall be prima facie members of the Democratic Caucus.
2. Any member of the Democratic Caucus of the House of Representatives failing to abide by the rules governing the same shall thereby automatically cease to be a member of the Caucus.
3. Meetings of the Democratic Caucus may be called by the Chairman upon his own motion and shall be called by him whenever requested in writing by twenty-five members* of the Caucus or at the request of the Party Leader.
4. A quorum of the Caucus shall consist of a majority of the Democratic Members of the House.

* Later increased to fifty.

5. General parliamentary law, with such special rules as may be adopted, shall govern the meetings of the Caucus.

6. In the election of officers and in the nomination of candidates for office in the House, a majority of those present and voting shall bind the membership of the Caucus.

7. In deciding upon action in the House involving party policy or principle, a two-thirds vote of those present and voting at a Caucus meeting shall bind all members of the Caucus: *Provided,* The said two-thirds vote is a majority of the full Democratic membership of the House: *And provided further,* That no member shall be bound upon questions involving a construction of the Constitution of the United States or upon which he made contrary pledges to his constituents prior to his election or received contrary instructions by resolutions or platform from his nominating authority.

8. Whenever any member of the Caucus shall determine, by reason of either of the exceptions provided for in the above paragraph, not to be bound by the action of the Caucus on those questions, it shall be his duty, if present, so to advise the Caucus before the adjournment of the meeting, or if not present at the meeting, to promptly notify the Democratic leader in writing, so that the party may be advised before the matter comes to issue upon the floor of the House.

9. That the five-minute rule that governs the House of Representatives shall govern debate in the Democratic Caucus, unless suspended by a vote of the Caucus.

10. No persons, except Democratic Members of the House of Representatives, a Caucus Journal Clerk, and other necessary employees, shall be admitted to the meetings of the Caucus.

11. The Caucus shall keep a journal of its proceedings, which shall be published after each meeting, and the yeas and nays on any question shall, at the desire of one-fifth of those present, be entered on the journal.

These rules indicate that members were bound to follow the party line only in a comparatively few cases and were allowed freedom of action in many instances.

Operation of the Caucus System[32]

During the Wilson administration, a strong system of party government was erected in the House of Representatives. Set up in place of Cannonism, this system was modeled upon "Aldrichism" in the Senate and was based on the party caucus. The essence of the new system was direct control of legislative action by the caucus itself. This control was effected by the caucus rules quoted above and by binding resolutions through which a majority of two-thirds of those voting at the caucus bound the Democrats in the House (except for Rule 7), and hence the action of the House itself.

For example, on April 11, 1911, the Democratic caucus adopted a resolution by Mr. Underwood, as follows:[33]

> Be it resolved, by the Democratic caucus that we endorse the bills presented by the ways and means committee . . . and pledge ourselves to support said bills in the house . . . with our votes, and to vote against all amendments, except formal committee amendments, to said bills and motions to recommit, changing their text from the language agreed upon in this caucus.

Another instrument of caucus control of legislative action was through the standing committees whose Democratic members were chosen by the majority members of Ways and Means, subject to caucus approval. The caucus often controlled the committees by forbidding reports on other than specified subjects, or by other than specified committees, without its express consent; by issuing instructions to the Rules Committee as to the terms of special rules under which bills could be taken up in the House; and even by developing legislation in the caucus itself and bringing it to the floor after formal committee reference.

Under the new regime the majority floor leader, Oscar Underwood, also emerged as a powerful figure. He derived his personal ascendancy from his control of majority committee assignments as chairman of Ways and Means, his chairmanship of the Steering Committee, and from his right to be recognized at any time on the House floor. He could use this right of recognition to determine the conduct of business in the House, subject to the right of the three privileged committees—Ways and Means, Appropriations, and Rules—to report at any time.

In addition to the party caucus and the floor leader, the Rules Committee was a major factor in the new system of party government during the period under review. Under Cannonism this committee had been a "sleeping giant." But after Cannon was dethroned and the majority floor leader succeeded to the scepter, Rules became an active power. Only by the laborious discharge petition procedure could the House force the Rules Committee to act upon any subject over which it had jurisdiction. By the exercise of its powers, Rules could function as a steering committee, steering the House in whatever direction the exigencies of the hour seemed to demand.

A contemporary observer of the caucus during this period concluded a description of its organization and operation by remarking that[34]

> the tendency of democratic government seems to be toward a system of party-responsibility; the party program is formulated by the national convention and transformed into legislative form by the congressional caucus; the party is collectively responsible. The legislative instrument of the party is represented in its most highly developed form by the Democratic caucus

of the sixty-second and sixty-third Congresses, the operation of which is based on two principles: strict party-unity on questions of essential party-policy; individual liberty in non-essentials.

This observer felt that the caucus had certain defects which could be remedied by the adoption of reforms in the House itself. And he concluded that

> once the rotten foundations of the caucus—patronage, perquisites, and "pork"—are destroyed, or, rather replaced; the sinister, throttling domination of the caucus will largely disappear of itself, and the institution may be left free to develop as a legitimate instrument of majority control and party-responsibility on the open floor of the house.

By way of summary, it can be seen that during its heyday in the House the party caucus performed the following functions. First, it chose the officers of the caucus: a chairman and a secretary. Then it nominated the party's candidates for Speaker and other elective House officers. It selected its floor leader and its Committee on Committees and approved their slate of committee assignments. It considered proposed amendments of the House rules and, occasionally, questions of legislative policy. It elected the party campaign committee and considered matters of Capitol patronage. It was also used by the leadership to test the temper of the House, to "gauge the relative strength of different opinions."[35] In performing these functions the Democratic caucus did not run itself. It was controlled by its own majority which was dominated in turn by the floor leader (Underwood), backed by his power over committee appointments. When necessary the power of the floor leader was reinforced by the other two members of the caucus cabinet: the Speaker (Clark), with the prestige of his position, and the chairman of the Appropriations Committee (Fitzgerald), with his hands upon the purse strings.

Developments During the 1920's

As regards party organization in the House of Representatives, the intervening years have been characterized by certain long-range tendencies and have witnessed several significant developments. Between the two World Wars, the party caucus disintegrated, party discipline declined, and party government was replaced by loose coalitions of voting blocs with shifting leadership. Attempts to bind the party membership to vote for measures designed to carry out platform pledges were rarely made by House Democrats and never by the Republicans. These trends reflected the growing diversity of interests in a pluralistic society, the emergence of deeply divisive political issues, such as civil rights, isolationism versus internationalism, and the extent of the "welfare state," the force of localism in American politics, and the decentralized, compromise character of our national parties constructed, as they are, of loose alliances of strong state and local parties.

The decade of the 1920's was marked by the diffusion of leadership in the House among a numerous group of men. The inner circle came to include the Speaker; the floor leader; the chairmen of Rules, Appropriations, and Ways and Means; the chairman and secretary of the party caucus; and the members of the Steering Committee and the Committee on Committees, which were enlarged. This tendency toward the dilution of leadership was reflected in a ruling of the Republican caucus in 1919 that no chairman of a major House committee should sit on their Steering Committee, and in a Republican caucus rule of 1925 that no chairman of a House committee should also serve on the Rules Committee. The development in the same period of "exclusive" committees, whose members were limited to one committee assignment, a practice approved by both party caucuses, illustrated the same trend.[36] On the other hand, the removal of the floor leaders from service on the standing committees of the House helped to strengthen leadership by relieving them from other distractions and giving them time to function as leaders.

Several other developments during the 1920's also affected the distribution of political power in the House. A series of rulings by the Speaker, overruling points of order raised against specific resolutions reported by the Rules Committee, served to clarify the scope of its powers and to expand its jurisdiction. In 1920 the chair ruled that although the "Committee on Rules is not permitted to do anything which directly dispenses with Calendar Wednesday or the motion to recommit . . . it can bring in a general rule . . . which indirectly produces that result as a minor part of its operation."[37] In the same year Speaker Gillett ruled that "the Committee on Rules may report a resolution providing for the consideration of a bill which has not yet been introduced."[38] Another ruling in 1922 held that the Committee on Rules could originate a resolution for the consideration of a bill regardless of whether the subject matter had been referred to it by the House, "because the Committee on Rules is the executive organ of the majority of the House."[39] And in 1933, Speaker Rainey held that the Rules Committee could report a resolution authorizing consideration of a bill on which suspension of the rules had been denied by the House.[40]

Abuses of the powers of this committee led to the adoption of two restrictions in the rules revision of 1924. One provision sought to protect the House from "snap" tactics by providing that the Rules Committee could not call up a report on the same day on which it was presented, except by a two-thirds vote of the House, unless during the last three days of a session. The other restriction was designed to prevent the chairman of Rules from defeating the will of his committee by the "pocket veto" method. In the early twenties Chairman Campbell had abused his discretion by pocketing several resolutions which his committee had authorized him to report several weeks before. When Mr. Campbell took this means to suppress an investigation of contracts by the Departments of Justice, War, and Navy in 1922, there were loud complaints, to which Mr. Campbell replied: "Even though every Member wants this investigation, what will that avail you? I have the resolution in my pocket and shall keep it there." And to the Committee on Rules his language was even stronger. "You can go to . . . ," he said; "it makes no difference what a majority of you decide; if it meets with my disapproval, it shall not be done; I am the Committee; in me reposes absolute obstructive powers."[41] Campbell's right to bury the resolution in his pocket was upheld by the Speaker and, on appeal, by the House. As a result of these and other instances of the exercise of autocratic power by the chairman of Rules, the House amended its rules in 1924 by adding the following paragraph:[42]

> The Committee on Rules shall present to the House reports concerning rules, joint rules, and order of business, within three legislative days of the time when ordered reported by the committee. If such rule of order is not considered immediately, it shall be referred to the calendar and, if not called up by the Member making the report within nine days thereafter, any Member designated by the committee may call it up for consideration.

As later amended, this rule now provides that if the rule is not called up by the member making the report within seven legislative days, "any member of the Rules Committee may call it up as a question of privilege and the Speaker shall recognize any member of the Rules Committee seeking recognition for that purpose."[43]

Dissatisfaction with the Rules Committee during the 1920's also led to a noteworthy amendment of the discharge rule in January, 1924. The question was whether access to the House floor should be completely controlled by the majority party leadership or whether a bipartisan coalition could override the leadership and get its bill considered, i.e., whether a majority of the House could work its will. As amended on January 18, 1924, the discharge rule, first adopted in 1910, was changed in several respects of which the most important concerned the number of signatures required on discharge petitions. Mr. Crisp of Georgia favored 100 signatures as sufficient to bring a discharge motion before the House; Mr. Fish of New York favored a majority of the whole House, or 218. The number was fixed at

150 in 1924. The discharge rule of 1924 was another step in the long struggle to strike a balance between centralized leadership and majority rule in the House of Representatives.[44]

In 1925, Mr. Longworth of Ohio, the Republican floor leader who was elected Speaker at the opening of the Sixty-ninth Congress, raised the question of the party status of some thirteen Republican insurgents who had supported La Follette for President in 1924. The bolters should be disciplined, he thought, for deserting the Republican party in the presidential election. Ten of the insurgents were from Wisconsin, and their leaders, Representatives Frear and Nelson, were ousted from their seats on the Ways and Means Committee and the Rules Committee respectively before the new House met in December, 1925. Discipline of the other insurgents would depend, Longworth indicated, upon how they voted on the Speakership and on restoring the strict discharge rule. When the insurgents failed to satisfy these acid tests of sound Republicanism, holding instead their own caucus and voting again for Cooper for Speaker and against the discharge rule, they were excluded from the Republican party caucuses and demoted on their committees to the bottom of the list. Later on, however, on the eve of the organization of the Seventieth Congress, the insurgents were restored to their party councils.[45]

When Nicholas Longworth became Speaker of the House in 1925, he affirmed his faith in the principles of party responsibility and set forth his conception of the role of the chair as party leader. "I believe it to be the duty of the Speaker," he said on assuming his new office, "standing squarely on the platform of his party, to assist in so far as he properly can the enactment of legislation in accordance with the declared principles and policies of his party and by the same token to resist the enactment of legislation in violation thereof."[46] In some quarters these remarks evoked shades of Cannonism; in others they elicited praise as promising a return to effective party leadership.

Development During the 1930's

Several developments during the decade of the 1930's bearing upon party government in the House of Representatives are worth noting.

The first of these in point of time was the adoption of the "Lame Duck" Amendment to the Constitution. Ratified in 1933 when the thirty-sixth state approved it, the Twentieth Amendment eliminated the short session of Congress which ended automatically on March 4. The House leadership had long liked the short session because it facilitated their control of business and helped them to prevent the consideration or passage of bills they opposed. The amending resolution had passed the Senate three times during the 1920's and had been pigeonholed in the House Rules Committee each time. Finally, the spur of public opinion forced the amendment to the House floor where Representative Snell, chairman of Rules, remarked:[47]

> If it had not been for the significant application of these two words, lame duck, the propaganda that has been spread throughout this country would never have been one-half as effective as it has been, and if it had not been for that propaganda I doubt whether this proposition would be on the floor at this time.

And Representative Kvale observed:[48]

> We have waited . . . for eight long years for a chance to vote on this resolution . . . the leadership of the House has denied us the opportunity to express our opinion and our vote on the subject. . . . Three men, the Speaker of the House and the majority floor leader and the chairman of the Committee on Rules . . . have prevented this House from having a chance to vote on this proposition all these years . . . [but] they did not dare block it any longer.

The ratification of the "Lame Duck" Amendment in January, 1933, was regarded as a victory over the House leadership by those members who were seeking to democratize control of the chamber.

A second development came in March, 1933, when the House Democrats set up a Steering Committee and assigned it the responsibility of watching legislative developments and making day-to-day decisions on party policy and action. This committee was composed of: the Speaker; floor leader; chairman of the caucus; party whip; the chairmen of Ways and Means, Appropriations, and Rules; and one representative from each of the fifteen zones into which the country was divided for party purposes, each such representative being elected by the Democratic delegation in the House from the zone. The committee elected its own chairman, vice chairman, and secretary, and co-operated with the party leaders in the planning and execution of party policy. Although this Steering Committee occasionally played an influential role in the early days of the New Deal, as when it induced the party to adopt the bill to guarantee bank deposits in 1934, it later fell into disuse and virtually disappeared from the political scene until its re-emergence as the Steering and Policy Committee in the Ninety-third Congress.

The role of the Rules Committee as agent of the majority party during the first Roosevelt administration is also noteworthy. During this period that committee used its broad powers to facilitate the achievement of the desires of the Democratic leadership in the House and the enactment of the administration's legislative program. Thus, in the Seventy-third Congress (1933-1934), almost all the economic recovery measures of the New Deal reached the House floor under closed rules restricting debate and amendments. Chairman Bankhead of Alabama justified this procedure, stating that "the Committee on Rules is the political and policy vehicle of the House of Representatives to effectuate the party program and the party policy."

Many of the most crucial tests of party loyalty took place on the votes to accept or reject the special rules reported by the Committee on Rules for the consideration of the legislative measures of the administration. Closed rules were used ten times during the first session and twice during the second session of the Seventy-third Congress. The House leadership justified their use on grounds of the emergency conditions of the times, the necessity of protecting the coherence of complex bills from confusing amendments, and the requirements of party control over the legislative program. All but one of the closed rules proposed during the Seventy-third Congress were accepted by the House. This record led Lewis Lapham to conclude that "in the Seventy-third Congress it appears to be a valid conclusion that a sympathetic and cooperative Rules Committee was an instrument by which the leadership of the House exercised a measure of control over the proceedings of the House and the content of legislative measures. . . . The Rules Committee in the Seventy-third Congress operated very definitely as an arm of the leadership and the House generally approved that kind of working relationship."[49]

During the Seventy-fourth Congress, the Rules Committee played a less active role in the management of the business of the House, reporting only three closed rules during 1935-1936, all of which were approved. The role of the Rules Committee in 1935 was explained to the House by its chairman, Representative O'Connor, as follows:[50]

> To some of you new members I might state in advance that the Rules Committee is an arm of the leadership of this House. It is sometimes called an "arm" of the administration in power in the Nation. Some people have also referred to it as the "political committee," or the committee which shapes or brings before the House the policies of the leadership of the House and the administration.

It is interesting to note that the Rules Committee was then regarded as the agent of both the House majority leadership and the administration. Doubtless it was with a view to strengthening party responsibility, as well as to protecting members from the pressures of organized interest groups, that the discharge rule was again amended in 1935 by increasing the number of signatures required on discharge petitions from 145 to 218.

Coalition Control: 1937-1946

During the decade 1937-1946, party government in the House of Representatives was seriously impaired by changes that occurred in the composition and tactics of the Committee on Rules. Instead of acting in the traditional manner as the responsible agent of the majority party and its leadership, the Rules Committee came under the control of a bipartisan coalition of Southern Democrats and North Central Republicans who used its power to block measures favored by the majority party and the administration. After the Seventy-fourth Congress, this coalition controlled well over half the seats on the Rules Committee, as the table shows:

PARTY COMPOSITION OF RULES COMMITTEE

Congress	Republicans	Southern Democrats	Northern Democrats	Total
75th	4	5	5	14
76th	4	5	5	14
77th	4	6*	4	14
78th	5	6*	3	14
79th	4	4	4†	12

* Includes one from Oklahoma.
† Includes one from Kentucky and one from Missouri.

During this period the Rules Committee repeatedly framed rules designed to facilitate its own views of public policy rather than those of the House leadership and the Roosevelt administration by including special provisions in its resolutions granting a "green light" for bills to the floor of the House. The coalition in control of the committee also repeatedly used its powers to obstruct and dilute important measures in the majority party program. Thus, as the decade advanced, this powerful committee became an instrument, not of the majority party and its legislative program, but of a bipartisan majority in the House. Upon occasion, remarked a close student of its activities, members of the Rules Committee "asserted a power independent of any party and almost without responsibility to any political institution."[51]

Domestic labor and public welfare legislation designed to implement Democratic platform planks, such as the Wage and Hour Bill, were pigeonholed in the Rules Committee. Chairman Sabath could not control his own committee whose turbulent meetings witnessed recurring battles between the veteran chairman from Illinois and Representative Cox of Georgia, ranking Democratic member and leader of the coalition. Only the influence of Speaker Rayburn was able to restrain the conflicts between these men.

During the Seventy-sixth Congress, the Rules Committee opposed the majority leadership, not by denying major bills access to the House floor, but by making their admission depend upon its own terms that were often distasteful to the leadership. During the early years of World War II (1941-1942) the split in the Democratic party in Congress was partly smoothed over as the legislature concentrated on defense and war legislation, while the Rules Committee for the most part co-operated with the desires of the majority party leadership and the President.

During the Seventy-eighth Congress, however, when the party division in the House was very close, the bipartisan coalition frequently succeeded in controlling the fate of legislation. And much of the success of the coalition was attributed to its ability to adapt the rules of the House to its own advantage through its control of the Committee on Rules.[52] After citing several examples of rules granted during the Seventy-eighth Congress that were deemed objectionable to the Democratic majority, Lapham concludes that "in each case the majority leadership and the administration could not look to the Rules Committee for action which would assist them in the promotion of the Democratic program or in avoiding outright defeat by coalition forces."[53]

During the Seventy-ninth Congress, the coalition consolidated its control of the legislative process in the House. Lapham summed up the situation when the first session convened:[54]

> It is clear that by 1945 the Rules Committee was exercising an increasingly influential role in the development of legislative policy on many of the domestic issues before Congress. Furthermore, this power was exercised in many cases independent of the organized leadership and frequently in opposition to its efforts. The instances in which the Committee facilitated the exercise of responsibility by the leadership or refrained from obstructing it had become almost a matter for comment.

By this time it had become a custom for the committee to examine the substance of bills reported by the legislative committees of the House and to use its powers to force them to amend their bills as the price of getting a "green light" to the House floor. In one instance a rule was reported that would have made it in order to consider a price-control bill which had been rejected by the Banking and Currency Committee and had never been reported to the House. This time the House evidently felt that the Rules Committee had gone too far, for it rejected the rule after Speaker Rayburn took the floor and attacked the proposed rule. The Speaker asserted that the Committee on Rules "was never set up to be a legislative committee."

If the issue were settled right, he said, there would be "an end to the trespassing of one committee in the House upon the rights, prerogatives, and privileges of other committees."[55]

In another notable instance, after the Senate had passed the Full Employment Bill of 1946, the House Rules Committee granted a rule allowing the weaker House bill to be substituted for the Senate bill. This and other episodes led Lapham to conclude that "the Rules Committee was simply not at the service of the majority party to assist it in enacting into law the kinds of programs to which it was committed as a party."[56]

While the Committee on Rules failed to function during the decade under review as the responsible instrument of majority party government in the House of Representatives, nevertheless it apparently did faithfully reflect majority sentiment in the House. The rules it granted or denied were calculated to facilitate the expression of the will of a bipartisan majority in the House, which may or may not have reflected majority sentiment in the country, while obstructing adoption of the program of the majority party. The experience of these eventful years raises the fundamental question: Should the Committee on Rules function as the agent of the majority party in the House so as to enable that party to carry out its platform pledges to the American people; or should it function as the instrument of a bipartisan coalition which can control a majority of the votes in the House? This question goes to the roots of our two-party system of government.

It is interesting to recall that during the Seventy-sixth Congress the Democratic party in the House of Representatives held two party caucuses to deal with the problem presented by coalition control of legislative action. At the first meeting, held on February 14, 1939, the Democratic leaders, including Speaker Bankhead, Floor Leader Rayburn, and John McCormack of Massachusetts, chairman of the caucus, treated the problem as one of absenteeism rather than as a split in the party, urged members to co-operate with the administration, and threatened, if necessary, "to crack the whip to compel Democratic members to attend the sessions." When these efforts failed, a second caucus was held on July 28, 1939, at which a resolution was adopted which in effect censured the dissident Democrats who had failed to support the New Deal program and pledged the party in the House to continued support of the Roosevelt program.[57]

The reappearance of coalitions in Congress after World War II led observers to comment upon "the looseness of party lines" and the "rather meaningless pattern of our so-called two-party system" and to speculate about the need for a political realignment. "Until the major parties are realigned," wrote Arthur Krock, "and two parties are formed in each of which there is a common set of political views and principles, these occasional combinations will appear in the House, as they also have in the

Senate. There is both oil and water in the bottle that bears the label 'Demo-crats,' and attempts to mix them will be less and less successful as the cata-lyst of war disappears."[58]

Professor Clarence A. Berdahl of the University of Illinois, a lifelong student of American politics, completed a 1949 study of party membership in Congress by expressing his belief that the solution of the problem of party government would be found in "the development of a more genuine and meaningful party system, with fairly precise criteria of party member-ship, with more closely knit party organizations in Congress, with the House and Senate parties more closely tied together and both closely re-lated to the respective national party organizations, with a keener sense of responsibility as a party, and with a better system of party discipline to keep members mindful of the party position on legislative problems and of their obligations as members of a responsible party group."[59]

Later Developments

A number of significant developments over a period of nearly thirty years merit attention. First was the recommendation for the creation of party pol-icy committees in both houses, made in the 1946 report of the Joint Com-mittee on the Organization of Congress. "Strong recommendations were made to your committee," said the report, "concerning the need for the for-mal expression within the Congress of the main policies of the majority and minority parties. These representations called for some mechanism which could bring about more party accountability for policies and pledges an-nounced and made in the national platforms of the major political parties." While provisions for policy committees were in the version of the Legisla-tive Reorganization Act of 1946, which passed the Senate, the opposition of House leaders, including Speaker Rayburn, prevented their inclusion in the act.

In January, 1949, the Republican party in the House converted its steer-ing committee, which had been in existence since the Sixty-sixth Congress, into a policy committee. According to the resolution creating it:

> The Republican Policy Committee shall be an advisory committee to the leadership, and to the Republican membership of this House, and as such will meet prior to any important action on the Floor, and shall discuss these issues with members of the regular and special committees handling the bills, and with such other Republican members as the Floor Leader may invite to the meetings, and shall report its suggestions for Republican action and policy to the House Members, at a Conference of all Republican mem-

bers, or through the Whip organization, or shall report its failure to determine a policy; and until such determination is made by the Policy Committee, no announcements and no publicity regarding policy shall have any official significance. No Republican Member of Congress shall be bound by the decisions of this Policy Committee, but its suggestions should guide the minority to a firmer national policy. . . . No issue of major importance affecting national Republican policy shall be brought to the Floor of the House with the consent of the Republican leadership until after a Republican conference has been held, with adequate time for a full discussion of the subject; and the Chairman of this Conference shall see to it that time is provided members capable of presenting the various viewpoints on the issue. In addition, time should be arranged, under a shorter time rule if necessary, for comments and suggestions from other members. So far as possible, these conferences of the entire Republican membership shall be held sufficiently in advance of Floor action to permit the new Policy Committee to function on the basis of the information secured from the full Conference, and to report its policy suggestions to the membership.

We have already noted the present structure of the House Republican Policy Committee. It should also be pointed out that in 1961 the Policy Committee appointed a Subcommittee on Special Projects, which in 1965 became the Committee on Planning and Research. Both committees were staffed and issued position papers on many issues.[60] Writing in 1970, Charles O. Jones stated:

> The organizational changes in the House Republican Party since 1959 are the most important developments in the role of the minority party in policy making in this century. By certain subjective measures of what party reformers think the minority party should be, these efforts may seem feeble, halting first steps. But by comparison to the organization, leadership, and actions of congressional minority parties in this century, the efforts are remarkably innovative.[61]

According to the resolution adopted by the Republican Conference for the Ninety-fourth Congress, the Committee on Research has seventeen members, including all of the party's leaders. The remaining members are selected by the leaders, subject to conference approval. After consulting with the ranking members of the standing committees, the leadership may appoint task forces. In 1975, task forces were established on economic reforms, antitrust and regulations reforms, energy and environmental problems, elections and Congressional reforms, and health policy. Essentially the task forces supplied background position papers for their colleagues.

During the Eightieth Congress (1947-1948), the Committee on Rules returned to its traditional role as agent of the majority party, this time the Republican party, which was back in power in the House after sixteen

years in the wilderness. In sharp contrast to its conduct during the preceding decade, the committee now co-operated with the party leaders to
promote the majority party program and to translate its campaign pledges
into legislative action. Just as the Democrats in the Seventy-third Congress
had relied on closed rules to avoid internal dissension and expedite passage
of their measures, so now in the Eightieth Congress the Republicans did
likewise. The Rules Committee reported nine closed rules during the bien-
nium: five in the first session, and four in the second. It also made frequent
use of the rule waiving points of order on appropriation bills in order to
clear the way for the elimination of "wasteful" governmental bureaus and
functions. The committee also long tabled rules for the consideration of
bills for American membership in the World Health Organization and for
Selective Service, only releasing the WHO bill upon the receipt of a directive so to do from the Republican Steering Committee and only then after
securing restrictive amendments as its price for clearance. The Rules Committee also successfully pigeonholed the UMT Bill and the O'Mahoney-
Kefauver Bill prohibiting the purchase of assets of competitors. After reviewing its performance during the Eightieth Congress, Dr. Lapham
concluded:[62]

> Although the Rules Committee took a lot of abuse during the Eightieth
> Congress, the record is pretty clear that the House leadership, including the
> Speaker, Majority leader, Majority whip, and the Republican Steering Com-
> mittee, could get a bill out of the Rules Committee if it wanted to badly
> enough, although occasionally some face-saving was necessary in the form
> of amendments. . . .

The most exciting development of recent years in this field was the fight
that led to the adoption of the so-called twenty-one-day rule in 1949 and
to its repeal in 1951. The highlights of this struggle have already been described in Chapter 5. It will be recalled that under this rule, which was
adopted by the House on January 3, 1949, the chairman of a legislative
committee reporting a bill and requesting a special rule for its consideration could request recognition for the purpose of calling it up if it had been
adversely reported by the Rules Committee or if that committee had failed
to report the rule for twenty-one calendar days after reference. It was in
order to call up such special resolutions on the second and fourth Mondays
of each month, and it was provided that the Speaker "shall recognize the
Member seeking recognition for the purpose. . . ." In practice, however,
if more than one chairman sought recognition under the rule, the Speaker
could exercise discretion as to whom he would recognize.

The twenty-one-day rule, which was in effect during the Eighty-first
Congress, was thrice the subject of bitter debate in the House: first, at the

time of its adoption in 1949; second, when an effort to repeal it failed on January 20, 1950; and third, when it was repealed on January 3, 1951. The first debate indicated that the new rule was not designed by its framers to strengthen party government in the House, but was conceived rather as a device to deal with a specific situation, i.e., the alleged "dictatorship of the Rules Committee." The second debate, in 1950, was more closely addressed to the problem of majority party responsibility for mangement of the business of the House and control of the legislative program than the 1949 debate had been. And a few of the debaters in 1951 considered the effects of the twenty-one-day rule on the exercise of responsible leadership in the House. But the rationale of responsible party government in Congress and the proper role of the several party agencies in the House of Representatives were never fully spelled out in these debates.

All told, some eight measures reached the House floor and were passed during the Eighty-first Congress by invoking the twenty-one-day rule, while the threat of its use forced the Rules Committee to grant clearance to a few other bills. But no major measures in the majority party program were actually taken up under this procedure. Several reasons were advanced for such limited use of the new device: the prestige of the Rules Committee based on a long tradition, fear of retaliation if it were thwarted, the feeling that the new rule should be reserved for use in emergencies, the disinclination of the leadership to develop its potentialities, their desire that certain bills should not be called up, and the availability of other routes to the floor, e.g., via suspension of the rules and Calendar Wednesday.[63]

Insofar as the Rules Committee is concerned, the situation following the repeal of the twenty-one-day rule in 1951 reverted substantially to what it had been prior to the adoption of the rule in 1949. In both foreign and domestic affairs, the majority party official leadership and some committee chairmen were often at odds with the majority members of the Rules Committee, except during the first Eisenhower Congress, with the result that a bipartisan coalition on the committee continued to exercise a strong influence on legislation. Meanwhile party leadership in Congress and in the country at large has been the subject of lively public discussion and debate during the past two decades.[64]

At the opening of the Eighty-sixth Congress in January, 1959, a group of Democratic liberals in the House contemplated a move to curb the Rules Committee by changing its party ratio and by reviving the twenty-one-day rule. After a conference with the Speaker, however, the liberals called off their drive and issued a joint statement saying: "We have received assurances from Speaker Rayburn that legislation which has been duly considered and reported by legislative committees will be brought before the House for consideration within a reasonable period of time. Our confidence in the Speaker is great, and we believe he will support such procedural steps as may become necessary to obtain House consideration of reported bills from legislative committees." Despite these assurances, the Rules Committee in 1959 and again in 1960 was criticized for keeping legislation from the House floor. Eventually, however, most of the major bills reported by House committees during the Eighty-sixth Congress reached the floor of the House either by action of the Rules Committee or by the rarely used Calendar Wednesday route.[65]

As the Eighty-seventh Congress approached, it became evident that enactment of President Kennedy's legislative program would hinge upon overcoming the conservative coalition's control of the Rules Committee. All signs indicated that a determined effort would be made, when the House met in January, 1961, either to curb the powers of the committee or to change its composition so as to enable the House to work its will on such Kennedy measures as medical aid to the aged under Social Security, a minimum-wage increase, federal aid to education, and a housing bill. Liberal and conservative forces in Congress and the country girded their loins for the impending test of strength.

On one side was the Democratic Study Group composed of a hundred or more liberal Democrats, led by Representatives Chet Holifield of California and Frank Thompson of New Jersey. On the other side was Representative Howard W. Smith of Virginia, powerful chairman of the Rules Committee, the Republican leaders of the House, and many influential Southern Democratic Congressmen. Speaker Rayburn kept his own counsel until the eve of the session when he came out on the side of the reformers with a plan to enlarge the membership of the Rules Committee from twelve to fifteen. His plan called for increasing the number of committee Democrats from eight to ten, and of Republicans from four to five, thus giving the liberal leadership a close eight-to-seven control of the committee.

The issue hung fire for several weeks while the leadership of both parties, the Kennedy administration, and lobby groups brought intense pressures to bear on House members. Finally, on January 31, four weeks after Congress convened, the House approved the Rayburn plan by the close and crucial vote of 217 to 212. Voting for expansion were 195 Democrats and 22 Republicans; against it were 64 Democrats and 148 Republicans. Southern Democrats divided 63 against and 47 for the resolution. Speaker Rayburn rejected last-minute efforts at compromise. Taking the House floor in one of his rare appearances, he said the issue was simple: the nation had elected a new President who had programs he considered vital to the country's welfare and the whole House should have an opportunity to vote on them. The split in the Democratic vote on enlarging the Rules Committee presumably indicates why the Democratic caucus could not be effective in the preceding two decades, especially when dissident members held most of the committee chairmanships.

Subsequently Representatives Carl Elliott of Alabama and B. F. Sisk of California were appointed to fill the two new Democratic seats on the Rules Committee; while the Republicans named Representatives Katharine St. George of New York, Elmer J. Hoffman of Illinois, and H. Allen Smith of California to fill their two vacancies and one new place on the committee. After Carroll Reece, second-ranking minority member of the Rules Committee, died on March 9, 1961, he was replaced by William H. Avery of Kansas.

Behind the scenes a key role in the recapture by Speaker Rayburn of the House Rules Committee was played by one of its Democratic members— Richard Bolling of Missouri. As described by a close observer, Bolling "is an occupational, professional anticipator of difficulties; a smoother-out of ruffled feelings; an estimator of the human weaknesses and strengths of other Democrats; a worker of small and sometimes large miracles. . . ."[66] In the 1961 struggle over control of the Rules Committee, he was "a kind of unsung field commander in a great war between the generalissimos, Mr. Sam and old 'Judge' Howard Smith of Virginia. . . ."

There have been occasions since the 1961 struggle when the Rules Committee has been accused of obstructionist tactics. But it is noteworthy that the committee has also been charged with allowing a considerable amount of legislation to go to the floor when further delay might have assisted the proposals. A *Congressional Quarterly* study showed that in 1973 the House rejected thirteen rules approved by the committee, compared to only fifty rejections from 1929 through 1972. Certainly it is possible to suggest that the full House may have been more conservative than the Rules Committee.[67]

The rule changes adopted by the Democratic caucus since 1972 also have great significance for the future of the Rules Committee. One rule allows the Speaker to name the chairman and all the other members of the committee, subject to caucus approval. Another, in effect, allows a majority of the caucus to direct the committee to allow a floor vote on "a particular germane amendment." All of this means that it should be easier in the future to equate the actions of the Rules Committee with the desires of the party or its leadership.

Revival of the Democratic Caucus

We have already noted the apparent reincarnation of the Democratic caucus as a formidable instrument of party policy. Almost dormant for fifty years, the caucus in 1974 rejected three committee chairmen. Its present rules call for monthly meetings when the House is in session and permit meetings to be called upon the request of any fifty members.

In addition to the changes in procedure and the selection of committee chairmen, the caucus engaged in two actions in 1975 that once again raised fundamental questions about the relationship of the member to his party as well as the relationship of the committee system to the caucus.[68] On February 25, the Democratic caucus voted to allow two amendments to a tax-cut bill to go to the floor. The amendment offered by Representative William J. Green of Pennsylvania would have eliminated the oil-depletion allowance; a second amendment by Representative Charles Wilson of Texas would have restricted the use of the oil-depletion allowance. In 1974 Chairman Wilbur D. Mills of the Ways and Means Committee had defied a similar action by the caucus on the grounds that the committee had voted to request a closed rule that would bar any amendments. In 1975, however, the Rules Committee sent the two amendments to the floor.

Whether the action of the caucus was merely procedural or whether it was a policy decision on the oil-depletion allowance made by the party in caucus was a matter of considerable conjecture. Presumably the full House was being given a choice between two approaches to the question, although it would be difficult to suggest that they were the only two ways to go at the problem or that the timing was most appropriate. Representative Green put the matter as follows, "In the case of my amendment, the Rules Committee was instructed merely to make it in order, and the substantive issue of depletion was technically not before the Committee, although many of the individual members saw fit to raise substantive questions." In other words, insofar as the caucus voted to instruct the Rules Committee to submit two amendments to the floor, it raised substantive policy questions in the minds of many members because they were taking positions on matters which were customarily before a standing committee.

That issue was posed even more clearly on March 12, 1975, when the Democratic caucus voted overwhelmingly in support of a resolution offered by Representative Bob Carr of Michigan which opposed any further military assistance to South Vietnam or Cambodia during the 1975 fiscal year. The next day the House International Relations Committee was scheduled to consider a presidential request for funds but adjourned without acting. Presumably the action of the caucus had been so definitive that any other recommendation by the committee would have been futile. Representative David R. Obey of Wisconsin noted that the caucus action compelled the members to examine more thoughtfully the exact role of the caucus. It is one thing to use the caucus to settle intra-party leadership problems, such as the "firing" of committee chairmen who have either abused their prerogatives or have thwarted the policy preferences of the majority of the party. In such instances, it is possible to articulate a position which holds that insofar as the caucus has selected the leaders, they are agents of the caucus and are responsible to it. It is the next step that becomes more complicated. If the caucus is too casual about voting on major policy questions, then it is running counter to one of the most unique characteristics of the Congress—the specialization of its legislative committees.

There are additional problems. If the caucus does adopt a position on a policy question, the likelihood is that it cannot force the members to follow that policy. The caucus rules contain escape hatches for the members, and in the real world the leadership simply does not have the incentive or the sanctions to deal with such a problem. The House tradition does not equate disagreement with mutiny. If the caucus persists in taking policy stands and they are not sustained by the full membership on the floor, then the party itself loses stature. One result would be that party members would even boycott caucus meetings.

In the case of the Carr resolution, Representative Obey and several other members who had been active in earlier attempts to strengthen the caucus believed that the substantive issue should have been discussed in the more deliberative atmosphere of the Steering and Policy Committee, which has only 24 members, rather than a caucus of about 290 people. Their position was that the Carr resolution could have been the basis for achieving consensus on an issue and then could have been discussed more profitably by the caucus.

The Carr resolution did have the effect of cutting off further aid to Indochina. But it also set in motion considerable criticism. The Republicans spoke about the return of King Caucus and the possibility that the House could be run by votes from a party caucus that might only be half a quorum of that caucus plus one. The likelihood is that the Democratic caucus will hesitate to re-enact an incident comparable to the Carr resolution; one Democratic staff member who had been an architect of the strengthened caucus labeled its action on Indochina aid as an attempt by the freshmen to "have some kicks." If the caucus does undertake specific policy questions, they will be considered only after clear evidence has been shown that the party's leadership and an overwhelming majority of the members are convinced that the regular channels of deliberation have been found wanting.

By September, 1975, criticisms of caucus actions by Democrats led to the adoption of a new rule which opened virtually all caucuses to the public and to the repeal of an old rule which allowed the caucus, in rare circumstances, to bind its members on policy questions. The caucus also voted to require five-days notice prior to meetings. It was hard to believe that the furtive reappearance of "King Caucus," a mirage at best, could long survive the new rules of the game.

Role of the Opposition Party

During the latter part of the nineteenth century, public policy in America emerged typically from legislative leadership and from acts formulated in the halls of Congress and the state legislatures. During the twentieth century, prior to World War II, with the growing development of powerful interest groups in a pluralistic society, public policy was increasingly generated in separate centers of power as a result of the interplay of pressure groups, their legislative spokesmen, and administrative agents. Congressional committees came to be composed in large part of spokesmen for organized interests in various sections of the country, and administrative agencies likewise had their sectional clientele among the groups whose pressures had influenced their establishment. Thus "the trilogy of the pressure group, the agency, and the appropriate congressional committee" gave rise to a pattern of public policy formation that Ernest Griffith has aptly described as "government by whirlpools."

As the mid-century approached, group conflicts combined with the demands of depression, the dangers of war, and recurring international crises to shift the leadership in public policy formation from Congress to the Executive, as the times called for quick decisions, continuous intervention, and administrative adjustment of the national economy. Regulatory boards and commissions were set up by the Congress in growing number to regulate and supervise the various forms of transport and communication, public utilities, monetary policy, federal trade, labor relations, security exchanges, and other important segments of our economic life.

After World War II, the Executive continued to dominate the field of policy determination and "government by whirlpools" continued. "Pressure politicians" inside Congress collaborated closely with the legislative agents of organized groups in the country and with likeminded administrators in the administrative agencies of the federal government to protect and advance their mutual special interests. Congressmen were more susceptible perhaps than the President to the pressures of organized minorities because of the different manner in which they are elected. Legislators are chosen in local elections on local issues, the President in a national election on national issues.

As the decade of the 1950's advanced, Congress reasserted its role in the formulation of public policy and showed promise of arresting the long-run trend toward executive leadership in policy formation. This shift seemed to be due to a variety of factors, including the division of the government between opposing parties, the apparent vacuum of leadership in the White

House, the reorganization of Congress in 1946 and the streamlining of its committee structure, equipped with new professional staff aids and assisted by overall policy committees. Thus policy formation became the product of the interplay of legislators, administrators, and lobbyists acting under the apprehensive impact of a growing foreign menace on the threshold of the Space Age.

It is in this political and historical framework that we have now to consider the modern role of the opposition party in policy formation.

The job of the opposition is at least fourfold. First, perhaps its most important function is to provide an alternative slate of party leaders who can replace the party in power in the White House and in the leadership posts on Capitol Hill in Washington. Democracy could not function without an opposition party to which the voters can turn at all levels of American government when they are dissatisfied with the party in power. In totalitarian countries with single-party systems, the voters have no real choice and general elections are a farce. Under our inflexible system of biennial and quadrennial elections, the chance to change the government peacefully occurs, of course, only at fixed calendar intervals, unlike the arrangement in parliamentary democracies like Britain where the government of the day can be displaced at any time and where a "Shadow Cabinet" is waiting on the Front Bench on the opposition side to take over. But in America we can always "kick the rascals out" every two or four years and install a new President in the White House and a new leadership in Congress.

The second function of the opposition party is to watch and criticize the majority party, to inspect and review the way in which it is conducting the government, to point out its errors, and to expose its misdeeds. In the classic phrase, "It is the duty of the Opposition to oppose." Such opposition should not be blind and irresponsible, especially in days of national danger. The opposition must be responsible and constructive, reflecting the principles of the minority party and the attitude of public opinion. Under our system of separated powers this "oversight" function, as we call it, is largely performed by the Congress through its committees and individual members. In a real sense, especially in a divided-government situation, Congress is itself the opposition to the Executive. By subjecting the administration to public scrutiny, the opposition is able not only to turn the spotlight on its sins of commission and omission, but also to inform the country about the conduct of public affairs and to gain votes on Election Day.

The third great task of the opposition is to try to influence governmental policy so that administrative decisions will approximate the principles and interests of the minority. This, of course, has long been a familiar role of the opposition and of Congress as a whole. Congressional direction and control of administration is carried out in various ways: (1) by the initiation of legislative proposals and the amendment of Administration measures; (2) by providing or reducing or denying funds for administrative programs; (3) by creating the administrative organization and reserving the right to veto changes therein proposed by the President; (4) by conducting investigations of administrative conduct; (5) by vesting in legislative committees the power to approve or disapprove proposed actions of executive officials; (6) by holding question periods at the committee stage where administrative officers may be "called on the carpet"; (7) by passing simple or concurrent resolutions designed to control administrative action; and (8) by participating in the appointment and removal of governmental officials. All these devices have been increasingly used in recent years to strengthen the watchdog function of Congress and to force concessions in administrative policy and program. In all these efforts to influence governmental policy the opposition plays an important role at every stage of the legislative process.

Finally, it is a special duty of the opposition to watch over the rights and interests of minorities. In a vast country like ours, with so many diverse economic and social interests, there are many minority groups—local and sectional, religious and racial, the small farmer and the small businessman—that might be crushed or forgotten in the massive sweep of social forces. Part of the task of the opposition, often performed by individual members of Congress, is to mitigate the impact of majority rule on minority groups.

Congressional Campaign Committees

In conclusion, mention may be made of the Congressional Campaign Committees. These groups are not agents of party government in the House and have no disciplinary or policymaking functions; they are essentially service agencies that render financial and other forms of assistance to Congressmen regardless of their party regularity. They date from 1866 when the Democratic members of both houses of Congress, who were supporting President Andrew Johnson against the attempt to impeach him, appointed a committee to manage the campaign of that year. The committee continued as a joint group through succeeding campaigns until the midterm election of 1882 when separate campaign committees were set up in the House and Senate. Today both the Democratic and the Republican Congressional Campaign Committees are autonomous groups that have no organic connection with the national committees or conventions and are primarily concerned with electing party members and maintaining party majorities in the House. Both committees maintain offices in Washington, employ a permanent secretariat, and are supported by voluntary contributions.

The Congressional Campaign Committees are each composed of one member of the House from each state having party representation in the chamber. They are chosen at the opening of each Congress by their respective state delegations. Each committee elects a chairman, several vice chairmen, a secretary, a treasurer, and other officers. In the Ninety-fourth Congress, the Democratic Campaign Committee had a total of fifty-three members. It was chaired by Representative Wayne L. Hays of Ohio and the deputy chairman was the Majority Leader. Among the ex officio members were the Speaker, the majority whip, two deputy whips and the caucus chairman. It had a full-time staff of eight. In 1974 the committee disbursed approximately $300,000 in assisting 202 candidates.

The Republican Campaign Committee in the Ninety-fourth Congress had a total of forty-four members. It was chaired by Representative Guy Vander Jagt of Michigan and had three senior vice chairmen and nine vice chairmen, elected by the committee. It had a full-time staff of thirty-five. In 1974 the committee spent $2.3 million in helping 375 candidates.

Both committees stay out of primaries, and both frequently supply staff support and advice even when they make no financial contributions. Writing in 1958, Hugh Bone described the Congressional Campaign Committee as "a device for catering to certain of the congressman's needs in campaigning, in his constituent relations, and in his work at the Capitol. . . . The lawmaker can be an isolationist or an internationalist, for or against the Bricker Amendment, for or against rigid farm price supports; but as long as he wears the party label, asks for help (and presumably needs it), and has an outside chance of election he will be served. . . . As far as these committees are concerned, party platform and program are clearly subordinate to organization."[70] The issues may have changed, but the description is just as accurate today.

10

Performance of the Legislative Function

KNOWLEDGE OF the various steps in the enactment of a law is part of the stock-in-trade of experienced members of Congress. But the nature of the legislative process is more or less of a mystery to the general public.

Let us suppose that a matter comes to congressional attention with the suggestion that it would be desirable to pass a law relating to it. There are at least a dozen steps that might be taken to translate a legislative proposal into a statute. Let us list these steps first and then try to explain each one in some detail.[1]

1. Research and fact-finding.
2. Drafting the bill.
3. Getting sponsors.
4. Timing the introduction.
5. Planning the campaign.
6. Organizing group support.
7. Propaganda and pressure.
8. Staging committee hearings.
9. Getting the bill to the Floor.
10. Floor debate and passage.
11. Getting the President's approval.
12. Implementation of the statute.

Research and Fact-Finding

Considerable research is ordinarily required in order to determine, first, that some governmental action is desirable; second, that there is no legislation already on the statute books which covers the situation; third, that the problem could not be better handled by appropriate administrative action or at the state or local level or by resort to the judicial process.

When it appears that no suitable legislation exists and that the problem calls for congressional action, despite all the risks and disadvantages involved in this procedure, then the next step will be to collect and comprehend the principal facts relating to the problem so that the author may be sure that the legislative proprosal has merit. For law is subsequent to the facts, as Woodrow Wilson once remarked, and the facts are precedent to all remedies. In gathering the facts the interested Congressman may call upon his own staff and/or committee staff and the experts in the administrative agencies concerned and in the Congressional Research Service of the Library of Congress, as well as those who are acquainted with the matter at first hand in the community or the pressure groups involved. He may also call upon representatives of the state or local governments for their comments and recommendations regarding the proposal.

Of course, he is not under the illusion that legislation is, or can be made, a strictly scientific business or that facts alone can solve our political and economic problems. But he appreciates that it is essential to obtain the basic facts with respect to an important problem so as to establish an area of agreement from which to proceed to consider their meaning for policy-making.

Drafting the Bill

Then, with all the relevant facts at hand, the next step is that of drafting a bill which, in appropriate legal terms, will carry out the intended purpose of the law. For this purpose the Congressman may call upon the Office of Legislative Counsel, a group of skilled lawyers who are experts in the art of bill-drafting. This office has a branch on the House side and another branch on the Senate side. First established in 1918, it has today a combined staff of some forty lawyers and law clerks whose services are of the highest quality.

The Chief Legislative Counsel of the House will send one or more members of his staff to the member's office to confer with him about the form and substance of his bill. Depending upon the scope and complexity of the proposal, they will have a series of conferences. The Congressman will tell the draftsmen what he is driving at, what objectives he has in view, what problem he would solve by legislative action. The draftsmen will incorporate his ideas into appropriate legal language, but they will not advocate any particular policy.

The drafting of a major measure is a complicated and time-consuming process that requires decisions regarding the distribution of costs and benefits, the assignment of functions to federal agencies, the creation or reorganization of governmental machinery, relationships with private organizations, judicial review and congressional oversight, administrative discretion, and the delegation of power. The form of a bill also raises important questions for author and draftsmen.

Getting Sponsors

The steps enumerated thus far may, in the case of comprehensive legislation, consume weeks or even months, before the member is satisfied that he has come up with a proposal suitable for the purpose at hand. Sometimes, of course, there are occasions where the facts are clear from the start, where the remedy needed is a simple one that may be accomplished with the passage of a short, concise bill.

In any event, once the bill is drafted, the next step is the choice of sponsors. The rules of the Senate have long permitted multiple sponsorship of bills, a strategy that sometimes has the advantage of mobilizing mass bipartisan support. Since 1967 the House has allowed multiple sponsorship, although the number is limited to twenty-five.

In order to improve the prospects of his bill, the member will try to get his bill co-sponsored by influential members of the majority party and by members of the committee, preferably the chairman, to which the bill will be referred. Unless he is a member of the committee to which the bill will be referred, it might not even get a hearing in the absence of good committee connections. He will also try to get some influential Senator to introduce a companion bill in the Senate and to fight for its passage by that body.

The sponsor of a bill is not necessarily the author of it. "In 1890 a bill was passed," wrote Senator Hoar in his autobiography, "which was called the Sherman Act for no other reason that I can think of except that Mr. Sherman had nothing to do with framing it whatever."[2]

Many measures are drafted in the executive departments and agencies or by private parties outside the government and then are introduced in Congress by sympathetic members who often play an important part in their eventual enactment.

Timing the Introduction

After the member has lined up his sponsors, the next step in the legislative strategy is the choice of time for the introduction of his bill. Several alternatives are available in the matter of timing. Shall the bill be introduced in the first or the second session of a Congress? Shall it be put in at the beginning of the session, or in the middle, or toward the end of the session? Shall it be introduced simultaneously in both houses of Congress, or in one house only, or in one house first and then in the other?

The answer to these questions depends upon a variety of factors: the climate of opinion in the country, the legislative program of the Administration and the congressional leaders, the condition of the economy, the state of the nation and the world, the character of the legislation, and other factors. It is wise to wait until the time is ripe before dropping the bill in the "hopper." For example, a presidential election year is usually considered a favorable time for introducing a tax-reduction bill, but a bad time for raising taxes.

Early introduction is usually the best strategy for a big complicated measure like a farm or consumer-protection bill that is apt to encounter a filibuster in the Senate or dilatory tactics in the House. Sometimes it is deemed best to take up a controversial bill in one house during the first session and in the other house during the second session. That strategy was followed in the Eighty-fourth Congress by Speaker Rayburn and Senator Lyndon Johnson in the case of the Natural Gas Bill. The end-of-the-session legislative jam is ordinarily not a propitious time for the introduction of major measures. But the suspension-of-the-rules procedure during the last six days of a session in the House of Representatives, when debate is limited to forty minutes, is sometimes used to rush through controversial bills without serious amendments. This technique was frequently used by the Roosevelt administration in obtaining extensions of price control and war powers legislation.

It is interesting to watch the ebb and flow of legislative tides. Times of crisis during the twentieth century produced the great reform legislative achievements of the New Freedom and New Deal eras and the legislation granting the President vast powers after the Japanese bombed Pearl Harbor, while the calmer days of the conservative administrations of Harding, Coolidge, and Hoover were comparatively barren of this type of legislation. During the recession of 1974, the Congress reacted quickly to the announcement of record postwar unemployment rates by enacting an emergency public jobs program and expanding the program of unemployment compensation. As the recession moved into 1975, the Congress again responded with quick action on a $21.3 billion tax cut.

Planning the Campaign

If the member's bill is a major measure that affects the vital interests of some powerful group in the country, such as the veterans or the farmers or the trucking industry, then it will be necessary to develop a basic plan of campaign. Planning a legislative campaign calls for the definition of objectives, the determination of priorities, and attention to strategic positions such as committee chairmen and party leaders. It also involves the use of weapons of propaganda and pressure, the development of sources of intelligence on the progress of the battle, and the arts of compromise in negotiating legislative settlements. Effective legislative campaigns require skilled and experienced leaders who are familiar with every phase of the legislative process and with all the tricks of the legislative trade.

Legislative campaign planning also involves co-operative arrangements with the "legislative departments" and "legislative representatives" (lobbyists) of the private interest groups that are back of the bill. Most of the great organized interest groups in this country have their legislative units and agents who work with the Congress and with the administrative agencies that function in their field of interest. The Congressman who is trying to get a bill passed will be in close and constant touch with the representatives of the organized interest groups and with the officials in the administration. During debates on farm bills, for example, agents of the Department of Agriculture and of the National Grange, the Farmers Union, and the Farm Bureau Federation are always in evidence on Capitol Hill. In 1974, when the House was considering the proposals for committee reform, some of the most vigorous lobbying came from the AFL-CIO which was opposed to the attempt to divide the Committee on Education and Labor into two committees. Virtually every measure of significance will generate lobbying activity if only because of the enormous stake so many Americans now have in the legislative process.

Sometimes special campaign organizations are retained for a fee. Law firms may be hired to help on bill drafting and the development of government support, while public-relations firms may be utilized for propaganda purposes and to develop the support of private groups. Legislative campaigning costs money for advertising, radio and television, and grass-roots lobbying, so that fund raising is an essential part of the total effort. The Buchanan Committee—a select House committee that investigated lobbying during the Eighty-first Congress—estimated that lobbying in all its ramifications had become a billion-dollar industry. The forms of lobbying are now so various—when an oil company tells us on nightly television of their interest in the environment, it is lobbying us—that the total costs are incalculable.

Organizing Group Support

The next step in the legislative battle is that of lining up the support of the groups in the country that are friendly to the bill. Much persistent effort is required to arouse the sustained backing of friendly groups. Not only the national and regional leaders of private organizations must be lined up, but also the officials of the executive agencies that have a stake in the legislation. In the campaign that led to the passage of the Employment Act of 1946, according to Stephen K. Bailey, "the lining up of a strong phalanx of political forces was considered to be politically necessary and in truth it is doubtful if [the bill] would ever have passed, even in modified form, without active support of these liberal organizations."[3]

The mobilization of group support also involves the effort to win over neutral groups who are not directly affected by the bill and have only a secondary interest in it. On most legislative issues the national political parties remain neutral in order to avoid alienating large segments of the electorate. But the chances of getting the bill enacted will be greatly enhanced if the author can secure the support of one or both of the political parties.

In trying to get his bill passed, a Congressman will also resort to the venerable strategy of "divide and conquer" by splitting the opposition. For example, the friends of the original Full Employment Bill tried to split the business opposition to the measure. Where a legislative proposal has originated in an executive department, a time-honored tactic of private opponents of the bill is to try to promote internal dissension within the executive branch or to create a conflict between Congress and the executive.[4]

Other tactics sometimes used in legislative campaigns are to hold an *ad hoc* conference on the subject of the measure and to organize an advisory committee to aid in the formulation of the proposal and to provide a center for the development of public support. From time to time, for example, White House Conferences on Education have met in Washington, and advisory committees have been used by the finance committees of Congress to assist them in the preparation of revenue and social security bills.

Propaganda and Pressure

The next step in the legislative campaign, if the member is working on a major bill for which public opinion is not yet fully prepared, is the distribution of propaganda and the application of pressure. Congress will not adopt a legislative proposal until it is convinced that it expresses the general will of the people and until there is sufficient public steam behind it. In an interest-group society, Congress yields only to the strongest influences that play upon it. It becomes necessary, therefore, for the sponsors of the legislation to employ all the arts of modern propaganda and publicity in order to build a convincing case and to disseminate it through all the media of mass communication.

We are all familiar with the techniques of publicity and propaganda that have been perfected in the world of advertising. They include the indirect methods of grass-roots lobbying that seek to influence public opinion through the mass distribution of books and pamphlets, full-page advertisements in the newspapers and periodicals, radio and television programming, and literature for use in schools and churches. The development of institutional advertising in which particular business, labor, and other groups set forth their views on public issues in the form of full-page ads and illustrated pamphlets is a modern method of influencing public opinion on legislative questions. Whenever they can arrange to do so, pressure groups will seek to take advantage of television's enormous ability to transmit a message to millions of people. This can mean attention-getting demonstrations as well as carefully prepared testimony delivered before the cameras.

Meanwhile the old-style direct techniques of contacting legislators are still employed. Interested groups will make their views known to members of Congress by letters, telegrams, and telephone calls. Congressmen will be personally contacted in their offices, their homes, and in the corridors and lobbies of the Capitol itself. Delegations will march en masse on the Capitol, a method sometimes used in recent years by civil rights groups and anti-Vietnam War activists. Senators and representatives will receive personal letters from influential friends in their states and districts, a technique perfected, for example, by the National Association of Real Estate Boards and the National Rifle Association.

In this stage of the campaign the member will endeavor to show that his proposal will promote the interests of this group and that group by indicating the exact benefits that will flow from its enactment. A full bill of particulars on the probable consequences of the proposal will be presented, directed at the special interests of different groups in the country, but embraced in terms calculated to promote the general welfare. Long-range objectives of unquestionable value will be avowed, such as peace, prosperity, and the preservation of the private-enterprise system; and the bill will be dressed up in all the accepted symbols of "democracy," the "public interest," and "the American way of life." In short, all the devices of propaganda and all the weapons of pressure—patronage, campaign contributions, chances for gain, the social lobby, petitions and memorials, letters and telegrams—will be employed to turn on the heat behind his bill.

Staging Committee Hearings

The next step in the legislative campaign is the committee stage. As sponsor of the bill, the member will have sought its reference to a friendly committee. Prior to the Eightieth Congress, there was often some choice in the matter of bill referrals. But the Legislative Reorganization Act of 1946 and the committee reforms of 1974 have considerably narrowed the parliamentarian's discretion as regards the reference of bills by its more precise definitions of committee jurisdiction. However, the 1974 changes also allow the assignment of a bill to more than one committee, either at the same time or in sequence.

Of the various steps in the legislative process, the committee stage is by far the most important. For it is through the committee hearings that Congress is informed of the merits of the measure. Here the friends and opponents of the bill marshal their arguments pro and con. Here the members of the committee interrogate the witnesses in a long and intensive study of the proposal. And here in executive sessions the committee amends the bill, seeks to compromise conflicting interests, and reaches a decision to report it favorably to the House. In the modern practice a committee will seldom report a bill without a hearing that may last for several weeks. But the mere holding of a hearing does not guarantee a favorable report.

In staging committee hearings several questions of strategy must be answered. Shall the hearings be held soon after the introduction of the bill before its opponents can marshal their resources? Or shall they be postponed for several months so as to allow ample time for the mobilization of friendly support and for the advance planning of the hearings? If companion bills have been introduced in both houses, shall the House or the Senate committee hold the first hearings?

Shall the hearings be short or long? For example, the House Subcommittee on District of Columbia Home Rule and Reorganization in the Eightieth

Congress held hearings from June 30 to July 25, 1947, and from February 2 to 10, 1948, and heard 159 witnesses before reporting a home-rule bill. In 1964, Chairman Emanuel Celler of the Judiciary Committee held six weeks of hearings on a resolution amending the First Amendment to allow Bible reading in the public schools; many of his critics charged that Celler was prolonging the hearings merely to allow critics of the proposal to dominate the limelight. Shall the hearings be open to the press and public so as to publicize the proceedings, or shall closed hearings be held so as to prevent unfavorable publicity and external criticism? Shall hearings be held in Washington only or also in the field? What witnesses shall be heard, in what order shall they appear, and how shall the available time be divided among them? Shall joint hearings be held with the twin committee of the other house and shall the power of subpoena be used?

In planning the presentation of testimony, the author will sit down in advance of the hearings with his friends and allies among the organized groups which have persuaded him to sponsor the bill. In a series of conferences they will develop and document the case for their proposal. They will select the best witnesses they can find and will brief them in advance of the hearings on their testimony and on the attitudes of the committeemen. They will utilize all the techniques of modern research and fortify their case with elaborate charts, tables, and statistics. In this event, the hearings may take on the atmosphere of an economic seminar—something that has actually happened in recent years in the case of hearings held by the House Committees on Interstate and Foreign Commerce, Ways and Means, and Banking, Currency and Housing.

Getting the Bill to the Floor

When at last the committee is satisfied that no new facts will be brought to light, the hearings are terminated, and the committee goes into what is called executive session. At this stage the committee will examine the merits of the proposal and perhaps vote to report the original bill pretty much in the form in which it was introduced, with a recommendation that the House approve it. Or the bill may be revised in committee and be reported out with majority and minority reports or by unanimous agreement. These reports usually outline the provisions of the bill, giving a section-by-section analysis of it, and summarize the committee's reasons for recommending passage of the measure. A minority report may call attention to sections of the bill that the minority does not endorse and give the reasons for its opposition.

Of course it is possible that the committee may decide to report out no legislation at all, thus bottling up the bill in committee and, in effect, killing it. When this happens, all the author can do is to circulate a petition in the House to discharge the committee from further consideration of his bill. Under the discharge rule, first adopted in 1910, it now takes the signatures of 218 members of the House, a simple majority of the entire body, on a discharge petition to take a bill away from a committee and bring it to the floor of the House.

Once the bill has been reported out of committee, it is placed upon the appropriate calendar of the House. The calendars are simply lists of bills upon which committee work has been completed and that are ready for floor action. The House has five calendars; the Senate has one. Getting the bill from the calendar to the floor is easier said than done. Shall they try to get it called up for floor consideration early or late in a session? In the House or Senate first? Enough time must intervene between the committee stage and the floor stage for the friends of the bill to get ready for the floor debate, prepare floor statements, and map their floor strategy.

Then there is the more perplexing problem of how best to reach the floor. In the House of Representatives there are five routes by which bills and resolutions can reach the floor: (1) by the right of certain committees to report at any time—a privilege enjoyed, for example, by the Appropriations and the Budget Committees; (2) by unanimous consent on the call of the consent calendar or the private calendar; (3) on special days when certain bills have the right of way, e.g., District Day when District of Columbia business is considered; (4) under suspension of the rules on the first and third Mondays and the last six days of the session, when debate is strictly limited and no amendments may be offered; and (5) under special rules reported by the Committee on Rules. Most major bills depend upon a "green light" from the Rules Committee for access to the floor of the House. The Committee on Rules is the instrument of the majority leadership for determining the order of business in the House.

Since the hypothetical measure under consideration is a major controversial one, the leadership will probably try to get it to the House floor via a special rule from the Rules Committee. To this end, the chairman and ranking minority member of the legislative committee that has favorably reported the bill will ask the chairman of the Rules Committee for a hearing. Their request will probably be granted, and the chief sponsor of the bill may be invited to attend. The members of the Rules Committee, of whom there are sixteen—eleven for the majority party and five for the minority—will question them closely about the background and merits of the measure. It is possible that they may disapprove of certain provisions of the bill and require the reporting committee to amend it to suit their predilections as a condition of its admission to the floor of the House.

Floor Debate and Passage

The floor stage of the bill is a story that need not long detain us, for it is short-lived and "after the fact" in the sense that the key decisions have already been made in committee. If strong opposition to the bill develops on the floor, it may be recommitted or postponed or become the victim of dilatory tactics or be killed by having its enacting clause struck out or be emasculated by amendments. But its fate will soon be determined, for debate in the House is strictly limited and rarely lasts more than one or two days per bill.

Assuming that the bill passes the House, it will then be sent over to the Senate where it will repeat its long journey through the same stages of the legislative process that it took on the House side. All told, there are twenty-eight stages in the enactment of a law, including its final approval by the President.

If our bill is approved by the Senate without amendment, it will be enrolled, signed by the Speaker and Vice President, and sent to the White House for the approval of the President. But if the bill is passed by the Senate with amendments, and if there is disagreement between the two houses on any amendment, a conference is asked by one house and agreed to by the other. In this case, a conference committee is appointed by the Speaker and the Vice President composed of members of the appropriate committees in each house that handled the legislation.

In the appointment of House conferees, the chairman of the committee which reported the bill recommends the majority party conferees to the Speaker while the ranking minority member of the committee recommends the minority conferees. In most cases the chairman and the ranking minority member will honor requests to serve on the conference committee according to the seniority of the applicants. The Speaker may or may not agree with the recommendations of the committee chairman either as to the names or the number of the conferees for the majority party. It may make a great deal of difference as to the outcome of the conference whether there are three or five majority party conferees from the House. The chairman may recommend five because he wants to achieve a certain objective and he knows the views of the five, while the Speaker may wish another result from the conference and so insists on having only three conferees, or vice versa. If the chairman resists the Speaker's suggestions, the Speaker may tell the chairman: "You must remember that I am the one who has the final say on conferees. If you will not agree to have three, then I will simply name them myself, but that may be an embarrasment to you." The power to select conferees who represent the wishes of the leadership is a little-noticed but powerful weapon in the hands of the Speaker who, to be sure, rarely uses it, but it is a telling weapon in reserve. It should also be noted that the rules adopted by the House for the Ninety-fourth Congress stated that "in appointing members to conference committees the Speaker shall appoint no less than a majority of members who generally supported the House position as determined by the Speaker." Furthermore the vote of the House (and Senate) conferees is the vote of the majority of each group.

The conferees, as they are called, meet and endeavor to compose the differences between the two houses. Under the provisions of the Legislative Reorganization Act of 1970, the House managers in a conference cannot agree to any amendments which would not have been germane had they been offered in the House unless the members of the House can vote on each of those amendments by majority. Prior to this change, the House was forced to deal with such amendments either by accepting or rejecting the bill in its entirety. If the conferees succeed, as they usually do, they prepare a conference report embodying their recommendations and submit it simultaneously to House and Senate. The report of the conference committee is almost always accepted by both houses.[5] This done, the bill is enrolled, signed by Speaker and Vice President, and sent to the White House for consideration of the President.

Conclusion

Such in sketchy outline are the major steps that a member of Congress takes to get a bill passed. Several months or even years may elapse between the original conception of a legislative proposal and its final birth as a statute. After its enactment and approval by the President, the implementation of the statute with adequate funds, competent personnel, and effective administrative action is another story—a sequel to this biography of a legislative campaign—that would require another chapter to tell.

I I

Performance of
the Oversight Function

IN THE COURSE of exercising its constitutionally delegated powers, the Congress impinges in many ways upon the administration of the laws. Congress can limit administrative discretion by detailed prescription of legislative standards, or by the adoption of resolutions otherwise limiting administrative action or subjecting it to some form of congressional approval or veto. It can fix the location of administrative responsibility and the form of organization; enact legislation affecting administrative personnel and procedures; itemize its appropriations; provide for review and audit of expenditures; require periodic and special reports from administrative agencies; and conduct investigations of the conduct of administration.

It would not be feasible to attempt to review even in summary fashion the history of the part played by the House of Representatives in these varied aspects of congressional surveillance of administration. This chapter will focus rather on three major areas of inspection and review: the selection of administrative personnel, the expenditure of public funds, and the economy and efficiency of administrative management. The specific role of the House of Representatives is stressed, but it cannot always be sharply differentiated from the actions of the Congress as a whole.

Control of Appointments

From the earliest days, members of the House have sought to influence appointments to federal office by corresponding with the President and department heads in favor of their friends and constituents. In important cases state delegations have acted as a group in submitting their recommendations. While the Constitution conferred upon the Senate the power to confirm nominations to superior offices, it had become customary by the end of John Adams' administration for representatives to be consulted concerning nominations to inferior federal offices in their districts. The annals of the Federalist period record numerous examples of attempts by representatives to influence the appointment of postmasters, revenue officers, land-tax commissioners, and army officers.[1]

Congressional influences continued to be strong during Jefferson's Presidency. According to Carl Russell Fish: "The New Yorkers, already becoming adept at businesslike politics, agreed upon a slate, to be submitted to the president by Burr in the name of the whole delegation in Congress. This was accepted, but with a few changes. Although this form was not always followed, the successful candidate seems generally to have been the one who had the support of his state delegation; and if congressmen did not take the initiative, the president usually consulted some of them in regard to names presented."[2]

During the Jeffersonian period, writes White, "local claims to local offices of the federal government, buttressed by the political interests of Congressmen in their constituents, became well-nigh irresistible. . . . Congressmen hovered around the executive offices to gain what they could for their friends. . . ."[3]

In 1821, John Quincy Adams declared: "About one-half the members of Congress are seekers for office at the nomination of the President. Of the remainder, at least one-half have some appointment or favor to ask for their relatives."[4] The low salaries of Congressmen at that time stimulated their appetite for more lucrative public offices, and the indebtedness of the President to the congressional caucus for his nomination during this period encouraged the feeling that his partisans in Congress were entitled to "an interchange of good offices," as Representative Quincy phrased it.

Toward the end of this period, portents of the spoils system were seen in the Tenure of Office Act of 1820. This act embodied the concept of rotation in office and provided that the principal officers concerned with the collection or disbursement of money should henceforth be appointed for fixed terms of four years and that the commissions of incumbents should expire at stated intervals.

During the age of Jackson, which was marked by historic battles between the President and the Senate over the control of appointments to presidential offices, department heads tended to defer to Congressmen in the appointment of inferior officers in their districts. Democrats in Congress actively solicited appointments to these offices for their friends and constituents during the Jackson and Van Buren administrations, while members of Congress sought executive appointments and military commissions for themselves during the Polk administration and the Mexican War. The adoption of an apportionment rule in 1853 for clerical jobs in the Washington agencies increased the potential influence of representatives over local appointments. By the time of the Civil War, they had acquired control over inferior appointments in the field services.[5]

According to Paul Van Riper, Congressmen themselves sought office during the period before the Civil War: "The information is most complete for Jackson's administration, though the tendency antedated his term. One list shows fifteen ex-senators and twenty-six ex-representatives as recipients of presidential appointments between 1829 and 1834. Nor did all of these appointments represent 'lame ducks.' "[6]

Local federal appointments to inferior positions continued to be regarded as the patronage of House members in Lincoln's Presidency and in succeeding administrations. Adherence to the patronage system was accepted as the price the President had to pay for congressional approval of executive measures. The conflict between President Hayes and Senator Conkling over the New York Customhouse is the best remembered of the period, but famous episodes involving the President and members of the House are not lacking.

Lincoln had hardly entered the White House before he was besieged by an army of office seekers anxious to participate in the spoils of Republican victory. Among the applicants for federal jobs, Carl Sandburg cites two Wisconsin Congressmen who went to see Secretary of State Seward in behalf of the appointment of Carl Schurz to be minister to Spain. Sandburg also describes an interview that Lincoln had with Congressman William Kellogg of Illinois, who called at the White House to solicit an appointment for one Major Hinshaw. Congressman White of Indiana asked Lincoln to give the job of postmaster at Lafayette, Indiana, to a certain man. And Speaker Grow visited the Executive Mansion to seek an appointment for a friend in the Treasury Department.[7]

In an attempt to transfer control of federal patronage from the executive branch to Congress, that body passed the famous Tenure of Office Act of 1867 over President Johnson's veto. Henry Adams wrote in 1870 that "the success of any executive measure must now be bought by the use of the public patronage in influencing the action of legislators."[8] And John Sherman declared in 1871 that "the position in which the President is now placed with regard to Congress is a constant source of irritation. Members of Congress, especially of the House of Representatives, claim the right to dictate local appointments, and if their wishes are not yielded to in every case it creates at once a cause of quarrel, which finds its outlet in some legislation or other. . . ."[9]

Increasing recognition of the limitations of the patronage system, accelerated by the assassination of President Garfield by a disappointed office seeker, led to the passage of the Civil Service Act of 1883. From this point on, political influence in appointments to public office declined, and the merit system was steadily expanded by congressional and presidential action, notwithstanding occasional countermovements. In 1883, 10 per cent of the positions in the executive civil service were under the merit system; in 1959, 86 per cent; in 1975, over 90 per cent. A series of executive orders and of major laws, including the Classification Act of 1923, the Postmaster Act of 1938, and the Ramspeck Act of 1940 were important landmarks in the evolution of the federal career service. Another important step was the creation of the U.S. Postal Service in 1970 as an independent agency of the federal government. The post of Postmaster General, long the headquarters of extensive patronage activity, was eliminated, and all political qualifications were abolished for postmasterships.

The decrease in the number of patronage jobs means that the members are still involved in responding to many inquiries about civil service positions and may seek to influence appointments in those situations where bureaucrats may select from a list of eligibles. Probably the greatest influence the members have in personnel selection derives from the system of annual appropriations. The members may well influence the agencies to appoint personnel who are sympathetic with their policy objectives.

Professor Louis W. Koenig has noted that for modern Presidents, the ability to produce programs and projects that will be of special benefit to a member's constituency has virtually supplanted the historical clout of patronage. He recalls, for example, how President Nixon persevered on behalf of the textile industry as part of his strategy to court Southern members and how President Johnson distributed funds from the Model Cities program to the districts of key committee chairmen. He also recalls the time when Senator Frank Church of Idaho explained his opposition to the Vietnam War by enclosing an article by Walter Lippmann, and President Johnson replied, "All right, the next time you need a dam for Idaho, you go ask Walter Lippmann."[10]

Control of Public Expenditure

The second main area of congressional oversight of administration has been in the field of finance. During the Federalist period (1789-1801), the prevailing practice was to pass annually two general appropriation acts granting lump sums: one for the civil list, the other for the military establishment. The Federalists favored general grants and broad executive discretion;

the Republicans, especially under the leadership of Albert Gallatin, who served in the House from 1795 to 1801, sought to limit administrative discretion in public expenditure by making specific appropriations. The Republicans had little success in their efforts during the 1790's, when the form of the supply bills was typically cast in very general terms. The pros and cons of executive discretion versus legislative restraint in fiscal affairs—a perennial issue in legislative-executive relations down through the decades—were clearly set forth in the debate on the resolutions of censure of Alexander Hamilton offered by Representative William B. Giles of Virginia in 1793. Giles sought to censure the Secretary of the Treasury for not strictly observing the laws making specific appropriations, but the House rejected the Giles resolutions and confirmed, at least for the time being, the Federalist viewpoint on administrative discretion.[11]

During the Jeffersonian period (1801-1829), the concern of the House with spending manifested itself in the creation of a standing Committee on Public Expenditures in 1814 and in the establishment in 1816 of six standing committees on expenditures, one each for the State, Treasury, War, Navy, and Post Office Departments, and one on public buildings. These committees were set up under the leadership of Henry Clay and reflected the intention of Clay and his friends "to take control of the government." They were mainly concerned with checking up on administrative economy and efficiency rather than with substantive policy, and they operated sporadically.

As regards the control of expenditure, the struggle continued throughout this period between the theory of executive discretion and that of congressional control, the Federalists favoring the former concept and the Republicans urging the doctrine of specific appropriations. The actual practice at this time was for Congress to pass three annual appropriation bills: the civil list for the support of the government, which was fully itemized and closely controlled; and the Army and Navy supply bills, which granted lump sums with ample room for administrative discretion. Beginning in 1809, Congress sought to restrict the transfer of funds between branches of expenditure, and in 1817 certain types of transfers were forbidden. During the depression of 1819-1820, Congress undertook a widespread program of retrenchment in public expenditures, reducing the size of the army, Indian outlays, the construction of ships, and the erection of forts. By the end of the period, White concludes, "the tug of war between Republicans in Congress and Republicans in the executive branch thus ended in a clear-cut victory for neither. . . . The balance in fiscal affairs between the executive and legislative branches remained about where the Federalists had left it."[12]

The struggle for power between Congress and the several executive departments over the control of public expenditures, which has gone on from the beginning of the Republic down to the present day, gained momentum during the age of Jackson. Congress now became more specific in its expectations as to the form and breakdown of the estimates and tended to demand better justifications for the funds requested. During this period, the financial struggle involved five major issues: the form and details of the estimates, the itemization of the appropriations, limitation of authority to transfer funds from one appropriation head to another, the control of deficiencies, and the prevention of expenditures or commitments not authorized by Congress. In the long fight for full control of federal expenditures, the guiding principle of Congress was expressed by Representative John Sherman of Ohio, who sat in the House from 1855 to 1861, as follows: "The theory of our government is, that a specific sum shall be appropriated by a *law* originating in this House, for a specific purpose, and within a given fiscal year. It is the duty of the executive to use that sum, and no more, especially for that purpose, and no other, and within the time fixed."[13]

Such full control does not appear to have been achieved in practice. Leonard White sums up his illuminating account of the battle over the control of federal expenditures during the period 1829-1861 by saying that:[14]

> Congress never succeeded in making such a rigid interpretation of the Constitution a reality. It did not appropriate specific sums for the armed services; it regularly held appropriations open for two years; it did not punish executives for using more money than had been appropriated nor for requiring more time than had been planned.
>
> The executive branch, on its side, found means, where necessary or useful, to avoid or to evade many of the fiscal limitations that Congress deemed it proper to impose. It drew the teeth out of some requirements by interpretation, it pleaded necessity in other cases, it confused Congress by its accounts, it made commitments that Congress had to honor, and it spent more than Congress had appropriated. In all of this there was a ready acquiescence on the part of individual Congressmen or party factions that wanted some particular payment made or task undertaken. The interests of the Congressmen were often different from and contrary to the interests of Congress. So also the interests of administration were often contrary to the requirements of an appropriation act.

After the depressions of 1837 and 1857, the House set up select committees on retrenchment in public expenditures which reported lack of cooperation from the departments and failed to achieve substantial results.

In the decades following the Civil War, Congress was described by Woodrow Wilson as "the central and predominant power of the system." One of the reasons for this impression was the nature of the postwar major supply bills. They followed a uniform pattern of detailed itemization for the civil establishments, specifying the objects and amounts for which money could be spent down to the last dollar, severely restricting executive discretion in the use of available funds, combined with lump-sum appropriations for the basic operations of the Army and Navy, based, however, on itemized estimates that were subject to congressional oversight and required departmental justification.

Restrictions on the spending power, which had been largely relaxed during the Civil War, were soon restored. Power to transfer funds from one purpose to another was repealed. Unexpended balances were recovered into the Treasury. Contract obligations in excess of appropriations were forbidden. The only escape for the departments from these limitations was to incur coercive deficiencies, a long-standing practice in which Congress acquiesced until it enacted the Anti-Deficiency Act of 1905 which apportioned expenditures at monthly or quarterly intervals.

Oversight of both revenue and spending was concentrated in the House in the Committee on Ways and Means down to 1865 when the Committee on Appropriations was created in order to divide the work load of handling both revenue and supply bills which had become very burdensome. During this period the House Committee on Appropriations was chaired by a succession of three strong men: James A. Garfield (1871-1875), Samuel J. Randall (1875-1877, 1883-1887), and Joseph G. Cannon (1889-1891, 1895-1901). Reacting to the dominant role acquired by the Appropriations Committee over both supply and general legislation, the House dispersed jurisdiction over the supply bills among half a dozen committees during the period 1879-1885. The Committee on Appropriations lost control of the rivers and harbors bill and the agriculture, Army, Navy, Indian affairs, and foreign affairs bills. As a result of this decentralization of fiscal control among several spending committees, the House of Representatives lost an overall coordinated view of income and outgo, and the several appropriation committees tended to become protagonists rather than critics of the fiscal needs of their departmental clientele.

The twentieth century has been replete with developments in the arena of fiscal control. A major change occurred in the House in 1920 when jurisdiction over all appropriations was consolidated in a single committee. Of great significance also was the Budget and Accounting Act of 1921, which provided for a budget system and an independent audit of government accounts, the latter by the General Accounting Office. Further improvements in financial administration were provided by the Budget and Accounting Procedures Act of 1950.

In 1945, the House Appropriations Committee was authorized to conduct studies and examinations of the organization and operation of executive departments and agencies, and it has made numerous such studies since. The Legislative Reorganization Act of 1946 contained several sections designed to strengthen congressional power of the purse. Outstanding among them was that for the creation of a Joint Budget Committee which was to formulate a legislative budget and fix a ceiling on expenditures. However, the Joint Budget Committee failed to function after 1949. A short-lived attempt at co-ordination in the fiscal field was the consolidation of all the general supply bills in a single package in 1950. In the 1955 session, the House Appropriations Committee established a special Subcommittee on Budget Reform. Chairman Clarence Cannon of the full committee described its creation as aimed at exploring all fields and proposals relating to improving procedures for balancing the budget.

With respect to control of expenditures, the General Accounting Office, its original authority considerably strengthened by the Government Corporation Control Act of 1945 and the Budget and Accounting Procedures Act of 1950, audits the financial transactions of executive departments and agencies. In addition, the Legislative Reorganization Act of 1970 gave the office the responsibility of analyzing the costs and benefits of government programs. Within sixty days after the GAO makes a report with recommendations to a federal agency, that agency is now required to report to the Committees on Government Operations of both houses. The GAO is also required to file the report with the Appropriations Committee so that the information will be available for hearings.

In illustrating the 1973 oversight activities of the GAO, the Comptroller General told the Select Committee on Committees:

> [we have done] a major study on the relation between social services and removal of people from the welfare rolls. Other work we've done includes a study on progress and problems in achieving the objectives of the school milk lunch program; a review of the effectiveness of programs for the elderly; a survey of the reading programs funded under the Federal program to aid educationally deprived children; a study of the adequacy of the minority business enterprise program; control of dangerous drugs under the law enforcement assistance propram; occupation health and safety; rail passenger service; Federal water pollution control research and development programs, etc. . . .[15]

In 1974, the GAO had a staff of 3,250; over 900 were from disciplines other than accounting.

The most significant budget legislation since 1921 came in 1974 with the enactment of the Congressional Budget and Impoundment Control Act. The act's basic objective was to assert the primacy of Congress in establishing the nation's priorities by way of the appropriations process. The most apparent feature of the act was its direct challenge to the concept of presidential impoundment of funds. This resulted from the intense controversy between President Nixon and his congressional critics. According to one estimate, President Nixon in his first term had impounded approximately $12 billion which the Congress had appropriated, including $6 billion in sewage-treatment funds which Congress has passed over a presidential veto. While other modern Presidents had impounded funds, their actions had not generated nearly as much controversy; most prior impoundments had involved military expenditures where a strong case could be made for greater presidential discretion. Furthermore, when previous presidential impoundments had resulted in negative congressional reaction, the issue was a subject for compromise. The distinctive features of the Nixon impoundments were their frequency, their size, and the obvious attempt by the President to make policy judgments on the value of particular social and domestic programs or on the impact of those expenditures on the economy of the country. It was as though the President had taken the relatively dull tool of impoundment and with it, fashioned a scalpel-like item veto power. By September, 1975, the courts had ruled in about thirty cases involving the impoundment of funds, and the President had lost in all but five.[16]

The act now requires the President to send a rescission bill to Congress when he wishes to impound funds because he seeks to terminate a program or merely wishes to cut spending. However, the President must spend the money if the rescission bill is not passed by the House and Senate within forty-five days.

During late 1974 and early 1975, President Ford sent three package rescission bills to Congress, which covered eighty-one separate items for a total of $2.46 billion. Congress approved $391 million or only 16 per cent. In only one instance was the President upheld by a floor vote on a rescission that had not been approved by the Appropriations Committees—this was on a $123 million procurement program for the F-111 bombers.[17]

While those who had anticipated this feature of the act as a congressional technique for reducing spending were obviously disappointed, the fact is that it is a provision which compels Congress to assume greater responsibility for actual expenditures.

The act also established separate Budget Committees in the House and Senate, and a staff—the Congressional Budget Office—of about 150. While the Senate's committee of fifteen members is chosen in the same manner as its other committees, the House requires that five of its twenty-three members be from the Ways and Means Committee, five from the Appropriations Committee, and one each from the majority and minority leadership.

The intent of the act is to compel Congress to look at the budget in its entirety prior to acting on authorizations and appropriations. All the committees are required to follow new timetables that will allow an estimate of total spending and revenue and anticipated deficits. Presumably this will encourage Congress to establish priorities with greater precision. Whether the Budget Committees will be able to achieve the stature required for such an assignment or whether Congress will continue to place emphasis on the traditional process of individual authorization and appropriation bills is most assuredly one of the large questions of the future.

Oversight of Administration

The conduct of administration in its multifarious aspects has been a third major focus of legislative oversight since the founding of the republic. The House early asserted its right to supervise the executive branch by the investigation in 1792 by a select committee of the defeat of General St. Clair by the Indians, by the Baldwin Committee investigation of the Treasury in 1794, and by frequent calls upon department heads for information. In 1793-1794 a House committee conducted an inquiry into Hamilton's management of the public debt and exonerated him from any misuse of power.

The St. Clair investigation, which was the first formal inquiry into the conduct of executive officers, raised at the beginning of our national history deep constitutional issues that are still rife in Washington. When the House committee called upon Secretary of War Knox for the St. Clair documents, President Washington conferred with his Cabinet and laid down the rule that has stood ever since as executive policy in response to congressional requests for executive papers, i.e., that "the Executive ought to communicate such papers as the public good would permit, and ought to refuse those, the disclosure of which would endanger the public." The St. Clair inquiry was highly successful in its primary purpose of informing the Congress, but it failed to determine who was to blame for St. Clair's defeat.[18]

During the Jeffersonian period, congressional supervision of the executive manifested itself through calls for papers, the requirement of regular annual departmental reports, requests for special reports on alleged cases of maladministration or malfeasance, and by frequent *ad hoc* investigations of executive conduct after 1815. White reports that "in the decade from 1815 to 1825 the power to investigate became well fixed as an important means by which Congress discharged its duty of supervising the conduct of administration."[19] The first comprehensive administrative reorganization was achieved during 1815-1817 after the War of 1812 had demonstrated the need of administrative reform. Important changes were made in the organization of the State, Treasury, War, and Navy Departments. Congress co-operated in effecting these necessary reforms by providing the legislative basis wherever it was needed.[20] "The evidence leaves no doubt," says White, "that a new spirit of enterprise and a different sense of responsibility animated Congress after the close of Jefferson's administration, and notably after the achievement of peace in 1815 gave the country opportunity to look at its domestic institutions."[21]

By 1829 the House had become very active in its exercise of the oversight function, thanks not only to the vigorous conduct of legislative inquiries into administrative behavior but also to the development of factionalism within the Republican party and a sense of responsibility on the part of the House to hold the executive responsible for its performance of public affairs. Suspicious critics of the executive like William B. Giles and John Randolph of Virginia were also a contributing factor.

After Jefferson's administration, select and standing committees of the House conducted a series of investigations of the economy and efficiency of administrative affairs that were unprecedented in scope and reflected a growing congressional sense of responsibility for supervision of the administration. A fairly complete list of the topics and years of these inquiries follows:[22]

> 1810—Conduct of General Wilkinson
> 1815—Expenses of the state militia
> 1816—Charges against Colonel Thomas
> 1816—Army expenditures on the northern frontier
> 1816—Fiscal affairs of the Post Office Department
> 1818—Conduct of General Jackson in the Seminole War
> 1818—Conduct of clerks in the executive departments
> 1818—Fees exacted by a district attorney
> 1819—Application of Army appropriations
> 1819—Embezzlement by a clerk of court
> 1819—Failure of a judge to hold court
> 1820—Illegal loans of powder to private persons
> 1821—Administration of the Post Office
> 1822—Conduct of the Post Office Department
> 1822—Accounts and expenditures of the War Department
> 1823—Refusal of a judge to admit an attorney to practice
> 1823—alleged suppression of documents by Gales and Seaton
> 1823—Conduct of superintendent of Indian trading houses
> 1824—Charges against Secretary of the Treasury Crawford
> 1825—Navy contingent fund
> 1826—Conduct of Calhoun as Secretary of War

Many of these investigations were conducted by select committees of the House that were frequently given power to send for persons and papers. Others were carried on by the new standing committees on expenditures in the executive departments, six of which were established in 1816. These and other inquiries during this period indicated that the House was conscious of its role as overseer of the public business.

During the Jacksonian era, Congress extended its requirements for departmental reports to include annual reports of finances, contracts, and personnel and payrolls. Beginning in 1836, each house of Congress also required its clerk to prepare an annual statement of all appropriations, a list of all new offices with their salaries, and a statement of all pay raises. This period was also marked by frequent congressional investigations of executive agencies, including the Post Office Department, the New York Customhouse, public buildings, the Brooklyn Navy Yard, and political corruption under the Buchanan administration. One of the outstanding inquiries at this time was that in 1842 by the House Select Committee on Retrenchment under the chairmanship of Thomas W. Gilmer of Virginia. If the achievements of these investigations were not conspicuous, they at least succeeded, as Leonard White remarks, in turning the spotlight of publicity on wrongdoing and in arousing public indignation over official misdeeds.[23]

The annals of Congress reveal that at least thirty-six investigations were conducted by committees of the House during the years 1829-1861: thirty-two of them by select committees, and four by standing committees. The agencies most frequently examined were the executive departments in general (seven times), Treasury (six), the Post Office Department (three), War Department (five), and Navy Department (four). The following list shows the subjects and dates of most of these inquiries.[24]

    1830—Post Office Department
    1832—Bank of the United States
    1832—Conduct of Secretary of War Eaton
    1834—Post Office Department
    1834—Bank of the United States
    1836—New York Customhouse
    1837—Management of deposit banks
    1837—Condition of the executive departments
    1839—Conduct of Captain Elliott
    1839—New York Customhouse
    1842—Economy in public expenditures
    1842—New York Customhouse
    1846—Charges against Daniel Webster
    1848—Administration of Indian affairs
    1850—Party patronage
    1850—Galphin claim
    1850—Secretary of Interior Ewing
    1850—Activities of office holders in elections

1855—Smithsonian Institution
1856—Affairs in Territory of Kansas
1857—Charges of congressional corruption
1859—Brooklyn Navy Yard
1860—Control of public printing

During the Civil War period, the House of Representatives continued to be active on the investigative front. In the Thirty-seventh Congress (1861-1863), it set up select committees to investigate government contracts, the defenses of the Great Lakes and rivers, Emancipation, and the confiscation of rebel property. In the Thirty-eighth Congress (1863-1865), select committees were appointed to investigate certain charges against the commissioner of patents, on emancipation, on the Northeastern defenses, on the rebellious states, on immigration, the Pacific Railroad, and on the railroad from New York to Washington. This period also witnessed the establishment of one of the most important joint select committees of the two houses Congress has ever known. This was the so-called Wade Committee on the conduct of the Civil War. It originated primarily to investigate the disaster of Ball's Bluff, but it exercised a roving commission thereafter to look into all sorts of matters connected with the war effort. This committee was given wide powers and played an important part in the successful prosecution of the war. Commencing its labors at a time when the government was still engaged in organizing its first great armies, it continued them until the rebellion had been defeated. Ten distinct reports were submitted by the Wade Committee between December, 1862, and May, 1865. Its investigations consumed eight volumes.

During the post-Civil War period, congressional committees, stimulated by constituent complaints of delay and waste in the executive branch of the government, conducted a series of investigations into the organization and operation of the administrative departments with a view to promoting economy and efficiency, from the inquiry of the Joint Select Committee on Retrenchment (1869-1871) to that of the Dockery-Cockrell Joint Commission of 1893-1895. Their voluminous reports produced valuable basic data on departmental organization and methods of administrative management and effected substantial economies, but they contributed little in the way of general principles for the guidance of practitioners of the administrative arts. While successive Presidents prior to Theodore Roosevelt remained aloof from such mundane matters, Congress took the initiative in seeking specific improvements for particular administrative problems. But it was too preoccupied with individual cases to be able to modernize the administrative system as a whole. It remained for later studies by a series of presidential commissions on economy and efficiency to pave the way for widespread administrative reform.[25]

During the years from the Civil War to the end of the century, some seventy investigations were conducted by select and standing committees of the House of Representatives, many of them into various aspects of administrative management. The scandals of Grant's Administration (1869-1877) provoked upwards of thirty House inquiries alone. Among the outstanding investigations of this era were the Credit Mobilier inquiry of 1872-1873 and the investigation of the real-estate pool and Jay Cooke in 1876.

The sensational Credit Mobilier investigation was conducted by one House and two Senate committees. It involved the financing of the Union Pacific Railroad. A principal stockholder in both companies was Oakes Ames, a representative in Congress from Massachusetts. Charges appeared in the press that Ames had bribed men prominent in public life by distributing shares of stock in the Credit Mobilier. Among those involved in the alleged speculation were Speaker Blaine and Vice President Colfax. One House committee was appointed, on motion of James G. Blaine himself, to investigate the charges that members of the House had been "bribed by Oakes Ames, or any other person or corporation, in any matter touching his legislative duty." Representative Luke Poland of Vermont was named chairman of this five-man select committee. A few weeks later, another five-man select committee, chaired by Representative Jeremiah M. Wilson of Indiana, was set up to determine whether the government had been defrauded, because of possible conspiracy in high places, by the Credit Mobilier. Meanwhile, the Senate appointed its own committee, under the chairmanship of Senator Lot M. Morrill of Maine, to determine if any of its members were implicated. Each committee was empowered to send for persons and papers.

The Poland Committee recommended that both Oakes Ames and James Brooks, a representative from New York, be expelled from the House. The committee held that Ames had been "guilty of selling to members of Congress shares of stock in the Credit Mobilier of America, for prices much below the true value of such stock, with intent thereby to influence the votes and decisions of such members in matters to be brought before Congress for action." Brooks was found guilty of procuring stock for his son-in-law, intended for and used for his own benefit. In the final event, both Ames and Brooks were censured by the House, but not expelled.[26]

The Wilson Committee found that the profits of the Credit Mobilier had been grossly exorbitant and recommended that the Attorney General bring suit against all who had ever received stocks or bonds in the railroad without paying for them, or who had received dividends unlawfully declared from the profits made in the construction of the road.[27]

The Morrill Committee found that Senator James W. Patterson of New

Hampshire had purchased stock from Mr. Ames at below its "esteemed" value in the knowledge that such sales were in the nature of bribes. The committee recommended that he be expelled from the Senate.[28] But the Senate permitted Patterson, whose term was about to expire to retire, without having the expulsion resolution brought to a vote and without formal censure.

No evidence was found that Speaker Blaine had any dealing with the Credit Mobilier or with Ames other than to decline offers of stock. The political career of Vice President Schuyler Colfax, however, was ruined by the investigations.

Woodrow Wilson wrote in 1885 that "quite as important as legislation is vigilant oversight of administration. . . ." But he added that[29]

> it is quite evident that the means which Congress has of controlling the departments and of exercising the searching oversight at which it aims are limited and defective. The intercourse with the President is restricted to the executive messages, and its intercourse with the departments has no easier channels than private consultations between executive officials and the committees, informal interviews of the ministers with individual members of Congress, and the written correspondence which the cabinet officers from time to time address to the presiding officers of the two Houses, at stated intervals, or in response to formal resolutions of inquiry. . . .

And then follows this famous passage:[30]

> Even the special, irksome, ungracious investigations which it from time to time institutes in its spasmodic endeavors to dispel or confirm suspicions of malfeasance or of wanton corruption do not afford it more than a glimpse of the inside of a small province of federal administration. Hostile or designing officials can always hold it at arm's length by dexterous evasions and concealments. It can violently disturb, but it cannot often fathom, the waters of the sea in which the bigger fish of the civil service swim and feed. Its dragnet stirs without cleansing the bottom. Unless it have at the head of the departments capable, fearless men, altogether in its confidence and entirely in sympathy with its designs, it is clearly helpless to do more than affright those officials whose consciences are their accusers.

Wilson concluded on this question of controlling the administration that "members of Congress ought not to be censured too severely, however, when they fail to check evil courses on the part of the executive. [For] they have been denied the means of doing so promptly and with effect."[31]

Since Woodrow Wilson wrote these words, the problem of effective supervision of administration has been greatly magnified by the steady growth of executive power induced by recurring economic and political crises, two World Wars, the emergence of the United States as a world power, the traumas of Vietnam and Watergate, and the growing complexity of our economic, political, and social activities both nationally and internationally. Meanwhile, there has also been a notable increase in the means of legislative liaison with the executive and in the techniques of congressional control of administrative action.

Liaison with the President, while still not entirely satisfactory, has been improved by the weekly meetings at the White House with the leaders of Congress; the personal delivery of the State-of-the-Union messages before joint sessions (a practice revived by Wilson himself); and by the designation of a deputy assistant to the President to handle congressional relations. Meanwhile, liaison with the departments has been improved by the appointment in a few cases of assistant secretaries for congressional relations, by the opening of branch departmental offices on Capitol Hill, and by some recent experiments with question periods at the committee stage. A few House committees have developed the practice of holding periodic or sporadic question-and-review sessions with the officials of executive agencies under their jurisdiction, especially at the beginning of each session. These meetings afford an opportunity for the review of administrative action, the discussion of citizen complaints, and the reaching of informal understandings concerning administrative policies and procedures.

Even more significant than these steps toward closer liaison between the legislative and executive branches has been the extension of the function of standing committees from the consideration of bills to the study and control of administration. "Committee government," as Wilson described it in the middle 1880's, was a system primarily if not entirely concerned with "digesting schemes of legislation." Occasional investigations of the executive were conducted by select committees. The annals of the House reveal only eight such inquiries between 1885 and 1925, and nine between 1925 and 1946, as follows:[32]

> Administration of Government Printing Office—50th Congress (1887-1889)
> Reform in the civil service—50th-52d Congresses (1887-1893)
> Soldier's Home in Leavenworth, Kansas—54th Congress (1895-1897)
> Purchase of the Danish West Indies—57th Congress (1901-1903)
> Prevention of fraud in public service—60th Congress (1907-1909)
> Operation of U.S. Shipping Board and Emergency Fleet Corporation—66th Congress (1919-1921)
> Contracts and expenditures by War Department—66th Congress (1919-1921)
> Operations of U.S. Air Service—68th Congress (1923-1925)
>
> Shipping Board—69th Congress (1925-1927)
> Government organization—76th Congress (1939-1941)
> National Labor Relations Board—76th Congress (1939-1941)

Acts of Executive Agencies beyond scope of their authority—78th and 79th
Congresses (1943-1946)
Seizure of Montgomery Ward and Co.—78th Congress (1943-1944)
Federal Communications Commission—78th Congress (1943-1944)
National Defense program in re small business—78th Congress
Postwar military policy—78th and 79th Congresses
Disposition of surplus property—79th Congress (1945-1946)

Today "legislative oversight" has become *a,* if not *the,* principal activity
of the standing committees of both houses. There has been an extraordinary
increase in the exercise of the investigative function of Congress in recent
times. As many inquiries have been conducted by each Congress since 1950
as were carried on in the whole nineteenth century.[33] This development has
been due, at least in part, to the directive in Section 136 of the Legislative
Reorganization Act of 1946 that "each standing committee of the Senate
and the House of Representatives shall exercise continuous watchfulness
of the execution . . . of any laws" by the administrative agencies within
their jurisdiction and by the requirement of the Reorganization Act of
1970 that the committees report annually on their oversight activities. The
expansion of the investigative function has also been facilitated by the great
increase in standing committee staffs.

After 1885 the House made comparatively few inquiries into the conduct
of executive departments, while the Senate assumed the leading role as
"grand inquest" of the nation. The House shifted its inquiring eye, especially after the turn of the century, to studies of economic and social problems. Among its major inquiries in this area during the past sixty years
have been the so-called Money Trust (Pujo) investigation of banking and
finance in 1912-1913, the investigations of Fascism and Communism by
the Committee on Un-American Activities since 1945, the examinations of
the federal regulatory commissions by the so-called Legislative Oversight
Subcommittee since 1957, and the widespread investigations by the Committee on Government Operations since 1947.

Early in 1957 a Subcommittee on Legislative Oversight was appointed
by Oren Harris, chairman of the House Committee on Interstate and Foreign Commerce. This subcommittee was set up "to examine the execution
of the laws by the administrative agencies, administering laws within the
legislative jurisdiction of the committee, to see whether or not the law as the
Congress intended in its enactment has been and is being carried out or
whether it has been and is being repealed or revamped by those who admin-
ister it." The subcommittee listed some sixteen regulatory boards and commissions that it proposed to examine, and some eight subjects that it was
going to consider, in what promised to be the most sweeping investigation
of the organization and operation of the regulatory agencies of the federal

government in American history. Late in 1957 the scope of the inquiry was limited to the "big six" regulatory agencies: Civil Aeronautics Board, Federal Power Commission, Federal Trade Commission, Interstate Commerce Commission, Securities and Exchange Commission, and Federal Communications Commission.

Representative Morgan M. Moulder of Missouri was named chairman of the special subcommittee, and Professor Bernard Schwartz of New York University Law School was retained as chief counsel and staff director. Originally designed to determine whether the agencies had followed the intent of Congress, the investigation became in 1958 a probe of charges of influence-peddling by representatives of the regulated industries, commissioners, Congressmen, and members of the White House staff. Later, Schwartz was dismissed as subcommittee counsel. Representative Moulder resigned as subcommittee chairman and was replaced by Representative Harris, chairman of the parent committee. The subcommittee then held hearings on charges of misconduct by members of the Federal Communications Commission, which led to the resignation of Commissioner Richard A. Mack. Subsequently an inquiry into the affairs of Bernard Goldfine, Boston industrialist, led to the disclosure of his gifts and financial assistance to Presidential Assistant Sherman Adams and to some Congressmen. Later, Goldfine was indicted for contempt of Congress for his refusal to answer subcommittee questions, and Adams resigned his White House post.[34]

During the past fifteen years, various House committees and subcommittees have investigated an extraordinary variety of topics, such as the charge of "managed news" by the executive branch, the systems of measuring the size of television audiences, the uses of lie detectors by federal agencies, the activities of the Ku Klux Klan, the responsibility of Army officers in the My Lai massacre of 1968, whether the behavior of Supreme Court Justice William O. Douglas could be the basis for impeachment, allegations of mismanagement in the Small Business Administration, and questions of whether the Central Intelligence Agency violated the law.

Another recent important development was the revival in 1946 of the long-moribund Committee on Expenditures in the Executive Departments. As redefined by the Legislative Reorganization Act of that year, this committee was given the duties of (1) receiving and examining the reports of the Comptroller General and of reporting to the House thereon; (2) studying the operation of government activities at all levels with a view to determining their economy and efficiency; (3) evaluating the effects of laws enacted to reorganize the legislative and executive branches of the government; and (4) studying intergovernmental relationships. It was thus designed to be a public accounts and machinery of government group. In 1952 its name was changed to the Committee on Government Operations.

It has forty-three members and has subcommittees on commerce, consumer, and monetary affairs; conservation, energy, and natural resources; government activities and transportation; government information and individual rights; intergovernmental relations and human resources; legislation and national security; manpower and housing.

This committee has held hearings on a wide range of subjects and has published numerous staff studies and reports. It handled most of the Hoover Commission legislation and has reviewed the audit reports of the General Accounting Office. The committee has become the principal investigative agency of the House in the field of government operations. Among the wide-ranging subjects of inquiry by this panel have been government information policies and practices, military procurement, the operations of Federal Prison Industries, of the Institute of Inter-American Affairs, of the Maritime Commission, of the General Accounting Office, of the Rural Electrification Administration, of the Veterans Administration, and of the Office of Education, federal supply management, U.S. relations with international organizations, and many other matters. In the Ninety-third Congress (1973-74), for example, the committee transmitted to the House 28 investigative reports, studied 550 bills and resolutions and analyzed 291 audit reports of the General Accounting Office.[35]

With a mandate to watch continuously, equipped with staffs and funds, "committee government" in our time has thus acquired new significance as a system of inspection and review of administrative performance. The Eighty-third Congress alone authorized upwards of $7,500,000 for various probes; for the Ninety-second Congress the authorization for investigations was $10,800,000 for only the first session.[36] Various oversight techniques are employed, some of ancient usage, some of recent vintage. They include question periods at the committee stage, field inspection trips at home and abroad, interim supervision of agency activities, and demands for documents and testimony—all of which have been increasingly used in recent years to strengthen the oversight function of Congress. And they have had many far-reaching effects.

Comparatively novel weapons in the oversight arsenal are the so-called legislative veto and committee veto. In the legislative veto, Congress includes in a statute that is to be administered by an executive agency a provision that certain kinds of decisions cannot go into effect unless they are first submitted to Congress during a specific period. Some statutes require Congress then to approve or disapprove the action; other statutes allow the agency to act in the absence of any action by Congress.

Beginning in the 1930's, Congress included provisions for a legislative veto in the legislation that authorized the President to reorganize executive agencies. This is a power that has been taken seriously. Between 1949 and

1973, ninety-three reorganization plans were submitted to Congress, nineteen of which were rejected.[37]

Congress has also made use of the legislative veto to suspend the deportation of aliens by the Attorney General, and to disallow the sale of federally owned property and obsolete naval vessels. The Federal Highway Act of 1956 stipulated that the apportionment of funds among the states required congressional approval by concurrent resolution. In the area of foreign affairs, Congress has legislated in a manner which prevents the President from negotiating an executive agreement that allows the exchange of atomic-energy materials unless Congress approves. A 1958 act stated that in instances where the President refused to raise import duties when the Tariff Commission recommended that he do so, the presidential decision could be overridden by a two-thirds vote of Congress.

The committee veto power is a function of statutes that require the executive agency to submit decisions to certain committees for their consideration during a specified time before those decisions can be implemented. Some statutes insist that the decisions be formally approved by those committees; others do not, although as a practical matter the agency is unlikely to proceed if the decision generates an adverse reaction from the committee.

A 1967 study by the Legislative Reference Service outlined nineteen statutes that contained the potential for committee vetoes.[38] Many of the statutes showed an especially close surveillance of the activities of the Atomic Energy Commission by the Joint Committee on Atomic Energy. The Civil Rights Act of 1964 illustrated how the committee veto provision allowed day-to-day scrutiny of the executive branch by providing that any attempt to deny federal funds to any political entity on the grounds of racial discrimination must first be reported to the legislative committees which have jurisdiction over those programs and the programs cannot be ended until thirty days after the report is filed. In 1965, President Johnson vetoed the Military Construction Authorization Act because it provided that no military base could be closed until 120 days after reports were made to the Senate and House Committees on Armed Services. The following year, Congress modified the act by reducing the waiting period to thirty days, and the President found the measure acceptable.

Understandably Presidents have chafed under the congressional and committee veto powers, frequently asserting that they violated the separation-of-powers doctrine and made difficult effective administration. Yet the excesses of executive actions in recent years have reversed the argument. For example, the power of Congress to prevent presidential impoundments of funds that have been appropriated is now defended as a restoration of the balance between executive and legislative authority. Indeed a forthcoming study by the Congressional Research Service will show that between January, 1973, and July, 1975, Congress enacted twenty-six statutes which contained fifty-two separate provisions that allowed for either a congressional or a committee veto, far more than in any other comparable period in our history. Another study counts 126 laws which include congressional veto provisions, 47 having been enacted since 1970. That study showed increasing sentiment in the House for a bill that would subject any federal regulation with a criminal penalty subject to rejection by either house within sixty days.[39] The contribution of the Nixon administration to the development of legislative oversight may become incalculable.

Another major development as regards congressional control of administration has been in the field of administrative regulation. Beginning with the Interstate Commerce Commission in 1887 and continuing through every decade to the Atomic Energy Commission in 1946, ten regulatory commissions have been created and granted rule-making powers. Congress exercises oversight of these "floating ribs of government" through statutes prescribing the terms and qualifications of their members, through the power of the Senate to reject nominees to them, through the annual appropriation hearings and interim amendments of the basic statutes, through sporadic committee question periods and occasional full-dress investigations of their work, and by requiring them to submit periodic and special reports.[40]

Despite the variety of weapons in the armory of congressional oversight of delegated powers, these methods of inspection and review apparently proved inadequate, especially under the emergency conditions of depression and war. Recurring complaints of the abuse of the rule-making power finally led, after long study, to the Federal Administrative Procedure Act of 1946. This act laid down a series of procedural safeguards for the guidance of the rulemakers, prescribing the minimum requirements of fair administrative procedure. It was supplemented by the Administrative Conference Act of 1964, which provides for continuing review of the procedures of administrators.

When the Select Committee on Committees held its hearings in 1973, many members who came before the committee to testify expressed their concern that the House was not doing an adequate job of legislative oversight. The *Report* and recommendations show that the committee shared that concern. For example, the *Report* summarized the oversight activities of the legislative committees from January 1, 1973, to September 5, 1973, and noted that of the 2,095 days devoted to hearings and meetings only 231, or 1.1 per cent, were devoted to oversight.[41]

Given the emphasis of the Reorganization Act of 1946 on "continuous watchfulness" and the requirement of the 1970 act that each standing committee issue a biennial report on its legislative review activities, the Select

Committee concluded that "there is a wide gap between what is required by law and what is actually done."

The committee's recommendations included the following:[42]

1. The establishment of oversight subcommittees on all standing committees, except the Committee on Appropriations.

2. The development of an oversight report for each Congress by the Committee on Government Operations, in consultation with the Speaker and minority leader, that would help coordinate and define the program review priorities of the House. Within the first sixty days of the convening of a new Congress, this report would be developed with the cooperation of the committee chairmen and would therefore serve as a coordinated oversight agenda for the House.

3. The institutionalization of several coordinative devices between the Committee on Government Operations and the authorizing, appropriating and taxing committees. For example, the Committee on Government Operations would have been privileged to offer amendments to authorization or appropriations bills on the floor, after the committee amendments had been considered, assuming, of course, that the amendments were based on review findings.

The reforms that were finally enacted were less formidable. In essence, the House reaffirmed the responsibility of every standing committee to engage in legislative oversight, and seven of the standing committees were allowed to conduct oversight functions on topics that were not within the exact areas of their legislative jurisdiction. The formation of a subcommittee on oversight became an alternative, but not a requirement. Three of the standing committees have added oversight subcommittees in the Ninety-fourth Congress—Agriculture; Banking, Currency, and Housing; and Ways and Means—bringing the number of standing committees with oversight subcommittees to eight. The House did accept the oversight-report concept. At the outset of the Ninety-fourth Congress, staff members of the Committee on Government Operations met with their counterparts on all the standing committees for the purpose of developing oversight plans. By March, 1975, it was possible for the committee to publish a document that outlined in considerable detail the plans of each committee.[43]

The unwillingness of the House to require oversight subcommittees may be the result of other pressures on the members. As Professor Morris S. Ogul stated to the Select Committee on Committees, the urgent problems that most members feel in their quest for "political survival" tend to leave little time for many of them to be too concerned with the painstaking work of oversight.[44] Or it may be that the House believes it now enjoys a formidable arsenal of weapons to engage in all the oversight activities it wishes to undertake. Day-to-day casework frequently leads to a review of the activities of the executive branch agencies. Committee investigations, the appropriations process, and now the work of the Budget Committee, the special responsibilities of the Committee on Government Operations to take up the oversight slack, the many informal opportunities that allow members to view the executive branch, the congressional and legislative veto powers, the extensive work of the GAO, the studies by the Congressional Research Service, and the work of *ad hoc* groups, such as the Democratic Study Group—all add up to an extensive review of the executive branch. As the members of the House looked back on the summer of 1974 and recalled how the painstaking efforts of the Committee on the Judiciary led to the resignation of a President, they may well have concluded that their capacity for oversight is indeed awesome.

12

The Role of the House
in Foreign Affairs

THE RELATIONS of the House of Representatives to the foreign affairs of the United States stem from the days of the American Revolution. During that conflict, the Continental Congress conducted and controlled the foreign relations of the thirteen states. Colonial experience with the English king and royal governors had produced a deep distrust of executive authority. So Congress appointed our diplomatic agents abroad and referred their instructions and correspondence to a series of select committees. On November 29, 1775, a Committee of Secret Correspondence was set up to correspond "with friends in Great Britain, Ireland and other parts of the world" and to seek foreign aid; after April, 1777, it was known as the Committee for Foreign Affairs. In January, 1781, the drawbacks of the committee system induced Congress to establish the office of Secretary of Foreign Affairs, but the legislature continued to deliberate on foreign relations in committee of the whole and to refer particular problems to select committees.

During the period of the Confederation (1781-1789), congressional control of foreign affairs continued with little change. The Articles of Confederation gave Congress exclusive power over war and peace (unless a state were invaded), the right to send and receive diplomatic agents and embassies, and the right to make treaties. Robert Livingston and John Jay served as Secretary of Foreign Affairs during this period, but Congress inspected their correspondence, issued detailed instructions concerning their negotiations, and kept a tight rein on the conduct of foreign affairs. Historians have assigned credit, however, for the Treaty of 1783 with Great Britain less to the Congress than to the able American negotiators: John Adams, John Jay, and Benjamin Franklin.

230

It was thus against a background of congressional control of foreign affairs that the Constitutional Convention met in Philadelphia in May, 1787. Its discussions concerning the conduct of foreign relations dealt largely with the power to make treaties and to appoint ambassadors—functions which, in the first draft of the Constitution, were assigned to the Senate. This draft also provided that treaties as well as the acts of the legislature should be "the supreme law of the several States, and of their citizens and inhabitants," and it forbade the states to make any treaties or alliances save with the consent of Congress. These proposals evoked an amendment that no treaty should be binding on the United States unless "ratified by a law," thereby requiring concurrence of the House of Representatives.

This amendment was rejected, but after a revised draft of the Constitution assigned control of foreign relations to the President *and* the Senate, it was proposed that the advice and consent of the House, as well as that of the Senate, should be required in the treaty process. In the closing debate of the convention, James Wilson discussed the treaty clause and moved to add after the word "Senate" the words "and House of Representatives." Treaties, he said, were to have the sanction of laws and should therefore be ratified by both houses. But his proposal was not adopted. In the final draft the framers assigned to Congress the other important powers in the field of foreign affairs, i.e., the powers to regulate foreign commerce and to declare war, while the House of Representatives received a share in the treaty power through the commerce clause and through its power to originate appropriation bills needed to implement a treaty.

Whatever the expectations of the framers may have been with respect to the control of foreign affairs, in the perspective of history it appears, as Professor Edward S. Corwin has written, that "the Constitution, considered only for its affirmative grants of power which are capable of affecting the issue, is an invitation to struggle for the privilege of directing American foreign policy. . . . The verdict of history . . . is that the power to determine the substantive content of American foreign policy is a *divided* power, with the lion's share falling usually to the President, though by no means always."[1]

1789-1800

During the first decade of the new republic, the House of Representatives participated in several decisions affecting the foreign relations of the United States. It helped enact the act of July 27, 1789, which established a Department of Foreign Affairs whose name was changed to the Department of

State some weeks later. By the Appropriation Act of July, 1790, a lump sum of $40,000 was made available to the President for the support of our embassies abroad. In establishing the Post Office by the act of February 20, 1792, the Second Congress authorized the Postmaster General to make arrangements with the postmasters in any foreign country for the reciprocal receipt and delivery of letters and packets which, according to Wallace Mc-Clure, was the first use of the executive agreement under the Constitution.[2]

President Washington's famous proclamation of neutrality of April 22, 1793, during the war between France and Great Britain, gave rise to a public controversy and a lively pamphlet debate between Hamilton and Madison over the powers of President and Congress. Both houses subsequently approved the President's actions, and in June, 1794, Congress passed the first neutrality law, prohibiting certain acts and imposing penalties. These developments established the precedent that the President has power to determine a policy of neutrality toward foreign nations, and that Congress has legislative authority to enforce neutrality within the domestic jurisdiction of the United States. Meanwhile Congress placed a temporary embargo by joint resolution on all ships in American ports bound for foreign ports and authorized the President to lay an embargo pending the next session—the first uses by Congress of its commerce power as a lever in foreign relations.[3]

The question of the role of the House of Representatives in the implementation of treaties arose as early as 1796. John Jay had gone to England to negotiate a commercial treaty with Great Britain. Publication of the treaty after the Senate ratified it in June, 1795, was followed by an outburst of popular resentment against Jay's surrender of American neutral rights. After President Washington sent a copy of Jay's Treaty to the House, a prolonged debate ensued in that body concerning the constitutional obligation of Congress to supply the appropriations required to put the treaty into effect. When a bill was introduced in the House to vote the needed funds, supporters of the treaty (Hamilton, Chief Justice Ellsworth, and others) argued that the House must make the appropriation willy-nilly; that the treaty, having been ratified by and with the advice and consent of the Senate, was the "supreme law of the land," and that the legislative branch was bound thereby no less than the executive and judicial branches. James Madison, a member of the House, opposed this thesis in a series of resolutions that asserted the traditional doctrine: "When a Treaty stipulates regulations on any of the subjects submitted by the Constitution to the power of Congress, it must depend for its execution, as to such stipulations, on a law or laws to be passed by Congress. And it is the Constitutional right and duty of the House of Representatives, in all such cases, to deliberate on the expediency or inexpediency of carrying such Treaty into effect, and to determine and act thereon, as, in their judgement, may be most conducive to the public good." The upshot of the matter was that the House adopted Madison's resolutions, while at the same time it voted the required funds.[4]

As the eighteenth century approached its end, our relations with France reached a crisis induced in part by French annoyance over American neutrality and Senate ratification of Jay's Treaty. In 1798 the Fifth Congress enacted the Alien and Sedition Laws and abrogated all existing treaties with France. This was congressional regulation of foreign policy with a vengeance, and after two years of an undeclared naval war, the Convention of 1800 confirmed congressional action.

Nineteenth-Century Developments

During the nineteenth century, the House of Representatives was largely preoccupied with domestic affairs, but on at least a dozen occasions it played a prominent part on the international stage.

The first occasion occurred in 1803 in connection with the Louisiana Purchase. After Spain retroceded the Province of Louisiana, as it was then called, to France in 1800, President Jefferson sent James Monroe to Paris to negotiate with Napoleon for the cession of New Orleans to the United States. Napoleon was getting ready to renew his war with England; he needed money, and he feared that England or the United States might seize New Orleans. So he offered to sell the entire Province of Louisiana. Monroe and the American ministers to France and Spain—Robert Livingston and Charles Pinckney—accepted the offer, and the treaty of cession was signed at Paris on April 30, 1803. The price finally paid for the territory was $27,627,622 and has been called "the most gigantic real estate transaction of all times." News of the acquisition of Louisiana, which more than doubled the area of the United States and gave us complete control of the "Father of Waters," produced a sensation in this country. At a special session of Congress in October, 1803, the Senate promptly ratified the purchase, and both houses passed the necessary appropriation bills. The sentiment of Congress had been foreshadowed early in 1803 when it had appropriated $2,000,000 for the purchase of New Orleans and the land around the Mississippi River.

After the renewal of the Napoleonic Wars and the ensuing invasion of American neutral rights and damage to our foreign trade, Congress and especially the House of Representatives employed its foreign commerce power to retaliate against Britain and France. From 1806 to 1812 a series of nonimportation and embargo acts were passed in an unsuccessful effort to win respect for our neutral rights and to keep the United States out of war. Finally the activities of Henry Clay and his band of "War Hawks" in the House forced the hand of President Madison and led to the second war with England. Although referred to derisively as "Mr. Madison's War," it was largely a war of Congress' own making. The Treaty of Ghent, which terminated the conflict, was effectuated by the act of February 5, 1816, in which the House, conscious of its commerce power, enacted the clauses of the treaty seriatim, after debating at length the issue of legislative power in relation to the status of a treaty.

A few years later, the House for the first time challenged the authority of the President with regard to the recognition of the insurgent republics of Latin America. In 1818, Henry Clay proposed to appropriate funds to pay the salary for a minister to one of the new republics, although the President had not requested the money. Clay's proposal was defeated, but on February 10, 1821, the House passed a resolution giving its "constitutional support" to the President whenever he should consider it expedient to recognize the new states. Finally, in May, 1822, the congressional viewpoint prevailed when the President asked for and received $100,000 for diplomatic missions to Latin America.

In his annual message of December 2, 1823, President Monroe inserted the passage that was to become famous as the "Monroe Doctrine." He asserted "that the American continents, by the free and independent condition which they have assumed and maintain, are henceforth not to be considered as subjects for future colonization by any European power." This doctrine was purely an executive declaration of principle, and although it was favorably received by the American people, it was never adopted or sanctioned by Congress. In 1824, Henry Clay tried unsuccessfully to persuade the House of Representatives to pass a resolution embodying the doctrine. However, its basic principle had been foreshadowed by a congressional resolution of January 9, 1811, relating to East Florida, which stated that the United States could not see "with indifference, any part of the Spanish provinces adjoining the said States eastward of the River Perdido pass from the hands of Spain into those of any other foreign power." French intervention in Argentina and Uruguay in 1838 prompted Caleb Cushing, chairman of the House Committee on Foreign Affairs, to sponsor a House resolution based on the Monroe Doctrine questioning French intentions. But that and later attempts to secure the formal sanction of Congress for the doctrine proved ineffectual.[5]

The Civil War was marked by serious complications in our relations with England and France in which the House of Representatives was involved. During the war, Congress became aroused by the intervention of Napoleon III in Mexico and tried to force President Lincoln to adopt a more vigorous policy toward France. On April 4, 1864, the House unanimously passed a joint resolution offered by Henry Winter Davis, chairman of the Committee on Foreign Affairs, which declared:

> The Congress of the United States are unwilling, by silence, to leave the nations of the world under the impression that they are indifferent spectators of the deplorable events now transpiring in the Republic of Mexico; and they therefore think fit to declare that it does not accord with the policy of the United States to acknowledge a monarchical government, erected on the ruins of any republican government in America, under the auspices of any European power.

In a dispatch to the United States minister at Paris shortly after the House adopted this resolution, Secretary of State Seward instructed him to explain to the French government that this was purely an executive question beyond the constitutional power of the House, which had no authority in the determination of American recognition policy. After Seward's dispatch had been communicated by the President to the House at its request, Representative Davis offered another resolution which was adopted by an overwhelming vote on December 21, 1865, and which declared:

> Congress has a constitutional right to an authoritative voice in declaring and prescribing the foreign policy of the United States, as well in the recognition of new powers as in other matters; and it is the constitutional duty of the President to respect that policy, not less in diplomatic negotiations than in the use of the national forces when authorized by law; and the propriety of any declaration of foreign policy by Congress is sufficiently proved by the vote which pronounced it; and such proposition while pending and undetermined is not a fit topic of diplomatic explanation with any foreign power.

The tempest subsided, but the controversy over the respective roles of the Executive and the Congress in foreign affairs under the Constitution remained unresolved.[6]

The House again asserted its legislative power over foreign relations following the Senate's ratification of the treaty with Russia for the purchase of Alaska on April 9, 1867. Considerable opposition to the purchase was displayed in the House, which finally passed an appropriation bill on July 14, 1868, with a preamble asserting the authority of Congress over the subjects covered in the treaty and giving its "assent" thereto. The Senate balked, of course, at this presumption but finally conceded in the compromise bill that certain clauses of the treaty could not be executed "except by legislation, to which the consent of both Houses of Congress is necessary."[7]

The relation of congressional legislative power to treaties arose again in this period when the House challenged the traditional practice of governing relations with the Indian tribes by treaty. It refused in 1870 to make an appropriation for the execution of certain Indian treaties and succeeded in removing the regulation of Indian affairs from the field of foreign relations by a provision in the Indian Appropriation Act of 1871 that prohibited future recognition of an Indian tribe by treaty.[8]

During the closing decades of the nineteenth century, Congress was still mostly concerned with domestic matters, but in the final years of the century it played an active part in three foreign episodes. In 1893, Queen Liliuokalani of Hawaii was deposed, but Congress resisted efforts to use American troops to restore the monarchy. In 1894, both houses passed resolutions of noninterference in the Hawaiian situation; on July 4, Hawaii became a republic and was formally recognized by President Cleveland. Treaties for the annexation of the Hawaiian Islands failed during the Harrison and McKinley administrations, but after Admiral Dewey's electrifying victory at Manila, Congress approved the annexation of Hawaii by joint resolution, which passed the House by a vote of 209 to 91.

In 1895 the long-standing boundary dispute between Great Britain and Venezuela came to a climax. By joint resolution Congress backed up President Cleveland's demand that the dispute be submitted to arbitration. When Britain refused, Congress, in a burst of anti-British feeling, quickly granted the President's request for an appropriation for a commission to investigate the boundary controversy. The episode led the two countries to the brink of war, but Britain finally agreed to arbitration.

At the end of the century, congressional action led to the Spanish-American War. A vivid account of the role of Congress in this fateful conflict is given by Dorothy B. Goebel.[9]

> The Cuban revolution led to a complete reversal of the roles of President and Congress in our foreign relations. While in the Venezuela dispute, the President led with Congress close on his heels, in the case of Cuba, Congress dragged an unwilling Executive into an armed conflict. . . .
>
> As the revolution continued, the spreading desolation in Cuba (trumpeted by the "yellow press") brought a nationwide demand for American action. The pugnacious mood evoked by the Venezuela crisis found in Spain a fresh target. Congressional humanitarian feeling and wrath erupted in a concurrent resolution (April 6, 1896) declaring in favor of recognition of the belligerency of the insurgents, and urging that the United States should tender its good offices to obtain from Spain recognition of the independence of Cuba. Cleveland and McKinley, in turn, refused to adopt this course and sought to restrain the Congressional temper.
>
> The sinking of the Maine in Havana harbor (February 15, 1898) was a fuse that set off a charge of pent-up emotion. Cries for war against Spain and for American intervention to liberate Cuba echoed in the halls of Congress. While diplomatic negotiations with Spain dragged to an unsatis-

factory conclusion, McKinley surrendered to Congressional pressure. Following the Presidential message of April 11, 1898, Congress passed the famous joint resolution (April 19) declaring the independence of the Cuban people, authorizing American intervention for the liberation of the island, renouncing any intention of annexation. A few days later, Congress passed an act declaring that, as of April 21, war existed between the United States and Spain.

By its action, Congress abandoned the historic American principle of nonintervention, and set the United States on a new and uncharted course. . . . Not since the days of the American Revolution had Congress exercised so fateful an influence on American foreign policy.

Thus it will be seen in retrospect that Congress, and especially the House of Representatives, participated intermittently in the foreign affairs of the United States during the nineteenth century, and that at times, as in the War of 1812 and the intervention in Cuba, it exercised a decisive influence upon our foreign policy. But at the end of the century the long-standing disputes between House and Senate over the rival powers of legislation and treaty, and between Congress and the President over the right to recognize foreign states, remained unsolved.

Twentieth-Century Trends

While the twentieth century was destined to witness a remarkable growth in the influence of the House of Representatives in the foreign field, its role in foreign affairs was a comparatively minor one down to the end of World War I. It participated in the passage of a bill for reciprocity with Canada during the special session of the Sixty-second Congress, which that country promptly rejected; it approved the Underwood Tariff Bill in the Sixty-third Congress by a vote of 281 to 139; and on April 6, 1917, it voted for war with Germany by 373 to 50. President Wilson dominated the foreign relations of the United States during World War I. After the Senate rejected the Versailles Treaty in 1919, both houses adopted a joint resolution "declaring peace," but President Wilson vetoed this measure on May 27, 1920, on the ground that it did not seek to accomplish any of the objects for which the United States had entered the war, and the House declined to override his veto. Later a similar resolution was adopted and signed by President Harding on July 2, 1921. Meanwhile, on the issue of naval disarmament, both houses adopted the Borah amendment, which was designed to remove the danger of Anglo-American naval rivalry.

Between the two World Wars (1920-1940), the House of Representatives played a noteworthy part in legislative consideration of adherence to the World Court, proposals to prohibit the exportation of arms, and in neutrality legislation.

Adherence by the United States to the World Court was repeatedly urged by the President, but the Senate was slow to act. Finally the House in 1925, by a vote of 303 to 28, took the unprecedented step of adopting a resolution declaring its approval of such a course and its willingness to make the necessary appropriations. Whereupon the Senate, on January 27, 1926, adopted a resolution of adherence by a vote of 76 to 17, but attached reservations that proved unacceptable to other members of the Court. In 1932, Chairman Linthicum of the Foreign Affairs Committee of the House sponsored a joint resolution authorizing an appropriation as our share of the Court's expenses for that year, but the resolution of adherence was rejected by the Senate on January 29, 1935, by a vote of 52 to 36, seven short of the required two-thirds majority. The United States finally became a member of the World Court on October 24, 1945, when the Charter of the United Nations and the Statute of the Court became effective.

In 1922, Congress, at the request of the State Department, extended the Arms Embargo Resolution of 1912 to prevent the shipment of arms to nations engaged in civil war. During the ensuing decade, the House Committee on Foreign Affairs had arms embargo bills on its agenda on which extensive hearings were held. Finally, in May, 1933, the McReynolds Arms Embargo Resolution passed the House by a vote of 254 to 109. An amended version of this resolution passed the Senate on February 28, 1934, but was not called up in the House. But the long study of the subject by the House was not without some influence, for on April 19, 1934, the Senate set up the special Nye Committee to investigate the international traffic in arms, and in May, President Roosevelt asked the Senate to give its advice and consent to the Geneva Convention of 1925.[10]

Meanwhile, as the clouds of war were gathering in Germany under Hitler, in Italy under Mussolini, and in the Far East, Congress turned its attention to measures designed to keep the United States out of war. These included credits to belligerents, restrictions on travel by Americans in war zones, on the use of ports by submarines, and on the shipment of raw materials to belligerents. Between 1935 and 1939 the Committee on Foreign Affairs and the House itself considered a flood of bills and resolutions that sought to prevent American involvement in any conflict. For five years or more, Congress engaged in a futile quest to find neutrality in a world bent on war. The upshot of this effort was a series of five neutrality laws: the joint resolutions of August 31, 1935; February 29, 1936; January 8, 1937; May 1, 1937; and November 4, 1939. When World War II broke out in 1939, the country embarked upon a defense program, and Congress re-

GEORGE W. NORRIS
July 11, 1861–September 2, 1944

George W. Norris of Nebraska spent forty eventful years in Congress: ten of them in the House of Representatives (1903-1913) and thirty in the Senate (1913-1943). Although three-fourths of his public life is associated with the Senate, where Norris is remembered for his filibuster against Woodrow Wilson's Armed Ship Bill in 1917 and for his long fight to establish the Tennessee Valley Authority, among many other battles, his decade in the House is of particular interest here. It coincided with the Speakership of "Czar" Cannon, whose arbitrary dictatorship Norris rebelled against and finally overthrew with the help of fellow insurgent Republicans and the Democrats in the House. In his *Profiles in Courage,* John F. Kennedy painted a picture of George Norris as a man of deep conviction, fearless courage, and sincere honesty:

His chunky figure . . . clothed in the drab black suits, white shirts and little black shoestring ties he had worn most of his life and would wear until his death. His mild manners, disarming honesty and avoidance of the social circle of politics in favor of a quiet evening of reading set him apart from the career politicans of his country, whose popularity among the voters, however, he far outstripped.

OSCAR WILDER UNDERWOOD
May 6, 1862–January 25, 1929

Oscar W. Underwood represented Birmingham, Alabama, in the House from 1897 to 1915, and then served two terms in the Senate (1915–1927). During his last four years in the House, he served as Democratic floor leader, and chairman of the Ways and Means Committee, posts in which he demonstrated his capacity for leadership and his detailed knowledge of the tariff, a current issue in which Underwood stood in favor of a tariff for revenue only. He was one of the leading candidates in 1912 for the Democratic presidential nomination, and co-operated fully with President Wilson's legislative program, being the chief architect of the Underwood Tariff Act. In the Senate he became an outstanding member, supporting Wilson in the bitter fight over the League of Nations. He served two years as Democratic floor leader in the Senate, but was a strong critic of the Senate's rules. In the presidential campaign of 1924, Underwood denounced the Ku Klux Klan as un-American, which probably cost him the Democratic presidential nomination. In 1927 he retired from the Senate to his beautiful estate, Woodlawn, near Mount Vernon in Virginia, and wrote *Drifting Sands of Party Politics* (1928), setting forth his reflections on government and revealing his devotion to Jeffersonian principles.

JOHN NANCE GARNER
November 22, 1868–November 7, 1967

John Nance Garner was a member of the House of Representatives for thirty years (1903–1933), until he resigned to become Vice President of the United States during the first two terms of Franklin D. Roosevelt. Garner served as minority floor leader of the House in the Seventy-first Congress and as Speaker in the Seventy-second Congress. During his years in the House, Garner sat at different times on the Rivers and Canals Committee, the Committee on Expenditures in the State Department, the Foreign Affairs Committee, and the Committee on Ways and Means. He was an active member of the coalition that overthrew Cannonism in 1910, and he fathered the creation of a joint Democratic steering committee to define party policies in the Seventy-second Congress. Garner was a master of parliamentary practice and an able strategist who enjoyed the give-and-take of political debate. He combined a broad understanding of public problems with a strong personality and capacity for leadership. During his career in the first chamber he was identified with much of the national legislation of the first three decades of the twentieth century. Garner's wife was his secretary throughout his political career, establishing one of Washington's most famous partnerships. In 1941, he retired to private life in Uvalde, Texas, the town where he began the practice of law in 1891.

Claude Kitchin was elected to Congress from North Carolina in 1900 and served until his death. A fluent speaker with a fine voice, ready wit, and strong convictions, Kitchin became the most powerful debater in the House and always knew whereof he spoke. In 1915 he became chairman of the Ways and Means Committee and majority floor leader. Although he voted against war with Germany, for which he was bitterly criticized, once war was declared he devoted himself completely to its prosecution in the preparation and passage of the war revenue legislation. In a memorial address Clarence Cannon said that Kitchin had "the strength and courage of a gladiator, the wisdom and vision of a statesman, and with them all the intuition and tenderness of a woman." Woodrow Wilson said of him: "I never knew a man who could state his position more lucidly, or state yours more fairly."

CLAUDE KITCHIN
March 24, 1869–May 31, 1923

BERTRAND HOLLIS SNELL
December 9, 1870–February 2, 195(

NICHOLAS LONGWORTH
November 5, 1869–April 9, 1931

After serving four years in the Ohio legislature, Nicholas Longworth represented Cincinnati in Congress from 1903 to 1913 and from 1915 to 1931. He was Republican floor leader of the House in the Sixty-eighth Congress (1923–1925) and served as Speaker for three terms (1925–1931), succeeding Frederick H. Gillett of Massachusetts. Before his elevation to the Speakership, he had served on the Foreign Affairs Committee and the Ways and Means Committee. Longworth became a master of parliamentary procedure and was a strong advocate of responsible party government. In his management of the House of Representatives he earned a reputation for fairness and efficiency. Though a firm partisan, he took the House floor to oppose Coolidge's naval program and helped to pass the Soldier's Loan Bill over Hoover's opposition. His marriage at the White House to Theodore Roosevelt's daughter Alice was a brilliant social event. A stickler for observance of due decorum in intercameral intercourse, a genial host, and talented musician, Longworth was a popular personality in Washington during his time.

Bertrand Snell began his political career in 1915 when he was elected to the Sixty-fourth Congress as a Republican from the Thirty-first New York District. His service in the House continued until January 3, 1939, when he voluntarily retired from Congress. For eight years (1923–1931) he was chairman of the Committee on Rules, having begun his service on Rules in the Sixty-fifth Congress. From 1931 to his retirement in 1939, he served as minority leader of the House. Mr. Snell was active in Republican politics in New York State for thirty years and was a delegate to seven Republican National Conventions. He was permanent chairman of the 1932 and 1936 conventions. Bert Snell graduated from Amherst College with Dwight Morrow and had an active and successful business career in northern New York state before coming to Congress. In the history of the House he was one of its outstanding legislators: a talented leader, a fine parliamentarian, and a rugged fighter. His ambition was to become Speaker of the House, which he never achieved. One of his great legislative contributions was his sponsorship of the St. Lawrence Seaway; this was his pet project in the House and one he lived to see within sight of completion. At the suggestion of the New York delegation, the Grasse River lock of the seaway was named in his honor.

CLARENCE CANNON
April 11, 1879–May 12, 1964

Clarence Cannon represented Missouri's Ninth District in the House of Representatives for twenty consecutive terms, beginning March 4, 1923. This was the same district that Speaker Champ Clark had represented; Cannon was originally a protege and clerk of Clark's. During his forty-one years in Congress, he had two claims to fame: first, as the outstanding authority on congressional procedure; and second, as chairman of the Committee on Appropriations from 1941 to 1964, except during the four years of Republican control. Former parliamentarian of the House, he was co-author with Asher Hinds of *Hinds' and Cannon's Precedents of the House of Representatives,* a monumental eleven-volume codification of congressional practice. He was also the author of *Cannon's Procedure in the House of Representatives,* a synopsis of the subject. For many years, Mr. Cannon was the parliamentarian for the Democratic National Conventions. As chairman of the powerful spending committee of the House, the Missourian reported bills appropriating more than a trillion dollars. He ruled his committee with an iron hand and was known as a combative, economy-minded chairman who often feuded with his Senate counterparts as well as with the executive branch.

SAM RAYBURN
January 6, 1882–
November 16, 1961

Sam Rayburn was elected as a Democrat to the Sixty-third Congress (1913–1915) and was a member of the House until his death. He served as majority leader in the Seventy-fifth and Seventy-sixth Congresses and was elected Speaker on September 16, 1940. "Mr. Sam" was the Speaker of the House for more than twenty years, except during the Republican Eightieth and Eighty-third Congresses when he was minority leader, and he holds the record for the longest service in the chair. In earlier years he was a member and chairman of the Committee on Interstate and Foreign Commerce, where he played a key role in shaping much of the New Deal legislation which bore his name. Mr. Rayburn was a solid, sturdy, untalkative man who avoided fanfare or headline hunting and preferred persuasion to dictation. As majority leader and as Speaker, he regarded himself as a team player and not as an individual star. He often said that he was "one man in public life who's satisfied," having achieved the Speakership which was his highest ambition. Perhaps his greatest parliamentary feat was his gaveling of the Draft Extension Bill through the House in September, 1941, by a single-vote majority before any legislator could change his mind. A practical politician trained in a rough and rigorous school, Rayburn once advised his fellow Democrats prior to a crucial roll call that "if you want to get along—go along." On such pragmatic principles as this, he ran the House with an iron hand for longer than any other Speaker in American history.

CARL VINSON
November 18, 1883–

"Uncle Carl" Vinson was elected to the Sixty-third Congress (1913–1915) to fill a vacancy in the Sixth Georgia District. When he retired in 1964 after twenty-five additional terms, he had served longer than any member in the history of the House. Known as "the Old Fox," Vinson was a major architect of the nation's defense policies as the veteran chairman of the Committee on Armed Services and its predecessor, the Naval Affairs Committee. A firm believer in civilian control of the military, he was also known as the "Backstage Boss of the Pentagon." Most of the important defense legislation after World War II came from his committee and over the years he rarely lost a floor fight. The measures that preserved the Marine Corps, established the Air Force Academy, and consolidated military purchasing were formed by his committee. On the occasion of Vinson's ninetieth birthday in 1973, President Nixon announced that a nuclear-powered aircraft carrier would be named for him. Forty-eight Congressmen flew to the Vinson home in Georgia to honor the day.

HOWARD W. SMITH
February 2, 1883–

Howard W. Smith represented the Eighth Virginia District in the House of Representatives from 1931 to 1967. He was chairman of the powerful House Rules Committee from January, 1955, until 1967. A soft-spoken and shrewd veteran, Judge Smith used his power to control the access of bills to the House floor in a manner that made him one of the most influential members of the chamber. He frequently used his position to block civil rights and other measures distasteful to the South. At the opening of the Eighty-seventh Congress in 1961, Smith led the coalition forces against Speaker Rayburn in the historic battle to enlarge the size of the Rules Committee, losing by only five votes. In 1966 he was defeated in the primary election. A large factor in that defeat was a reapportionment that added many suburban Washington voters to his district.

JOSEPH WILLIAM MARTIN, JR.
November 3, 1884–March 6, 1968

After serving in the Massachusetts legislature (1912–1917) and in various local party offices, "Joe" Martin was elected as a Republican to the Sixty-ninth Congress (1925–1927), and he sat in the House continuously until 1967. He was minority leader of the House from the Seventy-sixth until the Eighty-sixth Congresses, except during the eightieth and eighty-third Congresses when he was Speaker. He served on the Foreign Affairs Committee from 1925 to 1939, on the Rules Committee from 1929 to 1939, and on the Science and Astronautics Committee after 1958. As Speaker he assisted in the enactment of the Greek-Turkish Aid Program and the Marshall Plan. He also sponsored in 1945 the amendment restricting the President to two terms and aided in its adoption. In a Republican caucus on January 6, 1959, Representative Charles Halleck of Indiana ousted Martin as minority leader by a 74-to-70 secret-ballot vote. Many House Republicans felt that Halleck, at fifty-eight, could give the party more vigorous leadership than the seventy-four-year-old Martin. Six years later, when Representative Gerald R. Ford defeated Halleck for the post, Martin supported Ford. In 1966, Martin was defeated in a primary by Mrs. Margaret M. Heckler.

JOHN WILLIAM MCCORMACK *December 21, 1891–*

After serving six years in the Massachusetts legislature (1920–1926), John W. McCormack was elected as a Democrat to the Seventieth Congress and served from 1928 through 1970 as a representative of the Twelfth (redistricted as the Ninth in 1962) District. He was majority leader from 1940 to 1961, except for the Eightieth and Eighty-third Congresses when he was minority whip. He became Speaker in 1962, following the death of Sam Rayburn. A New Deal liberal, he was a consistent if undynamic supporter of Democratic Presidents. In 1969 he successfully rebuffed a challenge for the Speakership by Representative Morris K. Udall of Arizona, and in 1970 a resolution of no confidence in the party leadership was tabled in the caucus. He subsequently agreed to allow the younger members a greater voice in policy matters. He also supported a permanent enlargement of the House Rules Committee and the "twenty-one-day rule." Remarkably, in twenty-one elections to the House, he never received less than 70 per cent of the vote.

CHARLES ABRAHAM HALLECK *August 22, 1900–*

Charles A. Halleck was elected as a Republican to the Seventy-fourth Congress and was a member of the House from 1935 through 1968 as the representative of the Second Indiana District. He was majority leader during the Eightieth and Eighty-third Congresses. In 1959 he defeated former Speaker Martin for the post of minority leader in a struggle over the role of the younger members of the party. He had served on the standing committees on Rules, Expenditures in the Executive Departments, and Interstate and Foreign Commerce, and on the special committees on lobbying activities and small business. A conservative, Mr. Halleck was one of the chief architects of the so-called conservative coalition that has often been able since 1938 to control legislative action in the House. A shrewd, tough, practical politician and an able orator, he frequently teamed up with his opposite member in the Senate, Everett M. Dirksen. Their joint appearances were often dubbed the "Ev and Charlie Show." In 1965, Mr. Halleck was defeated for the post of minority leader by Representative Gerald R. Ford, as the younger members once again asserted themselves in an attempt to give the party more positive leadership. Mr. Halleck retired at the end of the next Congress.

CARL ALBERT *May 10, 1908–*

On January 21, 1971, Carl Albert was elected forty-sixth Speaker of the House of Representatives. He has represented the Third District of Oklahoma continuously since 1947. He served as House majority whip from the Eighty-fourth Congress (1955–57) through the first session of the Eighty-seventh Congress, then as House majority leader from January, 1962, until chosen Speaker. He served on the Committee on Agriculture for thirteen years and has been a member of the committees on Science and Astronautics, Post Office and Civil Service, as well as the Select Committee to Investigate Lobbying Activities and the Democratic Congressional Campaign Committee. An attorney, Carl Albert graduated from the University of Oklahoma and won a Rhodes Scholarship to Oxford.

Neither aggressive nor dynamic, Speaker Albert has nevertheless done much to increase the power and the influence of the office. In the Ninety-Third Congress, he influenced the caucus to add him to the Committee on Committees and then succeeded in filling vacancies on the Committee on Rules with members who were in harmony with the leadership. When in the Ninety-fourth Congress the newly reorganized Democratic Steering and Policy Committee became the Committee on Committees, the Speaker became chairman of the twenty-four-member committee and was empowered to appoint nine of the members. Speaker Albert has been sympathetic to a more active caucus system, although he does not believe that the leadership had (or should have) the sanctions to engage in arm-twisting. In the opinion of many congressional observers Speaker Albert has been very successful in curbing the worst excesses of the seniority system and restoring to the leadership the power to regulate the flow of legislation.

THOMAS P. "TIP" O'NEILL, JR. *December 9, 1912–*

A consistent liberal Democrat, "Tip" O'Neill began his career as a politician when he was elected to the Massachusetts General Court (State House) in 1936. In 1952 he succeeded John F. Kennedy as the representative from the Eleventh (now Eighth) District. He quickly became a protégé of Speaker McCormack and was appointed to the Committee on Rules during his second term. In 1971 he was made majority whip. When Majority Leader Hale Boggs was lost in a plane crash in 1973, "Tip" O'Neill succeeded him.

A politician of the old clubhouse school, O'Neill has successfully represented an extremely complex district—one with an enormous constituency of university students and dozens of ethnic, working-class neighborhoods. He has consistently supported aid to education, consumer protection, and strong gun-control legislation. He broke with President Johnson in 1967 on the issue of the Vietnam War. Over the years he has also been effective in promoting legislative reform and party responsibility. In 1970 he helped draft and promote the Legislative Reorganization Act and supported the abolition of unrecorded teller votes, the limiting of each representative to one subcommittee chairmanship and the recording of votes in committees. In 1973 he also helped promote the idea of a vigorous steering and policy committee. During the discussions of impeachment of President Nixon, Representative O'Neill insisted that the issue be considered by the Committee on the Judiciary, rather than an *an hoc* committee, and was effective in assisting the committee to establish its procedures. Hardly an orator or a dynamic personality, "Tip" O'Neill believes in politics as compromise and negotiation, a position that has led critics to fault his leadership while others point to his achievements.

GERALD R. FORD *July 14, 1913–*

At a time when most observers had discounted the possibility that members of the House could succeed in presidential politics, Gerald R. Ford became the nation's thirty-eighth President. But it was an extraordinary sequence of events that led to his inauguration. On October 12, 1973, President Nixon nominated Minority Leader Ford to become Vice President after the resignation from that post of Spiro T. Agnew. On December 6, Ford was confirmed. When Richard M. Nixon resigned as President in the aftermath of the Watergate scandal, Gerald R. Ford succeeded to the Presidency on August 9, 1974, the ninth Vice President in our history to become President.

An attorney, he graduated from the University of Michigan in 1935 and Yale Law School in 1941. President Ford was elected to the House of Representatives as a Republican from the Fifth District in Michigan and was re-elected continuously through 1972. In 1963 he was elected chairman of the House Republican Conference in an election that was regarded as a victory for the so-called Young Turks. Two years later, he defeated Representative Charles A. Halleck of Indiana to become minority leader, a post he held for nine years.

During his House career, Gerald R. Ford was a party loyalist and a conservative. He consistently supported the Vietnam War and his record on civil rights and social welfare programs in general was that of a moderate. On a few occasions his partisanship appeared excessive to many of his colleagues, yet there was an overall warmth and civility to his manner that led to applause on both sides of the aisle as he moved from the legislative to the executive branch. When he became President he faced an enormous task—that of somehow restoring a sense of credibility to the White House. President Ford did that, and even when a succession of vetoes generated strong responses in the Democratic Ninety-fourth Congress, the dialogue had at least recovered the quality of honest disagreement.

Representative Rhodes had the unenviable task of being minority leader during the darkest moments of the Nixon Presidency. First elected to the Eighty-third Congress from the First District in Arizona in 1952, he has been reelected eleven times and has been a member of the House longer than anyone in that state's history. Prior to his election as minority leader, he had been chairman of the House Republican Policy Committee for nine years. He was reelected minority leader at the outset of the Ninety-fourth Congress.

An attorney with degrees from Kansas State University and Harvard Law School, Representative Rhodes has been a conservative and a party regular. During the 1972 Republican Convention, he was chairman of the Platform Committee. He was a member of the Committee on Appropriations and also served on the Joint Study Committee on Budget Control which recommended the formation of House and Senate Budget Committees. His low key but effective manner was credited for the considerable success the Republicans had in sustaining many of the presidential vetoes in the ninety-fourth Congress.

JOHN J. RHODES
September 18, 1916–

Elected to the Eighty-seventh Congress as a Republican in 1960, Representative Anderson has been reelected seven times from the Sixteenth District of Illinois. In 1969 he was elected chairman of the House Republican Conference (caucus) and has been reelected three times, although in 1971 he won in a close election against a very conservative Representative Samuel Devine of Ohio.

An attorney with degrees from the University of Illinois and Harvard Law School, Representative Anderson has been enough of a party loyalist to command the respect of his colleagues, yet liberal enough to win Democratic votes in his district and a reputation as something of a maverick among House Republicans. In 1968, he cast a critical vote on the Rules Committee which sent a civil rights bill on open housing to the floor. Known as an articulate, witty and forceful debater, he has also been a vigorous spokesman for such congressional reforms as open conferences, a ban on proxy voting, the realignment of committee reponsibilities, and the televising of floor proceedings. During the Ninety-fourth Congress he frequently criticized the Democrats for their renewed emphasis on the role of the caucus, raising the specter of major policy decisions being made in secret. When the Democrats voted to allow open caucuses, he hailed the death of "King Caucus", expressing the hope that the wake would be open so that all might observe the "King Caucus" carcass.

JOHN B. ANDERSON
February 15, 1922–

PHILLIP BURTON *June 1, 1926–*

If the early 1970s are recalled as a time when the long moribund Democratic caucus showed spasms of vitality, much of the responsibility will be assigned to Representative Phillip Burton. Elected to the Eighty-eighth Congress in a special election on February 18, 1964, he has been re-elected six times from the Fifth District of California, a district so polyglot that only 25 per cent of its residents are "white, English-speaking, third-generation Americans." Representative Burton is one of the most vigorous House liberals, specializing in legislation dealing with minimum wages, public assistance, and health care. He wrote the black lung compensation provisions of the Coal Mine Health and Safety Act of 1970. He was also one of the early House opponents of the Vietnam war.

During the Ninety-second Congress, Representative Burton headed the Democratic Study Group, and was a vigorous member during the Ninety-third Congress, promoting the idea of a more vigorous caucus as a formulator of party policy. He campaigned vigorously for the chairmanship of the caucus and won in late 1974 by a vote of 162 to 111 over Representative B.F. Sisk of California. Burton received considerable aid from the newly elected freshmen.

His efforts for a vigorous caucus seemed realized when the caucus deposed three committee chairmen and enacted many procedural reforms at a series of meetings prior to the opening of the Ninety-fourth Congress. However the caucus was subjected to considerable criticism when it later voted to deny further funds to Southeast Asia prior to the consideration of that issue by the Committee on International Relations. Subsequently, the appropriate role of the caucus became a topic of increasing intensity among Democrats. Somewhat as a reaction to many of the criticisms which had arisen, the caucus voted in 1975 to allow open meetings and modified its rules to soften the provision which allowed it to bind its members. The failure of the Democrats to override several presidential vetoes also detracted from the vigorous posture the caucus had assumed in the early days of the session. Yet the caucus—and Representative Burton—had demonstrated to chairmen who abused their prerogatives that the caucus enjoyed viable, meaningful sanctions.

As chairman of the caucus, Burton was an *ex officio* vice-chairman of the Steering and Policy Committee, the new Democratic committee on committees and a committee which could evolve into a body which may yet have a significant impact on how party policies are determined.

sponded generously to executive requests for grants of money and power to safeguard the nation. As part of the defense program, Congress enacted the Lend-Lease Act of 1941, which passed the House by a vote of 260 to 165.[11]

Thus the two decades prior to the outbreak of World War II were marked by expanding congressional activity in the foreign field. This activity found expression in committee hearings and inquiries, in extended floor debates and the adoption of resolutions, and in the legislative consideration of a wide-range of international problems. Albert Westphal concluded his survey of the role of the House in foreign affairs down to 1940 by observing that it was still inferior to that of the Senate for various reasons, including qualities inherent in the composition and organization of the House; that the Senate was "less amenable to presidential leadership in foreign affairs than the House"; and that the Foreign Affairs Committee, which had long been regarded as an "ornamental committee" whose members were "relatively obscure in the national scene" and had been apathetic toward obtaining a large role in foreign policy, had come since 1935 into public and legislative prominence with the increasing importance of legislation on foreign affairs.

World War II: The Aftermath

While the House of Representatives up to the mid-thirties had upon occasion played an important part in specific foreign policy issues, its emergence as a major force in the field of foreign affairs on a continuing basis dates from that period. It found expression, first, in the neutrality legislation of the latter half of that decade, and second, in the active participation of the House in the legislative underwriting of World War II. President Roosevelt set forth the goals of a new foreign policy for the United States in the form of the Atlantic Charter and the Four Freedoms. The war period was marked by the establishment of bipartisan and bicameral consultations between Congress and the State Department during the Hull-Welles regime; the extension of the lend-lease legislation in 1943, 1944, and 1945, which the House approved by votes of 407 to 6, 334 to 21, and 354 to 28; creation in 1943 of the United Nations Relief and Rehabilitation Administration by means of an executive agreement, which the House approved by a vote of 287 to 57 on the conference report; House adoption of the Fulbright resolution by a vote of 360 to 29, indicating together with the Connally resolution, congressional support for the postwar establishment of an international organization to keep the peace; and congressional participation at either the preparatory or conference stages in international conferences at Dumbarton Oaks, Mexico City, and San Francisco. Desiring to participate in the control of postwar policy, the House in 1945 passed a resolution amending the Constitution by giving itself equal power over treaties with the Senate by a vote of 288 to 88, but the Senate was unwilling to share its treaty power with the House and took no action on the resolution.[12]

Any President must depend upon congressional support in order to implement his foreign policy, for Congress has power to regulate foreign commerce, to raise armies and maintain navies, to lay and collect taxes for the common defense, and to declare war. Moreover it has the added power "to make all laws which shall be necessary and proper" for effectuating its own powers and those of the government of the United States. Before and during World War II, the foreign policy of the Roosevelt administration was implemented and sustained by a series of legislative acts of which the Lend-Lease Act of March 11, 1941, was the classic example. Under this act, as extended, the United States entered into mutual-aid agreements whereby our allies received $40 billion worth of munitions and other supplies. According to Professor Corwin, the Lend-Lease Act was "the most extensive delegation of authority ever made by Congress to the President to enter into executive agreements. . . ."[13] Corwin further comments that "the relations of President and Congress in the diplomatic field have, first and last, presented a varied picture of alternate cooperation and tension, from which emerge two outstanding facts: first, the overwhelming importance of Presidential initiative in this area of power; secondly, the ever increasing dependence of foreign policy on Congressional cooperation and support."[14]

The enhanced role of the House of Representatives in the foreign affairs field was seen during World War II in the composition of the Committee on Postwar Foreign Policy on which the House was represented by Representative Sol Bloom, chairman of the Committee on Foreign Affairs, Representative Charles A. Eaton, ranking minority member of the committee, and Representative Luther A. Johnson of Texas. It was also reflected in Secretary Hull's consultations with various members of Congress prior to the Dumbarton Oaks Conference and in the presence of two representatives on the U.S. delegation to the San Francisco Conference. After the Senate ratified the United Nations Charter, it was implemented by the United Nations Participation Act of 1945, thus invoking the national legislative power to accomplish the objectives of the charter.

The importance of the role of the House in the international scene was also shown by the submission to the Congress of international agreements which required legislative implementation to become effective and which Congress approved by joint resolution. The original UNRRA legislation

(Public Law 267, Seventy-eighth Congress) was an early example of this procedure. During the Seventy-ninth Congress, both houses approved United States membership in the International Monetary Fund and the International Bank (Public Law 171, Seventy-ninth Congress) and in the Food and Agricultural Organization of the United Nations (Public Law 174, Seventy-ninth Congress). During the Eightieth Congress, the same procedure was employed to secure United States membership in the International Refugee Organization (Public Law 146, Eightieth Congress), the World Health Organization (Public Law 643, Eightieth Congress), the revised International Labor Organization (Public Law 843, Eightieth Congress), the Caribbean Commission (Public Law 431, Eightieth Congress), and the South Pacific Commission (Public Law 403, Eightieth Congress). Likewise the North Atlantic Treaty was implemented by a series of acts, beginning with the Mutual Defense Assistance Act of 1949 (Public Law 329, Eighty-first Congress), which were initiated in the House of Representatives, in accordance with its traditional function of originating supply bills.

Further evidence of the increasing share of Congress in the development and execution of American foreign policy can be seen in the evolution of our foreign-aid program. Beginning with the Economic Cooperation Act of 1948 and continuing through successive aid legislation, Congress spelled out in detail the conditions governing the administration and execution of our foreign policy in the field of economic aid. As a watchdog of the aid program, the 1948 act set up a Joint Committee on Foreign Economic Cooperation consisting of three members each from the House Foreign Affairs and Senate Foreign Relations Committees and two from each of the Appropriations Committees. Moreover, since all the various forms of foreign aid cost money that must be appropriated annually and since all appropriations bills originate in the House of Representatives, its Committee on Appropriations had a much stronger voice in the postwar conduct of our foreign relations than was traditionally true. The annual battle of the foreign-aid budget on Capitol Hill required the Administration to submit foreign-aid programs to periodic "agonizing reappraisals" in order to maintain continued congressional support.

In a single postwar year—1956—the State Department reported that the United States had concluded 260 treaties and other international agreements. Of these, only 5 were actually in the form of treaties that required the advice and consent of the Senate, while 95 per cent of the agreements were entered into under legislative enactments that specified their terms. In 1958 it could therefore be said that "in the most important areas of our formal relations with foreign countries, the negotiations of those relations by the President are conducted in a framework provided by the Congress and governed by conditions spelled out in advance by Congress."[15] The significance of these postwar developments was that, without any formal constitutional change, the role of the House in the foreign field was greatly enhanced.

The postwar years thus witnessed a resurgence of legislative activity in the conduct of foreign affairs. The Fulbright and Connally resolutions placed both the Senate and the House of Representatives on record as favoring United States participation in an international peace organization. They were followed in 1945 by congressional approval of the United Nations Charter. Postwar programs of economic assistance for Europe, such as the British loan in 1946, the Greek-Turkish aid program in 1947, and the European Recovery Program in 1948-1951, all had to be implemented by congressional appropriations.

Illustrations abound of congressional participation in the postwar conduct of foreign affairs. Under its constitutional power to fix import duties, Congress shared since 1934 in the reciprocal trade-agreement programs. Through its power over immigration, it also played a part in policy formulation on the entrance of displaced persons. By the National Security Act of 1947, it prescribed the process of policy formulation and co-ordination with respect to the use of force in the conduct of foreign affairs. The Eighty-first Congress alone enacted eighteen major public laws relating to international affairs, including the continuance of the Marshall Plan, extension of the reciprocal trade agreements, military aid to Western Europe and South Korea, and guarantees of private investments abroad under the Point Four program. Although the initiative was largely with the President, the conduct of foreign affairs continuously called for joint legislative-executive co-operation both in the determination of objectives and in the formulation and execution of policies.

The role of Congress in the conduct of our foreign affairs received increased recognition from the executive branch. The Department of State held many informal conferences on foreign policy with members of the foreign affairs committees of Congress after the outbreak of hostilities in 1939. The President and the Secretary of State reported in person to Congress upon their conduct of our foreign relations after their return from international conferences at Yalta and Moscow. The State Department named one of its assistant secretaries to supervise the department's liaison with Congress. Mr. Dean Acheson, who first functioned in this capacity, established a formal relationship with the Senate Committee on Foreign Relations and the House Committee on Foreign Affairs. And influential members of both houses of Congress participated by presidential invitation in the actual negotiation of great international agreements at Bretton Woods, San Francisco, and London—a practice that won widespread congressional approval and greatly improved the climate of legislative opinion, as well as congressional understanding, of international political and economic problems.

The period, then, saw an enormous increase in the foreign-affairs business of Congress. In 1925 only one bill in twenty-five had any direct bearing on foreign relations, whereas one out of every seven bills enacted in 1949 had some relationship to foreign affairs. In the 1950's, the responsibility for handling the rising work load was scattered among ten standing committees in each house of Congress and three joint committees: Atomic Energy, the Joint Economic Committee, and Immigration and Nationality Policy.[16] A study by Holbert Carroll showed that in the decade after World War II "ten committees of the House of Representatives pursued their sometimes inconsistent and usually uncoordinated philosophies in a fraction of one policy area, the area of international trade policy."[17] Meanwhile six House committees considered the subject of export control, and several committees were active in the field of shipping. The total picture was one of the widespread dispersal and unco-ordinated control of interrelated foreign policy matters among many autonomous committees.[18]

Under these circumstances the need of co-ordination in the work of the House on foreign affairs was generally conceded. But members have always been skeptical of proposals to solve the problem of integrating congressional control of foreign policy.[19] Among possible co-ordinating devices, the select committee, composed of members drawn from interested standing committees of the House, was tried in foreign affairs on three occasions in the 1940's: the Special Committee on Postwar Economic Policy and Planning (the Colmer Committee), established early in 1944; the Select Committee to Investigate Soviet Seizure of the Baltic States (the Kersten Committee), formed in the summer of 1953; and the Select Committee on Foreign Aid (the Herter Committee), created in July, 1947.[20]

Vietnam and Beyond

We have already noted Professor Corwin's observation that in foreign affairs the President and Congress alternate between co-operation and tension. The likelihood is that for many years to come, that relationship will emphasize the tensions. There seems every probability that Congress will legislate in the future with the memories of Vietnam as its catalyst. For many members, especially in the House, the sixties and the early seventies will be recalled as a period when a relatively supine Congress acquiesced time and again to presidential exhortations that the goals of the war could be achieved by one additional appropriation or yet another escalation or incursion. By 1970, Congress could look back at some twenty years of having reacted to presidential initiatives that either committed troops or could have committed troops under circumstances where Congress was relatively helpless to influence events. In 1950, President Truman had sent troops to Korea under his authority as Commander in Chief and a police action became a three-year war with over thirty thousand deaths. In 1955, President Eisenhower requested and received from Congress authorization in advance to use American troops to protect Taiwan if necessary. A 1957 resolution on the Middle East, which the House passed 355 to 61, also allowed the President to make the determination on the use of troops as did resolutions to defend Latin America and West Berlin in 1962. The cause for the greatest penance was the Gulf of Tonkin resolution of 1964, which passed the House without a dissenting vote, had only two negative votes in the Senate, and gave the President a seal of congressional approval to wage a seemingly endless and exhausting war without any further congressional endorsements. A 1968 review (by the Senate Committee on Foreign Relations) of the attack of the American destroyer cast doubt on President Johnson's version of the incident, thus further exacerbating congressional frustration.

The record of the period was clear; Congress, especially the House, had invariably acquiesced in one arms appropriation after another until it began to resemble the legislature of a parliamentary system. The questioning voices came mostly from the Committee on Foreign Relations beginning in 1967, but it was a committee with considerably more prestige than influence.

If the Congress now believes it has become a partner again in the making of foreign policy, perhaps the turning point can be traced to the Senate's 1969 resolution which stated that a national commitment (i.e., the use of armed forces) "results only from affirmative action taken by the executive and legislative branches of the United States Government by means of treaty, statute or concurrent resolution of both Houses of Congress specifically providing for such a commitment."[21]

In the same year, amendments were added to the defense budget which set a ceiling on expenditures in Vietnam, Laos, and Thailand and prohibited the use of American troops in Laos or Thailand. In 1970, Congress repealed the Gulf of Tonkin resolution and voted to forbid funds for the use of troops in Cambodia. An end-the-war amendment to the foreign-aid bill in 1971 by Senator Mansfield was tabled in the House, even though it passed the Senate twice. In 1972, no end-the-war amendments passed, but by then the focus was on the question of how to reduce the possibility that future wars might be exclusively presidential. The War Powers Act—at least a version of it—passed the Senate in 1972 and was finally enacted in 1973. When President Nixon vetoed the measure, the votes to override were 284 to 135 in the House (only four more than the needed two-thirds) and 75 to 18 in the Senate. Whether the act's provision that the President cannot commit troops for more than sixty days without congressional authorization is a genuine restraint on the Presidency or whether it in effect gives him a blank check to fight anywhere and is simultaneously an unconstitutional restraint on the powers of the Commander in Chief are disturbing questions, which will someday be resolved in a period of crisis. Yet the act must be read primarily as a troubled reaction by a Congress seeking to dispel its feeling of impotence.

Actions subsequent to the War Powers Act suggest that there will be continuing congressional involvement in foreign policy. In 1974, the foreign-aid bill contained a legislative veto; the President was required to advise Congress of any offer to sell defense items of $25 million or more to any nation, with Congress having twenty days in which to disapprove the sale. The provision was softened by the stipulation that if the President determined that the sale was in the national interest, he need only report it to Congress. In the same year, Congress also passed an act that restricted the President's ability to share nuclear technology, even for peaceful purposes. The measure required the President to submit the proposal to the Joint Committee on Atomic Energy, which then had thirty days to recommend approval or disapproval by Congress.

The legislative veto strategy was also a feature of several bills in the Ninety-fourth Congress which would limit the authority of the President to enter into executive agreements with foreign nations without congressional approval. While the Senate has the constitutional power to approve or disapprove treaties, the Congress has shown increased concern over the commitments which could be made by executive agreements. According to one count, there have been 157 treaties during the past decade, but 2,178 executive agreements.[22] At issue was not only the congressional attempt to define the concept of the executive agreement with greater clarity, but also the congressional intention of having a greater role in their further formulation. Thus the bill introduced by Representative Thomas E. Morgan of Pennsylvania, chairman of the House Committee on International Relations, and Representative Clement J. Zablocki of Wisconsin, chairman of the Subcommittee on International Security and Scientific Affairs, would require that any executive agreement involving a national commitment must be submitted to Congress and would take effect unless both houses, within sixty days, adopted a concurrent resolution of disapproval. A national commitment as defined by the bill would include any agreement involving United States troops in a foreign nation or any pledge of assistance to a foreign nation.[23]

More significant and certainly more dramatic was the 1975 action by the House in refusing to lift an embargo on the shipment of arms to Turkey. Despite vigorous pleas from President Ford and Secretary of State Kissinger that such action would imperil the existence of important bases in Turkey, the House took the position that Turkey should be penalized for its use of American arms in the invasion of Cyprus in 1974. The 1974 foreign-aid bill had also contained an amendment that ended arms shipment to Turkey, but the President was allowed to delay the ban if it assisted negotiations for a settlement of the Cyprus question. The House vote in 1975 was very close—223 to 206—and a presidential request that the action be reconsidered after Turkey had taken over twenty-six American bases was unsuccessful.[24] Four days after the House failed to lift the arms embargo on Turkey, the President suspended plans to sell $260 million of antiaircraft missile batteries to Jordan, because of the administration's doubts that the sale could survive the recently enacted congressional veto power. The wisdom of the post-Vietnam congressional actions could be debated; their frequency and their reality could not.

Committee on Foreign Affairs

The Committee on Foreign Affairs—whose name was changed to the Committee on International Relations in 1975—and the Committee on Appropriations have been the two principal agents of the House in the international area. Created in 1822, the Foreign Affairs Committee has long had a broad jurisdiction over our foreign relations, including the primary duty of authorizing all appropriations for the conduct of foreign affairs by the Department of State, the International Cooperation Administration, and the United States Information Agency. Long regarded as a minor committee, Foreign Affairs has become one of the more popular committee assignments in the House. After World War II, it was organized into several standing "consultative subcommittees" whose members became specialists on particular geographical and problem areas. With the aid of a small professional staff, this committee made a vital contribution to the development, implementation, and oversight of postwar foreign policy. The committee kept itself and the House informed of international developments by means of frequent conferences with top-level government officials, both civil and military; by sending special study missions to various parts of the world; by setting up special legislative subcommittees to hold hearings and report on specific legislative proposals; by the participation of members of the committee in important international conferences; and by the representation of the committee, beginning in 1951, on the U.S. delegations to the General Assembly of the United Nations.

Holbert Carroll summarized his intensive study of the Foreign Affairs Committee during the twelve-year period, 1945-1956, as follows:[25]

> Like the nation, the foreign policy committee only gradually adjusted to the role of world leadership that fell to the United States. Like the nation, the committee matured slowly. . . . In the second half of 1947, the group developed fresh strength and moved into a more constructive phase of its history; it began to play a more responsible role in the control of foreign affairs. . . .
>
> In testing and managing a large volume of bills and resolution, however, the committee did not alter the fundamentals of American foreign policy. Rather, it modified the measures to harmonize with its views regarding the objectives of that policy and to anticipate the political realities of the lower chamber. The committee's control resembled erosion; the essentials remained but were shaped to suit the congressional temper. In molding legislation, moreover, the Committee on Foreign Affairs, in contrast to many other committees, generally succeeded in keeping the foreign policy objectives dominant and unfettered by the more unenlightened proposals of pressure and propaganda groups.

During the past fifteen years, the reputation that the committee has earned is one of being essentially supportive of the executive branch. Put another way, if the Congress was restive and often critical of our Presidents during the Vietnam decade, the committee members have been more inclined to accept administration estimates and forecasts. For example, in 1972 the committee, for the first time, recommended an end-the-war amendment to a foreign-aid authorization bill, but it did so only after the Democratic caucus had instructed the Democratic members of the committee to do so. The amendment that finally emerged was unsatisfactory to most Democrats and was dropped.[26] In a study of the fate of foreign-aid bills during the period 1955-1966, Richard F. Fenno, Jr., noted that while the amounts requested were cut at every stage of the authorization and appropriations process, those requests fared better with the Foreign Affairs Committee than with any other committee in the legislative sequence.[27] Even when in 1975 the House voted to continue the arms embargo in Turkey, Representative Thomas E. Morgan of Pennsylvania, the committee chairman since 1963, defended the administration position, and the members of the committee voted for the resumption of the arms sales, 20 to 14.[28]

In the Ninety-fourth Congress, the Committee on International Relations had thirty-seven members and subcommittees on international economic policy, international operations, international organizations, international political and military affairs, international resources, food and energy, international security and scientific affairs, international trade and commerce, oversight, future foreign policy research and development, and investigations. Despite its formidable table of organization, there seems little likelihood that the committee will be a source of policy innovation. Perhaps it will make its most important contribution as an administration sounding board or critic, assisting the President in shaping opinions in Congress and in the country when it shares his views.

Committee on Appropriations

In the legislative process in Congress, supply follows authorization to spend. The role of the House Committee on Appropriations is therefore a powerful one, all the more because the House tends to ratify its recommendations. Down to 1959, jurisdiction over the financing of international affairs was scattered among several appropriations subcommittees, so that it was not possible to obtain an integrated view of the foreign affairs budgets. But the creation of a Subcommittee on Foreign Operations in 1950 has enabled its members to specialize in the financing of foreign affairs and has tended to consolidate the consideration of our international expenditures.

Holbert Carroll's analysis of the role of the Committee on Appropriations in handling foreign affairs since the end of World War II shows that it has employed five major types of control:[29]

> First, and most important, the committee determines how much money will be allowed for the foreign affairs purposes. Second, in the hearings it reviews policies and their administration. In the third place, it wields influence by the language employed in committee reports. Limitations and legislative provisions inserted in appropriation bills constitute a fourth type of control. Finally, the committee exercises year-round surveillance over the expenditure of funds.

The committee has continued in those roles and over the years has consistently appropriated considerably less money for foreign aid than a succession of Presidents have requested and usually less than Congress finally appropriates.[30] For many years, the foreign-aid bill was a target for conservatives who frequently described it as a "giveaway." Led by Representative Otto E. Passman, chairman of the Appropriations Subcommittee on Foreign Operations, they frequently succeeded in enacting cuts of from 20 to 30 per cent. During the Vietnam War, opposition to foreign assistance increased, with many members objecting to military aid to various governments ruled by dictators. In 1975, Congress reduced President Ford's request by 39.6 per cent, only slightly more than the cut recommended by the House Committee on Appropriations. The 1975 appropriation bill even contained another example of the "committee veto," requiring the executive branch to notify the House and Senate Appropriations Committees fifteen days in advance of any reprogramming of the funds which deviated from the presentation made to those committees during the budget process.[31]

In preparing legislation for 1976 and 1977, the Committee on International Relations decided to separate its authorizations for economic aid and military aid for the first time since the beginnings of the foreign-aid program in 1948. For many years, the legislative strategy had dictated the joining of those proposals in order to maximize the possibility of passage. By 1975 the problems of military assistance had become so involved in controversy that the linking was obviously a threat to economic development and food programs.[32]

Summary and Conclusions

Summarizing this chapter, we have seen that during most of the nineteenth century after the War of 1812, the House of Representatives, with intermittent foreign interruptions, was largely preoccupied with domestic issues; that down to World War II, the House was distinctly a junior partner of the Senate in foreign affairs; but that it became a co-ordinate member of the foreign policy team after World War II and that the foreign policy business of the House has greatly increased in recent decades and was in general supportive of the executive branch during most of the Vietnam war; that responsibility for foreign affairs is divided among numerous standing committees which have jurisdiction over important aspects of the field, with a resulting lack of integration and perspective; that the Committee on Foreign Affairs, now the Committee on International Relations, which experienced a rapid turnover among its chairmen and members during the nineteenth century, has become one of the more eminent and sought-after committees in the House; that the enhanced role of the House in foreign affairs since World War II reflects both the emergence of the United States as the leading power of the free world and the dependence of the far-flung activities of the Department of State and the mutual security program upon the power of the purse for their implementation; that the House Committee on Appropriations has a major voice in the determination of our foreign policy through its control over funds for foreign expenditure; and that in the post-Vietnam years the House as well as the Senate has sought a greater role in the day-to-day making of foreign policy by a more vigorous use of the appropriations process as well as by the passage of a War Powers Act.

It may be added, in conclusion, that the House of Representatives performs a special role in the foreign field. Representing local interests as it does, it furnishes a sort of recurrent plebiscite on the foreign policy of the United States, acting as a mediator between the foreign-policy specialists at Washington and the "public's" notions of what ought to be done. Moreover the House interprets and transmits to the country information on complicated world problems. Thus Congress functions as a forum through which public opinion is brought to bear upon the federal government, and as a medium for gathering and disseminating information for the instruction and enlightenment of the people.

13

The Role of
the Representative

THE MODERN SYSTEM of political representation as we know it in the United States today is a product of the evolutionary development of the national state which dates back to seventeenth-century England. The English Parliament had developed during the fourteenth century as a bicameral institution and had gradually acquired legislative power through its control over the purse, making its grant of funds to the king depend upon the redress of grievances. By the end of the fifteenth century, the consent of both the House of Lords and the House of Commons was recognized as necessary in the enactment of legislation. The seventeenth century witnessed the classic English statements of the right of the people through their chosen representatives to control the form and policy of government.

English Ideas in Colonial Times

By colonial times two ideas had developed in England regarding the proper role of the representative in relation to his constituents. One was the delegation theory, the idea that a member of Parliament was an agent of his constituency that had elected him, bound to obey its wishes. This idea was held by the Levellers during the Commonwealth period (1640-1660) and by the English Radicals in the late eighteenth century (1769-1800). It influenced the writings of political theorists like Harrington, Sydney, and Locke and the policies of colonial political leaders like William Penn and Roger Williams. One of the major items in the radical program was the

267

right of electors to instruct their members of Parliament. A clear statement of this concept was made by Henry Cruger, a Radical who was elected with Edmund Burke to represent the city of Bristol in Parliament in 1774. He said:[1]

> It has ever been my opinion that the electors have a right to instruct their members. For my part, I shall always think it my duty in Parliament to be guided by your counsels and instructions. I shall consider myself the servant of my constituents, not their master—subservient to their will, not superior to it. And let me add, I hold myself accountable to you for every action of my life which respects the public. By your upright judgment, I desire to stand or fall.

The other idea of political representation that developed in England during colonial times was the idea of virtual representation: the doctrine that the representative was a trustee for the entire nation and was free to decide matters according to his own independent judgment. This idea has been expressed as early as 1745 by Sir William Yonge who, speaking of members of the House of Commons, said:

> Every one knows that, by our Constitution, after a gentleman is chosen, he is the representative, or, if you please, the attorney of the people of England, and as such is at full freedom to act as he thinks best for the people of England in general. He may receive, he may ask, he may even follow the advice of his particular constituents; but he is not obliged, nor ought he, to follow their advice, if he thinks it inconsistent with the general interest of his country.

The classic statement of this position was contained in Burke's address to the electors of Bristol in 1774, replying to Cruger's challenge. The representative, Burke said, owed his constituents not his industry only, but also his judgment, and he betrayed instead of serving them if he sacrificed it to their opinion. To deliver an opinion was the right of all men, that of constituents was a weighty and respectable opinion, which a representative ought always to rejoice to hear, and which he ought most seriously to consider; but authoritative instructions, mandates which the member was bound blindly and implicitly to obey, to vote, and to argue for, though contrary to the clearest conviction of his judgment and conscience, were things utterly unknown to the laws of the land, and arose from a fundamental mistake concerning the whole order and tenor of the Constitution. Parliament was not a congress of ambassadors from different and hostile interests; it was a deliberative assembly of one nation with one interest, that of the whole, where no local purposes, no local prejudices, ought to guide. "You choose a member indeed, but when you have chosen him, he is not a member for Bristol; he is a member of Parliament."

Despite occasional departures, this idea of virtual representation was the prevailing theory and practice of members of Parliament during eighteenth-century England, especially after 1760 and at the time of the American Revolution.

Continental Ideas

Meanwhile, on the continent of Europe, theory and practice differed as to the nature of the representative's responsibility to his constituents. Writing in the later eighteenth century, Rousseau rejected the representative principle which he considered inconsistent with popular sovereignty. Whether the representatives sought to carry out an imperative popular mandate or to exercise their own judgment of the requirements of the general welfare, he felt that they would reach decisions essentially different from what the people would decide directly. The general will could be reliably expressed only in primary assemblies.

In the Cortes of medieval Spain and in the Netherlands from the fifteenth century until 1814, representatives were bound by the instructions of their constituents. On the other hand, the French revolutionary assembly of 1789 proclaimed that its members, representing the entire nation, could not be bound by instructions from their particular constituencies; and a similar principle of free representation was embodied in the mid-nineteenth-century constitutions of France, Prussia and Italy.[2]

Representation in Colonial Assemblies

Although the American colonists were deprived of the right of electing members of the English Parliament, every colony had a legislative assembly whose members were chosen on the basis of a limited popular suffrage. The colonial systems of representation were influenced by various factors. The colonial charters gave the colonists the full rights of English subjects, including the right to vote for representatives in the colonial assemblies. English customs and precedents exercised a controlling influence upon the qualifications of voters in the colonies. Tendencies toward direct democracy were seen in frequent elections of numerous officers, residence requirements, the decline of the real-property qualification for voting, and in the practice of instructions to representatives. Albert E. McKinley gives an interesting example of an instruction in 1773 by the inhabitants of Orange County, North Carolina, to their delegates in the assembly:[3]

> We have chosen you our Representatives at the next General Assembly and when we did so we expected and do still expect that you will speak our Sense in every case when we shall expressly declare it, or when you can by any other means discover it. In all other cases we suppose you left to your own discretion which is ever to be directed by the Good of our Country in general and of this County in particular. This is our notion of the Duty of Representatives, and the Rights of Electors.

"These practices all tended to reduce the representative to the delegate status, forcing the public servant to voice accurately and under pain of imminent defeat at the polls the sentiment of the majority of the constituency."[4] Over the long run, the trend in the colonies was thus away from the English idea of virtual representation, which the colonists strongly opposed, and toward the idea of direct representation, reminiscent of the Levellers of seventeenth-century England. This trend was influenced, at least in New England, by Puritan theology with its theory of the social compact, its idea of an organic society, and its doctrine of magistracy. It was also modified somewhat by the idea of the representation of the prevailing material interests of the rising commercial classes which found expression during the revolutionary period.[5]

Revolutionary-Constitutional Period

The years 1775-1790 were marked by the growth of two basic ideas concerning the relationship of the representative and its constituents. One school of thought was composed of the direct democrats like Benjamin Franklin, Thomas Jefferson, Tom Paine, and James Wilson who stressed the social compact doctrine and the natural rights of man, including the right to control his representatives in the popular chamber. This group placed its faith in the common people, direct representation, and majority rule. "Representation to them was a simple matter of making governmental officials an exact working model of the mass of people in action. A representative ought to be immediately responsible to his constituents, he ought to follow instructions, elections ought to be frequent, the recall and referendum might be used, a constitution ought to restrict the powers of the representatives rather than the powers of the people, any office of power ought to be elective, and the sovereignty and will of the people, expressed through the just principle of the majority rule, had almost a magical quality."[6]

A second school of thought, of which Madison and Hamilton were leading exponents, saw society as composed of constantly shifting and conflicting interests in an age of commercial expansion, and they sought in the Constitution to create a system of representation in which these contending interests would check and balance each other. Representation was regarded by them as a means of accommodating and controlling interest groups. Reflecting the interests of the commercial and landed classes, this group reacted against the delegation theory of representation, which had prevailed in the formation of the state governments, and seemed to favor a kind of pluralistic scheme of representation that would safeguard the rights of minorities and check the excesses of direct democracy. It was this balancing-of-interests view of the conservatives that found expression finally in the structure of government established by the Constitution of 1787.

Madison with customary clarity voiced this view of society in Number 10 of *The Federalist:*

> A landed interest, a manufacturing interest, a mercantile interest, a money interest, with many lesser interests, grow up of necessity in civilized nations, and divide them into different classes, actuated by different sentiments and views. The regulation of these various and interfering interests forms the principal task of modern legislation, and involves the spirit of party and faction in the necessary and ordinary operations of Government.

On the relations between a representative and his constituents, the authors of *The Federalist* also wrote: "It is a sound and important principle that the representative ought to be acquainted with the interests and circumstances of his constituents. But this principle can extend no further than to those circumstances and interests to which the authority and care of the representative relate."[7] Moreover: "If we consider the situation of the men on whom the free suffrages of their fellow-citizens may confer the representative trust, we shall find it involving every security which can be devised or desired for their fidelity to their constituents. . . . Duty, gratitude, interest, ambition itself, are the chords by which they will be bound to fidelity and sympathy with the great mass of the people."[8]

Debate in First Congress

After the ratification of the Constitution, the First Congress debated a proposal to amend that document so as to permit constituents to instruct their representatives. Madison opposed this proposal, and it was rejected by a vote of 41 to 10 after an extended debate in which seventeen members took part. The case for the amendment was presented by Mr. Page of Virginia and Mr. Gerry of Massachusetts. Page thought that instruction and representation were inseparably connected in a republic.

> I think, sir, [he said] to doubt the authority of the people to instruct their representatives, will give them just cause to be alarmed for their fate. I look upon it as a dangerous doctrine, subversive of the great end for which the United States have confederated. Every friend of mankind, every well-wisher of his country, will be desirous of obtaining the sense of the people on every occasion of magnitude; but how can this be so well expressed as in instructions to their representatives? . . . It is the sense of several of the [state] conventions that this amendment should take place; I think it is my duty to support it, and fear it will spread an alarm among our constituents if we decline to do it.

Gerry contended that instruction from the people would furnish an additional check against abuse which every government is subject to.

> To say the sovereignty vests in the people, and that they have not a right to instruct and control their representatives [he said], is absurd to the last degree . . . the amendment . . . only declares the right of the people to send instructions; the representative will, if he thinks proper, communicate his instructions to the House, but how far they shall operate on his conduct, he will judge for himself . . . much good may result from a declaration in the Constitution that they possess this privilege; the people will be encouraged to come forward with their instructions, which will form a fund of useful information for the Legislature.

Much of this debate revolved around the question whether or not instructions from the people would be binding upon their representatives; but most of those who participated in the discussion opposed the amendment. Hartley of Pennsylvania considered Congress to be the best judge of proper measures and anticipated that instructions would never be resorted to but for party purposes, that they would embarrass the best and wisest men, and make it impossible to accommodate various viewpoints. Clymer of Pennsylvania believed that a constitutional right of instruction would be "a dangerous principle, utterly destructive of all ideas of an independent and deliberative body, which are essential requisites in the Legislatures of free Governments." Sherman of Connecticut thought that

> when the people have chosen a representative, it is his duty to meet others from the different parts of the Union, and consult, and agree with them to such acts as are for the general benefit of the whole community. If they were to be guided by instructions, there would be no use in deliberation; all that a man would have to do, would be to produce his instructions, and lay them on the table, and let them speak for him. . . . It is the duty of a

good representative to inquire what measures are most likely to promote the general welfare, and, after he has discovered them, to give them his support. Should his instructions, therefore, coincide with his ideas on any measure, they would be unnecessary; if they were contrary to the convictions of his own mind, he must be bound by every principle of justice to disregard them.

Sedgwick of Massachusetts wondered how the sense of a majority of the voters in a large state could be obtained and communicated. Lawrence of New York opposed the amendment because he thought that every member ought to consider himself the representative of the whole Union and not of the particular district that had chosen him, whose interests might clash with those of the general good; unless instructions were to be considered as binding, they were superfluous. And Madison of Virginia did not believe that the inhabitants of any district could speak the voice of all the people. Far from it, "Their ideas may contradict the sense of the whole people; hence the consequence that instructions are binding on the representative is of a doubtful, if not a dangerous nature."[9]

Evidently it was the preponderant opinion of the House in the First Congress, despite the inclusion of the principle of instructions in several of the state constitutions, that representatives were to be trustees for the whole nation, not merely agents of their particular constituencies.

Development of Direct Representation: 1800-1860

Thomas Jefferson's triumph over the Federalists in 1800 marked the opening of a new century and a change in the prevailing theory and practice of political representation. The ideas of Madison and Hamilton were eclipsed, and faith in the common man and in the devices of direct democracy swept the country. The first decades of the nineteenth century witnessed the widening of the suffrage and the expansion of the electorate, a trend toward the direct election of officers, the dispersion of administrative functions, and widespread adoption of the practice of instructing representatives. The idea of direct representation now came into vogue, an idea which "exalted the majority principle, brought social institutions as close to the individual as possible, challenged the division of labor between officers and public, and decried any failure of the representative to reflect immediately and faithfully the mathematical sum of his constituents' desires and characteristics."[10]

The nature of the relations that prevailed at this time between the Congressman and his constituents was reflected in the practice of instructions which were generally obeyed. Some conception of the role of the representative as it was then conceived may be had from the tenor of a resolution adopted by the legislature of Virginia in 1812 when its Senators in Congress (Giles and Brent) had refused to follow legislative instructions. The resolution maintained that the instruction of representatives had been a legal practice in the English House of Commons since time immemorial, that it was "much more unquestionable in the United States, where the people are acknowledged to be the only legitimate source of all legislation," that the nature of representation required the right of instruction, and that the confidence and discretion with which a representative is endowed "is grounded on the supposition, that he is charged with the will, acquainted with the opinions, and devoted to the interests of his constituents."[11]

When Andrew Jackson was elected President in 1828, he received a letter of congratulation on his first annual message to Congress from the English philosopher Jeremy Bentham, who had published a pamphlet on parliamentary reform in 1817. Bentham sent Jackson a set of documents entitled "Anti-Senatica" which attacked the unrepresentative character of the American Senate, but approved the representative quality of the House of Representatives in which he saw a "unity of interest and affections with the body of its constituents."[12]

President Jackson set forth his own concept of the role of a representative in his proclamation on the South Carolina secession movement in 1832 when, speaking of the members of the House of Representatives, he declared: "However they may in practice, as it is their duty to do, consult and prefer the interests of their particular constituents when they come in conflict with any other particular or local interest, yet it is their first or highest duty, as representatives of the United States, to promote the general good."[13]

Not long after, Abraham Lincoln, then a young state legislator, expressed his own view upon the relation of a representative to his constituency. When he was a candidate for re-election to the Illinois legislature in 1836, he began his campaign by saying:[14]

> If elected, I shall consider the whole people of Sangamon my constituents, as well those that oppose as those that support me. While acting as their representative I shall be governed by their will on all subjects upon which I have the means of knowing what their will is, and upon all others I shall do what my own judgment teaches me will best advance their interests.

Not all legislators of that period, however, felt the same way as Lincoln did. Davy Crockett, Congressman from Tennessee, is said to have sent to his constituents whose demands he was unwilling to obey this brusque message in 1836: "I am going to Texas, and you can go to Hell!"[15]

Writing in 1851, John C. Calhoun, who was concerned for the protection of states' rights and minority interests, developed an original theory of representation that rejected the principle of majority rule and called for the separate representation of classes and interests, each of which should possess a veto over the acts of the others. Before any law of general application could be valid, he argued, it must receive the assent of each interest, in which event it has been enacted by a "concurrent majority." Otherwise, legislation is null and void in states that have rejected it. Calhoun's theory was liquidated by the Civil War, but echoes of it are still heard in the land.[16]

Post-Civil War Trends

The century since the Civil War has seen conflicting forces at work in the theory and practice of political representation in America. The psychological reaction of the Southern states to their defeat in the war, the emergence of many new economic groups with the postwar expansion of industry and agriculture and the growth of trade unions, the changes in the ethnic composition of the population as millions of European immigrants entered our gates, and the slow enfranchisement of the Negroes in recent decades, all combined to effect far-reaching changes in the ideas and tactics of representation.

The proponents of direct democracy and direct representation sought to democratize the political parties by substituting direct primaries for controlled conventions. They furnished much of the drive for the woman-suffrage movement, for the direct election of judges, and for the popular election of United States Senators. They advocated the initiative, referendum, and recall: a movement for the popular control of government that reached its crest in the late-nineteenth and early-twentieth centuries. Twenty states had adopted the initiative and referendum by 1938. The development of public-opinion polls after World War I was seen as another manifestation of the democratic surge and as a device for inducing the representative to comply with the expressed desires of his constituents. The third-party movements of the 1890's, of 1912 and 1924, all sought reforms in representation and political institutions that would strengthen the "people" as against the "interests" in the halls of Congress, in the executive departments, and on the Federal bench.[17] The most recent manifestations of this impulse have been the movements of the past decade in both political parties, although most dramatically in the Democratic party, to "democratize" the delegate selection process in our presidential politics, and to vastly increase the number of presidential primaries.[18]

Meanwhile, with the growing complexity of American society and the increasingly mixed character of many constituencies, the legislator tended to become a broker among competing interests in the political marketplace rather than a direct representative of the people. The development of powerful lobbies in Washington, described as "a third house of Congress," exposed members to the pressures of organized interest groups and converted the task of the representative into an effort to compromise their differences. As Representative T. V. Smith of Illinois expressed it:[19]

> Legislatures are the readiest exemplars of the process of compromise. This is a humble but honorable view of the democratic process. . . . Legislation is . . . a business in which you do something, then wait to see who hollers, and then relieve the hollering as best you can to see who else hollers.

In recent times the role of the representative has become increasingly that of broker for a member's constituency in its individual and collective dealings with the federal government. Legislative intervention in the life of the federal executive has become "more complex, more subtle, and more detailed" than ever before. Constituents expect their Congressman to intercede on their behalf with agencies to obtain a contract from the Navy or secure a favorable decision from a regulatory agency or what not. Congressional intervention in administration is apparently greater in programs involving loans, subsidies, contracts, franchises, and permits of various kinds. Marver Bernstein remarks that many members of Congress would be relieved of an awkward and time-consuming burden if they were forbidden to intervene in matters of formal adjudication in an agency. But almost all of them regard such services to constituents as a necessary and proper part of their representative function.[20]

Paradoxically the same basic developments that have brought an ever-increasing mass of constituent requests and claims and pressures have at the same time made the representative in some respects more and more a free agent in making his decisions. Interest-group organization and means of influence have been perfected; mass education, growing interest in public affairs, and greater ease of communication have all resulted in more and more demands on the member; but the increased diversity of interests in most constituencies makes it more difficult for any segment of the district or any particular interest to dominate. The member's increased "freedom" does not, of course, make his job easier; but it does help to explain why the mounting mass of constituent claims does not result in his functioning more and more in accordance with the Jeffersonian-Jacksonian theories.

Many members have regarded themselves and have behaved as free agents, enjoying a large range of discretion, guided by their own best judgment, their convictions, and the dictates of conscience. Other members have acted as delegates of their districts, bound to follow instructions received from or pledges given to their constituents, even when they have conflicted with their own judgment or principles. In actual practice most representatives have combined both roles with changing circumstances, acting at times as free agents in making decisions on matters on which they were uninstructed, and at other times as delegates with a mandate to follow the wishes of the folks back home. At still other times they have acted as brokers seeking compromises between conflicting interests in a system of checks and balances. In any session of Congress, members have had to make scores of voting decisions both in committee and on the floor. In so doing, they have been influenced, in varying degrees, by the wishes of their constituencies, by their political parties, by the pressures of special interests, and by their own views of the general welfare. Constituent instructions, personal pledges, party policies, interest group pressures, individual convictions, conceptions of the general welfare—all these factors have entered in varying proportions into the countless decisions made by representatives in Congress since 1789.[21]

A 1959 analysis of the role of the representative distinguishes between the focus of representation and the style of representation. In undertaking his legislative task, the representative may be guided by the view that legislation should benefit a geographical unit (district, state, or nation), or carry out his party's campaign promises, or favor some special-interest group, or support an administrative organization. Each of these "publics" is a possible focus of orientation for the representative. As regards his style of representation, he may take either the role of free agent, following his own convictions, or the role of delegate, bound by the instructions of his constituents.[22]

The same analysis identifies three major role types of representatives: the "trustee" who is a free agent and follows his own convictions, principles, judgment, or conscience; the "delegate" who is inclined to consult and follow the instructions of his constituents; and the "politico" who expresses both orientations either simultaneously or serially.[23] The writers think that, under modern conditions, the legislature has become "an agency for the coordination and integration of diverse social, economic, and political interests" and that "the representative has become less and less a Delegate and more and more a Trustee as the business of government has become more and more intricate and technical."[24]

Congressional Views of Representative Function

The congressional concept of the representative function is reflected in the views expressed by members themselves down through the years. In response to criticisms from some of his constituents, Representative Garfield in an open letter set forth his theory of the relations of a representative to his district. "I believe," he wrote in 1865, "a representative should get all the light on every matter of public importance that his position enables him to and then speak and vote in such a manner as will, in his judgment, enhance the best interests of his constituents and the whole country. If the constituency, in reviewing the action of their representative, find him deficient in ability, judgment or integrity they have always the remedy of choosing another in his place. But while he is in office his course should be guided by his own judgments, based upon the suggestions of his constituents and all other obtainable information. On no other ground could I have accepted the office I now hold, on no other ground could I continue to hold it."[25] Seven years later he confided to his diary: "It is a terrible thing to live in fear of their constituents to the extent which many members do. I would rather be defeated every day in the year than suffer such fear."[26]

Representative Robert Luce of Massachusetts, who sat in the House for twenty years, voiced his mature view of the role of the representative in 1926 as follows:[27]

> The lawmaker is not to be purely an agent, vainly trying to decide what the majority of his principals desire. He is not to be purely a trustee, making wholly independent decisions, self-conceived and self-sustained. He is to be both agent and trustee as far as may be. He is to feel it as much his duty to try to modify in others opinions with which he disagrees, as to try to let his own opinions be modified by the advice of others. He is to deal fairly both by his constituents and by himself. Such a man deems it necessary to break with constituency or with party only on those very rare occasions when Judgment must step aside and let Conscience rule. The great mass of legislation is matter of expediency. Not once in a thousand times is it matter of what is usually thought of as right and wrong. Only when right and wrong are at stake may the legislator refuse to concede, to compromise, or to yield.

During the 1945 hearings of the La Follette–Monroney Committee, many members discussed their relations with their constituents. The general theme was that the people had come to look upon a Congressman not as their representative in Congress but as their errand boy in Washington. Some members defended errand running on the ground that it won friends at home and helped to humanize relations between the people and the Washington bureaucracy. Other members complained that errand running left them little time for their primary legislative duties. They offered a variety of remedies for the problem, of which perhaps the most original was the suggestion of Representative Ramspeck of Georgia that the job be divided in two parts: the legislative part to be handled by elected representatives in Congress; the service function by elected agents before the executive branch of the government.

After a decade in the House of Representatives, Representative Jerry Voorhis of California disputed the view that Congress should merely echo the voice of the people. "The truly valid conception of 'representative government,' " he said, "holds that the people elect their representatives because they expect from those representatives better, more farsighted action than the people as a whole, with their limited access to all the facts, can provide."[28]

In 1958, Mrs. Coya Knutson of Minnesota responded to a questionnaire on the job, responsibility, and principles of representatives in Congress in part as follows:[29]

> Congressmen are elected on the basis of their party and personal principles. These principles govern our judgment and our actions. It would be impossible to let the various shadings of constituent opinion guide our actions. We would be stuck on dead center of every issue. It would be unrealistic to base actions on a numerical average of opinion-letters on various measures. These do not necessarily reflect cross-section opinion as there are many people who never write letters to their Representatives.
>
> There are always times when compromise is necessary—but never compromise with principle. We were elected by the people of our districts. They had to have confidence in us, else we would not have been elected, nor would we continue in office. They have given us the responsibility for making their laws and representing them to our best ability. Exchange of opinion between Congressman and constituent is fundamental to our democratic way of life, but the final decisions have to be ours.

Whether or not a member should compromise his principles in order to keep his seat in the House is a dilemma that sooner or later faces every politician. Former Senator William Benton of Connecticut put this question to some of his former colleagues and summarized their replies in an article in the *New York Times*. One of the replies came from Representative John Vorys of Ohio, then ranking Republican member of the Foreign Affairs Committee, who said: "I am extremely cautious about calling political decisions moral issues. On the other hand, I think that Congressmen and Senators are expendable rather than indispensable, and no Congressman or Senator should cast a vote he knows is wrong in order to be re-elected. It makes no difference whether the wrongness is on a moral, legal, economic, or other issue."[30]

Another reply was that of Representative John W. McCormack of Massachusetts, the then Majority Leader of the House, who wrote: "I never place myself mentally in the position of compromising principle and conscience. But there are times when I might harmonize differences in order to make progress, or maintain unity, and then start the journey from there. The extent of 'compromise' or 'harmonization' depends upon the circumstances of each case, the atmosphere, the strength of the opposition, as well as the support for a measure, and other factors. But sometimes there can be no 'compromise' or 'harmonization,' such as the extension of the Selective Service Act of 1941, three months before Pearl Harbor."[31]

In the course of participating in a reciprocal trade study, conducted under the auspices of the Center for International Studies of the Massachusetts Institute of Technology, Lewis A. Dexter interviewed several members of Congress. Subsequently he wrote an article based upon these congressional interviews in which he reached the following conclusions on the ways Congressmen today view representation:[32]

> The congressman represents his image of the district or of his constituents, or he fails to do so. . . . In large measure, their personalities, careers, and public images make them choose what they hear and how they interpret it.
>
> The first difference between some congressmen and others is how (consciously or unconsciously) they define their responsibilities . . . their conception of their "professional obligation." A few made explicit and many apparently hold implicit theories of representation . . . derived not from philosophical or academic sources, but from practical experience.
>
> Some members expressed themselves in terms of their obligation to select the right course, regardless of the views of their constituents. . . . Another member said: "My first duty is to get re-elected. I'm here to represent my district. . . . This is part of my actual belief as to the function of a congressman. . . ." Another member would see his responsibility on some issues as being almost exclusively to the district. On other issues he would be strongly inclined to emphasize national interest in some form as against district concern.
>
> Congressmen tend to see their obligations as being either to the nation or to their constituency. . . . The congressman's definition of national interest and responsibility on a particular issue depends in large measure upon his understanding of the facts of a particular issue. . . .
>
> A congressman's conception of his district confirms itself, to a considerable extent, and may constitute a sort of self-fulfilling prophecy. . . . A congressman hears most often from those who agree with him. Some men automatically interpret what they hear to support their own viewpoints. . . .
>
> In more general terms, what congressmen hear and how they interpret what they hear depends on who they are. . . . A congressman's reputation among those who might want to influence him determines in large measure what actually is said to him.

The author cited important instances when Congressmen were changed by their districts and concluded:

It should never be forgotten that most congressmen . . . respect the
right of petition. They have a general feeling that everyone should have a
right to talk or write to them about any public issues—that's what they're
there for. But they aren't as worried about each communication as college
professors might expect. They generally feel they have an equal right to
disregard the petitioner's point, once it has been courteously received and
acknowledged. . . .

Conflicting Responsibilities

Every national legislator is the focus of competing claims and pressures.
He takes an oath to support and defend the Constitution, to discharge the
duties of his office well and faithfully. But this obligation affords him no
unequivocal guidance when faced with the conflicting demands of district,
state, region, party, and special-interest group. To whom does a Senator or
Congressman owe his primary allegiance? To the people of his district—the
local interest? To the people of his state? To the special interests: the big
corporations, the big unions, the big farmers? Or to the people of the entire
country—the national interest? Does he have a greater responsibility to the
interests of the American people as consumers or to the interests of producers of such products as natural gas, potatoes, peanuts, petroleum, cotton, wool, silver, etc.? The great majority of the American people are not
members of special-interest groups and hence are much less articulate on
particular issues than are the interested minority whose affiliation with
some active organization gives them a greater political leverage. The result
is that the strongest pressures on Congress from outside are essentially
minority pressures representing particular local interests or specific occupational or political groups.

The primary responsibility of Congress is to promote the general welfare. No public policy could ever be the mere sum of the demands of the
organized special interests. For the sum of the organized special interests is
not equal to the total of all the interests of the nation, since there are vital
common interests that cannot be organized by pressure groups. For example, the general welfare is not the mere sum of Maine potatoes, Texas oil,
Wyoming wool, Colorado silver, Mississippi cotton, and Georgia peanuts.
Yet the member from a farm state, who hopes for re-election, faces a perplexing dilemma when he compares his responsibility for governmental
economy and national solvency with the demands of organized producers
of farm products for subsidies which drain hundreds of millions of dollars
a year from the pockets of taxpayers into the pockets of his constituents.
A similar dilemma arises in voting on subsidies for other organized groups.

Several measures, among thousands, offer graphic examples of conflicting responsibilities. The rivers-and-harbors bill posed the pork barrel-versus-economy issue most plainly. As Senator Douglas said in the debate: "Local groups demand that their Representatives and Senators bring home the 'bacon' or else. All too often these groups loudly proclaim their desire for economy, but at the same time they want their local pet projects at the Federal Government's expense. They want economy practiced on the other fellow, but not on themselves." Senator Douglas appealed not only to his colleagues in the Senate, but also to the public to support his economy campaign. "Citizen statesmanship," he said, "recognizes legitimate local or special needs, but it places the national interest first." On the final vote, members of both houses, including some who had earlier made eloquent economy speeches, voted to authorize more than $1 billion worth of public works projects.[33]

In the early days of foreign-aid bills during the Truman administration, Senator Tom Connally believed that an issue of great national concern had become the target of excessive narrow partisanship. In opening debate on one of those bills, he appealed for nonpartisan support for the measure. He said it would provide strength at points "where the Soviet Union is doing its best to create weakness and disunity," and he added, "On the battleground United States commanders do not order forward to the attack Republicans as a group, nor Democrats as a group. All owe to their country the same responsibility and . . . allegiance."

In 1974, the impeachment votes by the Committee on the Judiciary created immense pressures on those Republicans and conservative Democrats who represented districts which President Nixon has carried by extraordinary margins in 1972. When the critical vote came on the first article of impeachment, six Republicans and three conservative Southern Democrats voted yes, a vote which received considerable political assistance from the subsequent revelation that President Nixon had withheld an incriminating tape.

In cases of conflict between state and local organized-interest groups and party bosses, on the one hand, and the national interest, on the other, the national legislator faces a difficult decision. While he owes deference to the opinions of his constituents, and cannot ignore them if he seeks re-election, he is primarily an officer of the national government representing the whole people. In actual practice, to be sure, the typical member avows his first allegiance to his state or district. His chief aim usually is re-election to Congress, so as to gain power and prerogatives via seniority and political advancement to higher public office. And under the locality rule, his re-election depends on protecting local interests and avoiding perilous national issues. The typical member speaks for a coalition of local groups representing small business, farmers, veterans, and skilled workers. And he supports the measures they favor: tariffs, subsidies and price supports, bonus, and prevailing wages.

In the House the individual member must deal with the party leadership and the committee leadership. He generally follows the party leaders on matters of party procedure and organization. And he co-operates with the committee chairmen on matters of legislative policy, for they control the legislation of interest to his district. Since he is responsible to a local, not a national, electorate, he does not feel bound by the national platform of his party or by the promises and policies of his party's candidate for President. He spends his time mostly promoting the interests of his district and running errands for the folks back home. For this is the best way to get re-elected.[34]

14

Relations with the Senate

THERE IS A LEGEND that Thomas Jefferson, after his return from France, once asked Washington at breakfast why he had agreed to a second chamber in Congress. According to the story, Washington asked him: "Why did you pour that tea into your saucer?" "To cool it," Jefferson replied. "Just so," said Washington, "we pour House legislation into the senatorial saucer to cool it."

This anecdote may be apocryphal, but it reflects the expectation of the framers of the Constitution that the actions of the House of Representatives—the direct representatives of the people—might be more "emotional" than those of the Senate whose members were indirectly elected. The founders intended that the Senate should serve as a council of revision in relation to measures passed by the House, and as a forum where the states would be equally represented. Madison wrote during the Constitutional Convention that "I am fully of the opinion that the numerous and immediate representatives of the people composing the House will decidedly predominate in the Government," and Hamilton said that "the most popular branch of every government, by being generally the favorite of the people, will be generally a full match, if not an over-match, for every other member of the Government."[1]

Proposals were made in the Federal Convention, both in the Randolph plan and in Pinckney's plan, that the members of the second branch of the national legislature be elected by those of the first branch; but they were not adopted.[2] Another suggestion was that of Mr. Wilson who moved that the advice and consent of the House, as well as that of the Senate, be required in the making of treaties. As treaties, he said, were to have the operation of laws, they ought to have the sanction of laws also. But his motion was rejected.[3]

In the Constitution as it was finally adopted and ratified, the two branches were linked together in several important respects. They were to share in all legislative powers "herein granted." The House was to have the sole power of impeachment and the Senate the sole power to try all impeachments. All bills for raising revenue were to originate in the House of Representatives, but the Senate might propose or concur with amendments as on other bills. The House claims the exclusive right to originate all general appropriations bills, and does so in practice, but the approval of both houses is required for appropriations bills to become law. Neither house during a session should adjourn for more than three days, nor to any other place, without the consent of the other. Under the Twelfth Amendment (1804), the electoral count takes place at a joint session of the two houses on the sixth day of January following every meeting of the electors. The President of the United States is not elected directly by the people, but by electors in the several states who meet on a prescribed day and cast their votes for President and Vice President, respectively, in the manner directed by the Constitution. Certificates of the votes cast are forwarded by registered mail to the president of the Senate in Washington.

Representatives and Senators stand on an equal footing under the Constitution in that they receive compensation for their services which, in practice, has been the same for both groups; are bound by oath or affirmation to support the Constitution; are privileged from arrest during their attendance at sessions of their respective chambers, and in going to and returning from the same, except in case of treason, felony, or breach of the peace; and may not be questioned in any other place for any speech or debate in either house. They are also subject to the same prohibitions against holding any office under the United States or being appointed to any civil office which has been created or whose emoluments have been increased during their terms or serving as a presidential elector or engaging in insurrection or rebellion against the United States or giving aid or comfort to its enemies.

Intercameral Comity

Except for joint and conference committees, the passage of bills and joint and concurrent resolutions, and joint sessions for special occasions, the two houses of Congress generally operate independently of each other. Comity, courtesy, and mutual deference customarily characterize their relations.

Jefferson in his *Manual* early laid down the rule that debate and proceedings in one house are not to be noticed in the other house:

> It is a breach of order in debate to notice what has been said on the same subject in the other House, or the particular votes or majorities on it there; because the opinion of each House should be left to its own independency, not to be influenced by the proceedings of the other; and the quoting them might beget reflections leading to a misunderstanding between the two Houses.[4]

This rule of parliamentary law, when invoked, is usually followed in the House of Representatives. Reference to debates or votes on the same subject in the Senate, or to the action or probable action of the Senate, or to its methods of procedure, as bearing on the course to be taken on a pending matter has always been held a breach of order in the House. It is, however, permissible to refer to proceedings in the other house generally, provided the reference does not contravene the principles of the rule. But a member may not in House debate read the record of speeches and votes of Senators in such a way as might be expected to lead to recriminations.

Although the Senate may be referred to properly in debate, discussion of its functions, criticism of its acts, reference to a Senator in terms of personal criticism, even anonymously or complimentarily, or reading a paper making such criticism is out of order in the House. This inhibition extends to comment on actions outside the Senate. After examination by a committee, a speech reflecting on the character of the Senate was ordered stricken from the *Record* on the ground that it tended to create "unfriendly conditions between the two bodies . . . obstructive of wise legislation and little short of a public calamity."[5] But where a member of the House has been assailed in the Senate, he has been permitted to explain his own conduct and motives, without bringing the whole controversy into discussion or assailing a Senator. Resolutions relating to breaches of these principles are entertained in the House as questions of privilege.[6]

Jefferson's *Manual* also prescribes that "neither House can exercise any authority over a Member or officer of the other, but should complain to the House of which he is, and leave the punishment to them." In a notable instance in which a member of the House had assaulted a Senator in the Senate Chamber for words spoken in debate, the Senate examined the breach of privilege and transmitted its report to the House, which punished the member. But where certain members of the House, in a published letter, sought to influence the vote of a Senator in an impeachment trial, the House declined to consider the matter as a breach of privilege.

According to Jefferson, preventing expressions offensive to the other house is the duty of the Speaker:

Where the complaint is of words disrespectfully spoken by a Member of another House, it is difficult to obtain punishment, because of the rules supposed necessary to be observed (as to the immediate noting down of words) for the security of Members. Therefore it is the duty of the House, and more particularly of the Speaker, to interfere immediately, and not to permit expressions to go unnoticed which may give a ground of complaint to the other House, and introduce proceedings and mutual accusations between the two Houses, which can hardly be terminated without difficulty and disorder.

In the House of Representatives this rule of parliamentary law is considered as binding on the chair.

Contrasts in Political Control

The relations between the two branches of Congress down through the decades have also been affected by their political complexion. During the nineteenth century, when Senators were elected by the state legislatures, there were numerous occasions when opposing political parties controlled the two houses, a situation that tended to make for legislative deadlocks. Between 1854 and 1916 there were ten Congresses in which one party controlled the House of Representatives and the other party controlled the Senate. For example, in 1854, the Democratic per cent of the two-party membership of the House was 43.5 and of the Senate 73.7. In 1890 the situation was reversed when the Democrats had 72.4 per cent of the two-party membership of the House and 45.3 per cent of the Senate. Since 1913, however, when Senators have been directly elected by the people of the several states, the same political party has controlled both houses of every Congress, except the Seventy-second, and there has been a much closer correspondence in the measure of their majority in the two chambers than was normally the case before 1913.[7]

Behind the nominal control of Congress by the same political party in recent decades, however, have been internal cleavages in both parties and the frequent control of the legislative process by bipartisan coalitions in both houses. Fundamental divisions between liberals and conservatives have characterized both congressional parties for many years and have produced situations in which the balance of power in both chambers has been in the hands of moderate Republican–Southern Democratic coalitions that have largely dominated the national legislature during the past forty years. Many major measures of modern Presidents have depended for their passage upon coalition support. We have already noted the persistence of the conservative coalition down to the present day.* The relations between the House and the Senate in recent times have thus been marked by the collaboration of conservative coalitions in both chambers. Bipartisan combinations in Congress have often supported the foreign policy and moderate domestic programs of the President and offset the hazards implicit in periods of divided government.

The irregular movement of political tides has not only produced political contrasts between the House and the Senate in days gone by, but also within state delegations. It has frequently happened in the course of congressional history that one political party has dominated the House delegation from a particular state whose Senators belonged to the opposite party. In the Eighty-sixth Congress, for example, seven of the eight members of the House from Kentucky were Democrats, but both Senators—John Sherman Cooper and Thruston B. Morton—were Republicans. Another example from the same Congress was the Maryland delegation both of whose Senators were Republicans and all of whose Congressmen were Democrats. In the Ninety-fourth Congress, the New York delegation had a Republican Senator and a Conservative-Republican Senator, but twenty-seven Democratic and twelve Republican members of the House. Oklahoma had two Republican Senators and six Democratic members of the House; Oregon had two Republican Senators and four Democratic members of the House; and South Dakota had two Democratic Senators and two Republican members of the House.

Joint Machinery

Under a bicameral legislative system like ours the process of lawmaking is a dual one in that all bills must run the gauntlet of both houses and win the approval of each. In view of the differences between the two chambers in their politics, tenure, and membership, the possibility of their arriving independently at identical conclusions on legislative measures is quite remote. Obviously, therefore, some machinery and methods of co-operation had to be devised to avoid deadlock and impasse in the performance of congressional functions.

Several devices and procedures have been developed over the years to facilitate joint action. The principal mechanisms for the meshing of the legislative gears have been the joint committee and the conference committee. Congress has also made more or less use of joint hearings and joint

* See Chapter 9, page 187.

staffs, of joint and concurrent resolutions, of joint rules and joint sessions. The introduction of "companion bills" has also facilitated joint action.

Joint Committees

Joint committees have been used at intervals from the earliest days of the republic, mainly for ceremonial and routine administrative purposes and for the conduct of investigations. The First Congress set up select joint committees to prepare conference rules, choose chaplains, and arrange for the inauguration of President Washington, for the assignment of space in the Capitol building, and for fixing a time for adjournment. Henry Clay used a joint committee in 1821 to consummate the Missouri Compromise. Joint committees flourished during the Civil War and Reconstruction period when they were formed to investigate the conduct of the war, emancipation and reconstruction, retrenchment and Southern outrages, and the condition of the Indian tribes. During the Fifty-fourth Congress, the subjects of charities in the District of Columbia and free alcohol in the arts were referred to joint committees. More recent examples of their use have been on revision of the laws (1907), on the Ballinger-Pinchot controversy (1910), to investigate short-term rural credits (1920), to study tax policies and make recommendations (1926–), veterans' benefits (1932), governmental reorganization (1937), federal expenditures (1941-1973), the organization of Congress (1945-1946), the economic report (1946–), atomic energy (1947–), and defense production (1950–). And Congress has long used joint standing committees on enrolled bills (1789), the library (1806), printing (1846), and the disposition of executive papers (1889).

Since 1945, there has been a noteworthy increase in the use of joint committees for purposes of study, investigation, and oversight. The Atomic Energy Act of 1946 established a joint committee of eighteen members to "make continuing studies of the activities of the Atomic Energy Commission and of problems relating to the development, use, and control of atomic energy." The Employment Act of 1946 set up a joint committee of fourteen members to prepare an annual report "containing its findings and recommendations with respect to each of the main recommendations made by the President in the Economic Report. . . ." The Labor-Management Relations Act of 1947 charged a joint committee of fourteen members to investigate the entire field of labor-management relations. The Economic Cooperation Act of 1948 created a joint "watchdog" committee of ten members "to make a continuous study of the programs of the United States economic assistance to foreign countries, and to review the progress achieved in the execution and administration of such programs." The Defense Production Act of 1950 directed a joint committee of ten members "to make a continuous study of the programs authorized by the . . . Act . . . , and to review the progress achieved in the execution and administration of such programs." A Joint Committee on Indian Administration was set up in 1950; another on Immigration and Nationality was established in 1952; and a Joint Committee on District of Columbia metropolitan problems was created in 1959. In 1965 the Joint Committee on the Organization of Congress was established, and many of its recommendations were accepted in the Legislative Reorganization Act of 1970. That act created the Joint Committee on Congressional Operations "to continue the study of the operations of Congress and to recommend improvements." In 1972, Congress set up a thirty-two member Joint Study Committee on Budget Control, and its work led to the Congressional Budget and Impoundment Control Act of 1974.

In the Ninety-fourth Congress, the joint committees and the number of members on each included Atomic Energy (18), Congressional Operations (10), Defense Production (10), Economic (20), Internal Revenue Taxation (10), Library (10), Printing (6).

Over the years, many joint committees have done important work, publishing valuable reports which have frequently led to legislation. Only the Joint Committee on Atomic Energy has been given legislative authority and is widely regarded as one of the most powerful committees in Congress.

The achievements of some joint congressional committees have led to suggestions for even greater use of this device as a means of intercameral co-operation, to minimize the use of conference committees, and as watchdogs of the administration. Greater use of joint committees was the most favored proposal in replies by members of Congress to a 1950 questionnaire on congressional reorganization.[8] Representative Monroney of Oklahoma thought that a good case could be made for the establishment of the joint statutory committees on atomic energy, the economic report, and the European recovery program. But he felt that the most rigid tests should be applied to the creation of any more joint groups beyond those three. "Otherwise," he said, "the committee structure of the House and Senate will be badly confused again with duplicating and overlapping statutory joint committees."[9] There are also many members of Congress who have shared the view of Representative Bill Frenzel of Minnesota that joint committees are "heat generators rather than light producers."[10]

Joint committees have some obvious advantages. With the rising burden of the public business, they are more economical of the time and energy of busy legislators and administrators, substituting a single inquiry for two separate investigations. Moreover, they can accelerate the legislative process—an important consideration in periods of national emergency. The joint committee device also helps to maintain co-ordinate equality with the executive branch, by preventing it from playing one house off against the other. Furthermore, when measures are matured by joint action in this way, differences between the houses are not so likely to arise and require subsequent adjustment in conference. For these reasons, joint committees are widely and successfully used by American state legislatures and have been commended in recent times for more frequent use by Congress as well.

In actual practice, however, the House and Senate seldom co-operate in this manner on major matters of public policy, so jealous are the two houses of their independence and prerogatives and so desirous are they of maintaining a relationship with their own staffs. The question of which house shall supply the chairman was usually answered in favor of the Senate, with the lower house naming a vice chairman. However, the Joint Standing Committee on Internal Revenue Taxation began the practice of electing a chairman and vice chairman annually, alternating these offices between the chairman of the House Ways and Means Committee and the chairman of the Senate Finance Committee—a happy solution of this question and an example now followed by the other joint committees.

Conference Committees

One of the most important pieces of congressional machinery is the conference committee. As noted above, it is used to adjust differences between the Senate and the House of Representatives that arise when a bill or resolution does not pass both houses in identical form, and neither house is willing to yield to the other. Growing out of early English parliamentary practice, the conference committee system is an evolutionary product whose principal threads were woven on the loom of congressional practice into a unified pattern by the middle of the nineteenth century. "By 1852," wrote Ada McCown, "the customs of presenting identical reports from the committees of conference in both houses, of granting high privilege to these conference reports, of voting upon the conference report as a whole and permitting no amendment of it, of keeping secret the discussions carried on in the meetings of the conference committee, had become established in American parliamentary practice."[11]

Conference committees are composed of the senior members of the committees or subcommittees in charge of bills that the houses have disagreed upon, appointed by the presiding officers of House and Senate (with each body's approval) for the purpose of adjusting differences between bills they have passed. They vary in size from three to twenty members from each house, but do not necessarily have an equal number of Senators and Congressmen. The Senator first named usually serves as chairman; both parties are represented, with the majority party having the larger number; the members from each house vote separately on all questions; and a majority from each house must sign the conference report. A 1974 change in House rules requires the Speaker to appoint a majority of members to the conference committee who had supported the bill originally. For most of our history the proceedings of conference committees were secret and unrecorded, presumably to afford each member protection from external and internal pressures. However, in 1974 twelve conferences were opened to the public and at the beginning of the Ninety-fourth Congress the House amended its rules to require open conferences unless a majority of either chamber's conferees voted to close the session. The Senate was expected to adopt the same change.[12] Whether the "sunshine law" for conference committees would lead to open bargaining or merely increase the number of telephone calls and corridor conversations was a matter of considerable conjecture.

The jurisdiction of conference committees is presumably limited to the differences in the forms in which the same bill has passed both houses. Conferees are not authorized to delete matter agreed to by both houses or to include new matter. However, Section 135 of the Legislative Reorganization Act provided that

> (a) In any case in which a disagreement to an amendment in the nature of a substitute has been referred to conferees, it shall be in order for the conferees to report a substitute on the same subject matter; but they may not include in the report matter not committed to them by either House. They may, however, include in their report in any such case matter which is a germane modification of subjects in disagreement.
>
> (b) In any case in which the conferees violate subsection (a), the conference report shall be subject to a point of order.

In 1970 and 1972 the House rules were changed so that separate House votes could be taken on nongermane amendments that may have been added by Senate conferees.

The device of the conference has been used by every Congress since 1789. Most important legislation goes through the conference closet and is there revised, sometimes beyond recognition, by the all-powerful conferees or "managers," as they are styled. Whether the drastically revised version was the "package" that could survive a subsequent test in both houses is, of course, the major question. Of the 217 public laws enacted by the second session of the Eighty-second Congress, for example, ninety went through conference; of these, thirteen were the major appropriation bills. In the Ninety-third Congress, all of the appropriations bills and about one-third of the public laws were the results of conference committees.

From the outset the conference committee has been a medium of continuous struggle for legislative supremacy between the House of Representatives and the Senate. Here behind the legislative scenes many decisive battles of congressional history have been waged, lasting from a few hours to many weeks. Appropriation bills, for example, have always been sent to conference where the practice has long been to settle for sums somewhere between the upper and lower grants proposed by the two houses. Inter-cameral conflicts have customarily been compromised in conference, sometimes after protracted deadlocks. During the Seventy-ninth Congress, for example, the conferees on the "full employment" bill locked horns for two weeks. In the Eighty-first Congress, the Army civil functions supply bill was tied up in conference for four months.

In the Eighty-seventh Congress an extraordinary conflict between the House Appropriations Committee, chaired by eighty-three-year-old Representative Clarence Cannon of Missouri, and the Senate Appropriations Committee, headed by eighty-four-year-old Senator Carl Hayden of Arizona, held up all appropriations for three months. The ostensible issues involved challenges to the tradition of their conference meetings being held in the Senate committee room and chaired by a Senator. Also at stake was the right of the Senate to initiate appropriations. All the issues were eventually compromised, but the incident is a reminder of the persistence of institutional rivalry.[13]

It is also worth noting that the conference committee is one of the few places where Congressmen are in a position to act on the basis of their membership and loyalty to the house they represent. Yet one unintended consequence of opening up the committee's proceedings to the public may be to encourage the conferees to be much more responsive to constituency and White House pressures. In its coverage of an open conference committee on the energy bill in 1975, the *New York Times* noted that while most decisions were made in the open, "to avoid the public eye, individual conference members met at night and had caucuses in the back rooms during the day." The report also noted that White House staffers were in an adjoining room, listening to the proceedings over a loudspeaker and frequently sending in notes to conferees.[14]

Joint Hearings

The authors of the Legislative Reorganization Act of 1946 hoped that the correlation of the committee systems of the House and Senate, for which it provided, would facilitate joint action by the parallel committees. To this end the reorganization bill as it passed the Senate authorized "the standing committees of the two houses to hold joint hearings with respect to subject matter within their respective jurisdiction." Although this permissive provision was deleted from the bill on the House side, there were some instances of joint action by congressional committees during the post-World War II years. The Foreign Affairs Committees held joint meetings on several occasions for consultation purposes with the Secretary of State; their subcommittees met jointly; and they also held a few joint hearings on foreign aid and on the mutual defense-assistance programs. The Foreign Relations and Armed Services Committees of the Senate held extended joint hearings on Far Eastern policy during 1951. The special Small Business Committees of the two houses also held several joint hearings on matters of mutual interest.

A dozen witnesses who testified on the subject at hearings before the Senate Expenditures Committee in 1951, strongly advocated joint hearings on identical or similar bills as a means of saving the time of witnesses, printing costs, and the repetition of testimony. Joint hearings followed by separate committee action, it was urged, would not trespass upon committee prerogatives. "I think we could save a tremendous amount of time, a lot of money, and a lot of wear and tear on the heads of various departments," said Representative Multer of New York, "if we had joint hearings. I would make it mandatory to hold public hearings jointly so that . . . they would be held jointly by the twin committees of both Houses with the right on the part of either House or either committee to require additional public hearings, conditioned only upon their giving notice to the other. . . ."[15] Similar views were expressed by Representatives Holifield of California and Furcolo of Massachusetts.

On the other hand, some members are dubious of the practicability of joint action by the parallel committees of Congress. Their doubts were well expressed by Dr. Francis Wilcox, then chief of staff of the Senate Committee on Foreign Relations. He said:

> One of the main difficulties with joint hearings is that our calendars simply do not coincide. Take this session, for example, the Senate committee has been busy with the troops-for-Europe issue, and with the issues that have stemmed from the recall of General MacArthur. The House committee has not seen fit to launch a study of either one of those major problems. As a result, it would have been difficult for us to cooperate because they have been busy on other matters. Moreover, I am not sure that joint meetings would save much time, because if you add twenty-five members to thirteen members, you come up with a total of thirty-eight and that increases the questioning period time. I am not sure that joint sessions under such circumstances will in the long run save time. Furthermore, our

committee members do not seem to like it and to my mind that is probably the most conclusive argument that I can put forward.[16]

Whatever the abstract merits of joint hearings, most members of both houses believe the present system fits the needs of bicameralism more effectively. During the 1973 hearings by the Select Committee on Committees on Committee Organization in the House, the following exchange between Representative Charles Wiggins of California and Minority Leader Gerald R. Ford of Michigan undoubtedly typified the outlook of a majority of their colleagues:[17]

MR. WIGGINS. One final question, Mr. Chairman. Congressman Ford, can you foresee any circumstances where it would be helpful to the work of the Congress as a whole that there should be joint committee hearings by Senate and House personnel?

MR. FORD. I happen to believe in the legislative system, where you have a House and a Senate or a Senate and an Assembly, however you designate them. If you believe in that concept, I do not believe that you ought to favor proliferation of joint committee hearings.

I feel from my experience on the Committee on Appropriations that a presentation before a House subcommittee or a House committee is wholesome; it is good for the witnesses and it is good for the program and it is good for the country to have Senate committees go through the same process.

If you have joint hearings, I think you destroy that check and balance that we have by having a House and Senate act independently. I would raise this question: Let's take the Committee on Interstate and Foreign Commerce. They have 43 Members. How many do they have in the Senate side? If you had 18 Senators you would have a tremendous total. You would have to expand facilities in order to get a joint hearing of a House and Senate Interstate and Foreign Commerce Committee.

Maybe their subcommittees could meet, but even those are large. I like the check and balance hearings, and if you have a joint hearing, in my judgment, you do undercut that check and balance system.

One other practical problem—and that does not relate to us in the legislative branch—is the time the witnesses from the executive branch have to spend testifying when you have an authorization in the House and authorizations in the Senate, an appropriations in the Senate and an appropriations in the House.

In preparation for my testimony this morning, the executive branch, at my request, came up and indicated that from January 23 through the first 15 weeks of this Congress, that executive witnesses have testified 1,000 hours. I have the number of hours here on a chart.

The joint committee recommendation would help in that regard, but I think the more persuasive argument is that you ought to have a check and balance system and, therefore, you ought not to have joint hearings.

MR. WIGGINS. I understand your remarks to mean that there is more to this Government than efficiency and expedition.

MR. FORD. I certainly agree with that.

MR. WIGGINS Thank you, Mr. Chairman.

Insofar as the hearings process is an important outlet for interest groups and simultaneously allows members to demonstrate their concern, interest, and expertise, the duplication of hearings undoubtedly can serve the political interests of all those who participate and then seek to focus public attention on their activities. In 1975, for example, the proliferation of hearings on the energy crisis and the alleged wrongdoings of the CIA brought a spotlight on a very large number of Congressmen.

Joint Staffs

Congress has also had some experience with joint staffing through the staffs of its joint committees. The most noteworthy current examples of such joint staffs are those serving the joint committees on Taxation, Atomic Energy, and the Economic Report. The Joint Committee on Internal Revenue Taxation functions in large part through its staff of economists, statisticians, attorneys, and clerks. Created by statute in 1926 and appointed on merit, this joint staff has rendered invaluable service to the members of the Senate Finance Committee and the House Committee on Ways and Means. Its success has sometimes inspired proposals to equip the committees on Appropriations with a similar joint staff. Here again, the pride of possession that committee members have in their own staff and the services staff people perform for individual members have prevented any significant changes in those arrangements.

One novel staffing arrangement, which resulted from the Congressional Budget and Impoundment Control Act of 1974, merits note. That act created a Budget Committee for each house, and they have been staffed. The act also created a Congressional Budget Office headed by a director, appointed to a four-year term by the Speaker of the House and the president pro tem of the Senate in consultation with the Budget Committees. The director is required to staff the Budget Office in a nonpartisan manner, and one of the primary functions of that staff is to work closely with the staffs of the two Budget Committees. The director, when requested, may even assign staff persons temporarily to the staffs of the Budget Committees.

Aside from joint staffing, there has been some joint action through the collaboration of the staffs of the corresponding committees of the two houses. To a limited extent they consult with each other individually and collectively, and exchange information and memoranda. But it is difficult for them to engage in joint research on the same problems or to collaborate in the preparation of studies and reports because of the varying agenda of their committees, surviving disparities in their jurisdiction, and differing methods of operation and perspective among their members. With parallel committees in the two chambers considering the same problems at different times, it is difficult for their staffs to work together simultaneously on the same schedule or to integrate their research.

Procedural Links

In addition to the joint mechanisms described in the foregoing pages, the House and Senate have also been linked together by joint and concurrent resolutions, joint rules, joint sessions, and joint attendance at impeachment trials.

A *joint resolution* is a bill so far as the legislative process is concerned. All joint resolutions except those proposing constitutional amendments are sent to the President for approval and have the full force of law. They are used for incidental, unusual, or inferior legislative purposes, such as extending the thanks of the nation to individuals, the invitation to Lafayette to visit America, the welcome to Kossuth, and notice to a foreign government of the abrogation of a treaty. Joint resolutions have also been used to declare our intervention in Cuba, to correct an error in an existing law, to elect managers for the national Soldiers' Home, and to make special appropriations for minor and incidental purposes. In the Ninety-third Congress, forty-five House joint resolutions and forty Senate joint resolutions became law.

Congress has developed the *concurrent resolutions* as a means of expressing facts, principles, opinions, and the purposes of the two houses. Joint committees are authorized by this form of resolution which is binding on neither house until agreed to by both, and which is not sent to the President for approval. It was a concurrent resolution, for example, which early in 1945 launched the joint La Follette–Monroney inquiry into the defects and improvements of our national legislature.

In the Ninety-third Congress, 127 concurrent resolutions passed both houses, most of them relatively minor or ceremonial. However, under the 1974 Budget Act, each house is expected to agree by a concurrent resolution to budget targets which are subsequently to guide the standing committees in voting authorizations. Congress has on occasion drawn up a statute which allows a program to expire or allows for executive action by passage of a concurrent resolution, as we noted in our discussion of the "legislative veto." Since 1939, presidential reorganization plans can go into effect unless within sixty days they are disapproved by a concurrent resolution that passes both houses.

The two houses of Congress early adopted *joint rules* to govern their procedure in matters requiring concurrent action, but they were abrogated in 1876 after a continuous existence of eighty-seven years. Their most useful provisions continue to be observed, however, in practice.

Finally, *joint sessions* of Congress are held in the Hall of the House from time to time to hear the President deliver a message in person or for memorial or ceremonial purposes. Occasionally the House of Representatives or its managers have attended impeachment trials in the Senate chamber. It did not attend at all in the trials of Blount, Swayne, and Archbald; and after attending at the answer of Secretary of War Belknap, the House decided that it would be represented for the remainder of the trial by its managers alone. At the trial of President Andrew Johnson, the House in committee of the whole attended throughout the trial, but this was exceptional.

We may conclude this description of the joint machinery of Congress by saying that, by and large, there has been little formal co-operation between the House and Senate in the early formulative stages of the legislative process; but very considerable collaboration via conference committees in the concluding stages. Behind the scenes over the long years, however, there has been much friendly and informal intercourse between their members and staffs, and among the members of state delegations in the two chambers, as well as a spirit of mutual respect and comity, which have belied superficial and sometimes spirited signs of separatism.

15

Relations Between Congress and the President in American History

THE AMERICAN SYSTEM of government operates within a constitutional framework that provides for executive, legislative, and judicial powers, and assigns their exercise to separate branches of the government in Washington. Each branch is given some checks on the other two, so that we have a system of separated branches and shared powers coupled with a system of checks and balances. In setting up this system back in 1789, the purpose of our Founding Fathers was to prevent tyranny and the exercise of irresponsible power.

Historically, then, Congress and the President were cast for opposite roles. Not only do they have distinct functions to perform, but they operate at opposite ends of Pennsylvania Avenue and seldom come face to face. Alexander Hamilton and his colleagues in Washington's Cabinet had expected to submit their reports in person to the House, like parliamentary ministers, but the prompt adoption by the House of Elbridge Gerry's motion that they "report in writing" established a precedent followed ever afterward. One result was that department heads have appeared before committees of the House, rather than the House itself. Another effect, as Justice Story remarked, was: "The Executive is compelled to resort to secret and unseen influences, to private interviews, and private arrangements, to accomplish his own appropriate purposes instead of proposing and sustaining his own duties and measures by a bold and manly appeal to the nation in the face of its representatives."

This functional and physical separation between the legislative and executive branches of government has caused rivalry, suspicion, and hostility between Congress and the President at intervals throughout our national history. Conflict is a built-in feature of the American system of government. Our inherited system of shared powers has, however, prevented the rise of dictators, and has precluded the Executive from riding roughshod over Congress. There is no danger here of that "Cabinet tyranny" of which the British sometimes complain.

Several other historical developments and usages have also affected legislative-executive relationships in Washington. The fact that the President and members of Congress are elected in different ways and represent different electorates tends to promote conflict between them. On the one hand, the President is chosen in a nationwide election and has come to be practically the popular choice of the entire American electorate, or of a majority of the voters. As his office has evolved over the years, the American President has become the leader of *all* the people and the sole spokesman of *all* the people.

Members of Congress, on the other hand, are locally elected and locally responsible. Congressmen do not represent all the people; they represent primarily their own districts and states and the particular local and sectional interests which are vital to them. Under the usage called the "locality rule," a Congressman must be a resident of the single-member district that elects him: a condition that compels him to defer to the dominant interests of his constituency. By way of contrast, a member of Parliament need not reside in the district he represents at Westminster, a circumstance that leaves him comparatively free from constituent pressures.

A related factor that affects the chances of legislative-executive cooperation on particular measures is the fact that the President tends to represent the consumer-conscious masses of the metropolitan centers in the big states where presidential elections are decided; whereas most members of Congress represent the production-conscious interests of the smaller cities and towns and rural districts which have elected them. Successful presidential candidates must speak in the language of the consensus that unites most Americans. This means promising the retention or moderate expansions or contractions of those governmental programs that have a broad base of public support. Thus the two least successful candidates of the modern period—Senator Barry Goldwater and Senator George McGovern—were perceived as anxious to make drastic changes in our national policies. The typical member of Congress can, however, retain a seat in the House of Representatives by devotion to private and local interests and careful attention to the day-to-day problems of constituents.

Meanwhile legislative-executive relations have also been affected by the changing nature of American society. A familiar feature of American life in the twentieth century has been the development of a complex pattern of groups: economic and social, local and regional, each demanding action by the government to protect and promote its interests. The division of labor and specialization of function in an industrial age have given rise to a polity of pressure groups which seek to influence legislative and administrative action to their own ends. Within the executive and legislative branches of the federal government are administrative bureaus and legislative committees whose interactions and interrelationships with their affiliated interest groups form a complex pattern.

Another usage that makes co-operation between the President and Congress difficult, even when the same political party controls both branches, is the seniority system of selecting the chairmen of congressional committees. Under this system the chairmanships of the great legislative committees customarily are held by those majority-party members who have had the longest continuous service upon them. However, the majority party cannot control the chairmen, because it does not control their selection. This is important both because Congress has largely delegated control of legislative action to its standing committees and because the chairmen of these committees have great powers over their agenda. As Woodrow Wilson well said: "I know not how better to describe our form of government in a single phrase than by calling it a government by the chairmen of the standing committees of Congress." Over the years the power of committee chairmen has frequently been a major obstacle for Presidents seeking to achieve platform goals. This has been particularly so when liberal Democratic Presidents have confronted conservative Southern chairmen. However, the unseating of three chairmen by the Democratic caucus at the beginning of the Ninety-fourth Congress suggests that in the future all chairmen will be more sensitive to the views of the majority of their party.[1]

Aside from these basic difficulties, executive-legislative relations have been affected by the varying personalities of Presidents and Congressmen, by changing conditions of war and peace, of prosperity and depression, and by the increasing volume and complexity of public problems. Down through American history, leadership has oscillated between the legislature and the executive. We have had alternating periods of presidential government and of congressional government as the pendulum of power has swung back and forth.

From time to time, relations between the two branches have been handicapped by executive refusals to furnish information demanded by the House, or by alleged abuses of the investigative function of Congress, or by the executive submission of "must" legislation and attempts to "pack" the Supreme Court, or by opposition efforts to embarrass the administration by legislative inquests into the loyalty of government employees.

Relations have sometimes been embittered during periods of divided government when opposing political parties have controlled the White

House and one or both houses of Congress. This has happened several times in our history, as the accompanying table shows. We have had a government of fits and starts, marked by long periods of internal struggle and stalemate, in which the people have been the chief losers. Nineteen hundred and fifty-four to nineteen hundred and sixty was another period of divided government, but happily it proved to be largely an era of good feeling, thanks to the popularity of President Eisenhower, the eclipse of McCarthyism, and the "constructive opposition" of the Democratic leaders of Congress. The period of divided government between President Nixon and Congress was, however, very abrasive. The tensions of the Vietnam War, the "incursion" of Cambodia, repeated presidential impoundments, and finally the duplicities of Watergate made for persistent confrontations. In addition, Mr. Nixon had suffered the reputation of an overzealous partisan for many years. Although many Democrats continued to oppose many of the positions taken by President Ford, they did so without animus. The new President was assisted in his role by many years of experience in the House, where he had long enjoyed the reputation of a party loyalist who was nevertheless gracious in his relationship with all of the members.

DIVIDED GOVERNMENT SINCE THE CIVIL WAR

President	Party	Congress	Senate Control	House Control
Grant	Republican	44th (1875-77)	Republican	Democrat
Hayes	Republican	45th (1877-79)	Republican	Democrat
Hayes	Republican	46th (1879-81)	Democrat	Democrat
Arthur	Republican	48th (1883-85)	Republican	Democrat
Cleveland	Democrat	49th (1885-87)	Republican	Democrat
Cleveland	Democrat	50th (1887-89)	Republican	Democrat
Harrison	Republican	52nd (1891-93)	Republican	Democrat
Cleveland	Democrat	54th (1895-97)	Republican	Republican
Taft	Republican	62nd (1911-13)	Republican	Democrat
Wilson	Democrat	66th (1919-21)	Republican	Republican
Hoover	Republican	72nd (1931-33)	Republican	Democrat
Truman	Democrat	80th (1947-48)	Republican	Republican
Eisenhower	Republican	84th (1955-56)	Democrat	Democrat
Eisenhower	Republican	85th (1957-58)	Democrat	Democrat
Eisenhower	Republican	86th (1959-60)	Democrat	Democrat
Nixon	Republican	91st (1969-71)	Democrat	Democrat
Nixon	Republican	92nd (1971-72)	Democrat	Democrat
Nixon*	Republican	93d (1973-74)	Democrat	Democrat
Ford	Republican	94th (1975—)	Democrat	Democrat

* Gerald R. Ford succeeded Richard M. Nixon as President on August 8, 1974.

The basic causes of the recurring conflicts between Congress and the President have been functional and institutional, not personal. They have been functional as a result of the lack of an organic relationship between the two branches, a lack that might be remedied by the creation of truly national political parties. They have been institutional as a result of the separation of powers and personnel. Such monastic separation is not, however, a prerequisite of representative government. Under the British system of parliamentary democracy, for example, Parliament and Cabinet come face to face daily. Moreover, the House of Commons can oust the Cabinet, and the Cabinet can dissolve the Commons. It would be impossible under the British system for opposing political parties to control the two branches. Under such a system, if we had it here, when the President's party lost control of the House, he would resign and be replaced by the leader of the opposing party. It is improbable that the parliamentary form of government will be adopted in the United States, but the need remains of finding some way of integrating the determination and execution of public policies if what James M. Burns calls the "recurring cycle of drift, decision, deed, and deadlock" is to be ended.

Executive Leadership: 1789-1809

Throughout our national history, as we have mentioned, there has been an ebb and flow of political power between Congress and the President.

A struggle for power between the legislative and executive branches of the new government developed early in Washington's first administration. The Constitution did not define the boundaries of their respective powers, and early attempts to draw a line between executive and legislative functions were inconclusive. John Adams declared they were "natural enemies" and forecast the collapse of the system.

The Federalists, who were in control of the government during its first decade, believed in strong executive leadership in matters both foreign and domestic. As first Secretary of the Treasury, Alexander Hamilton sought to develop a ministry system on the British model, with the President serving as titular leader, the department heads exercising the initiative in legislation, the Treasury acting as a medium of communication between the two branches, and with himself functioning as a sort of prime minister. From 1789 to 1795, Hamilton actually acted like a prime minister, drafted bills and reports, helped to select congressional committees and attended their meetings, and largely dominated the legislative process in the House.

On his part President Washington recognized the co-ordinate position of

Congress in the new system of government. He was scrupulous to maintain correct formal relations with the legislature and careful to observe its statutory and financial limitations. During the early years of his administration, Washington frequently sought the advice of James Madison, then a member of the House. In the field of foreign affairs, a dispute arose in 1796 between the President and the House over Jay's Treaty. Washington rejected a House request for the Jay papers, while the House asserted its right to refuse funds for the execution of a treaty. The veto power was regarded as a weapon to defend the executive branch against congressional encroachment, but neither Washington nor Adams had occasion to use it for this purpose. Washington vetoed an apportionment bill in 1792 and an Army bill in 1797, but no bills were vetoed by John Adams.

On its part the House of Representatives during the early years frequently sought the advice and counsel of Secretary Hamilton on fiscal policy, the development of manufacturing and other matters; and he responded with the famous reports on the public credit, on national banking, and on manufactures. Meanwhile Thomas Jefferson, while Secretary of State, drafted legislation to promote the progress of the useful arts and to revise the patent law. These activities led some members of the House to fear executive domination. This apprehension was reflected in the debate on the Treasury bill in June, 1789, and led the House to empower the Secretary of the Treasury "to digest and prepare plans" rather than "to digest and report" them.

A basic issue of the Federalist period was whether matters should be referred by Congress to the department heads for information and report. The Federalists favored such references and denied that this procedure would impair congressional influence or authority. The Republicans opposed this procedure on the ground that the legislature should originate its own laws. Reference to department heads, especially to the Secretary of the Treasury, was the prevailing practice from 1790 to 1794 and confirmed Hamilton's leadership in the House. By 1794, however, the Republican position in favor of reliance by the House on its own committees won acceptance and led to Hamilton's retirement from the Treasury in January, 1795. Thereafter the House sought leadership internally on questions of future policy, although it continued to ask for departmental reports on past performance and on routine matters.

Another issue of this period was whether department heads should submit their reports in writing or orally to the House. The matter came up first in January, 1790, when Hamilton informed the House that he was ready to report the plan it had requested for the support of the public credit. After a brief debate, the House voted to receive the report in writing. A proposal in November, 1792, that Hamilton and Secretary of War Knox attend the House during the discussion of the defeat of General St. Clair by the Indians was opposed by Madison and other Republicans and rejected. No further attempts to admit department heads to the floor of Congress were made.[2]

The pattern of executive leadership, set during the Federalist period, was retained with some modifications by Thomas Jefferson. The Republicans in Congress had opposed the concept of presidential leadership of national affairs and favored the theory of legislative supremacy. But Jefferson, despite his Republican principles, kept the reins of government in his hands during his Presidency by using the machinery of party government, notably the caucus and the floor leader, behind the scenes to control Congress and promote his legislative objectives.

Recognizing the need of leadership in the House to guide the rank and file and to promote his legislative program, Jefferson converted the position of floor leader into a spokesman for the President. Under Jefferson the floor leaders of the House "were presidential agents, appointed by the executive, and dismissed at his pleasure."[3] They included William B. Giles, Caesar A. Rodney, John Randolph, and Wilson Cary Nicholas.[4] Giles' position of leadership in the House was currently described as "premier or prime minister of the day," "first lord of the treasury," and "chancellor of the exchequer," referring to his chairmanship of the Ways and Means Committee.[5] When Randolph refused to support the President's desire for the acquisition of Florida, he was deposed from the chairmanship of that committee. If the Republicans in the House lacked a leader with the requisite talents to expedite its business, Jefferson would persuade some private citizen whom he considered qualified to run for Congress and assume the floor leadership.

Jefferson also utilized the party caucus, a device first invented by the Federalists, to maintain close relations with Congress. There were frequent meetings of Republican party leaders at the home of Albert Gallatin, Secretary of the Treasury. "In this extra-constitutional agency President, Cabinet, and congressmen of both houses could meet and circumvent the sacred dogma of separation of powers without doing violence to the tenderest Republican conscience."[6] According to John Quincy Adams: "His [Jefferson's] whole system of administration seems founded on the principle of carrying through the legislative measures by personal or official influence."[7]

Another Federalist device, which the Republicans had formerly denounced but now adopted, was the practice of referring matters to the Secretary of the Treasury for report and recommendations. Gallatin revived Hamilton's practice of digesting laws and preparing plans on matters referred to him by the House. He also attended committee meetings, drafted their reports, and even suggested the names of their chairmen. "He seems," says Binkley, "to have been almost as active as Hamilton had been in steering measures through Congress."[8]

In short, by means of the floor leader and the majority party caucus,

Jefferson was able, with Gallatin's help, to maintain control of Congress and to continue the Federalist system of executive leadership.

Congressional Supremacy: 1809-1829

After Jefferson's retirement from the Presidency, the devices he had developed to maintain executive leadership were converted by Henry Clay and the leaders of the House into instruments of congressional control of the executive. After two years of indecision (1809-1811), the election of Henry Clay as Speaker and the appearance of the War Hawks marked the beginning of a period of legislative leadership of governmental affairs. Congressional supremacy during this period was based in part on the evolution of the office of Speaker and the expansion of his powers from a mere presiding officer to an active party leader. Clay's election and repeated re-election to the Speakership "marked a profound change in its character and in the effective leadership of the government."[9] According to Miss Follett, from 1811 to 1825 Clay was the most powerful man in the nation.[10]

Meanwhile the development of the standing committee system took place in 1816 and thereafter served to facilitate legislative-executive co-operation when cordial relations obtained between Congress and the President, but in times of conflict the committees became agents of legislative oversight and control of the administration. Another contributing factor was the emergence of the congressional party caucus and its use from 1800 through 1824 to nominate party candidates for President and Vice President. This practice tended to subordinate the President to his party leaders in Congress, since he owed his nomination to them, and hence to strengthen their authority in the government.

As Leonard White writes:[11]

> The story of the presidency under four Republican Chief Executives can be summed up briefly by stating that Jefferson fully maintained in practice the Federalist conception of the executive power; that Madison lost heavily to the legislative branch and carried the presidency to one of its lowest points; that Monroe, although hard challenged by the Speaker of the House, Henry Clay, was able to maintain executive leadership in foreign policy if not in domestic affairs; and that John Quincy Adams, as thoroughly committed in principle to executive leadership as his father, was unable to carry his principle into practice. He lost all opportunity to lead when factional opponents seized control of his second Congress in 1827. Leadership under the Republicans irresistibly followed the leaders—they were Jefferson and Gallatin for eight years, but for most of the remaining

twenty they were Giles, Smith, and others in the Senate; Clay, Calhoun, Lowndes, and others in the House of Representatives.

Presidential Leadership: 1829-1837

The election of Andrew Jackson in 1828 marked another swing of the pendulum from congressional sovereignty to presidential leadership. With their hero in the White House, the agrarians now reversed their stand on the doctrine of legislative supremacy, while the Whigs, who had appeared upon the public scene as successors to the defunct Federalist party, and the commercial and industrial interests they represented, likewise switched their historic allegiance from the Presidency to Congress, where Webster and Clay became the eloquent spokesmen of the interests of a rising capitalism.

As a tribune and direct representative of the people, Jackson made unprecedented use of the veto power to defeat bills on grounds of expediency, and employed patronage and the removal power as weapons in his recurring conflicts with Congress. A running feud ensued between the President and Henry Clay over the distribution of governmental powers.

During the "reign" of "King Andrew," executive-legislative relations were marked by bitter battles over the Bank of the United States. When Congress passed a bill to recharter the bank, Jackson vetoed it and withdrew the governmental deposits from the bank. The Senate responded by passing Clay's resolution of censure in March, 1834. Jackson's formal protest against this resolution precipitated a national debate on the proper limits of legislative and executive authority. Three years later, Jackson's friends in the Senate, led by Thomas Hart Benton, succeeded in expunging the censure resolution from the Senate *Journal*. The expungement, writes Binkley, marked "the final blow to the Republican system of congressional supremacy."[12]

The age of Jackson was marked by several fundamental changes in the American political system, including the shift from the congressional caucus to national party conventions as agencies for the nomination of presidential candidates, and a change in the method of choosing presidential electors from their appointment by the state legislatures to their election by the people in the several states by the general ticket system. The effect of these changes, coupled with the widespread adoption of white manhood suffrage, the building of party organizations throughout the country, and the presence in the White House of a strong popular leader, was to restore the vigor of the Presidency and to strengthen the Chief Executive in his struggles with the legislature.

Fluctuations in Power: 1837-1860

The quarter century from Jackson to Lincoln was a period marked by extreme fluctuations in power and influence between Congress and the President. Whig experience with Andrew Jackson's dominant personality led them to try to weaken the Presidency and to choose presidential candidates of less aggressive natures. During this period, legislative-executive relations were deadlocked in Van Buren's administration (1837-1841); Tyler antagonized Congress by his vetoes of two bank bills and two tariff measures (1841-1845); Polk restored the leadership of the Presidency and successfully administered the war with Mexico as Commander in Chief (1845-1849); while the decade of the 1850's witnessed a succession of weak Presidents—Fillmore, Pierce, and Buchanan—and a Congress also weak and divided by the baffling question of the extension of slavery.

Between Jackson's era and the Civil War, the Whigs repeatedly sought to subordinate the Executive to congressional control, but were frequently frustrated either by the vetoes of the unruly John Tyler or by the untimely demise of the two Whig Presidents: General William Henry Harrison in 1841, who had promised in his inaugural address to be duly subservient to Congress; and General Zachary Taylor, who threatened to veto the Compromise Bill of 1850.

Meanwhile the advocates of slavery, who were outnumbered in both houses of Congress, looked to control of the Presidency for the protection of their peculiar institution. "Their master stratagem for this purpose," writes Binkley, "was the fastening of the two-thirds rule for presidential nominations on the Democratic National Nomination Convention. The result was that even when they could not nominate a slaveholder they could, at any rate, prevent the nomination of a candidate unfavorable to slavery. In time the typical Democratic candidate became the 'doughface,' a Northern man with Southern principles. No matter what party controlled Congress, the veto power in the hands of a Pierce or a Buchanan made the slavocracy secure against legislation disadvantageous to their interest . . . The failure to retain this control [of the Presidency] in 1860 threw them into the panic that precipitated the secession movement."[13]

Lincoln and Congress: 1861-1865

After the secessionists withdrew from Congress in 1861, both houses were controlled by the Republican or Union party, which was split into conservative and radical factions. The Republicans strongly espoused the theory, inherited from the Whigs, of congressional supremacy. Radical Republicans in both houses regarded the President as "only the instrument of Congress." Said Senator Trumbull: "He is just as much subject to our control as if we appointed him, except that we cannot remove him and appoint another in his place."[14] Their theory of governmental powers was set forth most explicitly in the famous Wade-Davis Manifesto which declared that[15]

> the authority of Congress is paramount and must be respected; that the whole body of Union men in Congress will not submit to be impeached by him [the President] of rash and unconstitutional legislation; and if he wishes our support he must confine himself to his executive duties—to obey and to execute not to make the laws—to suppress by arms armed rebellion, and leave political reorganization to Congress.

In pursuit of this concept of congressional control, Congress created, in December, 1861, a Joint Committee on the Conduct of the War, composed of four Congressmen and three Senators. This committee carried on extensive investigations of the war effort, intervened in military operations, and exercised a roving commission to look into all sorts of matters.

On his part, President Lincoln outdid Jackson in his conception of the executive office. Under stress of the war crisis and impelled by his overriding determination to preserve the Union at all costs, Lincoln ignored the constitutional position of Congress and asserted and exercised powers that were unprecedented in American history and that brought him repeatedly in conflict with his fellow partisans in Congress. During his administration legislative-executive relations were embittered by controversies over the conduct of the war, the expansion of the Armed Forces, the expenditure of public funds, the emancipation of the slaves, and over plans for postwar reconstruction. In each of these areas Lincoln took steps that challenged the Republican theory of congressional dominance in the government.

By a proclamation of May 3, 1861, the President increased the size of the regular army and navy and called for volunteers, in disregard of the constitutional authority of Congress "to raise and support armies." He waited four months after his inauguration before summoning the legislature in special session to validate these measures. In 1863 he issued an elaborate code of rules for the regulation of the federal forces in the field, despite the constitutional delegation of this duty to the Congress. And he directed the Secretary of the Treasury to spend funds deemed necessary for the national defense without authority of law, far exceeding Jackson's irregularities in the removal of the deposits.

Lincoln outwitted and enraged the Radicals in Congress by sending them a veto message he would have used if they had not revised a confiscation bill as he wished, and by issuing the Emancipation Proclamation after Congress had adjourned. Thus, remarks Binkley in his vivid account of this era, "the President [gave] the final blow to the claims of congressional supremacy by the boldest stroke of executive policy of the war period."[16]

Soon thereafter, in another proclamation, the President suspended the writ of habeas corpus and declared himself a virtual dictator, thus answering the claims of Thaddeus Stevens and the Radicals who asserted that Congress itself had the "power of dictatorship." And in the Cabinet crisis of 1862, Lincoln cleverly outmaneuvered a congressional group that tried to reorganize his Cabinet.

In 1864, Congress and the President came into direct conflict over their respective constitutional powers of reconstruction in the Southern states. In response to a presidential proclamation of reconstruction on December 8, 1863, which ignored the role of Congress in this area, that body enacted the Wade-Davis Bill which was designed to transfer reconstruction matters from the President to Congress. When Lincoln pocket-vetoed the bill, the Radicals in Congress accepted the challenge by publishing the Wade-Davis Manifesto. "This manifesto," writes Binkley, "represents probably the most authoritative statement possible of the Radical congressmen's conception of the proper relation of the Executive to the legislature held during the Civil War. It describes perfectly the theory on which the party functioned during Johnson's administration. The fundamental idea of it can be traced more or less through Republican party doctrine to the present day."[17]

Binkley gives a succinct summary of legislative-executive relations during the Civil War:

> Unquestionably the high-water mark of the exercise of executive power in the United States is found in the administration of Abraham Lincoln. No President before or since has pushed the boundaries of executive power so far over into the legislative sphere. No one can ever know just what Lincoln conceived to be the limits of his powers. Even a partial review of them presents an imposing list of daring ventures. Under the war power he proclaimed the slaves of those in rebellion emancipated. He devised and put into execution his peculiar plan of reconstruction. In disregard of law he increased the army and navy beyond the limits set by statute. The privilege of the writ of habeas corpus was suspended wholesale and martial law declared. Public money in the sum of millions was deliberately spent without congressional appropriation. Nor was any of this done innocently. Lincoln understood his Constitution. He knew, in many cases, just how he was transgressing and his infractions were consequently deliberate. It is all the more astonishing that this audacity was the work of a minority President who performed in the presence of a bitter congressional opposition even in his own party. Of course, after the election of 1864 he probably considered that his reelection constituted a vindication of his record regardless of the question of the constitutionality of his practice.[18]

Congressional Government: 1865-1898

Thirty years of struggle between Congress and the President ensued after Lincoln's assassination. The Radical Republicans, who were in control of Congress, believed in the sovereignty of the legislature, and they promptly took a series of steps designed to cut the Presidency down to size and to restore Congress to a dominant position in the system of government. Their attitude was reflected in the oft-quoted words of Senator Benjamin F. Wade when the Joint Committee on the Conduct of the War called on the new President: "Johnson, we have faith in you. By the gods, there will be no trouble now in running the Government."

Their faith in Andrew Johnson, who had been a member of the Joint Committee, was soon severely shaken by his retention of Lincoln's entire Cabinet, his failure to convene Congress in special session, and his procedure in carrying out his own plans of reconstruction without consulting the legislature. Schuyler Colfax, who was re-elected Speaker of the House when the Thirty-ninth Congress met in regular session in December, 1865, doubtless voiced the feeling of many members of that body when he declared that it was the function of Congress and not the President to develop the program for the reconstruction of the conquered states.

Acting under the dominant leadership of Thaddeus Stevens and a Joint Committee on Reconstruction, controlled by the Radicals, Congress passed two bills: a Civil Rights Bill, over Johnson's veto; and a bill to continue the Freedmen's Bureau, on which his veto was sustained. They also barred the admission to Congress of representatives from the seceded states until both houses should declare them entitled to representation.

Emboldened by their victory in the congressional elections of 1866, the Radicals passed a Reconstruction Act in 1867, embodying their own plan for the reconstruction of the Southern states in place of Lincoln and Johnson's more conciliatory scheme. They also established Grant's headquarters as General of the Army in Washington, required all army orders and instructions to be issued through him, thus bypassing the President as Commander in Chief, and forbade the President to remove, suspend, or transfer the general without the prior consent of the Senate. Then they passed over the President's veto the Tenure of Office Act of March 2, 1867, and impeached Johnson in 1868 for not obeying it. This act required Senate approval of the removal of department heads and other officials who had been appointed with the advice and consent of the Senate. It was amended in 1869 and repealed in 1887. President Johnson dismissed Secretary of War Stanton to test the constitutionality of this law in the courts. In the impeachment trial, the Senate acquitted Johnson by the slim margin of a single vote, thus avoiding a possible revolution in the American constitutional system. But the net effect of these remarkable events was to destroy Johnson's leadership of the government, to humiliate the Presidency, and to produce a stalemate in legislative-executive relations. "From the day of the passage of the Civil Rights Bill over the President's head," writes Binkley, "Congress was master of the government and the President's initiative and usefulness as a constructive leader was at an end."[19]

In electing General Grant to the Presidency it was generally expected, in the light of his military achievements, that he possessed unique administrative talents, and that as a new tribune of the people he would be able, like Andrew Jackson, to provide strong executive leadership and to restore the balance of the constitutional system. In practice, however, Grant proved to be a weak and inept President, ignorant of the nature of the American system of government and indifferent to the conduct of public affairs. His two terms in the White House (1868-1876) were marked by executive compliance with the wishes of Congress. He accepted their advice on legislation and made the appointments they desired. He considered the President to be a "purely administrative officer" whose duties were those of "the commander of an army in time of peace." According to Henry Adams' analysis of Grant's philosophy: "It was the duty of the President to follow without hesitation the wishes of the people as expressed by Congress."[20] His administration was characterized by a degrading subservience to the Senate which attained the peak of its power during this period. Insensitive to his golden opportunity to restore the prestige of the Presidency, "he became little more than the political puppet of his flatterers and consequently he stands today in our history as the most pathetic figure that ever occupied the office of President of the United States."[21]

Rutherford B. Hayes (1877-1881) defended the powers of the Presidency against legislative encroachment both by a Republican Senate in the matter of Cabinet and customhouse appointments and by a Democratic House in regard to riders on appropriation bills. At the outset of his administration, Hayes defied the Senate spoilsmen by making his own Cabinet nominations, and he succeeded, with the support of an aroused public opinion, in forcing the Senate to confirm the entire list when it was in a mood to reject them. After a prolonged battle with the second chamber over the President's power of dismissal, Hayes also succeeded in winning Senate confirmation of his appointments to the New York Customhouse, stronghold of Senator Conkling's state political machine.

Meanwhile the Democratic House in the Forty-sixth Congress repeatedly attached riders to supply bills in an effort to obtain control of the government and to secure the repeal of measures for Southern reconstruction, lacking the votes to override executive vetoes of direct repeal bills. President Hayes firmly resisted this coercive practice in a series of seven vigorous veto measures that denied the validity of the House doctrine of "grievance before supply" and clearly restated the constitutional principle of separated powers. By his persistent use of the veto power Hayes succeeded in defending the independence of the Chief Executive and arrested the postwar decline in the prestige of the Presidency. "The action was defensive and protective," as Leonard White observes, "but it was important. Congress was forced to enact the long-delayed appropriation acts without imposing its will on the President; the integrity of the veto power was sustained; and the popularity of an unpopular President was repaired."[22]

After President Garfield's assassination by a disappointed office seeker, the decade of the 1880's was marked by lack of leadership in the White House and by congressional dominance of national affairs. Chester Arthur, Grover Cleveland, and Benjamin Harrison each seemed satisfied with the theory of separated powers and the practice of legislative leadership. "These were the years," as Leonard White remarks, "when the young but observant Woodrow Wilson was writing his *Congressional Government* and James Bryce was explaining why great men are not chosen Presidents."[23]

At the opening of his first administration, President Cleveland made numerous suspensions from and corresponding appointments to offices in the executive branch. A sensational controversy with the Senate ensued over its demands for information and the papers relating to these suspensions. The President denied the right of the Senate to the papers in a ringing message that stirred the nation. The upshot of the controversy was the confirmation of Cleveland's nominees and the repeal of the Tenure of Office Act.

During this period the Chief Executive used the veto power both on constitutional and on policy and judgment grounds. Chester Arthur and Benjamin Harrison rarely used this power; but in his two terms Grover Cleveland vetoed 345 bills, mostly private pension measures, three times as many as all his predecessors combined.[24]

While the doctrine of congressional supremacy was widely accepted in Washington, internal conditions in the House of Representatives were in a deplorable state. Binkley gives this picture of the situation:[25]

> The culmination of this vast assumption of power by Congress in the 1880s coincided almost exactly with the decline of the lower house to almost the nadir of incompetence. Despite its assumption of sovereign power in the government, it lay floundering in a confusion of warring committees. Spurning all suggestion of external leadership, it yet found no trace of leadership within. . . . The cause of the confusion lay in the fact that no rational system had been devised for sifting bills for consideration by

the House. Consequently among the tens of thousands of measures introduced during a session something like sheer caprice had come to determine which should reach the floor for consideration and vote. . . . The situation drew from Representative Thomas B. Reed the caustic remark that the "only way to do business inside the rules is to suspend the rules. . . . The object of the rules appears to be to prevent the transaction of business."

The vacuum of leadership in the government at Washington during Harrison's administration was finally filled by Representative Reed of Maine, who upon his election to the Speakership in 1889 brought the tactics of minority obstruction to an end, reformed the rules of the House, and established a strong system of internal leadership in the first chamber.

In conclusion, the period from Lincoln to McKinley was largely one of congressional primacy. Co-operative relations between the legislative and executive branches were handicapped during this period by the frequency of divided control of the government—in eight of the eleven Congresses between 1875 and 1897, the opposition party controlled one or both houses of the national legislature—by the determination of congressional leaders to curb the powers of the Presidency which had been expanded by the exigencies of war; and by their strong belief in legislative supremacy. Meanwhile, the position of the Presidency was weakened by the impeachment of Andrew Johnson, the scandals of Grant's administration when congressional investigations of the executive branch reached a highwater mark, by the fact that Hayes was a minority President whose title to office was clouded by a disputed election, by Arthur's association with the New York Customshouse controversy, and by Cleveland's insistence upon the independence of the executive and legislative branches as well as his uncompromising personality.

Executive Leadership: 1898-1918

In 1898, the pendulum of political power swung back to the executive branch, which continued to be the dominant partner in the federal system for twenty years. After thirty years of conflict, President McKinley restored the leadership of the Presidency by his tact, dignity, and his personal influence with Congress, both houses of which were controlled by the Republican party during his administration. The new President had enjoyed a distinguished career, having served six terms in the House of Representatives and two terms as governor of Ohio. His administration marked an era of good feeling between Congress and the President, who fully understood the psychology of the national legislature and respected its prerogatives. He was popular with the American people and possessed personal qualities that made for cordial and co-operative relations with Congress. The legislative and executive branches of the federal government achieved a closer integration during McKinley's Presidency than had existed since the administration of Thomas Jefferson.

After McKinley was shot by an anarchist in Buffalo on September 6, 1901, Theodore Roosevelt came to the White House. He had an expansive concept of the scope of executive power, considering himself to be in this respect a disciple of Andrew Jackson and Abraham Lincoln.

> I declined [he later said in his *Autobiography*] to adopt the view that what was imperatively necessary for the nation could not be done by the President unless he could find some specific authorization to do it. My belief was that it was not only his right but his duty to do anything that the needs of the nation demanded unless such action was forbidden by the Constitution or by the laws. Under this interpretation of executive power I did and caused to be done many things not previously done by the President and the heads of the departments. I did not usurp power, but I did greatly broaden the use of executive power.[26]

Teddy Roosevelt's dynamic exercise of the powers of the Presidency brought him into occasional conflict with Congress, which sought to restrain him by requiring him to file copies of his executive orders together with citations to their legal authority. Nevertheless, T.R. had remarkable success in securing enactment of the legislation he desired, an achievement attributed to the "organic connection" he established with Congress through the Speaker of the House, Joseph G. Cannon. After a long process of evolution, the Speaker had reached the peak of his powers and dominated the House of Representatives. Theodore Roosevelt and Speaker Cannon established a close working relationship. As Cannon described it:[27]

> I think Mr. Roosevelt talked over with me virtually every serious recommendation to Congress before he made it and requested me to sound out the leaders in the House, for he did not want to recommend legislation simply to write messages. He wanted results and he wanted to know how to secure results with the least friction. He was a good sportsman and accepted what he could get so long as the legislation conformed even in part to his recommendations.

On his part, the young President felt that both houses of Congress were controlled by conservatives and "reactionaries" who paid lip service to Lincoln but lacked his spirit. "I made a resolute effort," he later wrote, "to get on" with these men and with their followers, "and I have no question that they made an equally resolute effort to get on with me. We succeeded in working together, although with increasing friction, for some years, I pushing forward and they hanging back. Gradually, however, I was forced to abandon the effort to persuade them to come my way, and then I achieved results only by appealing over the heads of the Senate and House leaders to the people, who were the masters of both of us. . . . There were, of course, many senators and members of the Lower House with whom up to the very last I continued to work in hearty accord, and with a growing understanding. . . ."[28] Roosevelt illustrated the difference between what he called the "Lincoln-Jackson and the Buchanan-Taft schools" by comparing his own defense of his department heads, when attacked in Congress, with that of President Taft who asked Congress to pass judgment on the charges made against his Secretary of the Interior, Ballinger.[29]

William Howard Taft had a more limited view of the powers and duties of the President than his predecessor. He also lacked T.R.'s colorful personality and political adroitness. As President, Taft did not maintain the contact with the Speaker of the House that Roosevelt had established, both because he disliked "Uncle Joe" personally and because Cannon was soon "dethroned" in the parliamentary revolution of 1910. But Taft strongly favored giving members of the President's Cabinet access to the floor of each house of Congress "to introduce measures, to advocate their passage, to answer questions, and to enter into the debate as if they were members, without of course the right to vote."[30] This did not, however, come to pass. Meanwhile legislative-executive relations were handicapped by the fact that the Republicans in Congress were split internally by the struggle over the Payne-Aldrich tariff and by the Ballinger-Pinchot controversy over the conservation of natural resources. Then, in the mid-term congressional elections of 1910, the Democrats captured control of the House of Representatives, presaging a Democratic victory in the presidential election of 1912.

Woodrow Wilson entered the White House with a fully developed theory of executive leadership. From his student days he had considered the central problem of American government to be that of achieving effective cooperation between Congress and the President. His own thinking and Theodore Roosevelt's aggressive leadership had led Wilson by 1908 to regard the Presidency as the unifying force in our political system.[31] Long an admirer of the English parliamentary system, he revealed his conception of legislative-executive relations at Washington when, as President-elect, he wrote Representative A. Mitchell Palmer that "the President . . . must be Prime Minister, as much concerned with the guidance of legislation as with just and orderly execution of law . . ."[32]

After his inauguration, President Wilson employed a variety of techniques in his role of legislative leader. He began by delivering his State-of-the-Union message in person, reviving a practice that Jefferson had abandoned more than a century before. He conferred with congressional committees, sometimes in the President's room at the Capitol, sometimes at the White House. He sent up fully drafted bills, and he also lobbied personally with the legislators, soliciting their support of his measures. As a strong believer in party government, Wilson formed a smooth working relationship with the Democratic floor leaders in both houses of Congress: Oscar Underwood in the House of Representatives and John W. Kern in the Senate. Democrats in Congress listened to the eloquent voice of their leader in the White House and enacted the greater part of his legislative program via the caucus route in both houses. Historians have assigned the credit for the establishment of the Federal Reserve System, the Underwood Tariff Act, the currency and other domestic reforms of the New Freedom era to effective use of the legislative caucus in Congress. The Democratic party, operating through its party chief in the White House and its party caucus on Capitol Hill, became the hyphen that joined, the buckle that fastened, the legislature to the executive.

This system worked well during Wilson's first term and was largely responsible for the success of his domestic program.[33] But his leadership was sharply challenged on several matters of foreign policy. In 1914, both Speaker Champ Clark and Oscar W. Underwood, majority leader, opposed the President on the repeal of the Panama tolls. In 1915, Representative Jeff McLemore of Texas introduced a resolution requesting the President to warn Americans not to travel on armed merchant vessels, which Wilson regarded as a challenge to his leadership. On April 2, 1917, when the President appeared before a joint session of Congress to ask for a declaration of war against Germany, he was opposed in the debate by his own floor leader, Representative Claude Kitchin of North Carolina. Later, Speaker Clark denounced Wilson's military-conscription program in a floor speech. And Wilson's struggle with the Senate in 1919-1920 over ratification of the Treaty of Versailles was perhaps the most outstanding and fateful executive-legislative conflict in American history. Capture of both houses of Congress by the Republicans in the congressional elections of 1918, despite Wilson's appeal for a Democratic Congress, signaled the end of another period of executive leadership in the endless ebb and flow of political power.

Normalcy and Reaction: 1921-1932

Harding's administration marked a "return to normalcy" and a reaction against strong executive leadership of the Wilsonian kind. The Senator from Ohio was not equipped by training, experience, or temperament to be an aggressive leader. His senatorial colleagues, to whom he owed his nomination, did not desire to place a strong leader in the White House, and such also was the prevailing mood of the people. The election of 1920 reflected the reaction of public opinion to eight years of presidential government and political controversy. The people now wanted to return to tranquillity and the traditional system of checks and balances.

When President Harding addressed the Senate early in 1921 to urge a balanced budget, resentment was expressed in both houses. Senators criticized him for interfering in their business, while Congressmen felt that he had snubbed the House where all supply bills originate.

The lack of leadership in the executive branch was matched by a similar lack in Congress. The Sixty-seventh Congress, which was strongly Republican, mirrored the confusion and indecision of the public mind during this period. In the absence of guidance and direction from the White House, the legislative record of the Harding administration was largely devoid of constructive achievement, aside from adoption of the national budget system which had actually been formulated during the Wilson regime. This resulted in part from the breakdown of party government and party discipline in both houses and from the development of legislative blocs representing economic and sectional interests. In a searching critique of President Harding's first two years, William Bennett Munro wrote in 1923: "There has not been produced, during these two sessions, a single constructive piece of legislation that compares with the Congressional landmarks of the Wilson period."[34]

In launching the new executive budget system in 1921, the House of Representatives streamlined its fiscal machinery, consolidating control of appropriations in a single Committee on Appropriations which closely scrutinized the President's estimates and enhanced the prestige of the House. "For the first time since Joseph G. Cannon had been tumbled from the throne of Blaine and Reed," wrote George R. Brown, "there was an individual in the House [the chairman of the Appropriations Committee] who could put on his hat and walk to the other end of Pennsylvania Avenue and talk to the President of the United States eye to eye and man to man in the plain blunt language of 'yes' and 'no.' "[35]

In foreign affairs, Harding followed rather than led Congress. The Washington Naval Conference of 1921, the only notable achievement of his administration in the foreign field, was actually inspired by Senator Borah. The prestige of the Presidency declined during the Harding administration to a low ebb as a result of his weak and inept leadership in legislation and the sensational scandals in the government. After Harding's death on August 2, 1923, a series of congressional investigations revealed widespread corruption in many parts of his administration. As a result, Attorney General Daugherty and Secretary of the Navy Denby resigned under fire, and Secretary of the Interior Albert Fall, Director Forbes of the Veterans' Bureau, and Alien Property Custodian Miller went to prison. All told, it was an inglorious chapter in American history.

The relations between the House of Representatives and Calvin Coolidge during the mid-1920's were amiable and uninspired. It was a comparatively quiet time, after World War I and before the Great Depression. The Vermont President established no organic link with Congress the way McKinley and Roosevelt had done, and he had a limited conception of his role as legislative leader. His passive philosophy was reflected in his own words: "In the discharge of the duties of the office [of the President] there is one rule of action more important than all others. It consists in never doing anything that someone else can do for you. . . . About a dozen able, courageous, reliable and experienced men in the House and Senate can reduce the problem of legislation almost to a vanishing point."[36] There were such men in the House at that time, among them Frederick H. Gillett of Massachusetts and Nicholas Longworth of Ohio.

Coolidge made no effort to get his legislative program adopted by Congress, being content merely to submit it in the traditional messages and let the legislature take it or leave it. Congress responded to the President's indifference by passing a soldier's bonus bill over his veto, refusing adherence to the World Court protocol, drastically amending the Mellon tax measure, and enacting Japanese exclusion. The most exciting episode of this colorless administration was the Senate's rejection of the President's nomination of Charles B. Warren for Attorney General. The vote on Warren was a tie: 40 to 40. Vice President Dawes was taking a nap at the Willard Hotel; had he been present, the appointment would have been confirmed.

President Coolidge believed in party responsibility and felt it was the duty of political parties to perform their platform pledges. "It is the business of the President as party leader," he later wrote, "to do the best he can to see that the declared party platform purposes are translated into legislative and administrative action." The weakening of party loyalty in Congress, he said, "is one of the reasons that the Presidential office has grown in popular estimation and favor, while the Congress has declined. The country feels that the President is willing to assume responsibility, while his party in the Congress is not. I have never felt it was my duty to attempt to coerce Senators or Representatives, or take reprisals . . ."[37]

Personal contacts between Congressmen and the President were frequent and friendly during this period. Coolidge gave breakfasts at the White House, which were attended by fifteen to twenty-five members of Congress and which included wheat cakes and Vermont maple syrup. During his last session he invited all the members of the Senate and all the chairmen and ranking Democratic members of the committees of the House. These were purely social affairs at which matters of public business were not discussed.

Herbert Hoover was elected President in 1928 with an overwhelmingly Republican Congress, but he had to contend with a Democratic House of Representatives during his last two years in office. The mid-term election in 1930 reduced the Republican majority from 16 seats to 1 in the Senate and from 104 to 6 in the House. But deaths of Republican members, in the interval between the election and the meeting of the Seventy-second Congress in December, 1931, enabled the Democrats to organize the House and elect John N. Garner of Texas as Speaker.

Relations between the White House and Congress remained strained throughout the last two years of the Hoover administration. The President was provoked by what he regarded as lunatic bills and Democratic harassment. The Democrats wanted Hoover to call an international conference to reduce "excessive" tariff rates. The first session of the Seventy-second Congress enacted Hoover's measures creating the Reconstruction Finance Corporation and authorizing the Federal Reserve System to ease bank credit. But when Congress passed Garner's public-works bill covering 3,500 projects, Hoover vetoed it as "the most gigantic pork barrel ever proposed to the American Congress." Representative Patman of Texas moved to impeach Secretary of the Treasury Mellon on the basis of a 1789 statute prohibiting any person directly or indirectly interested in business or commerce from holding the Treasury post. But Mellon was appointed ambassador to Great Britain, and succeeded at the Treasury by Ogden Mills, before the Patman charges were taken up in the House.

Perhaps the most revealing account of Mr. Hoover's relationships with the leaders of Congress during his last two years in the White House is found in his own *Memoirs*. Referring to the Seventy-second Congress (1931-1933) he wrote:[38]

> The new Senate comprised 48 Republicans, 47 Democrats, and 1 Farmer-Labor. But actually we had no more than 40 real Republicans, as Senators Borah, Norris, Cutting, and others of the left wing were against us.
>
> Senator James Watson, Republican Senate leader, rejected my advice that the Democrats be allowed to organize the Senate and thereby convert their sabotage into responsibility. I felt that I could deal more constructively with the Democratic leaders if they held full responsibility in both houses, than with an opposition in the Senate conspiring in the cloakrooms to use every proposal of mine for demagoguery. Watson, of course, liked the extra importance of being majority leader, and the Republicans liked to hold committee chairmanships and the nicer offices in the Capitol.

The House had 219 Democrats, and of those quite a few were left-wingers. There were 214 Republicans, of whom 12, such as Fiorello La Guardia and Louis T. McFadden, were "Progressives." They almost invariably aided the opposition.

In an evaluation of the record of the Hoover administration, historian Allan Nevins concluded that although Hoover had been an able administrator, he had been inept in politics and parliamentary management:[39]

He several times displayed strong resentment against the Progressive-Democratic coalition which, during the summer of 1929, labored desperately to keep the tariff within the bounds of reason—intelligent observers were pained when Mr. Hoover threw his influence against the two most important of Senator Robert Wagner's bills dealing with unemployment and defeated them—bills endorsed by the best experts, and based on principles which Mr. Hoover himself had urged when Secretary of Commerce. . . . But the great initial loss of confidence in him occurred because at the outset, when the skies were brightest, he showed inability to lead; because he botched the tariff, he botched farm relief; he botched prohibition—because he showed a Bourbon temper and an inelastic mind. . . .

Roosevelt and Congress: 1933-1945

Franklin D. Roosevelt's relations with Congress were closer, more frequent, and occasionally more bipartisan than those of his predecessor. A disciple of Woodrow Wilson, in whose sub-Cabinet he had served, Roosevelt set forth his conception of the Presidency shortly after his first election, when he said:[40]

The Presidency is not merely an administrative office. That is the least of it. It is pre-eminently a place of moral leadership. All of our great Presidents were leaders of thought at times when certain historic ideas in the life of the nation had to be clarified. . . . Theodore Roosevelt and Wilson were both moral leaders, each in his own way and for his own time, who used the Presidency as a pulpit. That is what the office is—a superb opportunity for reapplying, applying to new conditions, the simple rules of human conduct to which we always go back. Without leadership alert and sensitive to change, we are bogged up or lose our way.

His attitude toward Congress was reflected at the outset in his opening address to the Seventy-third Congress, when he said:[41]

I come before you . . . not to make request for special or detailed legislation; I come rather to counsel with you who, like myself, have been selected to carry out a mandate of the whole people, in order that without partisanship you and I may cooperate to continue the restoration of our national well-being and, equally important, to build on the ruins of the past a new structure designed better to meet the present problems of modern civilization. . . . Out of these friendly contacts we are, fortunately, building a strong and permanent tie between the legislative and executive branches of the government. The letter of the Constitution wisely declared a separation, but the impulse of a common purpose declares a union.

President Roosevelt employed a variety of techniques in his congressional relations. He held frequent conferences at the White House with party leaders; these included Rainey, Byrns, Bankhead, Rayburn, and Doughton in the House, and Robinson, Harrison, Byrnes, and Barkley in the Senate. "In practice he evolved a 'master ministry' of congressional leaders, cabinet officers, and executive officials working through the White House."[42] According to Arthur M. Schlesinger, Jr., "He also spent long hours, in his office and over the telephone, persuading, reassuring, mollifying, and disciplining individual senators and congressmen. . . . He was a master of the art of providing congressional gratification—at the easy first name, the cordial handshake, the radiant smile, the intimate joke, the air of accessibility and concern, the quasi-confidential interview, the photograph at the White House desk, the headline in the home-town newspaper."[43] F.D.R. also revived Wilson's practice of delivering his State-of-the-Union messages in person, outlining general objectives and following them up with detailed legislative proposals that were drafted in executive departments and introduced in the House by sympathetic legislators. He obtained congressional cooperation, especially during his first term, by his adroit handling of legislative leaders, by generous use of the vast patronage of the New Deal agencies, by numerous and timely special messages, and by the skillful manipulation of public opinion.

Senator Barkley has given a graphic description of legislative-executive relations during the Roosevelt administration:[44]

> When President Roosevelt came into power in 1933, he inaugurated such a variety of legislative proposals that it was essential he keep in close touch with Congress through the leadership of the two branches. In the matter of the Economy Bill, the new Banking Law and many others, he consulted with the leaders of the two houses and the chairmen of committees, with respect to the measures before they were introduced. Senator Joseph T. Robinson of Arkansas, the Majority Leader of the Senate during the first four years of Mr. Roosevelt's Administration, usually introduced the proposed measures as Administration bills. . . .
>
> During the remainder of Mr. Roosevelt's Administration frequent conferences were held between the leaders of the two houses, in which the

Speaker and Vice President were always included because, while they were in theory mere presiding officers, they both had large influence with the membership of their respective chambers in advancing Administration measures. Frequently Mr. Roosevelt called either the Majority Leader of the House or of the Senate individually to the White House to discuss some problem peculiarly applicable to the one chamber or the other. When he had been abroad during the war he sometimes asked the Majority Leaders of each house to meet him in personal conference to bring him up to date on what had happened in the Congress during his absence.

In the pre-war days when President Roosevelt, to strengthen our defense, was urging measures which were, directly or indirectly, calculated to influence the tide of battle abroad, he had frequent conferences with both Democratic and Republican leaders in both houses of Congress.

During the first "Hundred Days," when Congress met in special session to deal with the banking crisis, it responded to Roosevelt's legislative leadership by enacting, almost sight unseen, a series of emergency bills sent up by the White House with supporting messages. The attitude of the House Republicans in this situation was summed up by Minority Floor Leader Snell who said, in urging support of the emergency banking bill: "The house is burning down, and the President of the United States says this is the way to put out the fire."

Meanwhile Congress itself was not found wanting. Professor Schlesinger pays it this deserved tribute for its performance in these early years:[45]

> The national legislature at this time contained strong, independent-minded, and intelligent men and on crucial occasions itself assumed the legislative initiative. Far from being a tame and servile body, it played a vital and consistently underestimated role in shaping the New Deal. A number of important measures—the federal deposit insurance system, the National Labor Relations Act, the public housing legislation—were entirely of congressional origination. At other times, congressional initiative forced the administration into action, as when Black's thirty-hour bill precipitated NRA, or when Elmer Thomas gave the administration an unsought flexibility in its monetary powers, or when the constant pressure of La Follette, Costigan, and Wagner helped increase appropriations for relief and public works. . . .

And historian Charles Beard, who frequently criticized the Roosevelt administration, surveying the labors of the legislature at the end of the 1935 session, said that "seldom, if ever, in the long history of Congress had so many striking and vital measures been spread upon law books in a single session."[46]

After the collapse of France in 1940, Congress granted President Roosevelt's requests for his military-preparedness program and gave it strong bipartisan support. In 1941 the national legislature passed the Lend-Lease Act, delegating the Chief Executive sweeping powers to establish an "arsenal of democracy" for the reinforcement of the beleaguered powers. In his 1942 Labor Day address, Roosevelt demanded that Congress repeal the Emergency Price Control Act. If it should fail to act adequately, he said, in effect, that he would repeal it himself. This, remarks Binkley, "was the most ominous threat ever delivered by a President face to face with Congress."[47]

Relations between Congress and the President deteriorated in Roosevelt's third term as the coalition of Southern Democrats and conservative Republicans launched an attack on his domestic program of social legislation. Riders on appropriation bills were used to eliminate some New Deal agencies; others were terminated by reducing their funds. Legislative-executive relations reached a low point in February, 1944, when F.D.R. vetoed a revenue bill and Senator Barkley resigned in protest as Senate majority leader, only to be promptly re-elected by acclamation by the Democratic party caucus. On the eve of Roosevelt's death, Congress was in open rebellion against the President's legislative proposals for postwar reconstruction. His sudden death on April 12, 1945, ended a public career that ranked F.D.R. among the nation's greatest Presidents.

Roosevelt's relations with the six Congresses that met during his twelve years in the White House illustrated what Professor Corwin called "the law of ebb and flow" in legislative-executive relations. The President's leadership waxed and waned during these eventful years. His influence flourished during the honeymoon sessions of the Seventy-third and Seventy-fourth Congresses, then receded during the Court Reform fight of the Seventy-fifth Congress and in the curtailment of his proposals for administrative reorganization in the Seventy-sixth Congress. His prestige revived with Hitler's invasion of Poland and the enactment of Lend-Lease in March, 1941, and ebbed again during the Seventy-eighth Congress when F.D.R. vetoed a revenue bill for the first time in American history. "Mr. Roosevelt's experience underscores a lesson to be drawn also from that of the first Roosevelt and of Woodrow Wilson, that presidential leadership is subject to a law of ebb and flow, or, as Professor Laski suggests, a 'law of honeymoon.' "[48]

Conflict and Collaboration: 1945-1952

Like his predecessor, Harry S. Truman faced Congresses (Seventy-ninth, Eightieth, Eighty-first, and Eighty-second) controlled by a coalition of

Southern Democrats and conservative Republicans that was hostile to his domestic program of social legislation, but continued to co-operate with the President in foreign affairs. Taft and Vandenberg were the opposition party leaders in the Senate; Martin and Halleck in the House. During the Eightieth Congress, both houses were controlled by the Republicans. The coalition clashed repeatedly with the President on domestic issues, and Truman later denounced it as a "do-nothing Congress." Yet the actual legislative record of the 1947-1948 session was impressive, at least in the field of foreign affairs.

Truman's domestic Fair Deal program was a source of constant friction and controversy between the legislative and executive branches. Aside from defense measures, few domestic proposals of the Democratic administration were enacted by the Republican-controlled legislature. Two leading measures promised by the Republicans in the 1946 campaign—the Taft-Hartley Act and income tax reduction—were enacted over presidential vetoes.

President Truman sent a series of special messages to Congress urging enactment of a long list of economic and social measures, including inflation-control legislation, social security expansion, federal aid to education, public housing and slum clearance, and a ten-point civil rights program. The opposition paid slight attention to these recommendations, and virtually none of the items on this program reached the statute books. Southern Democrats blocked legislative action on civil rights, and the conservative coalition overrode presidential vetoes of six major items of general legislation.

In foreign affairs, on the other hand, the legislative and executive branches continued to cooperate in a time of grave international tension. The fruits of bipartisan support of the Truman-Marshall-Acheson foreign policy are reflected in the record of the postwar Congresses. During the Seventy-ninth Congress (1945-1946), which marked the beginning of a new era in international relations with the participation of the United States in the United Nations, the votes on foreign policy questions were invariably bipartisan, thanks to the leadership of Chairmen Connally and Bloom of the Foreign Affairs Committees, and the aid of Senator Vandenberg and Representative Eaton, ranking Republican members of those committees. During the Eightieth Congress (1947-1948), which the Republicans controlled, the trend continued with bipartisan support of a series of measures relating to foreign affairs. Votes that commanded bipartisan support in the Eighty-first Congress (1949-1950) included appropriations for the European Recovery Program and the costs of Army occupation abroad, extension of the European Recovery Program, ratification of the North Atlantic Treaty, approval of the Foreign Military Assistance Act, and inauguration of the Point Four program. Considering the lack of party discipline in Congress, the postwar record of interparty co-operation in foreign affairs was indeed an impressive one. Its achievements were induced by the imminence of foreign dangers, the impulse of patriotism, farsighted leadership, and the spirit of compromise and tolerance. The Truman administration made many concessions to Republicans in Congress as the price of their support, while the Republicans refrained from dissolving the partnership when the Democratic Administration acted independently in forming policy or failed to consult them.

Several methods of executive-legislative collaboration were employed after World War II in the foreign-affairs field. They included:

1. Consultation by State Department officials with members of the Foreign Affairs Committees of Congress.
2. Formal designation, beginning in 1944, of an Assistant Secretary of State for Congressional Relations, to handle the department's relations with Congress.
3. Congressional representation on American delegations to international conferences.
4. Congressional resolutions assuring the President of legislative co-operation and support for some prospective action, e.g., the Vandenberg and troops-to-Europe resolutions.
5. Reports to joint sessions of Congress by the Secretary of State and top defense officials.
6. Creation during the Eighty-first Congress of a set of "consultative subcommittees" of the Foreign Affairs Committees of both houses, to facilitate legislative-executive co-operation in the formulation and execution of foreign policy.

These techniques of executive-legislative collaboration yielded valuable results after World War II. During the Eightieth Congress, despite the fact that the President was a Democrat and the Congress was Republican, the Foreign Aid Acts of 1947 and 1948 were passed; the Greco-Turkish loan and assistance to devastated countries were authorized; treaties of peace with Italy, Rumania, Bulgaria, and Hungary were ratified; the reciprocal interchange of students, teachers, and information with other nations was approved; the Trade Agreements Act was extended; the admission of displaced persons was approved; the Institute of Inter-American Affairs was re-established; the International Telecommunication Convention was ratified; United States trusteeship of the Pacific Islands formerly held by Japan under mandate of the League of Nations was approved; and American membership was provided for in the International Refugee Organization, the World Health Organization, and the South Pacific Commission. These were impressive achievements for a Congress that President Truman described as the "second worst in history."

In the field of international affairs, the first session of the Eighty-first Congress ratified the North Atlantic Pact, authorized and financed continuance of the Marshall Plan, extended aid to Greece and Turkey, restored and extended the reciprocal trade agreements program, authorized military aid to western Europe, Nationalist China, Korea, Iran, and the Philippine Republic, and again extended the Institute of Inter-American Affairs. The second session of the Eighty-first Congress amended the Displaced Persons Act to remove discriminatory provisions, authorized $3.1 billion economic aid to European Marshall Plan countries, South Korea, and non-Communist China, authorized $1.2 billion military aid for the North Atlantic Pact nations and other countries, passed the International Claims Settlement Act, and authorized increased contributions to various international organizations. Despite conflicts on the domestic front, the partnership was evidently working in relation to the outside world.

During the Eighty-second Congress, the fruits of executive-legislative co-operation in foreign affairs were seen in the adoption of measures concerned with the security of the United States and its free-world partners, and in the approval of the peace settlements of 1951-1952. The security measures included the Mutual Security Acts of 1951 and 1952, which assembled in a single package all foreign-aid programs on a global basis; the Mutual Defense Assistance Control Act of 1951, which provided for the control of exports to any nation or group of nations threatening the security of the United States; the Greek-Turkish Protocol, which admitted Greece and Turkey to the North Atlantic Treaty Organization in recognition of the valor of their troops in Korea and increasing instability in the Middle East; and Senate approval for sending four divisions of ground troops to Europe. The peace settlements included the termination of the state of war with Germany by joint resolution in October, 1951; Senate approval of peace and security treaties with Japan in March, 1952; ratification of a security treaty between the United States, Australia, and New Zealand, and of a mutual defense treaty between the United States and the Philippines in April, 1952; and the approval in June, 1952, of agreements with Western Germany that ended the occupation, restored her sovereignty, and brought her into the Western European defense system.[49]

Relations During Divided Government: 1953-1960

During President Eisenhower's first term, the Eighty-third Congress was controlled by the Republicans in both houses, while the Eighty-fourth Congress was under Democratic control in both chambers. The leaders of the opposition during these years were Senators Lyndon Johnson and Earle W. Clements, Speaker Rayburn, and Representative McCormack, the Democratic floor leader in the House.

Relations between the President and Congress, which during Hoover's administration had been sporadic, and infrequent, had now developed over the intervening years of depression and war and postwar to the point where they had become frequent and regular. The process of teamwork between the two branches, begun by Franklin Roosevelt and continued under the exigencies of recurring crises at home and abroad, reached a new stage of development with the Eisenhower administration. Beginning in 1953 and 1954, the President not only held Cabinet conferences to assist him in formulating legislative policies, but he called in Republican and Democratic congressional leaders to brief them in advance on his legislative program.

The following excerpt from Professor Neustadt's detailed account of these congressional briefings indicates how far cooperation developed:

> Periodic White House meetings with congressional party leaders have become the norm; agendas prepared for the President in Truman's time; minutes kept as well in Eisenhower's. And Eisenhower has established in his entourage an Army-type liaison operation, its several staff aides covering each corner of the Hill on regular patrols. But formal leaders' sessions tend to be ambassadorial encounters; organized liaison tends to create its own chores, if not, indeed, to confuse liaisoners' loyalties. So far as one can judge from the outside, it remains true in Eisenhower's time—as in Truman's and F.D.R.'s before him—that when the chips are down, there is no substituting for the President's own footwork, his personal negotiation, his direct appeal, his voice and no other's on the telephone. Naturally, such methods cannot guarantee success; to overwork them would be self-defeating; to institutionalize them may well be impossible. Yet these, not programming devices, must bear the weight, provide the test, of presidential "domination" over Congress.[50]

The response of the Democratic leaders of Congress to these developments was typified by Senator Lyndon Johnson's formula: "We will support the President when he is right and oppose him when he is wrong." Under this formula, of course, the opposition can define its own concepts of right and wrong. According to Johnson, partisan politics stops at the water's edge, and the only test of legislation is whether "it is good for the country." When Johnson saw the President at a White House meeting with congressional leaders, he told the President that these two simple standards would continue to be his guide. And he counted on Speaker Rayburn to follow the same principles in the House of Representatives.

Commenting on Johnson's method of supporting or resisting the President, Arthur Krock of the *New York Times* wrote:[51]

After the election of Johnson to the Senate leadership in the 83d Congress he set up and maintained these standards. He was criticized for doing this by some Democrats in the Capitol and more outside, their arguments being that (1) he was blurring the line of demarcation that should distinguish an opposition from the party in power if the opposition was to dislodge it, and (2) Johnson is congenitally "pro-Eisenhower." But in general he pursued the same course in the 84th Congress, and the return of Democratic majorities in both branches while the President was being reelected by a margin of more than nine millions has persuaded him that the country believes the opposition leadership acted on these two tests, and approves them.

President Eisenhower told the opposition leaders in Congress that it was "essential to have a continuing bipartisan approach to foreign affairs and national security matters, regardless of which political party controls the Congress." The Democratic leaders welcomed the President's assurances, but reserved judgment on how the bipartisan approach would work out in practice. Genuine bipartisanship, they contended, requires consultation before policy is made and implemented, and no mere blanket endorsement of policies initiated by the Executive.[52]

During the Eighty-fourth Congress, the Democrats generally supported the administration's defense and foreign-policy legislation. The defense budgets were overwhelmingly approved in both houses. More Democrats than Republicans voted for the foreign-aid authorization bill, and a large majority of Democrats backed the President's request for a three-year extension of the Reciprocal Trade Agreements Act. In many ways it appeared that President Eisenhower's relations with the Democratic leaders were more cordial than they had been with Republican leaders in the Eighty-third Congress. Eisenhower had many difficulties with Representative John Taber of New York, chairman of the Committee on Appropriations; Representative Daniel A. Reed, chairman of the Ways and Means Committee; Senator John W. Bricker of Ohio, the minority leader; and a very unique and vituperative brand of harassment from Senator Joseph R. McCarthy of Wisconsin.

In a special message delivered in person at the opening of the Eighty-fifth Congress, President Eisenhower sought to enlist the co-operation of Congress in his program for the Middle East. At the four-day Senate hearings on this program in January, 1957, Secretary of State Dulles was sharply attacked by some of the leading Democratic members of the Foreign Relations Committee, e.g., Senators Fulbright, Humphrey, and Morse. But Speaker Rayburn announced his support of the Middle East plan, and the House Foreign Affairs Committee gave it an overwhelmingly favorable report.

In planning his legislative program in co-operation with the leaders of Congress, President Eisenhower went "beyond the point of no return," according to Professor Rossiter. In an oft-praised book *The American Presidency,* Rossiter summed up developments as follows:[53]

The point was reached and passed in a press conference on January 13, 1954. During the first session of the Eighty-third Congress Mr. Eisenhower had submitted few proposals to Congress and had exerted little continuous pressure in their behalf. Observers were wondering aloud whether he was aware of the change that had come over the Presidency or of Congress's need for guidance. But as the second session approached the President began to gather steam, and within a few days of the opening of Congress in 1954 he was sending over detailed messages outlining his wishes on farm policy, social security, foreign policy, labor, and finance. And now at the press conference this exchange took place:

Q. Mr. President, could you say what percentage of your recommended proposals you would expect to be passed at this session?

A. The President said, Look, he wanted to make this clear, He was not making recommendations to pass the time away or to look good. . . . He was going to work for their enactment. Make no mistake about that. That was exactly what he was in the White House for and what he intended to do.

Twenty-five years ago this remark, especially as and to whom delivered, would have brought most members of Congress spluttering to their feet and set the President's few remaining friends to shaking their disbelieving heads. Even as late as ten years ago it would have been considered a gratuitous insult by the die-hards and a show of bad taste by the moderates in Congress. In 1954 it passed unchallenged and even unnoticed, except by those whose reaction was, "Well, it's about time."

Since that moment of awakening President Eisenhower has done his best to make good his pledge. He has used arts of persuasion that were once controversial but are now considered altogether regular, and that is the essence of this first ingredient of the modern Presidency: the irregular has become the regular, the unexpected the expected, in the area of executive-legislative relations. The President has no weapons that were not available to Harding or, for that matter, to McKinley. The appeal to the people is more easily brought off in the age of electronics; on the other hand, the dangled patronage has lost much of its influence thanks to the success of civil service reform. The White House conference, the appeal to party loyalty, the threat of a veto—these weapons, too, are no keener than they were a half-century ago. The President's own machinery for drafting legislative proposals and for maintaining good relations with Congress is vastly enlarged and improved, but the houses themselves, despite the pleas of Senators Kefauver and Monroney, have made no important institutional changes in recognition of his increased responsibility for providing them with leadership. And the Constitution, needless to say, reads exactly as it did 169 years ago in those passages that govern the relations of executive and legislature. The remarkable change in these relations has been neither institutional nor constitutional, but rather meteorological—a change in the climate of politics and custom. The country now expects the President to have a program and to work hard for its enactment. He is more likely to be criticized in today's press for timidity and inertia than for resolution and activity. What the country expects, Congress also expects. Henceforth, it will react with irritation rather than indignation to presidential attempts to goad it into action.

The President's right, even duty, to propose detailed legislation to Congress touching every problem of American society, and then to speed its passage down the legislative transmission belt, is now an accepted usage of our constitutional system. . . .

Congress and the President: Since 1961

The brief Presidency of John F. Kennedy was one of paradoxes. Though Kennedy had been a member of Congress for fourteen years—in the House from 1947 to 1953; in the Senate from 1953-1960—he had never developed the long-standing, cordial relations with many members that has so frequently assisted other Presidents who have emerged from Congress. The nation recalls him as a popular President, yet forgets that in 1960 he was elected by a popular plurality of about 112,000 votes out of nearly 69,000,000 votes cast. The Republicans actually gained twenty seats in the House and two in the Senate, and because of the religious question, Kennedy ran behind many victorious members of his party.

We have already noted that the initial problem Kennedy confronted was a Rules Committee heavily weighted against the New Frontier. Despite the Democratic majority of 263 to 174, the move to expand the committee won by only five votes. Kennedy's dependence on the votes of Southerners and Northern Republicans meant that the highly programmatic content of the 1960 campaign was considerably reduced as the President prepared his agenda for the Eighty-seventh Congress. Arthur Schlesinger, Jr., quotes President Kennedy as having said, "There is no sense in raising hell and then not being successful. There is no sense in putting the office of the President on the line on an issue and then being defeated."[54]

Although Kennedy worked hard at courting the Congress—even to arriving by helicopter at a birthday party for Senator Harry F. Byrd of Virginia—he continuously confronted the coalition of Southerners and Republicans. Not even a very effective congressional liaison team headed by

Lawrence O'Brien could alter the fact that the Congress was simply more conservative than the President. The new majority in the Rules Committee proved to be illusory. Eight to seven at best, the administration majority collapsed on the aid-to-education issue when Democratic Representative James J. Delaney of New York defected because parochial schools were excluded. The Rules Committee also held up proposals for a Department of Urban Affairs and greater aid for mass transit.

While there may have been a considerable gap between the energetic prose of the New Frontier and its achievements, the Kennedy record with Congress was quite good. The Eighty-seventh Congress did increase the minimum wage and social security benefits, created the Peace Corps and the Arms Control and Disarmament Agency, passed a Trade Expansion Act, sent to the states a constitutional amendment to outlaw the poll tax, passed a communications satellite bill, and enacted important housing, depressed areas, education, and drug-labeling legislation. In addition, the Kennedy administration undoubtedly generated much of the initial momentum for a tax cut, a civil rights bill, and medical care for the aged, all to be enacted during the Lyndon B. Johnson years.

In many ways the extraordinary output of the Eighty-ninth Congress was a consequence of the Republican party's nomination of Senator Barry M. Goldwater of Arizona as its presidential candidate. The legendary Johnson skills were important; he had, after all, achieved and earned a reputation as a master of the legislative process. Elected to the House as a New Deal representative from Texas in 1936, Johnson was elected to the Senate in 1948, became majority leader in 1955, and Vice President in 1961. His day-to-day effectiveness in the coalition politics of the Senate during the Eisenhower Presidency gave him renown of near mythical dimensions.[55] Yet the shrillness of the Goldwater campaign and the popular conception of him as an extremist, a view that was shrewdly re-enforced by the Democratic campaign strategy, led to a Johnson-Humphrey landslide. The ticket overwhelmed the Goldwater-Miller slate, receiving 61.4 per cent of the two-party vote, carrying all but six states, simultaneously adding thirty-eight Democratic Representatives and two Senators.

Despite frequent difficulties with conservative House chairmen—particularly Wilbur D. Mills of the Ways and Means Committee—Johnson was able to lead the Eighty-ninth Congress to enormous achievements. In 1965 alone, he sent sixty-three messages to Congress calling for legislative action. The mood of the nation was for reform, an outlook that was enthusiastically shared by an old New Dealer who now envisioned a Great Society. By the end of the 1966 session, Congress had enacted a major health bill, the landmark Voting Rights Act of 1965, an aid-to-education program, which adroitly compromised the parochial school question, and massive aid to the Appalachian region; it had initiated a "war on poverty," created the Department of Housing and Urban Development, and expanded consumer and environmental legislation. Perhaps the most dramatic statistic of the period involved the "conservative coalition" in the House. Where that coalition did appear in 1965, it was successful only 25 per cent of the time; in the first year of the Kennedy administration it succeeded on 74 per cent of the roll-call votes where it appeared.[56]

Yet even a shrewd President often confronts forces that elude solutions and responsibilities from which he cannot escape. When, as in the case of Lyndon Johnson, there is the absence of those charismatic qualities that lead to popular forgiveness, the problem is exacerbated. Riots in the black ghettos of the big cities, increasing inflation and rising hostility to the Vietnam War soon eroded the President's popularity, which had always been more wide than deep. In 1966 the President took a very modest role in the congressional campaign, much to the relief of many Democratic candidates, and when the Ninetieth Congress convened in 1967, it had forty-seven new Republicans in the House and three new Republicans in the Senate. On March 31, 1968, President Johnson made the extraordinary announcement that he would not be a candidate for re-election.

While most of the nation will recall the Johnson years in terms of the dispiriting, divisive, and ultimately unsuccessful war in Southeast Asia, for students of the legislative process that period will also be recalled as a time when a skillful politician could actually lead countless measures through that maze we call Congress.[57]

The nadir of executive-legislative relations in modern times came during the Nixon years. The confrontations were momentous and wrenching. It seems almost unkind to recall a speech of candidate Nixon in 1968 when he insisted that[58]

> surely one of a President's greatest resources is the moral authority of his office. It's time we restored that authority—and time we used it once again, to its fullest potential—to rally the people, to define those moral imperatives which are the cement of a civilized society, to point the ways in which the *energies* of the people can be enlisted in the *ideals* of the people.

Despite the lofty summons, the years were marked by such excesses in the use of presidential power that many of those who had viewed the Presidency as the prime source of energy in the American political system were compelled to re-examine their premises. Several of the Nixon actions have already been discussed, such as his abuse of the power to impound funds and his ignoring of Congressional directives while conducting an air war in Cambodia and military action in Laos. President Nixon also took the unprecedented position at one time that every member of his administration could invoke the doctrine of executive privilege. Two of his nominees to the Supreme Court (Clement F. Haynsworth, Jr., and G. Harrold Carswell) were obvious attempts to appeal to the rising Republican sentiment in the South, but in an unprecedented action, the Senate found both unqualified.

Throughout the Nixon Presidency, the Democrats, despite their internal divisions, controlled both houses of Congress. Even in 1972 when Nixon overwhelmed his Democratic opponent Senator George McGovern of South Dakota by carrying every state but Massachusetts and the District of Columbia, the Republicans gained only thirteen seats in the House while the Democrats actually gained two in the Senate. Thus much of the contention was the historical accompaniment of divided government. But much was also the consequence of a Congress that was often more liberal than the President. Even the Southern Democrats in the House had come to vote more often with their Northern colleagues as the full impact of the Voting Rights Act of 1965 manifested itself.

Thus the Nixon Presidency was frequently the scene of modest proposals receiving the blessing of the "conservative coalition" and occasional victories by a coalition of liberals and moderates. The struggle rarely involved a presidential attempt to abolish a program. Usually the struggle was over appropriations—the Democrats contending that the President was starving the agencies, the President insisting that the opposition was leading the nation to fiscal disaster. In 1970, President Nixon with great ceremony did seek the Family Assistance Plan, a form of guaranteed income, which passed the House and died in the Finance Committee of the Senate, but his critics contended that the President had not shown sufficient interest in pushing the bill. When the President led the drive for a revenue-sharing program in 1972, he then sought to reduce the various grant-in-aid programs to a degree that brought strong protests from many of the country's governors and mayors.

If Nixon did not dismantle the "welfare state" during his six years in office, it is nevertheless possible to suggest that much of its vitality was retained and some of it even expanded by a Congress that did not accept the President's recommendation and on many occasions confronted his veto. The antagonisms ended in the hell of Watergate, and the same President who carried forty-nine states in November, 1972, resigned less than two years later when confronted with three articles of impeachment from the House Judiciary Committee.

When Gerald R. Ford became the thirty-eighth President in 1974 (and the ninth Vice-President to be elevated) his major responsibility was to restore a sense of public confidence in our system of government and return executive-legislative relations to the more customary weaknesses of divided government. President Ford brought to his new office the reputation of being a conservative, zealous partisan whose friendly style nevertheless had made him many friends. He was a man of the House, having served there for twenty-four years, eight as minority leader.

The new President was well aware of the congressional concern with executive excesses, and his first address to Congress contained the following conciliatory sentiment:

> part of my heart will always be here on Capitol Hill. I know well the co-equal role of the Congress in our constitutional process. I love the House of Representatives. I revere the traditions of the Senate despite my too-short internship there. As President, within the limits of basic principles, my motto towards the Congress is communication, conciliation, compromise and cooperation . . . I do not want a honeymoon with you. I want a good marriage.[59]

Frictions were, of course, inevitable, and they came, perhaps beginning with his controversial pardon of the former President. In October, 1974, President Ford found it necessary to take the extraordinary step of testifying before a subcommittee of the House Judiciary Committee and assure the members and the nation that the pardon had not been part of any secret arrangement made prior to the Nixon resignation. His nomination of Nelson A. Rockefeller to become Vice President was accepted only after interminable hearings in both houses. When the Ninety-third Congress finally ended, a respectable record of social legislation had been compiled, much of it over presidential vetoes, but the major congressional energies had been directed at restricting presidential discretion in budgeting and foreign policy. Even a new law regulating campaign finances was an outgrowth of Watergate and was often defended on the grounds that it eliminated the power of an incumbent President to raise funds by veiled intimidation.

When the Ninety-fourth Congress convened in January, 1975, it was after a Democratic landslide. The Democrats had gained three Senate seats and forty-three House seats. In the House the Democrats technically had enough votes to override a presidential veto, although the realities always prevent such a calculation. Indeed, as the session progressed, it was possible for the Democrats to pass a great number of bills and then falter when hit by a presidential veto. A June, 1975, *Special Report* by the Democratic Study Group analyzed the votes on three major veto-override attempts and noted that 42 per cent of the House Democrats, including eight full committee chairmen, had voted to sustain one or more of the Ford vetoes. In many ways the confrontations were classic: somewhat liberal proposals passing a Democratic Congress; a conservative President, immensely knowledgeable in the ways of the Hill and the media, able to muster the one-third plus one. Often the conflict led to easy compromises; on other occasions the bargaining was arduous as both sides grappled with immensely complex issues like the energy crisis and an economy that persisted in high unemployment and high prices. But there was no doubt that a spirit of comity had returned to the executive-legislative relationship and that once again the dialogue was political in the best sense of the word.

Conclusions

The foregoing sketch of legislative-executive relations in Washington down through the decades indicates that they have been conditioned by a variety of factors and forces whose influence has varied with the changing circumstances of American political history. The personalities of the Presidents and their capacity for leadership has been one influential factor in the equation. Some Presidents like Jackson, Wilson, and the two Roosevelts have been dynamic men endowed with great personal force and talent for aggressive leadership. In his short time as President, John F. Kennedy showed those qualities, and until the Vietnam War made his Presidency untenable, Lyndon B. Johnson was extremely effective in dealing with domestic problems. Other Presidents, like Madison, Buchanan, and Coolidge have lacked these qualities.

The conception of the role of the President under the Constitution held by the occupant of the White House has been another major factor. Those like Jefferson and Wilson, who regarded themselves as both Chief Executive and chief legislator, were more successful in their relations with Congress than were the two Adams, father and son, who regarded the President as the leader of the whole nation and not of any combination of political factions or regional groups. Or contrast the theories of executive power held by Theodore Roosevelt and William Howard Taft. Roosevelt's view was that "every executive officer, and above all every executive officer in high position, was a steward of the people, and not to content himself with the negative merit of keeping his talents undamaged in a napkin. . . . My belief was that it was not only his right but his duty to do any thing that the needs of the Nation demanded unless such action was forbidden by the Constitution or by the laws."[60] Taft criticized this "stewardship theory" of the presidency. "The true view of the executive functions," he said, "is, as I conceive it, that the President can exercise no power which cannot be fairly and reasonably traced to some specific grant of power or justly implied and included within such express grant as proper and necessary."[61] The exigencies of foreign-policy crises and popular expectations that the President must take the initiative in dealing with our intricate economic problems will undoubtedly mean that our Presidents will always see themselves in the Theodore Roosevelt image; yet the events of the past decade will also mean a Congress that will persist in overseeing the President with far greater zeal.

The control of Congress by the administration or opposition party has been a vital factor affecting legislative-executive relations. When the same political party has controlled both houses of Congress and the Presidency, the situation has been more favorable to responsible party government and cordial working relationships than during periods of divided government. In the modern period, the first administration of Franklin D. Roosevelt and the first two years of the Johnson administration (the Eighty-ninth Congress) are perhaps the classical examples. On the other hand, seven Republican Presidents—Grant, Hayes, Arthur, Harrison, Eisenhower, Nixon, and Ford—and three Democrats—Cleveland, Wilson, and Truman—encountered serious difficulties in their relations with hostile Congresses. The loss of control of one or both houses of Congress at the mid-term elections, destroying the possibility of effective party government, has been the fate of nine Presidents and of three Vice Presidents who succeeded by accident to the presidency. The lack of party control of Congress, as Arthur Holcombe has shown in his *Our More Perfect Union,* means the frustration of presidential leadership in the legislative process.[62] But we have noted that recent reforms in the House, which have increased the role of the leaders and given both caucuses greater power, have also brought a fresh re-examination of the role of the party in the legislative process.

Relations between Congress and the President have also been affected by the latter's techniques of leadership, including his personal relations with the leaders and influential members of Congress, his skill in the use of patronage, his use of the veto power, and direct appeals to the voters. With the growth of modern methods of mass communication—press, television, and radio—the ability to appeal to public opinion over the heads of the legislature has become a factor of increasing potency of which every modern President has made effective use.

Still another important element in the equation has been the quality of congressional leadership. The role of Congress in the legislative-executive partnership has been enhanced, as we have seen, when strong and adroit leaders like Thomas B. Reed, Joseph G. Cannon, John W. Kern, Alben Barkley, Sam Rayburn, and Lyndon B. Johnson have held the legislative helm.

Notes

CHAPTER 1

1. Max Farrand, *The Framing of the Constitution of the United States* (1913), p. 204.

2. Wilfred E. Binkley, *President and Congress* (1947), pp. 21-22. Binkley adds, however, that "the framers probably greatly overestimated the inherent strength of the lower house and left it too weak . . . Is it not possible [he asks] that in their eagerness to establish a strong executive the framers left the lower house an 'incurably deficient and inferior organ of government'?" (pp. 22-23).

3. Charles Warren, *The Making of the Constitution* (1937), p. 400.

4. *Ibid.*, p. 618.

CHAPTER 2

1. Ralph V. Harlow, *The History of Legislative Methods Before 1825* (1917), p. 123.

2. Charles O. Paullin. "The First Elections Under the Constitution," *Iowa Journal of History and Politics,* January, 1904, p. 28.

3. Fisher Ames, *Works* (1854), Vol. 1, p. 33.

4. Paullin, *loc. cit.,* p. 31.

5. Fisher Ames, *op. cit.,* p. 126.

6. Madison, *Writings,* V, p. 373.

7. The language used here is taken *ad verbatim* from that in the second rule adopted by the House on April 7, 1789. It was probably influenced by the practice of the House of Commons where it is still a rule "that no Member who has a direct pecuniary interest in a question shall be allowed to vote upon it: but, in order to operate as a disqualification, this interest must be immediate and personal, and not merely of a general or remote character." (*Sir T. Erskine May's Parliamentary Practice,* 15th Edition, 1950, p. 418).

8. Fisher Ames, *op. cit.*, p. 64.
9. *Ibid.*, p. 61.
10. *House Journal,* Vol. 1, May 11, 16, August 18, 1789, and April 26, 1790.
11. *Ibid.*, September 11, 1789.
12. *Ibid.*, May 22, 1789.
13. *Annals,* 1st Congress, Vol. 1, p. 929.
14. *Annals of Congress,* Vol. 1, p. 987.
15. *House Journal,* January 9, 1790.
16. *Ibid.*, January 14, 1790.
17. Fisher Ames, *op. cit.*, p. 89.
18. *House Journal,* January 15, 1790.
19. *Ibid.*, February 23, 1791.
20. *Ibid.*, April 23, 1790.
21. *Ibid.*, September 17, 1789.
22. *Statutes at Large,* Vol. I, pp. 65-67.
23. William Maclay, *Journal,* p. 387.
24. *Ibid.*, pp. 209, 355, 385, 409.
25. Harlow, *op. cit.*, p. 143.
26. Maclay, *op. cit.*, pp. 208, 227, 235.
27. Harlow, *op. cit.*, p. 145.

CHAPTER 3

1. John Quincy Adams, *Diary,* Vol. VIII, pp. 471-72.
2. De Alva S. Alexander, *History and Procedure of the House of Representatives* (1916), p. 8.
3. For a detailed description of disparities in the size of congressional districts, see *Congressional Record,* March 26, 1956, pp. 5543-48. See also Andrew Hacker, *Congressional Districting* (1963), p. 3.
4. *Congressional Quarterly Weekly Report,* March 23, 1974, p. 726.
5. Kirk H. Porter, *History of Suffrage in the United States* (1918), pp. 11-14.
6. Charles Seymour and Donald P. Frary, *How the World Votes* (1918), Vol. 1, p. 232.
7. Porter, *op. cit.*, p. 148.
8. *Marston* v. *Mandt,* 410 U.S. 679; *Burns* v. *Forston,* 410 U.S. 686.
9. See U.S. Code, Title 2, Chapter 7. The procedures were modified in 1969 (PL91-138) so that the law now clearly states that only candidates on the ballot or bona fide "write-in" candidates can contest a House election rather than "any person."
10. Chester H. Rowell, *A Historical and Legal Digest of All the Contested Election Cases in the House of Representatives, 1789-1901* (Government Printing Office, 1901); and Merrill Moores, *A Historical and Legal Digest of All the Contested Election Cases in the House of Representatives, 1901-1917* (House Doc. No. 2052, 64th Congress, 2d session). See also *Congressional Quarterly's Guide to the Congress of the United States* (1971), p. 308.
11. Territorial delegates are persons whom the House by law admits to its

floor and allows to speak, but who have no right to vote. A territory is a possession of the United States that has not yet been admitted into the Union as a state.

12. *Hinds' Precedents of the House of Representatives,* Vol. 2, Chapter XLII. See also Robert L. Tienken, "Precedents of the House of Representatives Relating to Exclusion, Expulsion and Censure," Congressional Research Service, Library of Congress (1967; updated, 1973).

13. *Ibid.,* Vol. 6, § 236.

14. See *Powell* v. *McCormack,* 395 U.S. 486 (1969).

15. *Congressional Directory, 94th Congress, First Session,* pp. 238-250.

16. T. Richard Witmer, "The Aging of the House," *Political Science Quarterly,* December, 1964, p. 538.

17. "The Institutionalization of the U.S. House of Representatives," *American Political Science Review,* March, 1968, pp. 145-46.

18. *Ibid.,* pp. 146-47, 149. Data for 1975 compiled from *Congressional Directory.*

19. Plumer Letter Book, IV, 507. All but three of those mentioned in this letter were members of the House.

20. February 8, 1805. Foster Papers, II, 1864.

21. Cabell Phillips, "A Profile of Congress," *New York Times Magazine,* January 10, 1954, p. 16.

22. *Cf.* George B. Galloway, *Congress at the Crossroads,* pp. 32-37.

23. De Alva S. Alexander, *op. cit.,* p. 299. For a description of these successive congressional galaxies, see pp. 299-312.

24. Alexis de Tocqueville, *Democracy in America,* I, 204. Bradley edition (1945).

25. James Bryce, *The American Commonwealth* (1888), I, 143-44.

26. Stuart A. Rice, *Quantitative Methods in Politics* (1928), pp. 296-97.

27. See Morris P. Fiorina, David W. Rohde, and Peter Wissel, "Historical Change in House Turnover," in Norman J. Ornstein (ed.), *Congress in Change* (1975), p. 41. See also *Congressional Quarterly Weekly Report,* February 23, 1974, p. 392. Other data based on *Congressional Directory,* relevant editions.

CHAPTER 4

1. Prior to the adoption of the Twentieth Amendment in 1933, Congress met on the first Monday in December, in accordance with Article I, Section 4, of the original Constitution.

2. *Congressional Quarterly Weekly Report,* January 8, 1965, p. 33. The caucus vote was 157 to 115.

3. *Ibid.,* p. 34. See also Robert L. Peabody, *The Ford-Halleck Minority Leadership Contest, 1965* (1966) and Charles O. Jones, *The Minority Party in Congress* (1970), pp. 156-157.

4. *Congressional Quarterly Weekly Report,* January 22, 1971, p. 175.

5. *Congressional Record,* January 14, 1975, pp. H7-H18. See also *New York Times,* December 2, 1974, p. 1.

6. *Memoirs of John Quincy Adams* (1876), Vol. 10, p. 147.

7. *Ibid.,* p. 165. See also 1 *Hinds' Precedents of the House of Representatives* § 103.

8. *House Journal,* 31st Congress, 1st Session, p. 91.

9. *Ibid.,* p. 130.

10. Mary P. Follett, *The Speaker of the House of Representatives* (1896), p. 56.

11. *House Journal,* 34th Congress, 1st Session, p. 444.

12. Follett, *op. cit.,* p. 59. See also 5 *Hinds' Precedents* § 6647 and Paul T. Davil *et al., The Politics of National Party Conventions* (1960), p. 24.

13. *House Journal,* 36th Congress, 1st Session, p. 12.

14. *Ibid.,* pp. 16, 17.

15. *Ibid.,* p. 164. See also Follett, *op. cit.,* pp. 60-63.

16. *Congressional Record,* 68th Congress, 1st Session, p. 8.

17. Chang-Wei Chiu, *The Speaker of the House of Representatives Since 1896* (1928), pp. 32-33.

18. 1 *Hinds' Precedents of the House of Representatives* § 81.

19. James Bryce, *The American Commonwealth* (1888), Vol. I, p. 140.

CHAPTER 5

1. *Congressional Globe,* June 14, 1858, p. 3048.

2. House Report No. 1, 35th Congress, 2d Session.

3. *Congressional Globe,* 36th Congress, 1st Session, pp. 1178, 1209.

4. *House Journal,* 36th Congress, 1st Session, pp. 526-33, 545-51.

5. De Alva S. Alexander, *History and Procedure of the House of Representatives* (1916), pp. 192-93.

6. *Congressional Globe,* 42d Congress, 2d Session, p. 3819.

7. For report and debate see *Congressional Record,* 46th Congress, 2d Session, pp. 108-208, 478-91, 551-58, 575-79, 603-14, 658-65, 708-13, 727-35, 954-59, 1195-1208, 1255-67.

8. Alexander, *op. cit.,* pp. 194-95.

9. *House Journal,* 51st Congress, 1st Session, pp. 209, 214, 216, 219-21, 224-27, 227-33.

10. *Cf.* Alexander, *op. cit.,* pp. 165-68, 206, 220-21.

11. George Rothwell Brown, *The Leadership of Congress* (1922), p. 152. See also 8 *Cannon's Precedents* 3376.

12. *Ibid.,* pp. 158-59.

13. *Cf.* W. F. Willoughby, *Principles of Legislative Organization and Administration* (1934), pp. 544-45.

14. 7 *Cannon's Precedents* 1741.

15. Lucius Wilmerding, Jr., *The Spending Power* (1943), pp. 292-93. See also 7 *Cannon's Precedents* 2041.

16. *Cf. The Organization of Congress: Some Problems of Committee Jurisdiction.* Senate Document No. 51, 82d Congress, 1st Session. July, 1951.

17. In 1974, the Appropriations Committee opened 90 per cent of its hear-

ings, but closed half of its markups. *Congressional Quarterly Weekly Report,* January 11, 1975, p. 81. The issue of committee secrecy is discussed further in Chapter Six, *infra.*

18. See George B. Galloway, *Congressional Reorganization Revisited.* Bureau of Governmental Research, University of Maryland, 1956, pp. 9-14. See also J. Malcolm Smith and Cornelius P. Cotter, *Administrative Accountability: Reporting to Congress,* Stanford University Political Science Series, No. 60, 1957.

19. Walter Kravitz, "The Legislative Reorganization Act of 1970: A Brief History and a Summary of Its Provisions," Congressional Research Service, Library of Congress, 1970, expanded 1972, p. 2. The discussion of the 1970 act is based on this monograph and the same author's "The Legislative Reorganization Act of 1970; Summary and Analysis of Provisions Affecting Committees and Committee Staff of the House of Representatives," Congressional Research Service, Library of Congress, 1970. Mr. Kravitz had assisted the staff of the Joint Committee on the Organization of Congress in 1965. See also *Congressional Quarterly Weekly Report,* Oct. 9, 1970, pp. 2461-2462, and *ibid.,* December 25, 1970, pp. 3061-3064.

20. Select Committee on Committees, U.S. House of Representatives, Ninety-third Congress, *Report to accompany H. Res. 988* (March 21, 1974), pp. 12-13. See also the Committee's *Hearings on the Subject of Committee Organization in the House* (3 volumes: May 2–October 11, 1973). The final floor action on the proposals is summarized in *Congressional Quarterly Weekly Report,* October 12, 1974, pp. 2896-2898 and in *National Journal,* October 26, 1974, pp. 1614-1619. See also David E. Price, "The Ambivalence of Congressional Reform," *Public Administrative Review,* November/December, 1974, pp. 601-608.

21. *Congressional Quarterly Weekly Report,* November 12, 1965, pp. 2323-2325; October 28, 1966, pp. 2621-2622; January 13, 1967, pp. 39 and 84. See also James A. Robinson, *The House Rules Committee* (1963), pp. 63-71, and Lewis A. Froman, Jr., *The Congressional Process* (1967), pp. 97-99.

CHAPTER 6

1. On the evolution of the committee system see J. F. Jameson, "The Origin of the Standing Committee System in American Legislative Bodies," *Annual Report of the American Historical Association,* 1893.

2. 4 *Hinds' Precedents* §§4524, 4525, 4526, 4527, 4528, 4529.

3. 4 *Hinds' Precedents* §4513; 8 *Cannon's Precedents* §§2201-2.

4. Paul DeWitt Hasbrouck, *Party Government in the House of Representatives* (1927), p. 48.

5. *Congressional Quarterly Weekly Report,* February 12, 1971, p. 365.

6. *Ibid.,* January 27, 1973, pp. 136-138.

7. Mark F. Ferber, "The Formation of the Democratic Study Group," in Nelson W. Polsby (ed.) *Congressional Behavior* (1971); Arthur G. Stevens, Jr., Arthur H. Miller and Thomas E. Mann, "Mobilization of Liberal Strength

in the House, 1955-1970: The Democratic Study Group," *American Political Science Review,* June 1974, pp. 667-681.

8. *Report on House Committee Chairmen,* Common Cause, Washington, D.C., January 13, 1975. The report was extensively circulated prior to the "publication date."

9. *National Journal Reports,* January 25, 1975, p. 132.

10. In his unpublished doctoral dissertation, *Congress and its Committees: A Historical and Theoretical Approach to the Proper Role of Committees in the Legislative Process,* Harvard, 1960, on committee theory and practice in Congress. This excellent work analyzes committee theory and practice in the House of Representatives in three periods: The Jeffersonian, 1789-1829; the Progressive, 1909-34; and the Modern Reform, 1944-59. Portions of this dissertation were published under the title: *The Origins of the Standing Committees and the Development of the Modern House* as a monograph in Political Science by Rice University Studies, Summer, 1970. Subsequent references to Cooper are to the original dissertation.

11. *Annals,* 9th Congress, 1st Session, pp. 1114-15. Quoted by Cooper, *op. cit.,* pp. 35-36.

12. Woodrow Wilson, *Congressional Government,* pp. 56, 60-61, 102.

13. George B. Galloway, *The Legislative Process in Congress,* p. 289.

14. *Congressman's Report,* April 9, 1973, p. 3.

15. See also Raymond E. Wolfinger and Joan H. Hollinger, "Safe Seats, Seniority and Power in Congress," in Raymond E. Wolfinger (ed.), *Readings on Congress* (1971), pp. 36-57.

16. *Report, op. cit.,* pp. 18-19.

17. For a summary of the changes that were enacted, see *National Journal,* October 26, 1974, pp. 1616-1617.

18. For a description of the gradual evolution of the present system for the introduction of bills, see *Hinds' Precedents,* Vol. 4, Sec. 3365. For a lucid discussion of this subject see also Cooper, *op. cit., passim.*

19. *Ibid.,* p. 53.

20. *Congressional Record,* 82d Congress, 2d Session, p. 1334.

21. U.S. Congress, Joint Committee on Congressional Operations, *Interim Report, Broadcasting House and Senate Proceedings,* Report No. 93-1458, 93d Congress, 2d Sess., October 10, 1974, p. 54. See also Richard Dyer MacCann, "Televising Congress," *American Scholar,* Summer, 1975, pp. 466-72.

22. See article on "Governmental Investigations," by George B. Galloway in the *Encyclopedia of the Social Sciences.* For the House precedents see *Hinds' Precedents,* Vol. 3, Chapters 54-56; "Congressional Power of Investigation," Senate Doc. No. 99, 83rd Congress, 2d Session, pp. 36-39; Marshall E. Dimock, *Congressional Investigating Committees* (1929); Ernest J. Eberling, *Congressional Investigations* (1928); George B. Galloway, "The Investigative Function of Congress," *American Political Science Review,* February, 1927; and M. Nelson McGeary, *The Developments of Congressional Investigative Power* (1940).

23. Joseph Cooper, *op. cit.,* pp. 42-47.

24. *Ibid.*, p. 60.

25. For the history of this rule, see *Hinds' Precedents,* Vol. 4, Sec. 4621.

26. Mary P. Follett, *The Speaker of the House of Representatives* (1896), p. 246.

27. For a detailed and intriguing description of the factors that have been involved, see Nicholas A. Masters, "Committee Assignments in the House of Representatives," *American Political Science Review,* June, 1961, pp. 345-57.

28. In explaining this move to the House, Rep. Halleck said: "It does not in any way represent any retreat or departure from the original purpose and intent of the Reorganization Act." (*Congressional Record,* 83rd Congress, 1st Session, January 13, 1953, p. 368.)

29. Data for 1975 from *Congressional Directory, 94th Congress, 1st Session;* for 1973 from *Report of the Select Committee on Committees, op. cit.,* p. 265; for previous years from Louis C. Gawthrop, "Changing Membership Patterns in House Committees," *American Political Science Review,* June, 1966, p. 366.

30. Rep. Oakes Ames of Massachusetts and Rep. James Brooks of New York.

31. *Weekly Report,* January 11, 1975, p. 81.

32. *Congressional Record,* March 10, 1975, p. H1489.

33. Thomas B. Reed, *Saturday Evening Post,* December 9, 1899. Quoted by De Alva S. Alexander, *History and Procedure of the House of Representatives,* p. 116.

34. Kravitz, *op. cit.,* pp. 9-10.

35. *National Journal Reports,* October 26, 1974, p. 1619.

36. *Congressional Record,* February 6, 1975, p. H676.

37. Woodrow Wilson, *op. cit.,* p. 79.

38. *Cf.* Julius Cohen and Reginald Robson, "The Lawyer and the Legislative Hearing Process," *Nebraska Law Review,* May, 1954, pp. 526-27.

39. For an interesting discussion of this case, see W. F. Willoughby, *Principles of Legislative Organization and Administration* (1934), pp. 364-66. For a summary of the procedure and practice concerning "quorum of the standing committees," see *Cannon's Procedure in the House of Representatives,* fourth edition, pp. 289-290.

40. *Congressional Record,* March 3, 1975, pp. E834-835; John T. Welsheimer, "Constitutionality of Proposed House Rule Which Would Permit Its Committees to Conduct Business with Less Than a Majority Quorum," March 27, 1975, p. 8.

41. For early examples of discharge action see *Annals,* 4th Congress, 1st Session, pp. 288-90; 9th Congress, 1st Session, pp. 409-12.

42. For history of the discharge rule see *Cannon's Precedents,* Vol. 7, Section 1007.

43. *Ibid.*

44. See Mildred L. Lehmann, "The Discharge Petition in the House of Representatives: Background and Statistics," Congressional Research Service, Library of Congress, January 10, 1974. Also *Congressional Quarterly Weekly Report,* March 16, 1974, p. 702.

CHAPTER 7

1. Ralph V. Harlow, *The History of Legislative Methods in the Period Before 1825* (1917), pp. 176-77.
2. *Ibid.,* p. 192.
3. *Ibid.,* p. 208.
4. Woodrow Wilson, *Congressional Government* (1885), pp. 60-61.
5. David B. Truman, *The Congressional Party* (1959), pp. 198 ff. See Chapter 6 of this case study for an intensive analysis of House leadership roles in the 81st Congress. See also Randal B. Ripley, *Party Leaders in the House of Representatives* (1967).
6. Ripley, *op. cit.,* p. 146.
7. William S. White, "Sam Rayburn—The Untalkative Speaker," *New York Times Magazine,* February 27, 1949, p. 48.
8. De Alva S. Alexander, *History and Procedure of the House of Representatives* (1916), Chapter VII, "Floor Leaders," pp. 110-11.
9. Floyd M. Riddick, *The United States Congress: Organization and Procedure* (1949), Chapter V, "The Floor Leaders and Whips," p. 86n.
10. Lynn Haines, *Law Making in America* (1912), pp. 15-16.
11. Alexander, *op. cit.,* p. 109.
12. *Congressional Record,* 70th Congress, 1st Session, p. 8439.
13. Floyd M. Riddick, *Congressional Procedure* (1941), pp. 345-46.
14. Paul H. Hasbrouck, *Party Government in the House of Representatives* (1927), p. 117.
15. *Congress: Process and Policy* (1975), pp. 134-136.
16. See *The History and Operation of the House Majority Whip Organization,* House Document 94-162, 94th Congress, 1st Session (1975); *Congressional Record,* January 23, 1975, p. H241. In 1974 the Democratic caucus, by a vote of 32 to 138, rejected a proposal to elect the whip. *Congressional Quarterly Weekly Report,* December 7, 1974, p. 3247.
17. George R. Brown, *The Leadership of Congress* (1922), pp. 221-22, 224.
18. Atkinson and Beard, "The Syndication of the Speakership," *Political Science Quarterly,* September 1911, p. 414.
19. Hasbrouck, *op. cit.,* pp. 95-96.
20. Robert L. Peabody, "Committees from the Leadership Perspective," *The Annals,* January, 1974, p. 137.
21. For further discussion of White House leadership meetings, see Paul T. David *et al., The Politics of National Party Conventions* (1960), pp. 67-69. For a discussion of out-party congressional leadership roles in presidential politics, see *ibid.,* pp. 90-94.

CHAPTER 8

1. In 1967, the nation had ratified the Twenty-fifth Amendment to the Constitution. Section 1 states that in case of the removal of the President from of-

fice or his death or resignation, the Vice President shall become President. Section 2 states that whenever there is a vacancy in the office of the Vice President, the President shall nominate a Vice President who shall take office upon confirmation by a majority vote of both houses of Congress. The amendment also clarified the procedures to be followed in the case of presidential disability.

2. *Cf.* Roland Young, *Congressional Politics in the Second World War* (1956).

3. For an excellent summary of congressional initiatives during most of the Nixon administration, see Gary Orfield, *Congressional Power: Congress and Social Change* (1975).

4. George B. Galloway, *The Legislative Process in Congress* (1953), p. 417.

5. Donald G. Tacheron and Morris K. Udall, *The Job of the Congressman* (1966), p. 46.

6. Milton S. Gwertzman, "The Bloated Branch," *New York Times Magazine*, November 10, 1974, p. 31.

7. *Congressional Quarterly Weekly Report,* July 12, 1975, p. 1476.

8. Data complied from Galloway, *op. cit.,* p. 408; Walter Kravitz, "The Congressional Research Service and the Legislative Reorganization Act of 1970," Library of Congress (1975); letter from Charles A. Goodrum, Assistant Director, Congressional Research Service, April 2, 1975.

CHAPTER 9

1. James Bryce, *Modern Democracies* (1921), Vol. 1, p. 113.

2. Ralph V. Harlow, *The History of Legislative Methods Before 1825* (1927), pp. 139-45. On January 22, 1941, Representative Clarence Cannon of Missouri, in submitting for the *Record* a partial list of caucus chairmen of both parties, stated that "the caucus had been co-existent with the Congress from its first session; political parties had their origin in the caucus; congressional committees were made up in the caucuses as early as 1797. . . ." *Congressional Record,* 77th Congress, 1st Session, Vol. 87, pp. A383-84.

3. Quoted by Irving Brant in *James Madison: Father of the Constitution* (1950), p. 368.

4. Harlow, *op. cit.,* p. 184.

5. In 1828 the state legislatures made these nominations, and in 1832 the present system of national conventions was introduced.

6. *Washington Federalist,* Feb. 6, 1802. Quoted by Harlow, *op. cit.,* p. 187.

7. *Annals,* 7th Congress, 1st session, p. 480.

8. *Annals,* 10th Congress, 2d session, p. 1143. Quoted by Harlow, *op. cit.,* p. 189.

9. Henry Adams, *History of the United States* (1889), Vol. 1, pp. 264-66.

10. Webster, *Private Correspondence,* Vol. 1, p. 233. Quoted by Harlow, *op. cit.,* p. 203.

11. *Annals,* 13th Congress, 2d session, p. 1966, April 6, 1814. Quoted by Harlow, *op. cit.,* p. 204.

12. Harlow, *op. cit.,* pp. 249-51.

13. Clarence Berdahl notes that a Whig House caucus met in 1849 to organize the 31st Congress. "Some Notes on Party Membership in Congress," *American Political Science Review,* April 1949, p. 311.

14. Woodrow Wilson, *Congressional Government* (1885), pp. 98-100.

15. *Ibid.,* pp. 267-68.

16. January 7, 11, and 16, 1889, and February 7.

17. April 8, 1889.

18. April 22, and May 6, 1889.

19. For a good account of the situation in the House at this time, see William A. Robinson, *Thomas B. Reed: Parliamentarian* (1930), Chapter IX, "Legislative Impotence."

20. *Ibid.,* p. 215.

21. *Ibid.,* pp. 388, 389.

22. *Ibid.,* pp. 233-34.

23. W. F. Willoughby, *Principles of Legislative Organization and Administration* (1934), p. 540.

24. L. White Busbey, *Uncle Joe Cannon* (1927), p. xviii.

25. See Chapter 5, pp. 56-59.

26. Wilder H. Haines, "The Congressional Caucus of Today," *American Political Science Review,* November 1915, p. 697n.

27. Berdahl, *loc. cit.,* p. 725n.

28. *Ibid.,* p. 317.

29. Hasbrouck states that the House Republicans gave up the binding caucus after the Cannon regime, but returned to it before the 69th Congress. *Party Govenment in the House of Representatives* (1927), pp. 31-32.

30. Hasbrouck, *op. cit.,* p. 34.

31. The House Republicans have not adopted caucus rules, but have used the rules of the House itself wherever applicable.

32. For a detailed description of party organization in the House during the period, 1913-36, see *Cannon's Precedents in the House of Representatives,* Vol. 8, Chapter 278.

33. Wilder H. Haines, *op. cit.,* p. 698n.

34. *Ibid.,* p. 706. The reforms in the House advocated by Wilder Haines included reconstruction of the House rules, so as to require the Rules Committee to report within a certain time any proposed amendment to the rules which might be referred to it; reform of the committee system by abolishing dead committees and letting the committees select their own chairmen; self-government for the District of Columbia; voting by electricity; reduction in the size of the House; and the election of representatives in groups from a few large districts in each state, in place of election by single districts. *Ibid.,* pp. 702-03.

35. M. I. Ostrogorski, *Democracy and the Party System* (1926), p. 288.

36. Hasbrouck, *op. cit.,* pp. 92-94.

37. *Cannon's Precedents of the House of Representatives,* Vol. VIII, § 2667.

38. *Ibid.,* § 3388.

39. *Ibid.,* § 3389.

40. *Ibid.,* § 3392.

41. Floyd M. Riddick, *The U.S. Congress: Organization and Procedure* (1949), p. 123.

42. House Rule XI, clause 22.

43. This paragraph was amended December 8, 1931, January 3, 1949, and January 3, 1951. However, the language quoted in this paragraph is still intact.

44. For a searching discussion of this and related questions, the writer is indebted to an unpublished doctoral dissertation at Harvard University by Lewis J. Lapham entitled *Party Leadership and the House Committee on Rules,* April, 1953.

45. Berdahl, *loc. cit.,* pp. 497-503.

46. Hasbrouck, *op. cit.,* p. 23.

47. 70th Congress, 1st Session, House Doc. No. 331, *Fixing Presidential and Congressional Terms: Proceedings and Debate,* p. 43.

48. *Ibid.,* p. 42. Quoted by Lapham, *op. cit.,* pp. 46-47.

49. Lapham, *op. cit.,* pp. 66-67.

50. *Congressional Record,* 74th Congress, 1st Session, p. 13. Quoted by Lapham, *op. cit.,* p. 76.

51. Lapham, *op. cit.,* p. 88.

52. *Ibid.,* p. 124.

53. *Ibid.,* pp. 130-31.

54. *Ibid.,* p. 136.

55. *Congressional Record,* June 7, 1944, p. 5471. Quoted by Roland Young, *Congressional Politics in the Second World War* (1956), p. 116.

56. Lapham, *op. cit.,* p. 151. See also Stephen K. Bailey, *Congress Makes a Law* (1950), pp. 174-77.

57. Berdahl, *loc. cit.,* pp. 730-31.

58. Arthur Krock in *New York Times,* March 12, 1946, p. 24, c. 5. Quoted by Berdahl, *loc. cit.,* p. 732.

59. Berdahl, *loc. cit.,* p. 733. Judged by votes on the floor, the years have not been kind to this hope. The conservative coalition of Southern Democrats and Republicans has persisted in Congress. Acocrding to a *Congressional Quarterly Weekly Report* study (January 25, 1975, p. 190), the percentage of "coalition roll calls" in the House between 1965 and 1974 ranged from 20 per cent to 30 per cent. The "coalition roll call" is one on which a majority of voting Southern Democrats and the majority of voting Republicans are opposed to a majority of voting Northern Democrats. Where that coalition did appear in the House during that period, its victories ranged from 25 per cent in 1965 to 79 per cent in 1971 and 1972. The conservative coalition has been even more effective in the Senate.

60. Charles O. Jones, *The Minority Party in Congress* (1970), pp. 158-160. See also Jones, *Party and Policy-Making: The House Republican Policy Committee* (1964). John F. Bibby and Roger H. Davidson have pointed out that during the Nixon administration, the Policy Committee frequently refrained from taking strong positions when the leadership believed that the appearance of excessive partisanship might jeopardize needed Democratic votes. However, on such an occasion as the controversial Family Assistance Plan in 1969, the

Policy Committee "was used to help gain support among the more conservative members of the President's party." *On Capitol Hill* (1972, second edition), p. 155.

61. Jones, *The Minority Party in Congress,* p. 160.

62. Lapham, *op. cit.,* p. 183.

63. Lapham, *op. cit.,* pp. 235-37.

64. Much of the academic controversy surrounding the question of party responsibility resulted from the publication of "Toward a More Responsible Two-Party System: A Report of the Committee on Political Parties, American Political Science Association," *American Political Science Review,* September, 1950. The most recent scholarly analysis of that report is Evron M. Kirkpatrick, " 'Toward a More Responsible Two-Party System': Political Science, Policy Science, or Pseudo-Science?" *American Political Science Review,* December, 1971, pp. 965-90. See especially footnote 3, pp. 968-69 for a listing of the voluminous literature generated by the report. See also David Broder, *The Party's Over* (1971); James Sundquist, *Dynamics of the Party System* (1973); Lanny Davis, *The Emerging Democratic Majority* (1974); William Rusher, *The Making of the New Majority Party* (1975).

65. For a lucid description of "The Role of the Rules Committee in Arranging the Program of the U.S. House of Representatives" during the 80th-85th Congresses, inclusive, see James A. Robinson, *Western Political Quarterly,* September 1959, pp. 653-69.

66. William S. White, "The Invisible Gentleman from Kansas City," *Harper's,* May 1961, p. 84.

67. *Congressional Quarterly Weekly Report,* March 30, 1974, p. 808.

68. See *Congressional Quarterly Weekly Reports,* April 5, 1975, pp. 693-95, and May 3, 1975, pp. 911-15; Bruce F. Freed, "Raucous Caucus," *New Republic,* July 5 and 12, 1975, pp. 5-7; David Cohen, "The Continuing Challenge of Congressional Reform," *Democratic Review,* February-March, 1975, pp. 21-24.

69. For a full and informative account of the congressional campaign committees, see Hugh A. Bone, *Party Committees and National Politics* (1958), Chapter 5, "The Capitol Hill Committees."

CHAPTER 10

1. A vivid and profusely illustrated description of most of these stages may be found in Bertram M. Gross, *The Legislative Struggle* (1953), *passim.* This chapter is based both upon my own observations and on this excellent book by Mr. Gross. An absorbing recent study of how a bill works its way through the labyrinth is Eric Redman, *The Dance of Legislation* (1973). See also the case studies in John F. Bibby and Roger H. Davidson, *On Capitol Hill,* 2d edition (1972), and Daniel P. Moynihan, *The Politics of a Guaranteed Income* (1973).

2. George F. Hoar, *Autobiography of Seventy Years* (1930), Vol. II, p. 363.

3. Stephen K. Bailey, *Congress Makes a Law* (1949), p. 76.

4. On this point see Moynihan, *op. cit.,* Chapter 4. Moynihan contends that the strategy of the organized welfare professional groups in opposing President

Nixon's Family Assistance Plan in 1970 was to insist "on benefit levels that no Congress would pass and no president would approve . . . ," p. 306.

5. For detailed analyses of the actions of conference committees, see Ada C. McCown, *The Congressional Conference Committee* (1927); Gilbert Y. Steiner, *The Congressional Conference Committee* (1951); and David J. Vogler, "Patterns of One House Dominance in Congressional Conference Committees," *Midwest Journal of Political Science,* May, 1970, pp. 303-20.

CHAPTER 11

1. Leonard D. White, *The Federalists* (1948), pp. 82-87.

2. Carl Russell Fish, *The Civil Service and the Patronage* (1904), p. 47.

3. White, *The Jeffersonians* (1951), pp. 362, 365.

4. Adams, *Memoirs,* Vol. V, p. 238. Quoted by White, *The Jeffersonians,* p. 92.

5. Leonard D. White, *The Jacksonians* (1954), pp. 115-18.

6. Paul P. Van Riper, *History of the United States Civil Service* (1958), p. 49.

7. Carl Sandburg, *Abraham Lincoln: The War Years* (1936), Vol. 1, pp. 168, 175, 373, 375.

8. Henry Adams, "The Session," *North American Review,* Vol. CXI, p. 58.

9. *Congressional Globe,* 41st Congress, 3d Session, p. 293 (Jan. 4, 1871).

10. Louis W. Koenig, *The Chief Executive,* 3d edition (1975), p. 125. See also *New York Times,* August 5, 1975, p. 1, for a story of how members of Congress exercised influence in selection of personnel for the Small Business Administration during the Nixon administration in apparent disregard of Civil Service regulations. The story was based on a Civil Service Commission report and was released by the House Subcommittee on Manpower and Civil Service.

11. Leonard D. White, *The Federalists,* pp. 326-34.

12. White, *The Jeffersonians,* pp. 110-16.

13. John Sherman, *Recollections,* Vol. I, p. 155. Quoted by White, *The Jacksonians,* p. 141.

14. White, *The Jacksonians,* p. 141.

15. *Committee Organization in the House,* Vol. 2, p. 224.

16. *Congressional Quarterly Almanac* (1973), p. 253.

17. *New York Times,* April 6, 1975, section, 3, p. 14.

18. Telford Taylor, *Grand Inquest: The Story of Congressional Investigations* (1955), Chapter 2. The claim of executive privilege has even survived Watergate. When the Watergate special prosecutor sought to obtain certain tapes and was rebuffed by the President, the Supreme Court (8-0) upheld the prosecutor only because the tapes involved possible criminal conduct. The Court simultaneously recognized a "special privilege" which could presumably cover all other matters, although the Court left open the possibility that the determination would be made by the Court on a case-by-case basis: U.S. v. Nixon, 418 U.S. 683 (1974). One scholar has noted that "the President lost this battle, but the Presidency emerged a victor, encumbered with handicaps of only modest proportions." See D. Grier

Stephenson, Jr., "The Mild Magistracy of the Law: U.S. v. Richard Nixon," *Intellect,* February, 1975, p. 289.

19. Leonard D. White, *The Jeffersonians,* p. 100.

20. *Ibid.,* pp. 117-19.

21. *Ibid.,* p. 106.

22. Compiled from 3 *Hinds' Precedents,* Chapter LIV, and Leonard White, *The Jeffersonians,* pp. 99-100.

23. White, *The Jacksonians,* pp. 148-54.

24. Compiled from 3 *Hinds' Precedents,* Chapter LIV; Marshall E. Dimock, *Congressional Investigating Committees* (1929); and Ernest J. Eberling, *Congressional Investigations* (1928).

25. White, *The Republican Era* (1958), pp. 84-92.

26. 2 *Hinds' Precedents of the House of Representatives,* § 1286.

27. House Report, No. 78, 42d Congress, 3d Session.

28. Senate Report No. 519, 42d Congress, 3d Session.

29. Woodrow Wilson, *Congressional Government,* pp. 270-71.

30. *Ibid.,* p. 271.

31. *Ibid.,* p. 302.

32. *Records of the U.S. House of Representatives,* 1789-1946, 2 vols., Preliminary Inventories. National Archives and Records Service, General Services Administration, Washington, 1959.

33. M. Nelson McGeary, *The Developments of Congressional Investigative Power* (1940), p. 8. Floyd M. Riddick in his review of the session articles in the *American Political Science Review* and the *Western Political Quarterly.* Nelson McGeary reports that House committees conducted fifty investigations during 1929-38, and Floyd Riddick states that 107 inquiries were carried on by House committees during 1942-50.

34. For a full account of this episode see *Congressional Quarterly Almanac,* Vol. XIV, 1958, pp. 687-701. See also Report of the Subcommittee on Legislative Oversight, House Report No. 2711, 85th Congress, 2d Session; Bernard Schwartz, *The Professor and the Commissions* (1959); J. Sinclair Armstrong, "Who's Overseeing the Oversighters?" *Congressional Record,* February 2, 1959, pp. A707-10. For a critique of legislative participation in the administrative process, see Frank C. Newman and Stanley S. Surrey, *Legislation: Cases and Materials* (1955), chap. 4, sec. 2.

35. *Activities of the House Committee on Government Operations,* 93d Congress, 2d Session, p. 12.

36. *Congressional Quarterly Almanac, 1971,* p. 195. For earlier sessions, see *Congressional Quarterly Weekly Report,* July 4, 1969, p. 1197.

37. *Congress and the Nation* (Congressional Quarterly) 1973, p. 960; *Congressional Quarterly Almanac, 1973,* p. 730.

38. *The Committee Veto: Its Current Use and Validity,* Congressional Research Service, January 16, 1967. See also Joseph P. Harris, *Congressional Control of Administration* (1964), pp. 217-248.

39. *National Journal,* October 18, 1975, p. 1460.

40. For a description of the behavior of members of a congressional com-

mittee in their role as overseers of an independent regulatory commission, see Seymour Scher, "Congressional Committee Members as Independent Agency Overseers: A Case Study," *American Political Science Review,* December 1960, pp. 911-20.

41. *Report, op. cit.,* p. 268.

42. *Ibid.,* p. 63 ff.

43. Committee on Government Operations, U.S. House of Representatives, Ninety-fourth Congress, 1st Session, *Report on Oversight Plans of the U.S. House of Represntatives.*

44. *Committee Organization in the House, Panel Discussions,* Vol. 2, p. 702.

CHAPTER 12

1. Edward S. Corwin, *The President: Office and Powers,* 3d edition revised (1948), p. 208.

2. Wallace McClure, *International Executive Agreements* (1941), p. 38.

3. Dorothy B. Goebel, "Congress and Foreign Relations Before 1900," *Annals of the American Academy of Political and Social Science,* September 1953, pp. 28-29. I have made extensive use of Dr. Goebel's excellent article in this and the following sections.

4. *The Constitution of the United States* (1953), Corwin annotated edition, p. 418.

5. Goebel, *loc. cit.,* p. 32.

6. *Ibid.,* pp. 34-35.

7. *Ibid.,* p. 35.

8. *Ibid.,* p. 36.

9. *Ibid.,* pp. 37-38.

10. For a detailed account of the role of the House Committee on Foreign Affairs in arms embargo legislation during these years see A. C. F. Westphal, *The House Committee on Foreign Affairs* (1942), Chapter VI.

11. For a full account of the part played by the Committee on Foreign Affairs and by the House in shaping the various neutrality laws and the Lend-Lease bill, see Westphal, *op. cit.,* Chapter VII.

12. For a fuller account of these wartime developments see Roland Young, *Congressional Politics in the Second World War* (1956), Chapter 7.

13. Corwin, *The Constitution of the United States,* p. 443.

14. *Ibid.,* p. 470.

15. Walter S. Surrey, "The Legislative Process and International Law," *Proceedings* of the American Society of International Law, 1958, p. 13. Mr. Surrey was formerly Assistant Legal Adviser on Economic Affairs of the Department of State.

16. For a list of these twenty committees see L. Larry Leonard, *Elements of American Foreign Policy* (1953), p. 159.

17. Holbert N. Carroll, *The House of Representatives and Foreign Affairs* (1958; revised edition, 1966), p. 58.

18. For the details of this picture see Carroll, *op. cit.,* Chapter 5. Carroll has

since noted that "in the Ninety-second Congress (1971-1972) one could identify nineteen permanent (more than half of the total) and two joint House-Senate committees which dealt sufficiently with foreign affairs to require the serious, if sometimes episodic, attention of the executive branch. The committees spawned in the neighborhood of sixty subcommittees with titles indicating that their primary duties were in the international field." "The Congress and National Security Policy," in David B. Truman (ed.), *The Congress and America's Future*, 2d edition (1973), p. 182.

19. See Carroll, *op. cit.*, Chapter 11, for discussion of committee coordination.

20. For a brief description of these select committees see Carroll, *op. cit.*, pp. 211-18.

21. *Congressional Quarterly Weekly Report*, June 27, 1969, p. 1111. The vitality of this resolution was virtually destroyed in 1970 with President Nixon's announcement that U.S. forces had gone into Cambodia without his having consulted the Congress.

22. *Congressional Quarterly Weekly Report*, August 2, 1975, p. 1714. See also *New York Times*, August 17, 1975, section 4, p. 2.

23. *Congressional Quarterly Weekly Report, ibid.*

24. *Congressional Quarterly Weekly Reports*, July 26, 1975, p. 1607; August 2, 1975, p. 1736.

25. The best full-length histories of the Committee on Foreign Affairs are those by Albert C. F. Westphal, *The House Committee on Foreign Affairs* (1942), for the period before World War II; and by Holbert N. Carroll, *The House of Representatives and Foreign Affairs* (1966), for the postwar period.

26. Democratic Study Group, Special Report 93-12, June 4, 1974, p. 9; *Congressional Quarterly Weekly Report*, June 17, 1972, p. 1494.

27. *Congressmen in Committees* (1973), p. 219.

28. *Congressional Record*, July 24, 1975, p. H7445.

29. Carroll, *op. cit.*, pp. 154-72.

30. See Aaron Wildavsky, *The Politics of the Budgetary Process*, 2d edition (1974), pp. 47-61. See also Richard F. Fenno, Jr., "The House Appropriations Committee as a Political System," *American Political Science Review*, June, 1962, pp. 310-324.

31. *Congressional Quarterly Weekly Report*, March 29, 1975, p. 647.

32. *New York Times*, August 7, 1975, p. 8.

CHAPTER 13

1. Quoted by P. T. Underdown in "Henry Cruger and Edmund Burke: Colleagues and Rivals at the Bristol Election of 1774," *William and Mary Quarterly*, January 1958, p. 31n.

2. Article on "Representation" in the *Encyclopedia of the Social Sciences*, by Francis W. Coker and Carlton C. Rodee.

3. Albert E. McKinley, *The Suffrage Franchise in the Thirteen English Colonies in America* (1905), p. 113.

4. Alfred de Grazia, *Public and Republic* (1951), p. 56.

5. On theories of representation in England, on the continent of Europe, and in America, see Robert Luce, *Legislative Principles* (1930), Chapter XIX.

6. De Grazia, *op. cit.,* pp. 242-43.

7. *Federalist,* No. 56.

8. *Federalist,* No. 57.

9. *Annals of Congress,* Vol. 1, pp. 733-48. Gales and Seaton edition (1834).

10. De Grazia, *op. cit.,* p. 246.

11. *Ibid.,* pp. 126-27.

12. *Ibid.,* p. 122.

13. *Messages and Papers of the Presidents,* Vol. II, p. 648. Quoted by De Grazia, *op. cit.,* p. 128.

14. Nicolay and Hay, *Abraham Lincoln,* Vol. I, p. 129.

15. George H. Haynes, *The United States Senate* (1938), Vol. 2, p. 1030n.

16. John C. Calhoun, *Disquisition on Government* and *Discourse on the Constitution and Government of the United States.*

17. For a full discussion of these developments, see de Grazia, *op. cit.,* Chapter VI.

18. For a brief but excellent summary of those changes as well as some of the problems they have generated, see Austin Ranney, "Changing the Rules of the Nominating Game" in James D. Barber (ed.), *Choosing the President* (1974).

19. T. V. Smith, *The Legislative Way of Life* (1940), p. 71. On the legislator as broker, politician, parliamentarian, and party member, see Herman Finer, *The Theory and Practice of Modern Government* (1949), pp. 379-84.

20. Marver H. Bernstein, *The Job of the Federal Executive* (1958), p. 101.

21. *Cf.* Ernest S. Griffith, *The American System of Government* (1953), Chapter 6, "How Congress Makes up its Mind." See also Roger H. Davidson, *The Role of the Congressman* (1969), Chapter 4, "The Congressman as Representative." Davidson's data allowed him to suggest that "seniority probably works independently to stimulate the Trustee style of representation. To be sure, a large part of the effect stems from the fact that less experienced legislators are more likely to represent competitive districts . . ." (p. 136). Other recent studies on the process of representation include Aage R. Clausen, *How Congressmen Decide* (1973); John W. Kingdon, *Congressmen's Voting Decisions* (1973); and W. Wayne Shannon, *Party, Constituency and Congressional Voting* (1968).

22. Heinz Eulau et al., "The Role of the Representative," *American Political Science Review,* September, 1959, pp. 742-56.

23. *Ibid.,* pp. 749-50.

24. *Ibid.,* pp. 750-51. Davidson found that among the eighty-seven House members he interviewed, 28 per cent perceived of themselves as "trustees," 23 per cent saw themselves as "delegates" and 46 per cent thought they were "politicos" (*op. cit.,* p. 117). Since a Congressman is likely to respond to such a question with a reply that he believes will be most easily received by his constituency, it is probably unwise to overanalyze such data.

25. Theodore C. Smith, *Life and Letters of James A. Garfield*, Vol. I, p. 382.

26. James A. Garfield, *Diary*, Feb. 19, 1872, in Manuscripts Division, Library of Congress.

27. Robert Luce, *Congress: An Explanation* (1926), pp. 52-53.

28. Jerry Voorhis, "A Call to Congress to Lead, not Follow," *New York Times Magazine*, January 25, 1948, p. 12.

29. *Congressional Record*, June 28, 1958, p. A5889, daily edition.

30. William Benton, "The Big Dilemma: Conscience or Votes," *New York Times Magazine*, April 26, 1959.

31. *Ibid.* For two senatorial statements on the representative function, see Wayne Morse, "What do the American People Want from their Politicians?" James Lecture on Government, University of Illinois, 1951; and Richard L. Neuberger, "Are the People Ahead of their 'Leaders'?" *New York Times Magazine*, August 23, 1959. For a recent statement on the necessity for compromise in politics, see Garry Wills, *"Hurrah for Politicians," Harper's*, September, 1975, pp. 45-50. He states, ". . . compromise is just another name for the discipline all vote-getters must profess. It is representation. Without compromise, a politician would not represent anything or anyone but himself" (p. 46).

32. Lewis Anthony Dexter, "The Representative and His District," *Human Organization*, Spring, 1957, pp. 2-13. For additional views of House members on the various motives for their votes, see Charles L. Clapp, *The Congressman: His Work as He Sees It* (1963), pp. 420-43.

33. For a more detailed description of his unsuccessful attacks on the pork barrel, see Paul H. Douglas, *In the Fullness of Time* (1962), esp. pp. 314-18.

34. For an incisive presentation of the view that congressional behavior and indeed organization can be explained in terms of the quest for re-election, see David R. Mayhew, *Congress: The Electoral Connection* (1974). Mayhew states, ". . . if a group of planners sat down and tried to design a pair of American national assemblies with the goal of serving members' electoral needs year in and year out, they would be hard pressed to improve on what exists" (pp. 81-82). While the Congressman may be motivated primarily by his desire for survival, there are still many occasions when he can vote either way on a major question without jeopardizing his career, particularly if he has a relatively safe seat and is adept at explaining his vote. The conduct of the freshmen in the Ninety-fourth Congress could well be cited as an illustration of the Mayhew thesis. When they arrived in December, 1974, they were frequently described by the press as "issue-oriented." As the first session progressed, however, it became clear that many of them had concluded that the path to re-election was through greater attention to the traditional services required by constituents. Indeed, when the Committee on House Administration announced in 1975 the increases in staff, travel allowances, and newsletter costs, many Republicans charged that the measure was intended to assist the seventy-five freshmen Democrats to become sophomores. See *Congressional Quarterly Weekly Report*, August 2, 1975, pp. 1674-1679. The subtitle of the *C.Q.* report was, "How Democrats find House is changing them as much as they change it."

CHAPTER 14

1. George H. Haynes, *The Senate of the United States* (1938), Vol. 11, p. 999.

2. Madison's *Journal of the Federal Convention* (1893), pp. 61, 65.

3. *Ibid.*, p. 680.

4. Jefferson's *Manual of Parliamentary Practice*, Section XVII.

5. 5 *Hinds' Precedents of the House of Representatives*, § 5129.

6. *Rules and Manual of the House of Representatives* (1951), §§ 371-72. See also *Congressional Record*, September 27, 1951, pp. 12516-17, and 8 *Cannon's Precedents of the House of Representatives*, § 2516.

7. For party divisions of the Senate and House of Representatives from 1855 (34th Congress) to 1947-49 (80th Congress), see Louis H. Bean, *How to Predict Elections* (1948), p. 189, Table 10.

8. *Hearings on the Organization and Operation of Congress*, June 1951, p. 7.

9. *Hearings on Evaluation of Legislative Reorganization Act of 1946*, February 1948, p. 82.

10. *Hearings,* Select Committee on Committees, *op. cit.* (1973), p. 374.

11. Ada C. McCown, *The Congressional Conference Committee* (1927), pp. 254-55.

12. Recent changes in conference committee procedures are summarized in *Congressional Quarterly Weekly Report,* February 8, 1975, pp. 290-94.

13. For a dramatic account of this controversy, see Neil MacNeil, *Forge of Democracy* (1963), pp. 398-401.

14. *New York Times,* November 23, 1975, Section 4, p. 3.

15. *Hearings on the Organization and Operation of Congress*, June 1951, p. 507.

16. *Ibid.*, pp. 72-73.

17. *Hearings, op. cit.*, Vol. 1. Pt. 1, p. 41.

CHAPTER 15

1. During the first session of the Ninety-fourth Congress, the Americans for Democratic Action released a study that analyzed the votes of the chairmen of the twenty-two standing committees on ten "controversial" roll calls and concluded that "the new chairmen elected in the great Congressional reform wave earlier this year and other chairmen elected since 1973 show a marked trend toward unity with their Democratic colleagues" (*New York Times,* August 24, 1975, p. 34).

2. For a thorough account of legislative-executive relations during the Federalist period, see Leonard D. White, *The Federalists* (1948), Chapters V and VI. See also Stephen Horn, *The Cabinet and Congress* (1960), for a full history of this proposal.

3. Ralph V. Harlow, *The History of Legislative Methods in the Period Before 1825*, p. 177.

4. Leonard D. White, *The Jeffersonians* (1951), p. 48.

5. Wilfred E. Binkley, *President and Congress* (1947), p. 53.

6. *Ibid.*, p. 54.

7. John Quincy Adams, *Memoirs,* Vol. 1, p. 403. Quoted by Binkley, *op. cit.*, p. 53.

8. Binkley, *op. cit.*, p. 54.

9. White, *op. cit.*, p. 55.

10. M. P. Follett, *Speaker of the House of Representatives* (1896), p. 79.

11. White, *op. cit.*, pp. 30-31.

12. Binkley, *op. cit.*, p. 79.

13. Binkley, *op. cit.*, p. 291.

14. *Ibid.*, p. 117.

15. *Ibid.*, p. 125.

16. *Ibid.*, p. 120.

17. *Ibid.*, p. 125.

18. *Ibid.*, p. 126.

19. *Ibid.*, p. 135.

20. Henry Adams, "The Session," *North American Review,* Vol. CXI (1870), p. 34.

21. Binkley, *op. cit.*, p. 151.

22. White, *op. cit.*, p. 38.

23. *Ibid.*, p. 25.

24. *Ibid.*, p. 39.

25. Binkley, *op. cit.*, pp. 178-79. See also L. D. White, *The Republican Era* (1958), pp. 48-54.

26. *The Autobiography of Theodore Roosevelt,* Centennial Edition, 1958, pp. 197-98.

27. L. W. Busbey, *Uncle Joe Cannon* (1927), p. 219.

28. *The Autobiography,* pp. 195-96.

29. *Ibid.*, pp. 199-200.

30. William Howard Taft, *Our Chief Magistrate and His Powers* (1916), p. 31.

31. See his Columbia University lectures on *Constitutional Government in the United States* (1908), p. 60.

32. Binkley, *op. cit.*, p. 206.

33. See "Wilson the Domestic Reformer," by Marshall E. Dimock, *Virginia Quarterly Review,* Autumn, 1956, pp. 546-65.

34. W. B. Munro, "Two Years of President Harding," *Atlantic Monthly,* March 1923, p. 391.

35. G. R. Brown, *The Leadership of Congress* (1922), p. 241.

36. *The Autobiography of Calvin Coolidge* (1929), pp. 196, 197.

37. *Ibid.*, pp. 231-32.

38. *The Memoirs of Herbert Hoover, 1929-1941,* Vol. 3, pp. 101-3.

39. Allan Nevins, "President Hoover's Record," *Current History*, July 1932, pp. 388, 393, 394.

40. *New York Times*, November 13, 1932.

41. Franklin D. Roosevelt, *On Our Way*, p. 204.

42. E. P. Herring, *American Political Science Review*, Vol. XVIII, p. 854.

43. Arthur M. Schlesinger, Jr., *The Coming of the New Deal* (1959), p. 554.

44. Alben W. Barkley, "President *and*—Not vs.—Congress," *New York Times Magazine*, June 20, 1948, pp. 24-25.

45. Schlesinger, *op. cit.*, pp. 554-55.

46. Charles A. Beard, "The Labors of Congress," *Current History*, October 1935, p. 64.

47. Binkley, *op. cit.*, p. 266.

48. Edward S. Corwin, *The President: Office and Powers* (1948), p. 333.

49. For further discussion of postwar bipartisanship and cooperation in foreign affairs, see George B. Galloway, *The Legislative Process in Congress* (1953), pp. 177-87; and *Congress and Foreign Relations, Annals*, September 1953, *passim*.

50. Richard E. Neustadt, "Presidency and Legislation: Planning the President's Program," *American Political Science Review*, December 1955, p. 1016.

51. Arthur Krock, "The Democratic Leadership in Congress," *New York Times*, November 13, 1956.

52. In a Senate Speech on May 11, 1954, Senator Knowland, Republican Floor Leader, compared the Truman and Eisenhower records on bipartisan consultation on foreign policy and inserted a series of tables showing the consultations held during the 83rd Congress by executive officials with members and committees of Congress.

53. Clinton Rossiter, *The American Presidency* (1956), pp. 82-84.

54. *A Thousand Days* (1965), p. 709.

55. See William S. White, *The Professional: Lyndon B. Johnson* (1964); Rowland Evans and Robert Novak, *Lyndon B. Johnson: The Exercise of Power* (1966).

56. Congressional Quarterly *Congress and the Nation*, Vol. II (1969), p. 3.

57. See Lyndon B. Johnson, *The Vantage Point: Perspectives of the Presidency 1963-1969* (1971); Eric Goldman, *The Tragedy of Lyndon Johnson* (1969).

58. Reprinted in Sidney Wise (ed.), *Issues: 69-70*, p. 12. Underscoring in original text.

59. *Congressional Quarterly Weekly Report*, August 17, 1974, p. 2208. The full text is reprinted pp. 2208-2212.

60. Theodore Roosevelt, *Autobiography*, pp. 388-89.

61. William Howard Taft, *op. cit.*, p. 140.

62. Arthur N. Holcombe, *Our More Perfect Union* (1950), pp. 243-51.

Appendix A Speakers of the
House of Representatives

Congress	Speaker	State
1st (1789-1791)	Frederick A. C. Muhlenberg (Federalist)	Pennsylvania
2nd (1791-1793)	Jonathan Trumbull (Federalist)	Connecticut
3rd (1793-1795)	Frederick A. C. Muhlenberg (Federalist)	Pennsylvania
4th (1795-1797)	Jonathan Dayton (Federalist)	New Jersey
5th (1797-1799)	Jonathan Dayton (Federalist)	New Jersey
	George Dent (Democrat)	Maryland
6th (1799-1801)	Theodore Sedgwick (Federalist)	Massachusetts
7th (1801-1803)	Nathaniel Macon (Democrat)	North Carolina
8th (1803-1805)	Nathaniel Macon (Democrat)	North Carolina
9th (1805-1807)	Nathaniel Macon (Democrat)	North Carolina
10th (1807-1809)	Joseph B. Varnum (Democrat)	Massachusetts
11th (1809-1811)	Joseph B. Varnum (Democrat)	Massachusetts
12th (1811-1813)	Henry Clay (Whig)	Kentucky
13th (1813-1815)	Henry Clay (Whig)	Kentucky
	Langdon Cheves (Democrat)	South Carolina
14th (1815-1817)	Henry Clay (Whig)	Kentucky
15th (1817-1819)	Henry Clay (Whig)	Kentucky
16th (1819-1821)	Henry Clay (Whig)	Kentucky
	John W. Taylor (Democrat)	New York
17th (1821-1823)	Philip P. Barbour (Democrat)	Virginia
18th (1823-1825)	Henry Clay (Whig)	Kentucky
19th (1825-1827)	John W. Taylor (Democrat)	New York
20th (1827-1829)	Andrew Stevenson (Democrat)	Virginia
21st (1829-1831)	Andrew Stevenson (Democrat)	Virginia
22nd (1831-1833)	Andrew Stevenson (Democrat)	Virginia

Congress	*Speaker*	*State*
23rd (1833-1835)	Andrew Stevenson (Democrat)	Virginia
	John Bell (Whig)	Tennessee
24th (1835-1837)	James K. Polk (Democrat)	Tennessee
25th (1837-1839)	James K. Polk (Democrat)	Tennessee
26th (1839-1841)	Robert M. T. Hunter (Democrat)	Virginia
27th (1841-1843)	John White (Whig)	Kentucky
28th (1843-1845)	John W. Jones (Democrat)	Virginia
29th (1845-1847)	John W. Davis (Democrat)	Indiana
30th (1847-1849)	Robert C. Winthrop (Whig)	Massachusetts
31st (1849-1851)	Howell Cobb (Democrat)	Georgia
32nd (1851-1853)	Linn Boyd (Democrat)	Kentucky
33rd (1853-1855)	Linn Boyd (Democrat)	Kentucky
34th (1855-1857)	Nathaniel P. Banks (American)	Massachusetts
35th (1857-1859)	James L. Orr (Democrat)	South Carolina
36th (1859-1861)	William Pennington (Whig)	New Jersey
37th (1861-1863)	Galusha A. Grow (Republican)	Pennsylvania
38th (1863-1865)	Schuyler Colfax (Republican)	Indiana
39th (1865-1867)	Schuyler Colfax (Republican)	Indiana
40th (1867-1869)	Schuyler Colfax (Republican)	Indiana
	Theodore M. Pomeroy (Republican)	New York
41st (1869-1871)	James G. Blaine (Republican)	Maine
42nd (1871-1873)	James G. Blaine (Republican)	Maine
43rd (1873-1875)	James G. Blaine (Republican)	Maine
44th (1875-1877)	Michael C. Kerr (Democrat)	Indiana
	Samuel S. Cox (Democrat)	New York (pro tempore)
	Milton Saylor (Democrat)	Ohio (pro tempore)
	Samuel J. Randall (Democrat)	Pennsylvania
45th (1877-1879)	Samuel J. Randall (Democrat)	Pennsylvania
46th (1879-1881)	Samuel J. Randall (Democrat)	Pennsylvania
47th (1881-1883)	J. Warren Keifer (Republican)	Ohio
48th (1883-1885)	John G. Carlisle (Democrat)	Kentucky
49th (1885-1887)	John G. Carlisle (Democrat)	Kentucky
50th (1887-1889)	John G. Carlisle (Democrat)	Kentucky
51st (1889-1891)	Thomas B. Reed (Republican)	Maine
52nd (1891-1893)	Charles F. Crisp (Democrat)	Georgia
53rd (1893-1895)	Charles F. Crisp (Democrat)	Georgia
54th (1895-1897)	Thomas B. Reed (Republican)	Maine
55th (1897-1899)	Thomas B. Reed (Republican)	Maine
56th (1899-1901)	David B. Henderson (Republican)	Iowa
57th (1901-1903)	David B. Henderson (Republican)	Iowa
58th (1903-1905)	Joseph G. Cannon (Republican)	Illinois
59th (1905-1907)	Joseph G. Cannon (Republican)	Illinois

Congress	Speaker	State
60th (1907-1909)	Joseph G. Cannon (Republican)	Illinois
61st (1909-1911)	Joseph G. Cannon (Republican)	Illinois
62nd (1911-1913)	Champ Clark (Democrat)	Missouri
63rd (1913-1915)	Champ Clark (Democrat)	Missouri
64th (1915-1917)	Champ Clark (Democrat)	Missouri
65th (1917-1919)	Champ Clark (Democrat)	Missouri
66th (1919-1921)	Frederick H. Gillett (Republican)	Massachusetts
67th (1921-1923)	Frederick H. Gillett (Republican)	Massachusetts
68th (1923-1925)	Frederick H. Gillett (Republican)	Massachusetts
69th (1925-1927)	Nicholas Longworth (Republican)	Ohio
70th (1927-1929)	Nicholas Longworth (Republican)	Ohio
71st (1929-1931)	Nicholas Longworth (Republican)	Ohio
72nd (1931-1933)	John N. Garner (Democrat)	Texas
73rd (1933-1934)	Henry T. Rainey (Democrat)	Illinois
74th (1935-1936)	Joseph W. Byrns (Democrat)	Tennessee
	William B. Bankhead (Democrat)	Alabama
75th (1937-1938)	William B. Bankhead (Democrat)	Alabama
76th (1939-1941)	William B. Bankhead (Democrat)	Alabama
	Sam Rayburn (Democrat)	Texas
77th (1941-1942)	Sam Rayburn (Democrat)	Texas
78th (1943-1944)	Sam Rayburn (Democrat)	Texas
79th (1945-1946)	Sam Rayburn (Democrat)	Texas
80th (1947-1948)	Joseph W. Martin, Jr. (Republican)	Massachusetts
81st (1949-1951)	Sam Rayburn (Democrat)	Texas
82nd (1951-1952)	Sam Rayburn (Democrat)	Texas
83rd (1953-1954)	Joseph W. Martin, Jr. (Republican)	Massachusetts
84th (1955-1956)	Sam Rayburn (Democrat)	Texas
85th (1957-1958)	Sam Rayburn (Democrat)	Texas
86th (1959-1960)	Sam Rayburn (Democrat)	Texas
87th (1961-1962)	Sam Rayburn (Democrat)	Texas
	John W. McCormack (Democrat)	Massachusetts
88th (1963-1964)	John W. McCormack (Democrat)	Massachusetts
89th (1965-1966)	John W. McCormack (Democrat)	Massachusetts
90th (1967-1968)	John W. McCormack (Democrat)	Massachusetts
91st (1969-1971)	John W. McCormack (Democrat)	Massachusetts
92nd (1971-1972)	Carl B. Albert (Democrat)	Oklahoma
93rd (1973-1974)	Carl B. Albert (Democrat)	Oklahoma
94th (1975-)	Carl B. Albert (Democrat)	Oklahoma

Appendix B Floor Leaders of the House of Representatives: 1901-1975

Congress	Majority Leader	Minority Leader
57th (1901-1903)	Sereno E. Payne,[1] New York (R)	James D. Richardson,[2] Tennessee (D)
58th (1903-1905)	Sereno E. Payne,[1] New York (R)	John Sharp Williams,[3] Mississippi (D)
59th (1905-1907)	Sereno E. Payne,[1] New York (R)	John Sharp Williams,[3] Mississippi (D)
60th (1907-1909)	Sereno E. Payne,[1] New York (R)	John Sharp Williams,[3] Mississippi (D) Champ Clark,[4] Missouri (D)
61st (1909-1911)	Sereno E. Payne,[1] New York (R)	Champ Clark, Missouri (D)
62nd (1911-1913)	Oscar W. Underwood, Alabama (D)	James R. Mann, Illinois (R)
63rd (1913-1915)	Oscar W. Underwood, Alabama (D)	James R. Mann, Illinois (R)
64th (1915-1917)	Claude Kitchin, North Carolina (D)	James R. Mann, Illinois (R)
65th (1917-1919)	Claude Kitchin, North Carolina (D)	James R. Mann, Illinois (R)
66th (1919-1921)	Franklin W. Mondell, Wyoming (R)	Champ Clark, Missouri (D)
67th (1921-1923)	Franklin W. Mondell, Wyoming (R)	Claude Kitchin, North Carolina (D)
68th (1923-1925)	Nicholas Longworth, Ohio (R)	Finis J. Garrett, Tennessee (D)
69th (1925-1927)	John Q. Tilson, Connecticut (R)	Finis J. Garrett, Tennessee (D)
70th (1927-1929)	John Q. Tilson, Connecticut (R)	Finis J. Garrett, Tennessee (D)
71st (1929-1931)	John Q. Tilson, Connecticut (R)	John N. Garner, Texas (D)

Congress	Majority Leader	Minority Leader
72nd (1931-1933)	Henry T. Rainey, Illinois (D)	Bertrand H. Snell, New York (R)
73rd (1933-1934)	Joseph W. Byrns, Tennessee (D)	Bertrand H. Snell, New York (R)
74th (1935-1936)	William B. Bankhead, Alabama (D)	Bertrand H. Snell, New York (R)
75th (1937-1938)	Sam Rayburn, Texas (D)	Bertrand H. Snell, New York (R)
76th (1939-1941)	Sam Rayburn, Texas (D) John W. McCormack,[5] Massachusetts (D)	Joseph W. Martin, Jr., Massachusetts (R)
77th (1941-1942)	John W. McCormack, Massachusetts (D)	Joseph W. Martin, Jr., Massachusetts (R)
78th (1943-1944)	John W. McCormack, Massachusetts (D)	Joseph W. Martin, Jr., Massachusetts (R)
79th (1945-1946)	John W. McCormack, Massachusetts (D)	Joseph W. Martin, Jr., Massachusetts (R)
80th (1947-1948)	Charles A. Halleck, Indiana (R)	Sam Rayburn, Texas (D)
81st (1949-1951)	John W. McCormack, Massachusetts (D)	Joseph W. Martin, Jr., Massachusetts (R)
82nd (1951-1952)	John W. McCormack, Massachusetts (D)	Joseph W. Martin, Jr., Massachusetts (R)
83rd (1953-1954)	Charles A. Halleck, Indiana (R)	Sam Rayburn, Texas (D)
84th (1955-1956)	John W. McCormack, Massachusetts (D)	Joseph W. Martin, Jr., Massachusetts (R)
85th (1957-1958)	John W. McCormack, Massachusetts (D)	Joseph W. Martin, Jr., Massachusetts (R)
86th (1959-1960)	John W. McCormack, Massachusetts (D)	Charles A. Halleck, Indiana (R)
87th (1961-1962)	John W. McCormack, Massachusetts (D) Carl B. Albert, Oklahoma (D)	Charles A. Halleck, Indiana (R)
88th (1963-1964)	Carl B. Albert, Oklahoma (D)	Charles A. Halleck, Indiana (R)
89th (1965-1966)	Carl B. Albert, Oklahoma (D)	Gerald R. Ford, Michigan (R)
90th (1967-1968)	Carl B. Albert, Oklahoma (D)	Gerald R. Ford, Michigan (R)
91st (1969-1971)	Carl B. Albert, Oklahoma (D)	Gerald R. Ford, Michigan (R)
92nd (1971-1972)	Hale Boggs, Louisiana (D)	Gerald R. Ford, Michigan (R)

Congress	Majority Leader	Minority Leader
93rd (1973-1974)	Thomas P. O'Neill, Jr., Massachusetts (D)	John J. Rhodes, Arizona (R)
94th (1975-)	Thomas P. O'Neill, Jr., Massachusetts (D)	John J. Rhodes, Arizona (R)

[1] Sereno E. Payne was first appointed majority floor leader in the 56th Congress by Speaker Henderson. The Speaker made few changes in his appointments in the 57th Congress, and the bulk of evidence indicates that Congressman Payne continued in this post under Speaker Cannon through the 61st Congress. De Alva Stanwood Alexander, *History and Procedure of the House of Representatives,* 1916, pp. 110, 127. Brown, George R., *The Leadership of Congress,* 1922, pp. 158, 168. Clark, Champ, *My Quarter Century of American Politics,* 1920, V. 2, p. 339.

[2] Champ Clark, *My Quarter Century of American Politics,* 1920, V. 2, p. 271. Stealey, O. O., *Twenty Years in the Press Gallery,* 1906, p. 419.

[3] Gwinn, William R., *Uncle Joe Cannon, Archfoe of Insurgency,* 1957, p. 97.

[4] Champ Clark was elected to fill out the uncompleted term of John S. Williams as minority leader, when Williams was nominated for Senator from Mississippi in 1908. Champ Clark, *My Quarter Century of American Politics,* 1920, V. 2, pp. 27-28.

[5] John W. McCormack was elected majority leader on September 16, 1940, to succeed Sam Rayburn.

SOURCE: *Biographical Directory of the American Congress, 1774-1949,* Washington, U.S. Government Printing Office, 1950; *Congressional Directory,* 67th–94th Congresses.

Appendix C Political Divisions
of the House of Representatives

Congress	No. of Rep.	Dele-gates	Fed.	Whigs	Rep.	Dem.	Others	Vacant
1st	65		53			12		
2nd	69		55			14		
3rd	105	1	51			54		
4th	105		46			50		
5th	105		51			54		
6th	105	1	57			48		
7th	105		34			71		
8th	141	1	38			103		
9th	141		29			112		
10th	141	3	31			110		
11th	141	3	46			95		

Congress	No. of Rep.	Dele- gates	Fed.	Whigs	Rep.	Dem.	Others	Vacant
12th	141	4	36			105		
13th	182	4	67			115		
14th	183	4	61			122		
15th	185	3	57			128		
16th	187	3	42			145		
17th	187	3	58			129		
18th	213	3	72			141		
19th	213	3	79			134		
20th	213	3	85			128		
21st	213	3		71		142		
22nd	213	3		83		130		
23rd	240	3		93		147		
24th	242	2		98		144		
25th	242	3		115		117	10	
26th	242	3		132		103	6	1
27th	242	3		132		103	6	1
28th	223	3		81		142		
29th	225	2		78		141	6	
30th	227	1		115		108	4	
31st	227	2		111		116		
32nd	233	4		88		140	5	
33rd	234	6		71		159	4	
34th	234	7			108	83	43	
35th	237	7			92	131	14	
36th	237	5			113	101	23	
37th	178	8			106	42	28	2
38th	183	9			103	80		
39th	191	9			145	46		
40th	193	8			143	49		1
41st	243	9			170	73		
42nd	243	10			139	104		
43rd	293	10			203	88		2
44th	293	8			107	181	3	2
45th	293	8			137	156		
46th	293	8			128	150	14	1
47th	293	8			152	130	11	
48th	325	8			119	200	6	
49th	325	8			140	182	2	1
50th	325	8			151	170	4	
51st	330	4			173	156	1	
52nd	333	4			88	231	14	
53rd	357	4			126	220	8	
54th	357	4			246	104	7	
55th	357	3			206	134	16	1

Congress	No. of Rep.	Dele-gates	Fed.	Whigs	Rep.	Dem.	Others	Vacant
56th	357	3			185	163	9	
57th	357	4			198	153	5	1
58th	386	4			207	178		1
59th	386	4			250	136		
60th	386	4			222	164		
61st	391	4			219	172		
62nd	391	4			162	228	1	
63rd	435	2			127	290	18	
64th	435	2			193	231	8	3
65th	435	2			216	210	9	
66th	435	2			237	191	7	
67th	435	2			300	132	1	2
68th	435	2			225	207	3	
69th	435	2			247	183	5	
70th	435	2			237	195	3	
71st	435	2			267	163	1	4
72nd	435	2			218	216	1	
73rd	435	2			117	313	5	
74th	435	2			103	322	10	
75th	435	2			89	333	13	
76th	435	2			169	262	4	
77th	435	2			162	267	6	
78th	435	2			209	222	4	
79th	435	2			190	243	2	
80th	435	2			246	188	1	
81st	435	2			171	263	1	
82nd	435	2			199	234	2	
83rd	435	2			221	213	1	
84th	435	2			203	232		
85th	435	2			201	234		
86th	436	1			153	283		
87th	437				174	263		
88th	435				176	258		1
89th	435				140	295		
90th	435				187	246		2
91st	435				192	243		
92nd	435				179	254		2
93rd	435	3			187	245		3
94th	435	3			144	291		

SOURCE: De Alva S. Alexander, *History and Procedure of the House of Representatives* (1916), pp. 411-12; *Factual Campaign Information,* Office of the Secretary of the U.S. Senate (1960), p. 18; *Congress and the Nation,* Vol. III p. 51a; *Congressional Quarterly Weekly Report,* January 6, 1973, pp. 16-20, and January 18, 1975, pp. 122-127.

Appendix D Committee Structure of the House of Representatives in 1975

Standing Committees	Number of Members	Party Division	
		Dem.	Rep.
Agriculture	43	29	14
Appropriations	55	37	18
Armed Services	40	27	13
Banking, Currency, and Housing	43	29	14
Budget	25	17	8
District of Columbia	25	17	8
Education and Labor	40	27	13
Foreign Affairs	37	25	12
Government Operations	43	29	14
House Administration	25	17	8
Interior and Insular Affairs	43	29	14
Interstate and Foreign Commerce	43	29	14
Judiciary	34	23	11
Merchant Marine and Fisheries	40	27	13
Post Office and Civil Service	28	19	9
Public Works and Transportation	40	27	13
Rules	16	11	5
Science and Technology	37	25	12
Small Business	37	25	12
Standards of Official Conduct	12	6	6
Veterans Affairs	28	19	9
Ways and Means	37	25	12

Appendix E Stages in
Enactment of Law

1. Introduction of Bill. Informally dropped in basket on clerk's desk on floor of the House. Bills that the member does not desire to sponsor may be introduced "By request." All bills must be signed by the Member before accepted for introduction. Bills may be introduced by as many as twenty-five members; the signature of the member first named must, however, appear on the bill.

2. Reference to a Committee. If a public bill, the Speaker, with the assistance of the parliamentarian, refers it by indorsing the name of the proper committee (or committees) on the bill. If a private bill, the member indorses the name of the committee on the bill before introducing it.

3. Numbering and Printing. Journal clerk sends bill to bill clerk, who numbers it in the consecutive order in which received, and sends it to the Government Printing Office where it is printed. Available the next morning in the document room.

4. Delivery to Committee. Transmitted to office chairman of committee to which referred, where it is received by clerk of the committee and entered on committee calendar.

5. Hearings. If committee determines to consider the bill it may order hearings, and issue notice by announcement or by mail to those interested to appear before the committee and discuss the merits and demerits of the proposed legislation. Transcripts of such hearings may, in the discretion of the committee, be taken down by committee stenographers and printed under direction of the chairman of the committee and are distributed through his office and not through the document room.

6. Reference to Subcommittee. If committee elects, it may refer the bill to a subcommittee for preliminary or detailed consideration, and hearings may be held by the subcommittee.

7. Consideration by Subcommittee. Subcommittee meets and reads the hearings, and after reading the bill for amendment, reports it back to the committee with suggested amendments and recommendations as to its disposition. Committee and subcommittee meetings must be open to the public unless in open session and with a quorum present a roll call vote determines that the meeting shall be closed. All roll call votes must be made public.

8. Consideration in Committee. Committee receives and considers report of subcommittee and adopts or rejects its recommendations. If consideration is favorable the chairman is authorized to draft and file a report.

9. Report of Committee. If committee is authorized to report at any time,* the report is made from the floor by announcement, and delivery at the Clerk's desk. If unprivileged, the report is filed by dropping in the basket on the Clerk's desk. The Parliamentarian refers the report to the proper calendar and the Journal Clerk sends it to the Bill Clerk who numbers it and forwards it to the Government Printing Office, where printed. Available the following morning at the document room. Minority views must be submitted on same day on which report is made unless, at the time the report is filed, leave is obtained by unanimous consent to file minority views at later date. With certain exceptions, Members must have the report for at least three calendar days before House consideration. The report must also contain an estimate of the costs which will be incurred in carrying out the bill.

10. Consideration by Committee of the Whole. If on the Union Calendar, the bill is considered in the Committee of the Whole where, after general debate, it is read for amendment under the five-minute rule, and reported to the House. If not requiring consideration in Committee of the Whole, the bill is taken up in the House and read a second time in full, after which it is open to debate and amendment.

11. Consideration in the House. When reported from the Committee of the Whole the bill is not read again but is subject to debate and amendment unless the previous question is ordered. It is then ordered engrossed, read third time, and the question is taken on its passage.

12. Engrossment. Engrossment is by printing on special paper under supervision of the Enrolling Clerk. The law provides that House bills shall be engrossed upon a distinctive blue paper. Senate bills are engrossed on white paper. This blue paper indicates that it is the official copy of the measure as passed by the House.

13. Messaging to Senate. After passage, the engrossed copy is attested by the signature of the Clerk of the House and transmitted to the Senate by messenger, who is received in the Senate and announces the action of the House.

14. Reference to Senate Committee. The engrossed House bill goes to the desk of the Vice President on the floor of the Senate, from which it is referred to the appropriate committee.

15. Senate Printing and Filing. The bill retains the number assigned to it in the House but is again sent to the Government Printing Office for reprinting

---

* The privilege conferred by the right to report at any time authorizes immediate consideration when not in conflict with privileged matters entitled to precedence. However, matters so reported are merely privileged in the order of business and therefore yield to questions of privilege, to special orders, to call of committees, and are not in order on Calendar Wednesday.

as received from the House. Placed on the calendar of the Senate committee to which referred.

16. Senate Hearings. The Senate committee may consider the bill on the basis of the House hearings or may decide to hold hearings of its own.

17. Consideration in Senate Subcommittee. The Senate committee may refer to a subcommittee where consideration proceeds as in subcommittee of the House.

18. Consideration in Senate Committee. The subcommittee having reported the bill back to the committee, the recommendations of the subcommittee are taken up and adopted or rejected, and the committee chairman authorized to draft report, but Senate rules do not require a written report as in the House.

19. Report of Senate Committee. When reported to the Senate the report goes to the desk of the Vice President, where it is referred and sent to the Senate Bill Clerk who numbers it and dispatches it to the Government Printing Office to be printed. Copies are available at both House and Senate document rooms the following morning.

20. Consideration by Senate. The bill when taken up in the Senate has its several readings and is open to debate and amendment, after which vote is taken on final passage.

21. Return to House. If passed by the Senate without amendment, the bill when messaged to the House is at once enrolled and delivered to the Committee on House Administration, Subcommittee on Enrolled Bills. If returned with amendments requiring consideration in Committee of the Whole, the bill is referred to the committee having jurisdiction, which reports the bill back to the House for reference to the Calendar, and the Committee of the Whole having again considered and reported it, the Senate amendments are taken up by the House, although usually Senate amendments are considered in the House by unanimous consent or under special order. When Senate amendments need not be considered in Committee of the Whole, they are laid before the House direct from the Speaker's table.

22. Consideration of Senate Amendments. When taken up by the House, Senate amendments are considered separately and agreed to, disagreed to, or agreed to with amendment.

23. Conference. If there is disagreement between the two houses of Congress on any amendment, conference is asked by one and agreed to by the other, and a committee of conference consisting of managers on the part of the House and Senate appointed by the Speaker and the Vice President, respectively, meets customarily on the Senate side.

24. Conference Report. The committee of conference having composed the differences between the Houses, a report embodying their recommendations is written in duplicate and submitted simultaneously to the House and Senate.

25. Enrollment. The conference report having been adopted by both houses, the bill is enrolled by the house in which it originated. That is, it is printed at the Government Printing Office on parchment under the supervision of the enrolling clerk, and delivered to the Committee on House Administration.

26. *Signature in House and Senate.* The Committee on House Administration having approved the form in which enrolled, the enrolled bill is reported to House and Senate, where it is signed by the Speaker and Vice President, respectively, in open session.

27. *Approval by the President.* After signature by the Speaker and Vice President, the bill is returned to the Committee on House Administration, which sends it by messenger to the White House for consideration by the President. If signed within ten days or if retained more than ten days, Sundays excepted, without action thereon, the bill becomes a law unless Congress adjourns before expiration of the ten days. Such retention of a bill without signature on adjournment of Congress within ten days after receipt by the President, known as a "pocket veto," is effective on adjournment of interim session as well as on final adjournment at the close of the last session of the Congress. Signature after adjournment and within ten days validates. If returned by the President with objections, the bill may again be considered and becomes a law if repassed by a two-thirds vote of both houses.

28. *Proclamation.* If approved by the President, or if held for more than ten days without disapproval, the bill is deposited in the office of the Administrator of General Services and published. If passed by the two houses over the President's veto, it is transmitted to the Administrator of General Services by the house last acting on it.

SOURCE: Reprinted by permission from *Cannon's Procedure in the House of Representatives,* 1959 edition (House Document No. 122, 86th Congress, 1st Session), pp. 237-241.

EDITOR'S NOTE: These steps have been updated to take into account the major changes since the 1959 edition of *Cannon's Procedure.* However, for a much more detailed analysis, reference must be made to Lewis Deschler's *The Constitution, Jefferson's Manual, and Rules of the House of Representatives,* issued biennially by the U.S. Government Printing Office since 1959. A helpful brief summary is Dr. Charles J. Zinn's *How Our Laws Are Made,* 1974 edition [House Document No. 93-377, 93rd Congress, 2nd Session], revised and updated by Edward F. Willett, Jr., Law Revision Counsel, Committee on the Judiciary, House of Representatives.

Appendix F Number of Laws
Enacted by Congress Since 1789

Congress	Acts	Public Resolutions	Total	Acts	Private Resolutions	Total	Total
1st	94	14	108	8	2	10	118
2nd	64	1	65	12		12	77
3rd	94	9	103	24		24	127
4th	72	3	75	10		10	85
5th	135	2	137	18		18	155
6th	94	6	100	12		12	112
7th	78	2	80	15		15	95
8th	90	3	93	18		18	111
9th	88	2	90	16		16	106
10th	87	1	88	17		17	105
11th	91	3	94	25		25	119
12th	163	7	170	39		39	209
13th	167	18	185	88		88	273
14th	163	10	173	124	1	125	298
15th	136	20	156	101		101	257
16th	109	8	117	91		91	208
17th	130	6	136	102		102	238
18th	137	4	141	194		194	335
19th	147	6	153	113		113	266
20th	126	8	134	100	1	101	235
21st	143	9	152	217		217	369
22nd	175	16	191	270	1	271	462
23rd	121	7	128	262		262	390
24th	130	14	144	314	1	315	459
25th	138	12	150	376	6	382	532
26th	50	5	55	90	2	92	147
27th	178	23	201	317	6	323	524
28th	115	27	142	131	6	137	279
29th	117	25	142	146	15	161	303
30th	142	34	176	254	16	270	446
31st	88	21	109	51	7	58	167
32nd	113	24	137	156	13	169	306

Congress	Acts	Public Resolutions	Total	Acts	Private Resolutions	Total	Total
33rd	161	27	188	329	23	352	540
34th	127	30	157	265	11	276	433
35th	100	29	129	174	9	183	312
36th	131	26	157	192	21	213	370
37th	335	93	428	66	27	93	521
38th	318	93	411	79	25	104	515
39th	306	121	427	228	59	287	714
40th	226	128	354	380	31	411	765
41st	313	157	470	235	64	299	769
42nd	515	16	531	479	2	481	1,012
43rd	392	23	415	441	3	444	859
44th	251	27	278	292	10	302	580
45th	255	48	303	430	13	443	746
46th	288	84	372	250	28	278	650
47th	330	89	419	317	25	342	761
48th	219	65	284	678	7	685	969
49th	367	57	424	1,025	3	1,028	1,452
50th	508	62	570	1,246	8	1,254	1,824
51st	531	80	611	1,633	7	1,640	2,251
52nd	347	51	398	318	6	324	722
53rd	374	89	463	235	13	248	711
54th	356	78	434	504	10	514	948
55th	449	103	552	880	5	885	1,437
56th	383	60	443	1,498	1	1,499	1,942
57th	423	57	480	2,309	1	2,310	2,790
58th	502	73	575	3,465	1	3,466	4,041
59th	692	83	775	6,248	1	6,249	7,024
60th	350	61	411	234	1	235	646
61st	526	69	595	286	3	289	884
62nd	457	73	530	180	6	186	716
63rd	342	75	417	271	12	283	700
64th	400	58	458	221	5	226	684
65th	349	56	405	48	—	48	453
66th	401	69	470	120	4	124	594
67th	549[a]	105	654	275	1	276	930
68th	632	75	707	286	3	289	996
69th	808	71	879	537	7	544	1,423
70th	1,037	108	1,145	568	9	577	1,722
71st	869	140	1,009	512	1	513	1,522
72nd	442	74	516	326	1	327	843
73rd	486	53	539	434	2	436	975
74th	851	136	987	730	7	737	1,724
75th	788	121	919	835	5	840	1,759

Congress	Acts	Public Resolutions	Total	Acts	Private Resolutions	Total	Total
76th	894	111	1,005	651	6	657	1,662
77th[b]	850		850	635		635	1,485
78th	568[c]		568	589		589	1,157
79th	734		734	892		892	1,626
80th	905		905	458[d]		458	1,363
81st	921		921	1,103		1,103	2,024
82nd	594		594	1,023		1,023	1,617
83rd	781		781	1,002		1,002	1,783
84th	1,028		1,028	893		893	1,921
85th	1,009		1,009	845		845	1,854
86th	800		800	492		492	1,292
87th	885		885	684		684	1,569
88th	666		666	360		360	1,026
89th	810		810	473		473	1,283
90th	640		640	362		362	1,002
91st	695		695	246		246	941
92nd	607		607	161		161	768
93rd	649		649	123		123	772
GRAND TOTALS	39,571		39,571	44,836		44,836	84,407

[a] Last Act numbered 550, but Public Numbers 45 and 46 included in one chapter (42 Stat. 147).

[b] Beginning with 77th Congress no distinction is made between acts and resolutions; all are numbered consecutively as "Public Laws."

[c] Last Act number 733, but total includes Public Law 160A.

[d] Last Act number 457, but total includes Public Law 394A.

NOTE: The distinction between the terms Public and Private, as used in the Statutes at Large, is somewhat arbitrary. Prior to 1845 a number of laws were printed in both groups; these have been classed as Public only, in the above table. The decided reduction in the number of Private acts beginning with the 60th Congress was caused primarily by the combining of a large number of pension bills in a single omnibus pension bill.

Appendix G Organization of
the House of Representatives

THE SPEAKER is the presiding officer of the House; he decides questions of order, appoints chairmen of the committee of the whole, signs acts, warrants, subpoenas, and orders of the House, controls the unappropriated rooms and corridors in the House wing of the Capitol; appoints conference and special committees, the official reporters of debates, the committee stenographers, the parliamentarian, and his office force of clerks.

MAJORITY LEADER is elected in caucus by the majority party and has the responsibility of conducting the legislative program: appoints the legislative clerks and other assistants provided for his office, and selects the party whip.

MAJORITY WHIP acts under the direction of the majority leader in ascertaining sentiment on a given question and secures the attendance of members of his party for votes on important matters; keeps in touch with the legislative program and advises members of the time when certain bills are expected to be considered.

PARLIAMENTARIAN is appointed by the Speaker, under whose direction he indicates the reference of public bills and executive communications to committees; furnishes precedents to the Speaker and chairman of the committee of the whole, confers with them and with members concerning legislative propositions with respect to their parliamentary admissibility or otherwise, and prepares the House Manual.

OFFICIAL REPORTERS OF DEBATES report stenographically all proceedings of the House of Representatives.

LEGISLATIVE COUNSEL assist House committees in drafting bills and committee reports; likewise also assist members when not engaged in committee work.

HOUSE OFFICE BUILDINGS COMMISSION prescribes rules and regulations governing use of all rooms and space in the House Office Buildings, and directs protection, care, and occupancy thereof.

COMMITTEE ON RULES. This committee occupies a unique position in that it is not a legislative committee, yet it exercises influence upon legislation through special rules reported by it providing for the consideration of bills on the majority program and prescribing the methods of their procedure. It also reports proposed changes in the rules of the House, and brings in resolutions creating special committees.

CHAIRMEN OF COMMITTEES preside at committee meetings and hearings, report bills to House and conduct their consideration on the floor; may delegate these

377

Organization of the House of Representatives

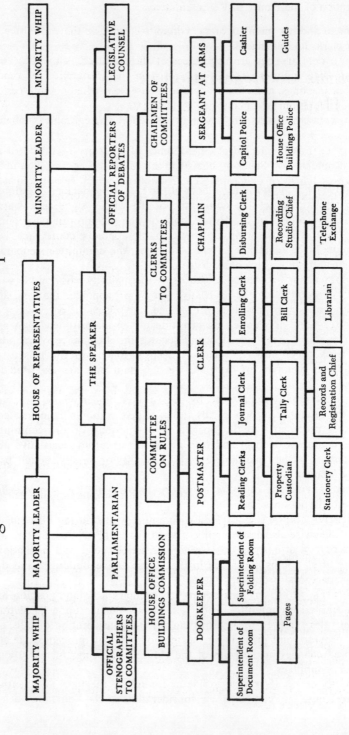

functions to another member of the committee; appoint the committee complement of clerks and assistants.

CLERKS TO COMMITTEES are appointees of the chairmen, subject to committee approval; keep minutes of meetings, assist in the preparation of reports and minutes of meetings, and are admitted to House floor when committees' bills are under consideration.

OFFICIAL STENOGRAPHERS TO COMMITTEES report stenographically hearings of House committees.

MINORITY LEADER is selected at a conference of Minority Members; usually his party's candidate for Speaker, chairman of Minority steering committee and chairman ex officio of Committee on Committees which selects and nominates minority members on House committees; is spokesman for his party and enunciates its policies. The minority whip functions in conjunction with him.

MINORITY WHIP acts under the direction of the minority leader in ascertaining sentiment on a given question and secures the attendance of members of his party for votes on important matters; keeps in touch with the legislative program and advises members of the time when certain bills are expected to be considered.

DOORKEEPER is charged with the enforcement of rules relating to the privileges of the House chamber and is responsible to the House for the official conduct of his employees; must enforce rules of decorum on the floor of the House, in conjunction with the sergeant at arms; is also charged with the operation of the Document Room and the Folding Room; supervises the janitor service, cloakroom men, pages, and messengers.

SUPERINTENDENT OF DOCUMENT ROOM receives, files, and keeps available for use of the House all bills, resolutions, and documents ordered printed by the House, as well as all public laws and resolutions; maintains a current card index giving the daily status of each piece of legislation introduced in the House and Senate.

SUPERINTENDENT OF FOLDING ROOM charged with the distribution of public documents by members of the House.

THE CUSTODIAN has charge of the laborers and janitors appointed by the doorkeeper.

POSTMASTER receives and delivers mail for members, officers, and employees of the House.

CLERK: The duties of the clerk of the House of Representatives are largely executive and quasi-judicial in their nature, and he derives his authority from the rules of parliamentary law, rules of practice (which have the force of common law), express statutes, and the printed *Rules* of the House of Representatives. He is a continuing officer whose duties do not terminate with the sine die adjournment of Congress. He attests bills, resolutions, and subpoenas, is the custodian of the seal of the House, prepares the roll of representatives-elect, and presides at the beginning of a Congress until the election of a Speaker.

JOURNAL CLERK keeps minutes of the proceedings of the House; writes the Daily Journal, and prepares and indexes it for printing; endorses all official papers at the clerk's desk.

ENROLLING CLERK has charge of the engrossment and enrollment of bills.

READING CLERKS. It is the duty of the reading clerks to read all matter presented to the House and to call the roll. They also keep a file of all bills, reports, etc., on the various calendars of business.

DISBURSING CLERK prepares the pay rolls and pays the salaries of all officers and employees of the House, including clerks to members; disburses all money appropriated for operating expenses of the House; also keeps all books, accounts, etc., for auditing purposes by the comptroller general of the United States.

PROPERTY CUSTODIAN is purchasing agent of the House; furnishes and repairs all office equipment and keeps property records; superintends furniture repair shop.

TALLY CLERK prepares and indexes the daily calendars of business of the House; records all votes by the yeas and nays and roll calls for quorum, and prepares the voting records of members.

STATIONERY CLERK has charge of the Stationery Room of the House, makes purchases, and keeps the accounts of the representatives, officers, and committees.

RECORDS AND REGISTRATION CHIEF receives and files all papers from committees of the House, as required by the rule, and is custodian of the archives of the House.

BILL CLERK has charge of numbering and printing bills and transcribing, for the *Congressional Record,* bills, resolutions, executive documents, and reports of committees; keeps a complete record of the reference of and action on bills, resolutions, executive documents, and reports of committees.

RECORDING STUDIO CHIEF receives all special orders for binding documents for members of the House, distributes House and Senate Journals, United States Statutes at Large, and bimonthly index to the *Congressional Record;* receives and files all House and Senate documents.

TELEPHONE EXCHANGE furnishes telephone service to all members of the House and Senate.

LIBRARIAN has supervision of the House Library and the Hall Library on the floor of the House.

CHAPLAIN opens the daily sessions of the House with prayer and officiates at memorial exercises.

SERGEANT AT ARMS: Disbursing officer of members' salaries and mileage; is charged with keeping order on the floor of the House; serves summonses to witnesses to appear before committees of the House; conducts obsequies of deceased members.

CAPITOL POLICE appointed by the sergeants at arms of the Senate and House of Representatives and are under the direction of the Capitol Police Board. It is their duty to police the Capitol building and grounds.

CASHIER keeps records of and handles all money in the sergeant at arms' office, assisted by tellers and bookkeepers.

HOUSE OFFICE BUILDINGS POLICE appointed by the sergeant at arms to police the House Office Buildings.

GUIDES appointed by the sergeants at arms of the Senate and House, are subject to the rules and regulations promulgated by the Capitol Police Board.

Appendix H Compensation, Allowances, Facilities, and Benefits of Representatives in the Ninety-Fourth Congress (1975-1976)*

The salary of members is at the rate of $42,500 per annum.†

Members are allowed mileage at twenty cents per mile for one round trip per regular session between Washington, D.C., and their place of residence. In addition, the representative may be reimbursed for twenty-six round trips to district during each regular session. Six of these round trips may be designated for use by a staff employee.

Members and members-elect have the privilege of sending mail under their frank from the date of election until the first day of April following the termination of office. Each member is furnished with up to 40,000 public-document envelopes per month in conjunction with the franking privilege. He or she also receives U.S. airmail and special-delivery stamps in an amount not to exceed $1,140 per session.

Each member is allowed $6,500 for stationery or other supplies. In the event of the resignation or death of a member, the stationery allowance remaining to his credit is payable to the member, his spouse, or his estate.

Each member is entitled to a constituent communications allowance of $5,000 per session for use in printing and production of newsletters, questionnaires, or similar correspondence eligible to be mailed under the frank.

Each member is allowed 125,000 units of long-distance telephone calls and telegrams per session. (One minute of a long-distance call is four units; one word of a telegram is two units.) Each member is entitled to be furnished,

* Excerpted from W. Pat Jennings, Clerk of the House of Representatives, *Information on Allowances and Services for Members of the House of Representatives,* November 6, 1974, and Committee on House Administration, *Regulations on Allowances and Expenses for Committees, Members and Employees of the U.S. House of Representatives,* August 1, 1975.

† In July, 1975, the Congress enacted legislation that tied future legislative salary increases to those that would be recommended by the President for other government employees. It was expected that a 5 per cent increase would become effective in October, 1975. The salaries would then be as follows: members of the House and Senate, from $42,500 to $44,625; Speaker of the House, from $62,500 to $65,625; leaders of the House and Senate, from $49,500 to $51,975.

through the clerk of the House, certain approved types of electrical or mechanical office equipment not exceeding a total cost of $5,500.

Each member may employ a staff of up to eighteen persons for his Washington and district offices. In addition, he may hire for any two months in any one year, a student or a teacher in government or social studies as a "Lyndon Baines Johnson Congressional Intern." The intern must serve in the Washington office and may be paid up to $500 per month. Members may use $1,000 a month of unused clerk-hire allowance for computer services in connection with official duties.

Members are entitled to suitable office space in their districts. Leases for more than $500 per month must be approved by the Committee on House Administration. The General Services Administration may outfit up to three district offices for each member.

Each member is authorized a quarterly allowance of $500 for official expenses incurred outside the District of Columbia.

The clerk of the House operates a modern full-color television and radio recording facility in the Rayburn House Office Building for the exclusive use of the members. The studio produces broadcast quality programs recorded on video tape, 16mm. film, color, and black and white, and audio tape for radio broadcasting.

A member may deduct $3,000 per year for living expenses for income-tax purposes.

A member is automatically covered under the Federal Employees Group Life Insurance Act. Members are covered by $45,000 of regular insurance while in Congress. Upon retirement, the insurance of a member over age sixty-five is reduced by 2 per cent each month he is over sixty-five until a reduction of 75 per cent is reached. The remaining 25 per cent stays in effect. A premium of $26.82 is withheld from monthly salary for this purpose.

Members have the opportunity to participate in the Federal Employees' Health Benefits program, partly paid for by the government.

A member may join the Civil Service Retirement System. If the member does so, an 8 per cent retirement reduction will automatically be withheld each month from his salary.

A participating member is entitled to annuity benefits when he has (1) completed at least five years of service and attained the age of sixty-two, (2) completed ten years of service and attained the age of sixty, (3) completed thirty years of service and attained the age of fifty-five, (4) completed twenty-five years of service upon an involuntary separation other than by resignation or expulsion, regardless of age, (5) completed twenty years of service or service in nine Congresses and attained the age of fifty upon an involuntary separation other than by resignation or expulsion.

The House Committee on Standards of Official Conduct provides each new member with a copy of the *Code of Official Conduct*. Each member also receives a financial-disclosure form which must be filed with the committee not later than April 30 of each year during incumbency. In addition, the committee sends new members a copy of an advisory opinion suggesting guidelines for properly representing constituents on behalf of their problems with executive agencies.

Appendix I Glossary of Legislative Terms

ADMINISTRATION BILLS: Bills drafted in the executive departments and agencies designed to implement the legislative program of the administration and sponsored in Congress by spokesmen for the government.

APPROPRIATION BILL: A bill that grants money for the support of the government and the financing of authorized programs. There are three types of appropriation bills: general, deficiency, and supplemental.

BICAMERAL: Consisting of two chambers or legislative branches.

CALENDAR: A record of the order in which bills are to be taken up for consideration. The House has five calendars: Consent Calendar, House Calendar, Private Calendar, Union Calendar, and the Calendar of Motions to Discharge Committees.

CALENDAR WEDNESDAY: Wednesdays are set apart for the floor consideration of unprivileged bills on the House and Union Calendars which are taken up under a procedure called the "call of the committees." Calendar Wednesday is not observed during the last two weeks of a session, and is usually dispensed with by unanimous consent.

CHAIR: The seat or position on the rostrum of the House floor occupied by the presiding officer; or, alternatively, the occupant of this position, who may be the Speaker, the Speaker pro tempore, or the chairman of the committee of the whole. Hence the expression: "the decision of the Chair."

CHAMBER: The Hall of the House of Representatives where the entire membership meets, as distinguished from the committee rooms. The House met in what is now Statutory Hall down to 1857 when the House wing of the Capitol was completed.

CLOSED HEARING: A committee hearing to which only members of the committee are admitted.

CLOSED RULE: A rule recommended by the House Committee on Rules that limits or prohibits amendments from the floor.

CLOSURE OR CLOTURE: A procedure for closing debate which is effected in the House by adoption of the previous question motion, or by unanimous consent, or by a motion to lay on the table.

COMMITTEE HEARINGS: (1) Meetings of committees at which interested parties give testimony during the consideration of proposed legislation or during the conduct of investigations. Only a small proportion of all bills introduced are sufficiently important to justify the holding of formal hearings. (2) The recorded testimony presented at such meetings.

COMMITTEE OF THE WHOLE: Any one hundred or more members of the House who may consider legislation on the Private or Union Calendars, adopt amendments without record votes, and report them to the House for further action. It is a device for expediting business since a quorum in committee of the whole is one hundred and no record votes are taken.

COMMITTEE ON COMMITTEES: A political party committee that draws up slates of standing committee assignments for the members of the party in the chamber.

COMMITTEE STAGE: That stage in the legislative process when bills are considered in committee.

COMPANION BILLS: Bills identical to those introduced in the other chamber.

CONFEREES: The representatives of the House or Senate on a conference committee.

CONFERENCE: A meeting of representatives of the two houses of Congress for the purpose of reaching an agreement on conflicting views on bills and joint resolutions or parts thereof.

CONFERENCE COMMITTEE: A committee appointed by the Speaker of the House and the president of the Senate, composed usually of the ranking members of the committees of each house that originally considered the legislation in disagreement. The members on the part of the House of Representatives are referred to as "managers" and those on the part of the Senate as "conferees." The purpose of the committee is to consider the points of conflict between the two houses on a specific bill with a view to reaching an agreement.

CONFERENCE REPORT: The report of a conference committee. Such reports cannot be amended on the floor, and if not approved by both chambers, the bill goes back to conference.

DILATORY MOTION: A motion, usually made upon a technical point, for the purpose of killing time and preventing action on a bill. The rules outlaw dilatory motions, but their enforcement is largely within the discretion of the presiding officer.

DISCHARGE RULE: A rule of the House which permits a committee to be relieved of jurisdiction over a measure before it. Under this rule, after the reading of the Journal on the second and fourth Mondays, a motion which has been signed by 218 Members, to discharge a committee from consideration of a public bill, which for thirty days has been referred to it, may be called up by any of the 218 Members, and the House shall proceed to consideration without intervening motion except one motion to adjourn.

DIVISION: A standing nonrecord vote on the House floor in which members stand and are counted for and against a proposal by the presiding officer who announces the result.

ENACTING CLAUSE: Key phrase in bills reading, "Be it enacted by the Senate and House of Representatives. . . ." A successful motion to strike this clause from a bill kills the measure.

ENGROSSED BILL: A bill that has passed the house of origin and is sent to the other house for further action, or having passed the other house also, is sent back to the house of origin for enrollment. The engrossed copy of a bill that has passed both houses together with its engrossed amendments is the official working copy from which an enrolled bill is prepared.

ENROLLED BILL: The final draft of an engrossed bill that has passed both houses, embodying all amendments. Such a bill is enrolled on paper (formerly on parchment) and is signed first by the Speaker of the House and secondly by the president of the Senate. On the back is an attestation by the clerk of the House or the secretary of the Senate, as the case may be, indicating the house of origin. This final draft is then presented to the President for his approval or disapproval.

EXCLUSIVE COMMITTEE: A standing committee whose members are excluded from serving on any other standing committee of the House.

EXECUTIVE SESSION: Committee meetings that are held behind closed doors and are not open to the public.

FILIBUSTER: A time-consuming tactic used by a minority in an effort to prevent a vote on a bill. The strict rules of the House make filibusters more difficult than in the Senate, but dilatory tactics are sometimes employed in the House through such devices as repeated demands for quorum calls.

FIVE-MINUTE RULE: A House rule dating from 1847 under which, when general debate is closed in committee of the whole, any member proposing an amendment has five minutes in which to explain it, after which the member who shall first obtain the floor is allowed to speak five minutes in opposition to it.

FLOOR: The ground level of the Hall of the House where its business is conducted and where members sit and speak and enjoy certain rights.

FLOOR STAGE: That stage in the legislative process when bills are considered in the Hall of the House.

FRANKING PRIVILEGE: The privilege of a Congressman to send mail postage-free in envelopes bearing his facsimile signature, used in lieu of stamps.

HOPPER: The container in which bills are placed when introduced. Placing a bill in the hopper is another way of saying that a bill has been introduced.

ITEM VETO: Disapproval by the Executive of portions of a bill such as separate items of appropriation or "legislative riders" on appropriation bills.

JOINT HEARINGS: Hearings held by members of two or more committees of Congress.

JOINT RULES: Rules governing the procedure of the two houses of Congress in matters requiring concurrent action. The joint rules were abrogated in 1876, but the most useful of their provisions continue to be observed in practice.

JOINT SESSION: A session of Congress attended by members of both houses.

JOURNAL: The official record of the proceedings of the House. It summarizes the actions taken in the chamber, but does not provide an *ad verbatim* transcript of the proceedings, which is given in the *Congressional Record*.

LEGISLATIVE COMMITTEES: Committees that report legislative measures as distinguished from investigating committees, study committees, party policy committees, etc.

LEGISLATIVE VETO: Disapproval by Congress or either house of a legislative proposal or an executive reorganization plan submitted by the President.

LOBBYING: Making representations to members and committees of Congress for or against the passage of legislative proposals.

LOCALITY RULE: The custom that requires a representative in Congress to reside in the district that he represents.

MAJORITY LEADER: Chief strategist and floor spokesman for the majority party in the chamber. He is elected by his party conference and is in charge of its program on the House floor.

MARKING UP A BILL: Going through a measure in committee, section by section, making changes, revising language, adding amendments, etc. If the bill is extensively revised, a "clean bill" with a new number may be introduced in place of the original one.

MINORITY LEADER: Chief strategist and floor spokesman for the minority party on the floor of the House.

MORNING HOUR: The time set aside at the beginning of each legislative day for the consideration of regular routine business. The House rarely has a morning hour, unlike the Senate where the first two hours of a daily session following an adjournment are usually devoted to morning-hour business.

OPEN HEARING: A committee hearing from which members of the press and the public are not excluded.

OPEN RULE: A rule recommended by the House Committee on Rules that allows a bill to be amended by the House.

OVERSIGHT FUNCTION: The function of exercising continuous watchfulness of the execution of the laws by the executive departments and agencies of the federal government. This function is assigned by law to the standing committees of Congress.

PAIRS: A pair is a written agreement between members on opposite sides not to vote on a specified question or during a stipulated time. It is available to members not wishing to be recorded on a proposition, or those desiring to preserve their vote or the vote of a colleague during absence from the House.

PARTY CAUCUS: A meeting of all the members of a political party in either house of Congress held to select party leaders in the chamber or to establish party policy on legislative questions and promote party unity. House Democrats customarily call such meetings *caucuses;* House Republicans refer to them as *conferences.*

PARTY CONFERENCE: A meeting of all the members of a political party in the House or Senate.

PARTY POLICY COMMITTEE: A political party committee set up to formulate party policy and to advise party leaders regarding the order of business on the floor.

PARTY WHIP: A party official chosen to assist his leaders in the management of the congressional party, by securing the attendance of party members on all necessary occasions, especially for votes, arranging pairs, and acting as a channel of information between the rank and file and the party chiefs.

PIGEONHOLE: The act of a legislative committee in laying aside indefinitely or shelving a report.

POINT OF ORDER: An objection raised by a member that the pending proceedings are in violation of some rule of the House and a demand for immediate return to the regular order. Questions of order are decided by the Speaker.

PREVIOUS QUESTION: The motion for the previous question is a debate-limiting device which, when carried, has the effect of cutting off debate and of forcing a vote on the subject at hand. It is not admitted in committee of the whole or in the Senate.

PRIVATE LAW: A law to grant a pension, authorize payment of a claim, or afford another form of relief to a private individual or legal entity.

PROXY VOTING: The practice of voting by means of an authorized agent or substitute. This is sometimes permitted in committee, but never in the House.

PUBLIC LAW: A law that is of universal application, that is clothed with any public interest, or that applies to a class of persons as opposed to a law that applies only to a specified individual or legal entity.

QUESTION PERIODS: Times at the committee or floor stage when legislators may put questions to administrative officials.

QUORUM: The number of members whose presence is necessary for the transaction of business. A quorum is 100 in the committee of the whole and 218 (a majority of the membership) in the House. If a point of order is made that a quorum is not present, the only business in order is either a motion to adjourn or a motion to direct the sergeant at arms to request the attendance of absentees.

RECOMMIT: To send a bill back to the committee that reported it.

RESOLUTIONS: There are three forms of resolution: simple, concurrent, and joint. A *simple* resolution is a measure whose authority extends only to the House. It does not contain legislation and does not require concurrence of the Senate or presidential approval. Simple resolutions are used to express the will of the House, to create special committees, to authorize the printing of reports, and to request information from administrative agencies. A *concurrent* resolution indicates joint action and requires the concurrence of the Senate. It contains no legislation, and its authority does not extend beyond Congress. It is used, for example, to set the time for a sine die adjournment, to correct enrolled bills, to express the will of Congress, and to create special joint committees. It does not require presidential approval. A *joint* resolution is a form of proposed legislation almost identical to a bill which requires the signature of the President or passage over his veto before it becomes law (except a joint resolution proposing an amendment to the Constitution).

REVENUE BILLS: Bills that originate with the Committee on Ways and Means and levy taxes.

RIDER: A provision tacked on to a bill in the hope of getting it enacted into law, even though it may not be germane to the main measure. The most familiar form of rider is that providing for legislation in appropriation bills. A rule bans such riders, but it is not always invoked.

ROLL CALL: (1) the calling of the roll of members for the purpose of determining the presence of a quorum or for recording the yeas and nays. The recording of yeas and nays is usually done electronically. (2) The record of roll calls taken.

SELECT COMMITTEE: A committee created by a simple resolution of the House to perform a special function. Its members are appointed by the Speaker and it expires upon the completion of its assigned duties.

SENIORITY: Tenure of Congressmen either in the House or on a particular committee.

SPEAKER OF THE HOUSE: The presiding officer of the House of Representatives, elected by its members at the opening of each new Congress.

SPEAKER'S TABLE: All bills transmitted by message from the Senate, whether Senate bills or House bills with Senate amendments, go to the Speaker's table. Under the rules, all bills on the Speaker's table are distributed by reference to the appropriate committees, with two exceptions.

SPECIAL ORDER: (1) A report by the Committee on Rules providing for the consideration of a measure, which is agreed to by a majority vote. (2) Permission to address the House for a specified period of time not to exceed one hour, following the legislative program.

STANDING COMMITTEE: A permanent group of members whose size and jurisdiction are prescribed in the standing rules of the House. The House had twenty-two standing committees in 1975.

STEERING COMMITTEE: A political party committee which formerly advised the leadership regarding the order of business on the House floor, but which in the later practice has fallen into disuse.

SUBCOMMITTEE: A subdivision of a standing committee that considers specified matters and reports back to the full committee.

SUSPENSION OF THE RULES: A time-saving House procedure in order on the first and third Mondays and the last six days of a session only, when the rules may be suspended by a two-thirds vote. Debate is limited to forty minutes, and no amendments from the floor are allowed. Permission of the Speaker must be secured to make the motion and is within his discretion. The practice has been for the Speaker to list the members he agrees to recognize in the order of their application and recognize them in turn.

TABLE: To dispose of a matter finally and adversely without debate.

TELLER VOTE: A method of voting in the House in which members file down the center aisle past tellers who count those for and against a measure, but do not record individual votes. Tellers are ordered upon demand of one-fifth of a quorum, which is forty-four in the House and twenty in committee of the whole. One-fifth of a quorum of the committee of the whole may also demand that teller votes be recorded.

VOICE VOTE: A method of voting in the House in which members answer "aye" or "no" in chorus and the presiding officer decides the result.

WHIP NOTICE: A weekend notice sent out to party members by the party whips about the following week's legislative program.

YEAS AND NAYS: The record of the vote on a matter by the members of the House.

Bibliography

(The following is not intended to be exhaustive. Major works and historical classics are included as well as several biographies. The emphasis is primarily on the House of Representatives. Much of the literature on the House is published in scholarly journals, and included here are several collections in which are reprinted many of the leading essays.)

Alexander, De Alva Stanwood, *History and Procedure of the House of Representatives* (Boston: Houghton, Mifflin, 1916)

Anderson, Lee F., *et al., Legislative Roll-Call Analysis* (Evanston, Ill.: Northwestern University Press, 1966)

Bailey, Stephen K., *Congress Makes a Law* (New York: Columbia University Press, 1950)

Bibby, John F., and Roger H. Davidson, *On Capitol Hill,* second edition (Hinsdale, Ill.: Dryden Press, 1972)

Bolling, Richard, *House Out of Order* (New York: E. P. Dutton, 1965)

————, *Power in the House* (New York: E. P. Dutton, 1968)

Busbey, L. White, *Uncle Joe Cannon: The Story of a Pioneer American* (New York: Holt, 1927)

Carroll, Holbert N., *The House of Representatives and Foreign Affairs,* revised edition (Boston: Little, Brown, 1966)

Chiu, Chang Wei, *The Speaker of the House of Representatives* (New York: Columbia University Press, 1928)

Clapp, Charles L., *The Congressman: His Work As He Sees It* (Washington, D.C.: Brookings Institution, 1963)

Clark, Champ, *My Quarter Century of American Politics,* 2 vols. (New York: Harper, 1920)

Clark, Joseph S., *Congress: The Sapless Branch* (New York: Harper and Row, 1964)

———, ed., *Congressional Reform: Problems and Prospects* (New York: Thomas Y. Crowell, 1965)

Clausen, Aage R., *How Congressmen Decide: A Policy Analysis* (New York: St. Martin's Press, 1973)

Cleveland, Frederic N., *Congress and Urban Problems* (Washington, D.C.: Brookings Institution, 1969)

Cooper, Joseph, *The Origins of the Standing Committees and the Development of the Modern House* (Rice University Studies, Vol. 56, No. 3, Summer, 1970)

Davidson, Roger, *The Role of the Congressman* (New York: Pegasus, 1969)

———, *et al.*, *Congress in Crisis: Politics and Congressional Reform* (Belmont, Calif.: Wadsworth, 1966)

De Grazia, Alfred, ed., *Congress: The First Branch of Government* (Washington, D.C.: The American Enterprise Institute for Public Policy Research, 1966)

Dexter, Lewis A., *How Organizations Are Represented in Congress* (Indianapolis: Bobbs-Merrill, 1969)

———, *The Sociology and Politics of Congress* (Chicago: Rand McNally, 1969)

Eidenberg, Eugene, and Roy D. Morey, *An Act of Congress: The Legislative Process and the Making of Education Policy* (New York: W. W. Norton, 1969)

Evins, Joe L., *Understanding Congress* (New York: Clarkson Potter, 1963)

Ewing, Cortez, *Congressional Elections, 1896-1944: The Sectional Basis of Political Democracy in the House of Representatives* (Norman, Okla.: University of Oklahoma Press, 1947)

Fenno, Richard F., *Congressmen in Committees* (Boston: Little, Brown, 1973)

———, *The Power of the Purse: Appropriations Politics in Congress* (Boston: Little, Brown, 1966)

Ferejohn, John A., *Pork Barrel Politics: Rivers and Harbors Legislation, 1947-1968* (Stanford, Calif.: Stanford University Press, 1974)

Follett, Mary P., *The Speaker of the House of Representatives* (New York: Longmans, Green, 1902)

Froman, Lewis A., *The Congressional Process: Strategies, Rules and Procedures* (Boston: Little, Brown, 1967)

Galloway, George B., *The Legislative Process in Congress* (New York: Thomas Y. Crowell, 1953)

Getz, Robert S., *Congressional Ethics* (Princeton, N.J.: D. Van Nostrand, 1966)

Goodwin, George, *The Little Legislatures* (Amherst: University of Massachusetts Press, 1970)

Harlow, Ralph V., *The History of Legislative Methods in the Period Before 1825* (New Haven: Yale University Press, 1917)

Harris, Joseph P., *Congressional Control of Administration* (Washington, D.C.: Brookings Institution, 1964)

Hechler, Kenneth, *Insurgency* (New York: Columbia University Press, 1940)

Hinckley, Barbara, *The Seniority System in Congress* (Bloomington, Ind.: University of Indiana Press, 1971)

Jewell, Malcolm E., and Samuel C. Patterson, *The Legislative Process in the United States,* second edition (New York: Random House, 1973)

Jones, Charles O., *Every Second Year* (Washington, D.C.: Brookings Institution, 1967)

————, *The Minority Party in Congress* (Boston: Little, Brown, 1970)

————, *Party and Policy-Making: The House Republican Policy Committee* (New Brunswick: Rutgers University Press, 1965)

Keefe, William J., and Morris S. Ogul, *The American Legislative Process,* third edition (Englewood Cliffs, N.J.: Prentice-Hall, 1973)

Kofmehl, Kenneth, *The Professional Staffs of Congress* (Lafayette, Ind.: Purdue Research Corp., 1962)

McGeary, M. Nelson, *The Developments of Congressional Investigative Power* (New York: Octagon Books, 1940)

McInnis, Mary, ed., *We Propose: A Modern Congress* (New York: McGraw-Hill, 1966)

MacNeil, Neil, *Forge of Democracy: The House of Representatives* (New York: David McKay, 1963)

McRae, Duncan, *Dimensions of Congressional Voting* (Berkeley: University of California Press, 1958)

Manley, John F., *The Politics of Finance: The House Committee on Ways and Means* (Boston: Little, Brown, 1970)

Martin, Joe, *My First Fifty Years in Politics* (New York: McGraw-Hill, 1960)

Mayhew, David R., *Congress: The Electoral Connection* (New Haven: Yale University Press, 1974)

Miller, Clem, *Member of the House: Letters of a Congressman* (New York: Scribner's, 1962)

Orfield, Gary, *Congressional Power: Congress and Social Change* (New York: Harcourt Brace, 1975)

Ornstein, Norman J., ed., *Changing Congress: The Committee System* (Annals of the American Academy of Political Science, January, 1974)

Peabody, Robert L., and Nelson W. Polsby, *New Perspectives on the House of Representatives,* second edition (Chicago: Rand McNally, 1969)

————, *et al., To Enact a Law: Congress and Campaign Financing* (New York: Praeger, 1972)

Polsby, Nelson W., *Political Promises* (New York: Oxford University Press, 1974)

Redman, Eric, *The Dance of Legislation* (New York: Simon and Schuster, 1973)

Rieselbach, Leroy N., *The Congressional System: Notes and Readings* (Belmont, Calif.: Wadsworth, 1970)

Ripley, Randall B., *Congress: Process and Policy* (New York: W. W. Norton, 1975)

———, *Majority Party Leadership in Congress* (Boston: Little, Brown, 1969)

———, *Party Leaders in the House of Representatives* (Washington, D.C.: Brookings Institution, 1967)

Robinson, James A., *Congress and Foreign-Policy Making* (Homewood, Ill.: Dorsey, 1962)

———, *The House Rules Committee* (Indianapolis, Ind.: Bobbs-Merrill, 1963)

Robinson, William, *Thomas B. Reed: Parliamentarian* (New York: Dodd Mead, 1930)

Saloma, John, III, *Congress and the New Politics* (Boston: Little, Brown, 1969)

Shannon, Wayne, *Party, Constituency, and Congressional Voting* (Baton Rouge: Louisiana State University Press, 1968)

Steinberg, Alfred, *Sam Rayburn* (New York: Hawthorn Books, 1975)

Tacheron, Donald G., and Morris K. Udall, *The Job of the Congressman* (Indianapolis: Bobbs-Merrill, 1966)

Truman, David B., ed., *Congress and America's Future,* second edition (Englewood Cliffs, N.J., Prentice-Hall, 1973)

Vogler David J., *The Third House: Conference Committees in the U.S. Congress* (Evanston, Ill.: Northwestern University Press, 1971)

———, *The Politics of Congress* (Boston: Allyn and Bacon, 1974)

Wilson, Woodrow, *Congressional Government* (New York: Houghton Mifflin, 1885)

Wolfinger, Raymond K., ed., *Readings on Congress* (Englewood Cliffs, N.J., Prentice-Hall, 1971)

Index